The Psychological Basis of Moral Judgments

This volume examines the psychological basis of moral judgments and asks what theories of concepts apply to moral concepts. By combining philosophical reasoning and empirical insights from the fields of moral psychology, cognitive science, evolutionary psychology, and neuroscience, it considers what mental states not only influence but also constitute our moral concepts and judgments. On this basis, Park proposes a novel pluralistic theory of moral concepts which includes three different cognitive structures and emotions. Thus, our moral judgments are shown to be a hybrid that expresses both cognitive and conative states.

In part through analysis of new empirical data on moral semantic intuitions, gathered via cross-cultural experimental research, Park reveals that the referents of individuals' moral judgments and concepts vary across time, contexts, and groups. On this basis, he contends for moral relativism, where moral judgments cannot be universally true across time and location but only relative to groups.

This powerfully argued text will be of interest to researchers, academics, and educators with an interest in cognitive science, moral theory, philosophy of psychology, and moral psychology more broadly. Those interested in ethics, applied social psychology, and moral development will also benefit from the volume.

John J. Park is an assistant professor of philosophy at California State University, Sacramento. He received his PhD from Duke University in philosophy. His research interests are in ethics, political philosophy, and philosophy of mind and cognitive science.

Routledge Research in Psychology

This series offers an international forum for original and innovative research being conducted across the field of psychology. Titles in the series are empirically or theoretically informed and explore a range of dynamic and timely issues and emerging topics. The series is aimed at upper-level and post-graduate students, researchers, and research students, as well as academics and scholars.

Recent titles in the series include:

Declarative Mapping Sentences in Qualitative Research
Theoretical, Linguistic, and Applied Usages
Paul M. W. Hackett

Post-Capitalist Subjectivity in Literature and Anti-Psychiatry
Reconceptualizing the Self Beyond Capitalism
Hans Skott-Myhre

A Scientific Assessment of the Validity of Mystical Experiences
Understanding Altered Psychological and Neurophysiological States
Andrew C. Papanicolaou

The Relevance of Alan Watts in Contemporary Culture
Understanding Contributions and Controversies
Edited by Peter J. Columbus

Eastern European Perspectives on Emotional Intelligence
Current developments and research
Edited by Lada Kaliská and John Pellitteri

The Psychological Basis of Moral Judgments
Philosophical and Empirical Approaches to Moral Relativism
John J. Park

Developing a Model of Islamic Psychology and Psychotherapy
Islamic Theology and Contemporary Understandings of Psychology
Abdallah Rothman

For a complete list of titles in this series, please visit: https://www.routledge.com/Routledge-Research-in-Psychology/book-series/RRIP

The Psychological Basis of Moral Judgments

Philosophical and Empirical Approaches to Moral Relativism

John J. Park

Routledge
Taylor & Francis Group
NEW YORK AND LONDON

First published 2022
by Routledge
605 Third Avenue, New York, NY 10158

and by Routledge
2 Park Square, Milton Park, Abingdon, Oxon, OX14 4RN

Routledge is an imprint of the Taylor & Francis Group, an informa business

Library of Congress Cataloging-in-Publication Data
Names: Park, John J. (Professor of philosophy) author.
Title: The psychological basis of moral judgments : philosophical and empirical approaches to moral relativism / John J. Park.
Description: New York, NY : Routledge, 2021. | Series: Routledge research in psychology | Includes bibliographical references and index.
Identifiers: LCCN 2020056772 | ISBN 9780367740757 (hbk) | ISBN 9781003155980 (ebk)
Subjects: LCSH: Psychology–Moral and ethical aspects. | Ethics–Psychological aspects. | Ethical relativism. | Psychology and philosophy.
Classification: LCC BF76.4 .P36 2021 | DDC 174/.915–dc23
LC record available at https://lccn.loc.gov/2020056772

ISBN: 978-0-367-74075-7 (hbk)
ISBN: 978-0-367-74076-4 (pbk)
ISBN: 978-1-003-15598-0 (ebk)

Typeset in Baskerville
by SPi Global, India

Contents

Tables

Acknowledgments

This book couldn't have been written without the help of numerous people. It is built on my dissertation, *Theories of Concepts & Ethics,* and the most gratitude I have for this work goes to my advisor, David Wong. Other members of my committee who I'm indebted in alphabetical order are Karen Neander, Wayne Norman, and Daniel Weiskopf.

In alphabetical order, I've also received valuable help from Coskun Cetin, Kevin DeLapp, James Dreier, Adam Gies, Chad Gonnerman, John Halpin, Joyce Havsted, Bryce Huebner, David Kaspar, Daniel Kelly, Joshua Knobe, Edouard Machery, Carlos Mariscal, Fritz McDonald, Garret Merriam, Shaun Nichols, Russell Powell, Jesse Prinz, Cindy Pury, Harvey Qu, Regina Rini, Bongrae Seok, Hagop Sarkissian, Charles Starkey, Mark Timmons, and Mark van Roojen.

Part I
The Constitution Project

1 The Groundwork for Theories of Moral Concepts

The basic unit of a moral judgment is a concept. For example, my judgment POLLUTING IS WRONG is made up of three concepts represented in all capitalized letters: POLLUTING, IS, and WRONG. Yet, what is a concept? More specifically, what is a moral concept? This book explores what theories of concepts apply to moral ones. It is concerned with examining the psychological nature of moral concepts and the implications this may have in moral philosophy. This chapter will lay down the groundwork for our inquiry into this foundational project in moral psychology.

Theories of concepts can have far-reaching ramifications in metaethics and normative ethics. In later chapters I will conclude that our moral concepts can be constituted by an array of cognitive mental states as well as by conative states like sentiments and emotions. When I say that a moral concept is constituted by a particular mental state, I mean that the moral concept just *is* that particular mental state, where I am using the "is" of identity. To discuss what constitutes a concept is to discuss what the nature of a concept is. My conclusion on the nature of moral concepts then will lead to a view that combines certain elements of metaethical cognitivism and non-cognitivism concerning the nature of our moral judgments in that our moral judgments generally express both beliefs and conative mental states. Since our moral concepts, like WRONG, are constituted by cognitive and conative states, then judgments that contain moral concepts, like POULLUTING IS WRONG, express both cognitive and conative states in virtue of containing moral concepts that just are certain cognitive and conative states. Although we will discuss metaethical cognitivism and non-cognitivism in much greater detail in later chapters, one aspect of cognitivism is that it generally holds that moral judgments express beliefs. On the other hand, one element of non-cognitivism is that it generally claims moral judgments express emotions, attitudes, and/or desires.[1] On an a priori approach, the cognitivism/non-cognitivism debate appears to be an interminable issue that is generally mired in philosophers having different a priori intuitions on the matter. However, the question of what mental state(s) constitutes our moral concepts is an empirically tractable question. I explore the nature of moral concepts based on experimental evidence and hope to shed new light on this debate.

Furthermore, my theory of moral concepts will lead to a certain internalist position in the motivational judgment internalism/ externalism debate. Although there are variants of it, motivational judgment internalism generally maintains that there is a necessary connection between making a sincere moral judgment and at least having some degree of motivation to act on the judgment. Externalism denies this necessary connection. I will contend that my theory of moral concepts, which includes motivating emotional states and dispositions to feel emotions, leads to a certain internalist position. This debate is also one that is commonly based on a priori intuitions drawn from thought experiments in which there is a lack of consensus. However, I will show how this issue can be put on better ground via a cognitive scientific approach to moral concepts.

In normative ethics, most philosophers presuppose that their moral concepts have representations of necessary and sufficient conditions to them. They assume that if we have the proper strict definition for our concepts in mind, such as for RIGHT ACTION, PERSONHOOD, or DISTRIBUTIVE JUSTICE, we can then apply it to real world cases. However, this assumption is one on the nature of moral concepts. It presumes that our moral concepts have classical structure in that it can be constituted by representations of necessary and sufficient conditions. For example, my RIGHT ACTION concept may be constituted by WHAT A HIGHLY VIRTUOUS PERSON WILL DO, where this represents a necessary and sufficient condition for being a right act. However, this assumption will be challenged, and the basic framework for how to approach normative ethics based on a psychologically real theory of moral concepts will be posited.

Moreover, through most of the history of philosophy and the study of concepts, most have believed that there is only one correct monolithic theory of concepts for all concept domains. Nevertheless, I will demonstrate that there are many different theories of concepts that apply to moral ones. Also, most a priori and a posteriori-based moral psychologists do not discuss what contemporary theories of concepts apply to moral ones, and those who do, fail to explore and assess all the major views. However, I will analyze all the major theories of concepts to see if they are viable for moral concepts. I will empirically prove that our moral concepts generally have four different psychological structures; three cognitive structures and one conative.

Examining the nature of concepts dates back to the likes of Plato and Aristotle. Descartes, Locke, Leibniz, Berkeley, and Hume called concepts *ideas* that are the materials of thought and the human understanding. For example, the British Empiricists claimed in varying degrees that our concepts, which are the building blocks of propositional knowledge claims, are pictorial images acquired from the senses. Rationalists who believe that not all knowledge comes from the senses deny this claim. Ideas or concepts are mental representations that are psychological states that represent or purport to refer to properties and categories. For example, my idea NIETZSCHE in my mind refers to, is about, or represents the historical German philosopher, Nietzsche. There are exceptions to this as there can be mental representations, like CHIMERA, that do not purport to refer at all. Furthermore, concepts largely are causally responsible for how we think and reason about the extension or referent of our ideas.

For those who are not familiar with the contemporary concepts literature but only its history, much has changed since Modern philosophers theorized about concepts. Although contemporary work on theories of concepts is recognizably built off of and indebted to such philosophers, today, the concepts field is interdisciplinary combining the work of philosophers, psychologists, linguists, and neuroscientists. Hence, this area concerning theories of concepts is an inquiry in cognitive science or the interdisciplinary study of the mind and cognition. What our concepts are is an empirically tractable question, and cognitive scientists have been running experiments on the nature of our concepts for decades now in order to justify concept constitution claims. Most philosophers who write about the theories of concepts tend to be philosophers of mind or of cognitive science rather than moral philosophers, so there has been far less work on examining the current theories of concepts in light of moral mental representations as compared to standard concrete concepts ordinarily tested for in the concepts literature like CAT, APPLE, and CUP that are of things like household objects and biological species. However, this book is the first to address all the major contemporary theories of concepts to see which ones apply to moral concepts.

The three books in Hume's *A Treatise of Human Nature: Being an Attempt to Introduce the Experimental Method of Reasoning into Moral Subjects* synchronically are of the understanding, emotions, and morals. Hume unifies the books of the *Treatise* by drawing from his first book on concepts and his second on emotions to conclude in his final book that moral concepts are constituted by emotions. Hume is standardly interpreted as claiming that moral concepts are only constituted by emotions. He writes, "To have the sense of virtue, is nothing but to *feel* a satisfaction of a particular kind from the contemplation of a character" (1738/2000, p. 303). Hume's work is an important precursor to and influence for metaethical non-cognitivism.[2] Influenced by Isaac Newton's revolutionary physics book, *Mathematical Principles of Natural Philosophy*, Hume, who was an empiricist, attempted to use empirical-based methods, such as common observation, in his examination of ethics and moral psychology. As indicated by the subtitle of his *Treatise*, his theory of moral concepts is an empirical claim based on observation. The advancements made in natural philosophy or, in other words, science impressed Hume, and he only believed it obvious that we should rely on experimental philosophy and the experimental method in moral psychology and ethics. Indeed, he referred to moral philosophy as the "science of human nature." He stated that in order to avoid fruitless debate in moral philosophy, we need to turn to the science of human nature and become "thoroughly acquainted with the extent and force of *human understanding*," and that we also should "explain the nature of the *ideas* we employ, and of the operations we perform in our reasonings" (1738/2000, p. 4).[3] In other words, we should first focus on moral concepts when examining ethics. He writes that for moral concepts and human nature,

> ...the only solid foundation we can give to this science itself must be laid on experience and observation. 'Tis no astonishing reflection to consider, that the application of experimental philosophy to moral subjects shou'd come after that to natural at the distance of above a whole century....
>
> (1738/2000, p. 4)

It is from his empirical claims about moral concepts and human nature that he builds his moral philosophy. For example, in contrast to another empiricist who also uses his view on human nature to ground his moral philosophy, Hume criticizes Hobbes' theory that we are fundamentally self-interested. Rather, in his *Treatise*, which Jerry Fodor (2003, p. 135) labels as the foundational book in cognitive science, Hume claims that human nature also contains a modicum of sympathy and benevolence. Hume argues that these sentiments, which he notes can be observed in non-human animals as well, cannot be reduced to self-interest, and such extended sentiments of humanity stored in our moral concepts are ultimately the very foundation of ethics. Similarly, I in part rely on experimental and empirical data to help inform my theory of moral concepts and foundation of ethics. I am a methodological naturalist, where my epistemology for arriving upon conclusions is informed by and is consistent with the sciences.

There were other philosophers during the Modern Era other than Hume who also examined the nature of our moral concepts based on observation. For example, Adam Smith's *A Theory of Moral Sentiments* and works by Smith's teacher, Hutcheson, also drew a British sentimentalist picture linking emotions with moral concepts based on empirical evidence. Nietzsche made relevant observation-based conclusions in moral psychology as well. For instance, Nietzsche, who influenced Freud, claimed that we have a subconscious, where emotions secretly are responsible for our moral judgments even though we may not be aware of it in all cases. He also made claims that most cognitive reasoning about ethics is post hoc and is formed only after our actual judgments are made. Reasoning largely is not a part of the process of moral decision-making. The empirically informed pursuit of a theory of moral concepts is also consistent with John Rawls' (1971) belief that the foundations of moral theory are built upon empirical moral psychology. Rawls writes, "I wish to stress that a theory of justice is precisely that, namely, a theory. It is a theory of the moral sentiments (to recall an eighteenth century title) setting out the principles governing our moral powers, or, more specifically, our sense of justice" (1971, pp. 50–51). In what is known as Rawls' linguistic analogy, in *A Theory of Justice*, Rawls provides an initial a posteriori argument that our moral psychologies contain innate moral principles. Also, Allan Gibbard (1991) contends for his conative-based theory of moral concepts in *Wise Choices, Apt Feelings* as being an empirical claim grounded on evolutionary psychology. Jesse Prinz (2007) relies on experimental psychology in order to conclude that all moral concepts are constituted by sentiments or emotions.

My claim about moral concepts should be understood as being a general empirical claim about human beings where there also may be certain exceptions to the rule. Many overall qualities attributed to human beings are general claims in which there can be exceptions to the exemplification of the relevant qualities. For example, humans generally want to eat at regular intervals. However, there are exceptions to this as some have a complete loss of appetite due to a serious illness such as cancer or liver failure. Human beings generally have complex rational capacities; however, children born from mothers who drank alcohol while pregnant may become severely mentally handicapped as a result and lack such capacities. Aristotle points out that humans are social animals. However, there are exceptions as some choose to be hermits. We generally have a fear of the use of atomic bombs, but some do not. Likewise, my theory of what moral concepts are should be understood as being a general empirical claim about human beings in which there can be certain exceptions and aberrations.

This first chapter will establish some of the proper groundwork in order to argue for which theories of concepts apply to or are viable for moral concepts. By stating that a theory is viable, I mean that a concept view and its concomitant structure is experimentally supported, and it can be used to successfully describe a structure of a moral concept that individuals generally do have. In this chapter, important basic distinctions will be made, the definition of concepts will be drawn, projects will be outlined, and the desiderata for theories of moral concepts will be laid down. What unifies these seemingly diverse topics is that they are rudimentary and important topics in laying down the groundwork for my project. In the next chapter, the main theories of concepts in the concepts field in cognitive science will be introduced and will be shown how they can apply to moral concepts. The third chapter will explain a new particular method of how to draw conclusions on what mental states constitute our moral concepts and judgments, and the fourth through nine chapters will establish which theories of concepts apply to moral concepts. They will demonstrate that my pluralistic theory of moral concepts best explains the desiderata of a theory of moral concepts. These first nine chapters will assess moral concepts predominantly from an empirical cognitive science-based approach, where later chapters will introduce and entertain a priori philosophical approaches and views on moral concepts that may be more familiar to moral philosophers. The tenth chapter will assess what implications my new theory of moral concepts has in the cognitivism/non-cognitivism and motivational judgment internalism/externalism debates. The final three chapters will examine the reference of moral concepts based in significant part on experimental philosophy studies I have conducted and contend for moral relativism in part by relying on semantic premises and the experimental method. I acknowledge that this will be a difficult undertaking to rely on empirical data to argue for moral relativism. However, I believe such an argument can be made in a promising fashion with the evidence available.

1.1 The Concept/Category and the Concept/Conception Distinctions

An important distinction will be made between concepts and categories. Categories generally are a class of objects that do not exist in the head; whereas concepts are mental representations of categories. Concepts are mental states that generally represent or refer to categories. For example, there is the class of gold objects with atomic number 79, where particular objects like gold nuggets and various gold jewelries fall within this class. Since I have knowledge about gold, in my mind I have the concept GOLD, which in turn is about or refers to the category *gold* out there in the world. *Gold* is the referent, extension, or content of GOLD. Thus, to mark this distinction between concepts and categories, when specific concepts are discussed, they will be marked in capital letters, such as the concepts MORAL and IMMORAL. However, when categories or properties are at issue, they will be italicized.

Another important and common distinction made is the concept/conception distinction. Concept theories may be thought to be concerned with immutable *correct* concepts that explain metaphysical facts such as what actually makes something a chair. Here, concepts are not presupposed to be mental representations and can themselves be abstract objects. Correct concept theories attempt to give the specifications of the metaphysical conditions for something to actually be categorized under the concept. Examples of such concept theories arise from Georges Rey (1983) and Christopher Peacocke (1992) who believe that concepts are abstract objects and have necessary and sufficient conditions for determining whether an entity may be classified under the concept.

As understood here, *conceptions*, on the other hand, are mental representations. Mental representations are psychological states that are in the head, and they are not abstract objects. Within the domain of conceptions, there are two major projects. The first project is providing a theory that determines what kinds of mental states constitute conceptions. Let us call this *the constitution project.* Some theories that are understood to be relevant to this first project are the prototype, exemplar, and theory views, where I will elaborate on the specifics of such theories in the next chapter. These are epistemic theories about how we, for example, judge something to be a chair. How we judge something to be a chair is dependent upon what constitutes our CHAIR conception. For instance, my CHAIR conception may be constituted by HAS FOUR LEGS, HAS A FLAT SURFACE, CAN BE SAT ON, IS MADE OF WOOD, and OF MEDIUM HEIGHT. These mental representations that constitute my conception are responsible for my decision that something is or is not a chair. When I walk into a classroom that I have never been in before, what constitutes my CHAIR conception allows me to quickly and unconsciously identify objects I have never seen before as being chairs so that I may sit down; a conception without which I would have extreme difficulty in judging where it is appropriate to sit. Thus, having a conception is for a subject to be in the epistemic state of having beliefs and/or potentially other mental states about the extension of a conception. In this respect, we may think of conceptions as pertaining to mental representations that, depending on the person, may change over time and may even be incorrect. At times, we can possess incorrect conceptions of things that lead to making erroneous judgments, and a conception theory still is interested in discovering what mental states constitute incorrect conceptions.

The second major project for conceptions is providing a theory that determines how such mental representations refer to properties or categories as well as to determine the meaning of conceptions.[4] Let us call this *the semantic project.* Those working on this aim will try to provide a theory of meaning and reference for conceptions, if the conceptions in question have any meaning and reference at all. As an example of such a theory, Richard Boyd (1988) argues that the reference of moral conceptions is determined by certain causal relations between the use of moral conceptions and the relevant natural properties. Boyd believes that moral conceptions rigidly refer to natural kind properties, such as *human need* and *well-being,* which causally regulate their use. For Boyd, meaning and reference is not determined by the internal moral descriptions held by agents or by mental states that may constitute their moral conceptions but rather by the fact that to a large extent, our moral conceptions are being causally regulated by the relevant natural properties. Moral conceptions refer and have meaning in virtue of certain causal relations to natural properties. On this view, moral meaning and reference of moral conceptions is not determined by or does not supervene upon what constitutes moral conceptions. Meaning just ain't in the head. Such semantic values lie independent of a theory of what constitutes moral conceptions. As we can see, the constitution and moral semantic projects may in principle be split apart from each other. For example, my GOOD conception may be constituted by KIND, HONEST, and BRAVE. These constituents are responsible for why I categorize or judge that someone is good. However, they may not constitute the meaning of my GOOD conception nor determine the reference of it. That in principle is a different issue where something else may be responsible for moral meaning and reference. It may be the case that the meaning and reference of my moral conception is determined by an external natural property, such as *human well-being*, which causally influences my thoughts of goodness. Hence, despite what may constitute this conception, since *human well-being* causes me to have GOOD thoughts, the meaning and referent of my GOOD conception is *human well-being*.

Our focus will not be on platonic concepts that are abstract objects. Rather, our focus will be on conceptions understood as being mental representations in the head. In fact, later arguments for moral relativism based on the semantics of moral conceptions will demonstrate that there are no abstract moral concepts that contain the objectively correct conditions for something to be categorized as, for example, *moral*, *virtuous*, or *just*. Furthermore, as the two main projects in regard to conceptions can in principle be split apart, where one potentially may only pursue one of these projects, I will pursue both. For example, Edouard Machery's (2009) book on conceptions only pursues the constitution project for standard concrete conceptions, and he does not provide a theory of meaning and reference. Meanwhile, it is common for many philosophers of mind and language who work on standard concrete conceptions largely to focus on the semantic project and not the constitution project.[5] On the other hand, there are efforts in the standard concrete conceptions field that discuss both projects (Carey 2009). In this book, I will attempt to address the constitution project as well as the semantic project for moral conceptions. In the first nine chapters, I will provide a pluralistic theory of what constitutes moral conceptions. The constitution project also will occupy the tenth chapter on the cognitivism/non-cognitivism debate. In the final three chapters, I will assess the reference of our moral conceptions by in part relying on experiments I have run on cross-cultural moral semantic intuitions from ordinary competent speakers of a language or the folk as well as from professional philosophers. I will then show how these experimental results help lead to a kind of moral relativism. Moreover, I will provide a new view on what moral properties are in light of moral relativism. From here forward, we will follow standard convention in cognitive science and understand any use of the term 'concept' to really be about conceptions unless otherwise noted.

1.2 Concepts Defined

Locke understands concepts as being the bare materials or constituents of thought. For example, the judgments KILLING IS WRONG and DO NOT RAPE are each constructed of three concepts. Each of the individual concepts is the building block required in order to have these thoughts. However, Machery offers an alternate understanding that is consistent with Locke's and is one which he believes plays a useful role in the understanding of human psychology. He gathers this definition by putting puzzle pieces together from the works of several psychologists such as Lawrence Barsalou et al. (2003) and Lloyd Komatsu (1992). His definition of a concept is as follows:

> A concept of *x* is a body of knowledge about *x* that is stored in long-term memory and that is used by default in the processes underlying most, if not all, higher cognitive competences when these processes result in judgments about *x*.
>
> (2009, p. 12)[6]

In Machery's definition, 'knowledge' is used in the psychological sense where it means any mental representation or information-bearing mental state that may be used in such higher cognitive competences as categorization and induction. It is not to be confused with the traditional philosophical definition of "true justified belief." This psychological understanding of 'knowledge' also will be adopted throughout this book unless otherwise specified. Long-term memory is memory that can last for days or decades while working memory refers to the relatively small amount of information one can attend to or maintain in a rapidly accessible state at one time. The higher cognitive competences in psychology are controversially distinguished from the lower competences, where both kinds of competences are defined functionally. Examples of lower competences are vision and motor planning, while instances of higher competences are categorization and induction. They may be differentiated in that the lower deal largely with perceptual and motor competences while the higher competences do not usually take perceptual stimuli such as the activation of rods and cones as direct inputs nor do they produce direct motor outputs. An exception is in the last stages of perception when what is perceived is categorized. This is a higher act of cognition. Moreover, the higher cognitive competences are to a certain extent under intentional control and their products can be conscious. The higher competences also are slower than the lower competences.

By 'default,' Machery means that concepts preferentially and presumptively are used in most of the higher acts of cognition such as deduction, induction, planning, categorization, and analogy-making. In other words, bodies of knowledge stored in a concept of *x* are preferentially used and readily available when thinking or reasoning about *x* rather than being knowledge that is less available and that does not come spontaneously to mind when cognizing about *x*.[7] Since working memory, where concepts are recruited and organized into complete thoughts, is understood to be a limited capacity, only default knowledge about *x* is stored in the concept of *x*. This has the added benefit of allowing us to generally reason and perform higher cognitive functions in real time without having to always systematically select from all the facts we may know about *x*.[8]

As we can see, concepts are defined functionally. In other words, concepts have a job description of playing a specified causal role of influencing most higher acts of cognition. This functional definition of concepts enjoys a wide consensus in the concepts field, and as concepts are properties in psychology, it has the additional benefit and usefulness of being an operational definition that allows us to measure or test what a concept is. However, as is unstated by Machery, this contemporary understanding of concepts as playing a causal role in higher cognition is also consistent with relevant aspects of the history of philosophy. For Hume, concepts are ideas that are derived from impressions or direct sensory experiences. Hume (1738/2000) claims that, "By *ideas* I mean the faint images of these [impressions] in thinking and reasoning…" (p. 7). For Hume, concepts are mental representations that play a causal role in thinking and reasoning. Locke (1689/1996) writes, "Every man being conscious to himself, that he thinks, and that which his mind is employed about whilst thinking being the *ideas*, that are there…" (p. 33). Locke, for instance, explicitly believes that our idea PERSONAL IDENTITY is responsible for how we reason about what the conditions are for being the same person across time.[9]

This understanding of concepts is also the same notion used by many of those who believe that a priori conceptual analysis is the analysis of our psychological concepts. On a general understanding of this approach, our concepts supposedly contain representations of the necessary and sufficient conditions for categorizing items as members of the corresponding category in question, and by introspecting on our concepts, we can unpack the constituents or implicit definitional knowledge contained within our concepts. For example, through the analysis of one's PERSONHOOD concept, one may come to realize that one's concept in part contains HAS THE ABILITY TO FEEL EMOTIONS. This definitional constituent in part is what is functionally or causally used when one categorizes certain things as being persons or not.

This causal understanding of concepts is also explicit at times in the metaethics literature. Hare claims that moral concepts have both evaluative and descriptive components, where the descriptive components are used to categorize whether persons or acts are members of the corresponding class (1952). An example he uses is that of a parson's GOOD GIRL concept, which may be in part constituted by GOES TO CHURCH REGULARLY and IS HELPFUL. Such constituents are used by the parson to help classify whether someone is a good girl. Likewise, the thin and thick moral concepts literature generally maintains that thin concepts like RIGHT and WRONG only have normative components. Meanwhile thick concepts have both normative and descriptive components. The descriptive components of one's thick moral concepts also play a causal or functional role of influencing one's categorization judgment as to whether a person or act falls within the corresponding moral category. For instance, my thick concept GENEROUS has a positive normative component, but it also has descriptive components like GIVES A LOT OF AID TO THOSE IN NEED that are used to categorize whether someone is *generous.*

As Locke's view that concepts are the building blocks of thought and Machery's more modern functional definition of concepts are philosophically and historically compatible with each other, we shall understand both views to be appropriate for the definition of a concept. They are consistent since when a concept of *x* stored in long-term memory is used by default in inferring the conclusion that X IS LARGER THAN Y, X is a constituent of this conclusion or thought. Although there may be various understandings of the term 'concept,' in this book, we shall understand 'concept' based on its standard usage in cognitive science. Concepts are the basic units of thought and mental representations that play a causal role in most higher acts of cognition. In essence, we shall define and understand the term in the same way Hume did when he claimed that all moral concepts are constituted by emotions.

1.3 Moral Concept Pluralism

I will now elaborate upon my moral concept pluralism thesis and my strategy for demonstrating that it is true. Most empirical psychological work on concepts has studied such theories in light of what are normally thought of as standard concrete concepts. Most work has focused on things like representations of three-dimensional household objects and biological species. Far less work has been done in relation to moral concepts. For the most part, when psychologists and philosophers offer or support a theory or theories of concepts in the cognitive science literature, they are usually only concerned with views that pertain to standard concrete concepts. However, as the question on the psychological nature of moral concepts and judgments is an empirically tractable question, I would like to explore the empirical evidence for the structure of moral concepts. The handful of explicit moral concepts empirical studies or, in other words, psychology experiments specifically designed to reach moral concepts-based conclusions, has only been for the prototype view, and even some of these tests on their own lack the rigor and systematicity to make a complete case that ethical concepts are prototypes. With the numerous extant theories of concepts out there, there is unquestionably a sizable lacuna in the concepts literature for moral concepts. However, it is my intention to help fill in this ethics gap. Elizabeth Anscombe has stated that there can be no ethics that is not grounded in a proper philosophy of psychology (1958).[10] By examining what a moral concept is, my overall theory on this subject attempts to make a significant and fundamental contribution to this endeavor.

As a qualification, while the extant theories of concepts may not be able to account for all the evidence that may exist for the nature of moral concepts and it may be the case that many new moral concept theories must be constructed due to this fact, the focus of this inquiry will be limited to the examination of moral concepts in light of the extant concept theories. Concerning the empirical exploration of the structure of moral concepts, there generally has not been sufficient support or an adequate examination of which psychological theories of concepts apply to ethical concepts. Many moral philosophers engage in analysis of moral concepts, but few have addressed which possible contemporary theories are viable for such concepts. Here, one of the main aims of a concept theory is to provide an account of the structure of concepts, where different theories provide different views of a concept's structure. A concept structure generally explains what kinds of mental representations constitute a concept, where a concept usually is thought to be constituted by other more basic concepts and mental representations. Instances of those few who have used such experimental data to attempt to examine the nature of ethical concepts are Mark Johnson, Jennifer Frei, and Philip Shaver for prototype structure and Jesse Prinz, using studies that are not explicitly concept experiments, for a conative-based structure. However, to my knowledge, no one has attempted an actual comprehensive examination of our moral concepts by taking into account all the potential theories of concepts. For example, to my knowledge no one has given experimental evidence for the exemplar view for moral concepts. No thinker has even explained what the theory-theory for concepts will look like in the moral domain, let alone has anyone explicitly stated that such a view is viable for moral concepts. Fodor (1998) claims that concepts are the very heart of cognition and cognitive science. It is not difficult to see why this is the case because concepts are in significant part responsible for how we think, reason, categorize, draw inductions and deductions, plan for the future, understand the world, make arguments by analogy, form complex thoughts, etc. However, very few moral psychologists have worked on the very heart of moral cognition by examining the various contemporary theories of concepts.

The aim of the constitution project is to provide this comprehensive analysis of which contemporary concept theories are viable for moral concepts by examining each extant psychological theory of concepts in turn. By using (1) the existent moral prototype concept studies, (2) studies in moral psychology on moral judgments that are not explicitly designed to draw conclusions in the domain of concepts but do in fact lead to viability concept conclusions for the exemplar, theory, and conative views, and (3) philosophical arguments in tandem with (1) and (2), the prototype, exemplar, theory, and conative accounts will be posited as the four viable theories for moral concepts based on proper experimental evidence. I will empirically prove that our moral concepts have such psychological structures. Moreover, at times, new analysis will be given for the viable theories of moral concepts as to what the relevant moral conceptual components will even look like.

I will contend that there is a plurality of theories of concepts that are viable for moral concepts rather than just one view. There is a moral concept pluralism.[11] Both Machery (2009) and Daniel Weiskopf (2009) argue that many to most thinkers working in the standard concrete concepts field believe that all concepts have a single uniform type of structure. Recall that philosophers like Locke, Berkeley, and Hume generally thought that all our concepts are pictorial images. Yet, there has been a general recent shift in cognitive science, where in order to account for the various desiderata of a theory of concepts, such as explaining categorization and concept combination, many theorists have adopted the view that our concepts can have various kinds of structure that apply (Murphy 2002, Machery 2009, Weiskopf 2009). Decision-making and cognition is complex, where different situational factors can lead to different kinds of cognitive processing and the use of different kinds of knowledge individually or conjointly in cognition. Thus, in order to explain all the intricate phenomena, several theories of concepts are viable in the standard concrete concepts domain rather than having a single monolithic view.

My pluralistic theory of moral concepts is not a monolithic view because it generally posits four different structures to our moral concepts in order to account for the desiderata of a theory of moral concepts; desiderata that will be discussed shortly. On my theory, the conceptual structures may be used individually or conjointly in cognition depending on the context, although I will argue later that there is an exception in that conative states must always work together with at least one cognitive state. As an example of the context dependency of the use of conceptual structures, for a certain issue in business ethics, I may rely on prototypes, and for a dilemma in politics, I may use exemplars and emotions to reach my decision.

Given that our domain of inquiry is ethics-related, some philosophers and psychologists who have studied moral concepts have held a prototype view. Several proponents are Coleman and Kay (1981), Paul Churchland (1989), and Mark Johnson (1993). First, I will show that none of these above concept theorists sufficiently have demonstrated that moral concepts have prototype structure. Furthermore, since they have not considered the further requisite evidence for other theories of concepts, there are no alternative conceptual structures for such thinkers from which a pluralism even may be recommended. It may be the case that such thinkers believe there are several viable moral concept structures beyond the prototype view. This may be the case even though they have not explicitly stated what the other viable structures are or that there is even a moral concept pluralism. Yet, since they have not considered the further requisite evidence for other structures, the question still remains as to what the other viable structures are as well as to what the argument is for moral concept pluralism. Contrastively, such evidence and arguments will be provided here. Even if they or others believe there are more viable theories of concepts in the cognitive science literature that apply to moral concepts that are not mentioned in their writings, there still is substantial and arduous work that needs to be done in assessing what those theories of concepts even will look like in the moral domain and how those theories fare with all the many desiderata of a theory of moral concepts. Much labor is required to demonstrate that a particular concept structure is viable. I will undertake such extensive work in this book.

In *The Emotional Construction of Morals*, Prinz holds the Humean-based view that all of our moral concepts are constituted by sentiments or emotions. Gibbard contends for a different conative theory of moral concepts. However, their a posteriori cases for their respective conative theories will be criticized in chapter seven. Nevertheless, the appropriate arguments for the conative view of moral concepts will be given in chapter eight.

Some philosophers can be read as having adopted a moral concept pluralism such as Alvin Goldman (1993), Stephen Stich (1993), Andy Clark (1996), David Wong (2006), Kim Sterelny (2010), and Gilbert Harman et al. (2012). They may be read as stating that it is plausible that there is a pluralism between prototype and exemplar theory. While I agree with this basic position, I contend that the above fail to provide sufficient support for this view. On the other hand, my inquiry provides sufficient justification for this conclusion. It also augments the purview toward which their pluralism applies by adding the theory-theory and the conative view as viable moral concept theories. They may not necessarily exclude the possibility that there are more viable moral concept structures even though they do not write about them, but the ensuing chapters will give the appropriate evidence for such structures in light of all the desiderata for a theory of moral concepts as well as explain how the theory view will look like in the moral concept domain. As with the general standard concrete concepts literature, I will claim that several theories of concepts are viable for moral concepts in order to account for the desiderata of a theory of moral concepts. I will argue that our moral concepts widely have one conative-based structure and three cognitive structures, which are the prototype, exemplar, and theory structures. This differs from the likes of A.J. Ayer and Prinz who contend that all of our moral concepts are only constituted by sentiments and emotions as well as from cognitivists like David Brink and Russ Shafer-Landau who claim that we widely have moral concepts that only have a cognitive component. Thus, sufficient experimental evidence for establishing the given plurality of fundamental moral concepts structures will be provided here in light of all the many desiderata. The actual empirical establishment of a new robust moral concept pluralism in moral psychology that is absent in the cognitive science literature uniquely will be attempted in this book.

My main argument in the constitution project is that my pluralistic theory of moral concepts best explains the relevant phenomena that pertain to moral concepts. In other words, it best satisfies the desiderata of a theory of moral concepts. My arguments are generally non-deductive. As we shall see, at times I use induction as well as abduction or inference to the best explanation to reach my conclusions. However, from a big picture perspective, my ultimate argument establishing my pluralistic theory of moral concepts generally hinges on an inference to the best explanation. My theory best explains the relevant phenomena or desiderata for moral concepts in moral cognition. At some points, inductive arguments will be made to help build up to this broad abductive contention I use to finally establish my theory of moral concepts. The general strategy is to first show how prototypes, exemplars, theories, and then conative states all together generally help to explain phenomena such as how we make moral categorization judgments, understand the moral world, and acquire moral concepts. Next, I will show how all four of these theories also contribute or can contribute to help explain how we draw moral inductive inferences and how we combine moral concepts to form more complex thoughts. As noted above, along the way, I will provide objections to others' arguments regarding the viability of particular moral concept theories. However, the main center of philosophical gravity in the constitution project is to provide a positive contention for my new pluralistic theory of moral concepts generally based on an inference to the best explanation. All four concept structures play important roles in order together to best explain the relevant phenomena and to best satisfy the desiderata of a theory of moral concepts. Hence, I argue that my pluralistic theory of moral concepts is true.

1.4 The Desiderata for Theories of Moral Concepts

The desiderata on an overall theory of moral concepts in cognitive science regarding the constitution project rather than the semantic project now will be explored. These are the explanatory roles any promising overall theory of what constitutes moral concepts must to a certain extent satisfy.[12] Only after establishing this will I then investigate a priori approaches to what constitutes moral concepts and examine the reference of our moral concepts. Laurence and Margolis (1999), Prinz (2002), and Machery (2009) have done much to clarify what the desiderata for theories of standard concrete concepts must be. A look at their relevant works will be beneficial to the reader. Many of these desiderata also will apply to a theory of moral concepts. To note, while there may be other desiderata relevant to the ethical domain of concepts, such as planning, only the conventional desiderata for theories of standard concrete concepts that also apply to ethical concepts will be examined here given the limited empirical resources available on such alternative desiderata that have not been much explored.

Before listing the desiderata, one common desideratum for theories of concepts will now be discussed as to why it is not included in the given list. A possible desideratum of theories of concepts is the scope requirement where, as understood here, one fundamental concept theory or a pluralistic theory of concepts has to be able to account for the different types of concepts that are abstract, concrete, and sensory. For example, a theory of concepts is thought by some to have to be able to encompass a diverse array of concepts such as TRUTH, FEAR, TURTLE, DOORKNOB, and JUSTICE. This desideratum is considered to be the bane of the traditional empiricism view held by Locke, Berkeley, and Hume. Traditional empiricism's demise is in part brought about due to its failure to account for moral concepts, such as PUSILLANIMITY, MORAL, WRONG, and VIRTUE, within an image-based perceptual theory.

For our purposes, we will be examining only ethical concepts. This inquiry is about ethical concepts concerning how we should or should not act inter- and intra-personally, and it is also about virtue trait concepts. For now, we may understand it as not being meant to be about conventional normative concepts that are thought to pertain to such actions as not blowing one's nose at the dinner table or always wearing formal clothing when at the clubhouse. As we will see later in this book, it is very difficult to come up with a principled distinction between the moral and the conventional. However, for now, suffice it to say that this inquiry concerns itself with normative concepts pertaining to those actions that are usually thought to be moral, although this in itself is contentious on some issues. Moreover, what is considered to be moral may be subject to things such as cultural variance. Thus, our area of interest is on a specified set of concepts and does not pretend to be about all types of concepts: concrete, sensory, and abstract. In this respect, the scope requirement does not apply here.

1.4.1 Desideratum #1: Categorization

A prominent desideratum for a theory of concepts is the ability to explain categorization. It is largely the need to satisfy this aim for which new concept views have arisen and have been sustained. As will be shown in the next chapter, the prototype, exemplar, and theory views for standard concrete concepts have gained their plausibility in part from this desideratum. For standard concrete concepts, the desideratum of categorization assesses how well concept theories can account for how human beings actually subsume more particular objects and classes within a more general or superordinate category. For example, psychologists may measure how and whether participants classify *bears*, *whales*, and *monkeys* as falling within the *mammal* category. For ethical concepts, one aspect of categorization will be how particular actions are classified as *moral* or *immoral*. For instance, a study may measure how and whether subjects classify acts of stealing food when one is poor as falling under *morally right* or *morally wrong*. For categorization, given the previously discussed functional definition of concepts, what constitutes a concept is what plays a causal role in categorization. For instance, one's VIRTUOUS PERSON concept may be constituted by JESUS, MARTIN LUTHER KING, JR., and MOTHER THERESA. Due to this fact, one may classify certain people as being virtuous if they are significantly similar to Jesus, Martin Luther King, Jr., or Mother Theresa.

As we shall see in much more detail in the next chapter, other aspects of categorization involve typicality effects, where some members of a category are classified as being more typical than others. More typical members are usually categorized faster than other less typical tokens of a class and are more easily learned. The ability for a theory of concepts to address and explain these phenomena of categorization add to the explanatory power of the view.[13]

1.4.2 Desideratum #2: Sense or Cognitive Content

The cognitive content desideratum is related to the constitution project in that the cognitive content of a concept is what constitutes the concept. The cognitive content of a concept can be traced back to Frege's (1892/1953) view on semantics. Frege described cognitive content, or what he called the *sense* of a term, as a mode or way of presenting the putative referent. Frege understood the sense of a term to be abstract objects. However, we will understand what Frege meant by the 'sense' of a term to be certain mental states in the head. As an example of cognitive content, although the concept UNICORNS does not refer to anything since unicorns are not real, there is still a sense to UNICORNS that describes the supposed yet non-existent referent. For example, it perhaps may include HAS WINGS, FLIES, and HAS A HORN. Moreover, Frege claimed that an identity statement between two co-referential terms can be informative. For example, the statement "Kierkegaard, who is not the penned author of *The Sickness Unto Death*, is really Anti-Climacus, who is the penned author of *The Sickness Unto Death*," could be surprising and educational to many people who lived during Kierkegaard's time. Despite the fact that both names refer to or denote the same man, the referential aspects of the names do not fully exhaust the content of them. Thus, there must be some additional aspect of understanding the terms that is over and above that of reference; namely, the mental state descriptions that one is not and the other is the original formally penned author of *The Sickness Unto Death*. It is this additional understanding that is what we shall call the sense of a term.

Frege also argued that substituting co-referential terms in certain linguistic expressions may alter the truth value of the expression. For instance, "Colleen thinks that Anti-Climacus is the penned author of *The Sickness Unto Death*" differs in truth value from "Colleen thinks that Kierkegaard is the penned author of *The Sickness Unto Death*." For, Colleen thinks or believes that Anti-Climacus is the penned author of the book, but she does not know that Anti-Climacus is the same person as Kierkegaard. She may think that Kierkgaard wrote some philosophy books but at the same time think that he did not write *The Sickness Unto Death*. Thus, both linguistic expressions have different truth values where the first sentence is true, but the latter is false. In spite of the fact that the two proper names refer to the same individual, there is an additional sense to them that accounts for this change in truth value.

These examples suggest that our concepts also have a sense to them. While the sense of concepts is concerned with ways of understanding the referent rather than necessarily drawing any conclusions in semantics about the meaning and reference of conceptual mental representations, concepts have a sense to them which makes important contributions to how human beings psychologically understand the world. Concepts or ideas are largely responsible for the human understanding. The sense of a concept, when discussed at the level of the corresponding linguistic terms, is a way of presenting the purported referent of a term that may allow a statement of the terms' being co-referential to be informative. Also, it may account for the change in truth value of certain linguistic expressions in which two co-referential terms are substituted for each other. Any overall theory of moral concepts must be able to account for the sense of such concepts in order to explain how human beings psychologically understand the moral world.

1.4.3 Desideratum #3: Acquisition

The acquisition desideratum is where theories of concepts in any domain must provide an account of or at least be consistent with the most plausible views on how concepts are ontogenetically and phylogenetically acquired. For ethical concepts, this primarily will be an issue of child development, how we learn right from wrong, examining the evolutionary history of our capacity to think about ethics, and seeing whether we have innate moral concepts. It may be the case that ostension, hypothesis testing, and learning from error, either considered individually or in combination, may be important means by which human beings generally acquire moral concepts. Acquisition may examine how both children and adults attain their moral concepts by, for example, encountering members of the concept's extension or by being instructed by others. It may be the case that some or all moral concepts are innate and we have innate moral principles that influence decision-making. While a theory of moral concepts need not necessarily put forth a view of how moral concepts are acquired, it must at least be consistent with the dominant views of moral concept acquisition.

It is important to note that our moral concepts in significant part are acquired through intense social learning, childhood development, moral education, cultural influence, and interaction with one's family, friends, and peers. Even moral nativists must somehow account for this fact. Through such external factors, others can influence and shape our moral concepts, and within a community, due to such interaction, it is the case that many members to a certain extent share some components of their moral concepts. It is not surprising that the moral concepts held by most Western moral philosophers are those that are heavily in line with the general spirit of a Christian ethics even though most Western ethicists are atheists.[14] For, the Christian influence and morality is a significant bedrock of contemporary Western culture. This, for instance, can be contrasted with those who happen to be born and raised in the ultraviolent Yanomami warrior society, where they participate in raiding excursions: raping, pillaging, and plundering others. As will be discussed later in this book, given the substantial social diversity in moral judgments held across cultures and time, as can be found in the fields of history, political science, anthropology, psychology, religion, and sociology, it is important that an overall theory of moral concepts be consistent with a view on moral concept acquisition that contains a significant element where social and environmental factors play an important role in developing and acquiring one's moral concepts and sense of right from wrong.

1.4.4 Desideratum #4: Induction

The induction desideratum is where theories of concepts must have a structure that allows and can explain how we make inductive inferences about the world. As induction is a crucial higher cognitive competence that is reliant on concepts, an ability to account for this desideratum may be important. An inductive argument is one in which the truth of the premises shows that the conclusion is likely to be true, not that the conclusion must be true. It is contrasted with deductive reasoning where the conclusion is necessarily entailed by the truth of the premises. There are many different types of induction, but induction in philosophy is commonly understood as a type of reasoning that draws general conclusions about the category *x* from particular cases of *x*, where the conclusion does not necessarily have to follow. *Philosophical induction* was the target of Hume.[15] An example of philosophical induction in category-based language is drawing the conclusion that all individuals within the category *evil persons* are dangerous to one's well-being based on previous limited experiences with particular instances of individuals who fall under this class. This kind of philosophical induction is fallibly in play at times in concept acquisition and how we form concepts of, for example, *evil persons.*

There are other kinds of inductive reasoning such as category induction. What is meant by 'category induction' in the concepts literature is the broadening of information from a previously known *given* class to a known but different or *target* category. Category inductions differ from philosophical inductions in that the given class in a category induction cannot be wholly subsumed as a subset under the target category and vice versa. An example of category induction is where if I am told that those classified under *humble person* have the property of being soft spoken, then I may induce that those under the target class *honest person* also may have this property. How the various viable views of moral concepts handle inductions will be discussed in chapter nine.

1.4.5 Desideratum #5: Concept Combination

It is thought that concepts have productivity and systematicity (Fodor 1975). Productivity is where with a finite set of concepts and rules of combination, we can have an infinite amount of new thoughts. For example, if we have the concept AND with the letters of the alphabet, we can have A AND B, A AND B AND C, AA AND B AND BCC, etc. ad infinitum. Systematicity is where if one understands the given concepts and combination rules, one can understand variations on a thought. An example of this is where if one can understand JONES SHOT A FEDERALLY PRESERVED AND ENDANGERED WOLF, then one may also understand the incredible idea A FEDERALLY PRESERVED AND ENDANGERED WOLF SHOT JONES.

Concept combination is the desideratum that attempts to explain how lexical or even compound concepts combine with each other in order to form even more complex concepts or ideas. This desideratum falls within the constitution project since it is largely what constitutes concepts that allow us to understand complex ideas in our minds. For example, Hume writes that our idea GOLD MOUNTAIN is formed by combining the image that constitutes our GOLD concept with the image that constitutes our MOUNTAIN concept. Combining the knowledge stored in the individual concepts that make up the compound is responsible for my idea of *gold mountain* that is in my mind or understanding even though I have never seen a gold mountain. Compound concepts still may be thought to be concepts. However, for clarification, they will be referred to as 'compound' or 'complex concepts' in order to mark the difference between them and lexical or one word concepts.

Combination must not only take into account the productivity and systematicity of thought, but it must also account for emergent features, or seemingly new components of a compound concept that represent features that apparently "emerge" from a complex class that are not ordinarily thought to be contained within the constituent classes. For example, the compound SENSIBLE KNAVE may have the component feature KNOWING WHEN ONE WILL NOT GET CAUGHT. However, this component feature does not appear to be contained within SENSIBLE or within KNAVE when considered individually. My SENSIBLE concept only may be constituted by constituents like MAKES GOOD FINANCIAL DECISIONS and MAKES PRACTICAL CAREER MOVES while my KNAVE concept is only constituted by representations like DECEITFUL and BAD. KNOWING WHEN ONE WILL NOT GET CAUGHT appears to not be contained in either lexical concept for me, but it somehow emerges when SENSIBLE and KNAVE combine. A discussion of how certain theories of moral concepts may account for this desideratum will be explored in chapter nine.

Notes

1 More nuanced positions that are exceptions to this general demarcation and hybrid views in this cognitivism/non-cognitivism debate will be discussed in chapter ten.

2 However, Hume does not adopt all aspects of non-cognitivism, generally understood.

3 My italics.

4 In the literature, theories that are focused exclusively on the meaning and reference project are usually discussed as also being about "concepts," and theories focused only on the constitution project are discussed as being about "conceptions." However, my use of the concept/conception distinction does not follow this literature as I believe my present demarcation of using "concept" for *only* abstract objects and "conceptions" more widely for mental representations is more clear.

5 For instance, we see in a later work that Fodor's (1998) informational atomism theory of conceptions should be understood as providing a theory of meaning and reference for conceptions and not necessarily providing a view of what constitutes conceptions, where a conception's constituents partake in higher acts of cognition. Fodor's atomism maintains that all conceptions have no constituent components and are atoms. However, without any conceptual structure, this means that we are not influenced by any relevant mental states, such as BARKS, PLAYS FETCH, HAS FUR, HAS FOUR LEGS, etc. when we make categorization judgments, such as whether something is a dog or not. Yet, this is false as experiments show that decision-making is influenced by conscious and/or subconscious states. Hence, we should really understand his project as being about the semantic rather than constitution project. His main argument for atomism will be criticized in chapter nine.

6 We may understand this definition to be represented with theory rather than classical structure.

7 There is concept and linguistic evidence that our concepts store default knowledge (Murphy and Medin 1985). For example, when we are told that a cheetah can outrun a man, representations of a one day old cheetah or an old gray feeble cheetah normally do not come to mind. Rather, we quickly understand and assent to the statement. This suggests that we have default knowledge stored in our concepts; knowledge that frequently comes readily and spontaneously to mind. More recently, Machery (2015) claims that default knowledge that constitutes a concept must be context independent and retrieved in any context. However, this has the problematic consequence that exemplars and theory knowledge then do not constitute concepts since they are not used in every context. Machery's context independence requirement is too strict. Rather, I suggest we understand context dependency as a continuum, where default knowledge is a vague concept that lies more on the context independent side of the continuum, but it still allows for a degree of context dependency. This will allow exemplars and theories to constitute concepts.

8 Machery initially stated that concepts are used in the higher competences rather than in *most* of the higher competences. However, he later adds in the term "most" in order to account for Piccinini and Scott's (2006) objection that if concepts are used in all of the higher competences, then this will allow such things as spatial maps to be concepts. However, Piccinini and Scott argue that things such as spatial maps are not ordinarily thought to be concepts. Thus, taking Piccinini and Scott's lead, Machery can be read as limiting the higher competences in his definition to ones that psychologists normally think concepts play a role in, such as categorization and concept combination. Furthermore, we more specifically may understand concepts to be constituted by those declarative representations, conative states, and/or perceptual mental states (neo-empiricism) that are used by default in the relevant higher acts of cognition.

9 While Hume and Locke viewed concepts as playing a causal role in reasoning, I do not necessarily attribute them as having a modern-day notion of a functionalist identification of concepts in mind, where concepts are those mental states that realize the causal role.

10 Her statement's focus was not on the nature of moral concepts, although the structure of moral concepts is a foundation to ethics.

11 In this book, I take no stance in the pluralism/hybridism debate, although I have sympathies with pluralism. See Machery (2009) and Weiskopf (2009) for arguments for pluralism. In the text, I use "pluralism" to mean that more

than one theory of concepts is viable for moral concepts. However, for the pluralism/hybridism debate, I understand "pluralism" to mean that there may be several individuated concepts of a category *X* in an individual's mind, where each concept of a category X contains different kinds of knowledge, such as prototypes and exemplars. Hybridism claims that in one's mind, there is only one super-structured concept of a class *X* that contains parts, where each part contains a different kind of knowledge. Despite remaining agnostic on this debate in this book, I generally assume the language of a hybridist throughout this book since it seems to fit more naturally with ordinary language.

12 A priori desiderata for a theory of moral concepts will be discussed in chapter ten.

13 There are no studies on the basic level of categorization for moral concepts, so it will not be part of the categorization desideratum for theories of moral concepts.

14 For data showing that most philosophers today are atheists, see Bourget and Chalmers (2014).

15 To note, Hume's inductive conclusions also included particular predictions that were not general.

References

Barsalou, L., Solomon, K., and Wu, L. 2003. "Abstraction in Perceptual Symbol Systems." *Philosophical Transactions of the Royal Society of London: Biological Sciences* 358, 1177–1187.

Bourget, David and Chalmers, David. 2014. "What do Philosopher's Believe?" *Philosophical Studies* 170, 465–500.

Boyd, Richard. 1988. "How To Be a Moral Realist." *Essays on Moral Realism.* Ed. by Geoffrey Sayre-Mccord. Ithaca, NY: Cornell University Press.

Carey, Susan. 2009. *The Origin of Concepts.* Oxford: Oxford University Press.

Churchland, Paul. 1989. *A Neurocomputational Perspective.* Cambridge, MA: The MIT Press.

Clark, Andy. 1996. "Connectionism, Moral Cognition, and Collaborative Problem Solving." *Mind and Morals.* Ed. by L. May, M. Friedman, A. Clark. Cambridge, MA: The MIT Press.

Coleman, Linda and Kay, Paul. 1981. "Prototype Semantics: The English Word Lie." *Language* 57, 26–44.

Fodor, Jerry. 1975. *The Language of Thought.* Cambridge, MA: Harvard University Press.

Fodor, Jerry. 1998. *Concepts: Where Cognitive Science Went Wrong.* Oxford: Oxford University Press.

Fodor, Jerry. 2003. *Hume Variations.* Oxford: Oxford University Press.

Frege, Gottlob. 1892/1953. "On Sense and Reference." Trans. M. Black. Ed. by P. Geach and M. Black. *Translations form the Philosophical Writings of Gottlob Frege.* Oxford: Blackwell.

Gibbard, Allan. 1991. *Wise Choices, Apt Feelings.* Oxford: Clarendon Press.

Goldman, Alvin. 1993. "Ethics and Cognitive Science." *Ethics* 103, 337–360.

Harman, G., Mason, K., and Sinnott-Armstrong, W. 2012. "Moral Reasoning." *The Moral Psychology Handbook.* Ed. by John Dorris and the Moral Psychology Research Group. Oxford: Oxford University Press.

Hume, David. 1738/2000. *A Treatise of Human Nature.* Ed. By D. Norton and M. Norton. Oxford: Oxford University Press.

Johnson, Mark. 1993. *Moral Imagination.* Chicago: The University of Chicago Press.

Komatsu, Lloyd. 1992. "Recent Views of Conceptual Structure." *Psychological Bulletin* 112, 500–526.

Laurence, Stephen and Margolis, Eric. 1999. "Concepts and Cognitive Science." In *Concepts.* Ed. by Eric Margolis and Stephen Laurence. Cambridge, MA: The MIT Press.

Locke, John. 1689/1996. *An Essay Concerning Human Understanding.* Ed. by Kenneth P. Winkler. Indianapolis, IN: Hackett Publishing Company.

Machery, Edouard. 2009. *Doing Without Concepts.* Oxford: Oxford University Press.

Machery, E. 2015. "By Default: Concepts Are Accessed in a Context-Independent Manner." *The Conceptual Mind.* Ed. by E. Margolis & S. Laurence. Cambridge, MA: The MIT Press.

Murphy, Gregory. 2002. *The Big Book of Concepts.* Cambridge, MA: The MIT Press.

Murphy, G. and Medin, D. 1985. "The Role of Theories in Conceptual Coherence." *Psychological Review* 92, 289.

Peacocke, Christopher. 1992. *A Study of Concepts.* Cambridge, MA: The MIT Press.

Piccinini, Gualtiero and Scott, Sam. 2006. "Splitting Concepts." *Philosophy of Science* 73, 390–409.

Prinz, Jesse. 2002. *Furnishing the Mind.* Cambridge, MA: The MIT Press.

Prinz, Jesse. 2007. *The Emotional Construction of Morals.* Oxford: Oxford University Press.

Rawls, John. 1971. *A Theory of Justice,* 2nd edition. Cambridge, MA: Belknap Press.

Rey, Georges. 1983. "Concepts and Stereotypes." *Cognition* 19, 237–262.

Sterelny, Kim. 2010. "Moral Nativism: A Sceptical Response." *Mind & Language* 25, 279–297.

Stich, Stephen. 1993. "Moral Philosophy and Mental Representation." In *The Origin of Values.* Ed. by Hechter, M., Nadel, L., and Michod, R. New York: Aldine de Gruyer, 215–228.

Weiskopf, Daniel. 2009. "The Plurality of Concepts." *Synthese* 169, 145–173.

Wong, David B. 2006. *Natural Moralities.* Oxford: Oxford University Press.

2 Concerning Human Understanding

I now will introduce the major concept theories concerning the human understanding in the concepts literature in cognitive science. We will examine concept theories in light of both standard concrete and ethical concepts, where initial theorizing of how such views will look in the ethical domain will be provided here. The evidence, arguments, and desiderata satisfaction for which theories are viable in the moral domain will be examined in later chapters. I will summarize the contemporary concepts literature for standard concrete concepts as well as provide my own views on how the extant theories of concepts will look like when they are applied to moral concepts. To note, there have been several philosophers and psychologists who have provided an even more detailed examination and summary of the contemporary concepts literature for standard concrete concepts (Murphy 2002, Prinz 2002, Machery 2009, Weiskopf 2009). While I understand my summary of the standard concrete concepts literature to be sufficient for our purposes of primarily examining moral concepts, I do not delve into even further detail of the standard concrete concepts literature, as there are numerous other resources available for those who wish to explore the standard concrete concepts literature even further.

2.1 The Classical View

The classical theory of concepts dates back to the likes of Plato, Aristotle, and Piaget. It maintains that concepts are constituted by knowledge that is about the individually necessary and jointly sufficient features of members of a class. The theory of concepts at hand is also known as "definitionism," as it claims that our concepts are kinds of knowledge that represent strict definitions that are used in the higher cognitive competences. This is a cognitivist theory in that it claims that our concepts are constituted by cognitive constituents. This view is widely and uncontroversially held to be a discounted theory in cognitive science for standard concrete concepts, although it is commonly thought to be viable for mathematical and logical concepts. The criticisms of this view will be provided in the fourth chapter. Illustrations of the kinds of concepts we have based on the classical theory are that our BACHELOR concept may be constituted by BEING UNMARRIED and BEING A MALE or that EVEN NUMBER may be made up of A NUMBER DIVISIBLE BY TWO WITHOUT REMAINDER. In the first case, if an individual satisfies the necessary and sufficient conditions of being both unmarried and a male, then we will classify this person as a bachelor. In the latter instance, any number that satisfies the definition of being divisible by two without remainder will be categorized as an even number. Therefore, if the classical theory is viable in the moral domain, one may have in mind a definition such as "maximizes the best consequences" when representing the category *right action*. In this circumstance, MAXIMIZES THE BEST CONSEQUENCES represents a necessary and sufficient condition, and it constitutes one's RIGHT ACTION concept.

2.2 The Prototype View

In the 1970s, psychologists started running studies which began pointing toward a different theory of concepts from the classical view. Spearheaded by the likes of Eleanor Rosch (1973), Caroline Mervis (Rosch & Mervis 1975), Edward Smith (Smith et al. 1974), and James Hampton (1979), the prototype theory was born as a view of concepts that could account for the new experimental data. Rosch and Mervis explicitly draw inspiration of the prototype view from Wittgenstein's (1953) notion of family resemblance, where members of a category may have one to several features or characteristics in common with each other, but zero or very few characteristics are common to all category members. For example, Wittgenstein argued that members of a family, such as the Smiths, do not all have necessary and sufficient physical characteristics in common with each other. Rather, they generally and more loosely share overlapping features that are not applicable to all members, such as eye color, hair color, nose size, head shape, etc. Such features are not necessary and sufficient conditions for being a member of the Smith clan. Wittgenstein maintained that this idea that our concepts are not constituted by representations of necessary and sufficient conditions but by representations of statistically frequent or family resemblance features also applies to other concepts such as GAMES.

There are various versions of the prototype theory, but it generally states that a concept is constituted by a prototype or knowledge that is about a list of statistically frequent features that are summary or general representations of members of a class. Such features are considered statistically frequent in that it is highly probable that a member of one's category will have them. Moreover, prototypes do not represent features that are necessary and sufficient conditions for determining membership. For example, one's prototype of DOG may be HAS HAIR, HAS FOUR

LEGS, BARKS, PLAYS FETCH, and WAGS ITS TAIL. The features that are represented may be arrived upon based on all of one's previous experiences with particular dogs. Furthermore, a dog may still be considered a dog even though it is hairless or even if it only has three legs. Such features are not necessary and sufficient conditions.

Some prototype or family resemblance theories may emphasize that features are based on cue validity rather than statistical frequency, or it may be the case that feature selection of a category is based on both. Cue validity is a measure that increases with the probability that a feature occurs within a category and also decreases with the probability that the feature occurs within members of a similar but different contrast category. For instance, *plays fetch* may be a feature that has high cue validity for *dog* in that while it may be a feature common among the members of *dog*, items in contrast categories such as *wolf* and *hyena* are unlikely to have this feature as well. On the other hand, *has hair* does not have high cue validity for *dog* in that it will most likely occur in members of *wolf* and *hyena*.

On some prototype views, based on statistical frequency or cue validity, features may be weighted more heavily than others. For example, *barks* and *plays fetch* may be weighed more heavily than *has hair*. When calculating how similar a potential or target member may be to a category, a prototype theory may take into account the number of features the instance may share with a category, or the instance's satisfaction of heavily weighted features, or both. Prototype theory is considered a similarity-based view because when an object or act is similar enough to the representation of summary or general features and passes a calculated similarity threshold, then the object falls within the class. Returning to the example, since my pet animal satisfies the important heavily weighted features of *barks* and *plays fetch*, along with several of the other features, it passes the similarity threshold and is categorized as a dog. When a token passes the similarity threshold of two or more classes, it is generally categorized in the class toward which it has the highest similarity score. At the same time, passing the similarity threshold for multiple categories can also explain the phenomena of ambiguous cases of membership where some individuals may categorize an item as a member of two different classes.

The prototype view also tends to be a linear model where a category's properties are independent cues for categorization in that the incremental increase of a similarity score occurs when one feature is matched between the potential member and a category despite the fact that it may not yet have been determined whether there is further feature matching between the target item and category. As we shall see in the non-linear exemplar theory, this cognitive processing contrasts with a non-linear model where the incremental increase of a similarity score is dependent on the sharing of other features between the target item and the category.

Moreover, prototype theorists believe that an item having a higher similarity score to a prototype explains why subjects understand such higher scored items to be more typical members of a category than others (Rosch & Mervis 1975, Hampton 1979, Armstrong et al. 1983). Due to this graded membership or typicality effects, for example, a golden retriever will be thought to be a more typical dog than a Chihuahua for some individuals. The prototype view explains typicality effects. Typicality effects usually are measured by asking subjects to rate how typical an item is of a category on a scale. An example of the scale may be: 1 = very typical; 4 = moderately typical; 7 = not very typical. Typical members are usually learned quicker by subjects and tend to be categorized faster as members. Members that are considered to be less typical are more difficult to learn and take a longer time to be categorized.

A common way to examine whether a given concept has prototype structure is by giving participants a feature-listing task or a variation thereof. In the first phase, participants are asked to list what they take to be the features of several categories. In order to tease out the features, several questions are provided to the subjects such as, "why is X only loosely speaking a kind of Y?" or "what characteristics of X make it a Y rather than a Z?" Once the questionnaires are gathered, the features are pooled together to create a much shorter list based on a production frequency measure. Those properties from the pool that score low on this measure are eliminated. The list of features that remain after the elimination round is considered to be the list of features associated with the category. In the second phase, experimenters provide a list of potential category members for each of the previously given categories. Subjects then rate how well they think each potential member belongs or does not belong in the category. Those that are rated highly are taken to be typical members while those that generally are still considered to be members but are not rated as highly are taken to be atypical members. Next, judges determine which features of a category from the first phase each member of the category possesses. Given that judges now have determined which features members possess, it may now be seen whether the number and degree of features a member satisfies makes a precise and accurate mathematical prediction in how items are categorized and in how typical subjects understand a member to be. If there is such an accurate prediction, then this provides evidence that the represented feature list is a prototype that influences the relevant judgments.

As further support that prototypes play a causal role in categorization and typicality judgments, studies were run using artificial categories. Artificial categories are usually a string of letters or numbers that are completely made up by experimenters, are meaningless, and are not intended to refer to any ordinary category used by human beings such as with natural and artifact kind concepts. For example, Rosch & Mervis (1975) used strings such as HPNWD and JXPHM to examine the prototype theory. Generally, typicality judgments in experiments may be made based on alternate factors, such as pleasantness, rather than similarity to a prototype. Using artificial categories eliminates these alternate possible confounding variables as causal influences. When subjects had to categorize and give typicality ratings as to whether, for instance, HPSWD belonged to the category HPNWD, Rosch and Mervis found that prototype similarity of letter-matching predicted and explained categorization and typicality judgments.

As another part of the feature-listing task, the feature list from the first phase is compared with the category members' and nonmembers' features derived from the judges. If the concept has prototype or family resemblance structure, then the feature list will not prove to be independently necessary and jointly sufficient conditions for determining category membership and for excluding instances as nonmembers. As we will see in the fourth chapter, the results of typicality effects and the absence of psychological evidence for the use of definitions combine to state a case against the classical theory of moral concepts.

Our examination of the concept DOG presupposes the featural model of the prototype theory. This more predominant model for prototype structure uses features for a class in which a potential member is calculated as either having the feature or not having the feature. The featural model does not allow for any middle ground where an object may be thought to only partially have some characteristic to a certain degree. For a featural calculation or cognitive processing, a potential member either has it or does not have it. For example, *has four legs, barks, plays fetch,* and *wags its tail* may be thought of as qualities that a potential member of *dog* either has or does not have. Under the featural model, whether it does or does not have such features will in part determine whether or not the token instance may be categorized as a dog.

A second, but less prevalent option as compared to the featural model, as illustrated by Edward Smith and Douglas Medin (1981), is the dimensional model where whether a potential member shares the properties of a category is taken to be a matter of continuous degrees rather than a matter of bluntly either having the property or not having it. For instance, when using a dimensional model, one may calculate the similarity of particular objects to *dog* based on the dimensions of *size, athleticism,* and *ferocity*. The object in question will have different degrees or measurements of these attributes. On this model, it is not an issue as to whether the object does or does not have these qualities. Rather, it is an issue as to what degree the object has such characteristics. At times, it may be the case that certain qualities can appropriately be used both in a featural and dimensional model. On the dimensional model, a prototype will be knowledge that represents the mean or average dimension values for given qualities that may have been abstracted from one's experiences of particular instances of a category. Such dimensions, like the featural model, may also be weighted in terms of importance. Thus, whether or not an object passes the similarity threshold of *dog* is a matter of degree based on whether or not the object is close to the average dimension values for the class.

If prototype theory is viable for moral concepts, then the prototype for the moral concept RIGHT ACTION for some individual may be BEING GENEROUS TO OTHERS, HELPING THE HOMELESS IS THE JUST THING TO DO BECAUSE IT BENEFITS THOSE IN NEED, PREVENT HARM, DOES NOT BREAK LAWS, and EXHIBITS FRIENDLINESS. Such representations, when understood as features of members of a class, are not necessary and sufficient conditions for categorizing something as a right action. As we can see, prototypes for moral concepts may be about such things as general features of moral situations, virtues, reasons for action, and basic moral principles or rules that happen to occur or be extracted from many particular instances of situations that fall under *right action*. When a person points out to another an instance where a stranger is helping homeless people that such is a case of moral rightness, the mentally represented reason or justification for action that HELPING THE HOMELESS SO LONG AS ONE IS NOT IN POVERTY ONESELF IS THE JUST THING TO DO BECAUSE IT BENEFITS THOSE IN NEED may now be a candidate to be a constituent component of this listener's prototype of RIGHT ACTION based on further particular experiences. The abstraction of such features may be based on personal experiences and moral education. For the individual in question, the virtue *friendliness* may carry less weight for this individual as compared to heavily weighted features such as the principles *prevent harm* and *does not break laws*. Thus, particular acts such as walking away from a potentially violent physical confrontation with a meddling person or calling the police when witnessing a homicide unfold can be understood by one as being more typical instances of right actions than going out of one's way to welcome a new resident to the neighborhood. All of the above given acts supposedly will pass her similarity threshold for RIGHT ACTION to be categorized as one of its members. However, as indicated, if moral concepts have prototype structure, there will be graded membership among the acts in question. Furthermore, the more typical members will tend to be categorized faster and learned more quickly as members of *right action*. The prototype theory is a cognitivist view in that moral concepts are constituted by cognitive mental representations.

Also, on the prototype model, assuming that she lives in a society where abortion is legal, acts such as abortion may be ambiguous for her in that it may barely pass the similarity threshold for both RIGHT ACTION and WRONG ACTION. For her, acts of abortion match the heavily weighted feature of *does not break laws*, but it also is a cause of harm in that she believes a fetus has personhood or moral status. Given that there are certain hard cases where individuals appear to suffer from moral ambiguity, the prototype theory nicely accounts for and predicts this phenomenon at times with its given structure and similarity-based algorithms.

If moral concepts have prototype structure, a featural model may work for such concepts, where qualities such as *does not break laws* may be considered to be features. However, some characteristics may be more amenable to a dimensional model. For example, the features *exhibits friendliness* and *prevent harm* may be accounted for by matters of degree and a dimensional value rather than by whether a particular act or person does or does not have these features. A person who invites and actively introduces a new, shy, and awkward individual to each person in a social group and attempts to include him in conversation may be considered as friendlier than one who merely says hello on a daily basis to this individual at work. We may certainly think that a good Samaritan has a higher degree of helping as opposed to someone who merely notifies the proper authorities when seeing an injured person on the side of the road. For moral prototype concepts, depending on the list of characteristics a prototype represents, the possibility will be left open that a dimensional model may be the actual way by which a person may calculate for similarity as to whether a particular act is categorized as moral or immoral. Nevertheless, for our purposes, when discussing the prototype theory we will assume what is considered to be the more predominant featural model, but this is not meant to preclude the possibility of the dimensional prototype model.

2.3 The Exemplar View

Soon after the arrival of the prototype theory, some cognitive scientists began hypothesizing the existence of a different theory of concepts. This exemplar theory, like the prototype view, is a cognitivist account that also calculates membership based on a similarity score measure. However, instead of accounting for similarity by comparing the potential member to a summary or general representation of features, it is compared to a set of particular members of a category. An exemplar is a mentally represented particular instance of a class. This view, in which concepts are constituted by exemplars, was initially proposed in contemporary times by Medin and Schaffer's (1978) exemplar theory context model (Brooks 1978, Medin & Schwanenfluegel 1981). However, it has its roots in the likes of Berkeley, who famously criticized Locke's view of concepts. In *An Essay Concerning Human Understanding*, Locke (1689/1996) states that one can have a general idea of a triangle that abstracts away from any particular kind of triangle. For instance, one may bring to mind a TRIANGLE concept that is, for instance, not scalene, equilateral, nor isosceles. However, Berkeley asks his readers to attempt to picture such an abstracted notion of a triangle in one's own mind that is not scalene, equilateral, or isosceles. He concludes that one cannot envision such an idea. For, when one thinks of a triangle, one is always envisioning a particular triangle that must be either scalene, equilateral, or isosceles. In contemporary terms, Berkeley (1710/1982) is claiming that our concepts are constituted by exemplar images or representations of particular members of a class.[1]

Like prototypes, exemplars are not considered to be about necessary and sufficient conditions for determining membership. There are various versions of the exemplar theory. However, depending on one's exemplar view, an exemplar may itself be constituted by knowledge about the set of features or dimensions of an instance, and such features or dimensions may or may not be weighted. Thus, what is stored in long-term memory for DOG is knowledge that represents particular instances rather than abstracted summary features. For example, one's concept DOG may have exemplar structure. Thus, based on one's experiences, it may be constituted by a set of exemplars such as THAT GREYHOUND ON THE TRACK, MY NEIGHBORS AMERICAN BULLDOGS, MY ROTWEILLER, and MY SISTER'S CHIHUAHUA. One's GREYHOUND exemplar may be constituted by knowledge that is about a set of dimensions of the extension of one's exemplar such as FAST, LARGE, and ATHLETIC. One's exemplars for AMERICAN BULLDOG and ROTWEILER are likely constituted by a body of knowledge that represents related values as compared to the dimensional values held by one's GREYHOUND exemplar. On the other hand, one's CHIHUAHUA exemplar will be constituted by knowledge that is about quite different values compared to one's other instances of dogs. Thus, in this case, one's concept DOG has exemplar structure and is constituted by knowledge that is about particular instances of a class. Each exemplar has components that are about a set of features or dimensions.

When one comes across an object that is a Doberman pincer, the exemplar theory holds that the target object will be categorized based on its similarity score with one's dog exemplars; a similarity score that must be higher than other similarity scores for contrast categories. Since one's DOG concept is constituted by exemplars and one has exemplars such as MY NEIGHBORS AMERICAN BULLDOGS and MY ROTWEILLER, it is likely that the Doberman pincer will be categorized as a dog. The set of dimensions for the Doberman pincer will be similar to the sets of dimensions contained by several of one's particular instances. Furthermore, since exemplars do not represent necessary and sufficient conditions, the Doberman still will be classified as a dog even though it comes nowhere close to matching the dimensional values of a Chihuahua. The exemplar theory also can claim to partially account for graded membership, where more typical members are categorized faster and learned quicker than less typical members. For example, given its high degree of similarity to most of one's particular instances, a Doberman pincer may be a typical member of *dog* and may be categorized faster than less typical dogs.

When calculating similarity as specified by Medin and Schaffer's (1978) context model of the exemplar view, its theory on cognitive processing uses a non-linear model, where the incremental increase of a similarity measure depends on what other features a target item and category share. For example, if there is a pig in my presence, it may have only one instance of feature matching with MY ROTWEILLER concept in that a pig is large. However, a pig is neither fast nor athletic. On a non-linear model of computational processing, there is very little to no increase in the similarity score measure, as compared to a linear model used by the prototype theory, since there is only one instance of feature matching. However, if the pig happened to match many more features, then there would be a dramatic increase in the similarity score. A non-linear model allows for the fact that if a target is highly similar to a few or possibly one particular instance, then it is more likely to be classified as a member of the category as compared to if it is only moderately similar to all the particular instances that make up the class. This leads to the fact that the exemplar theory is better suited to account for the classification of novel and odd member items of a category as compared to the prototype theory; items that may share few if any properties with a representation of summary or general features. This is a specific respect in which the exemplar theory may be superior to the prototype view. For example, if one comes across a pug, then, with a non-linear model, this will receive a higher similarity score for the exemplar theory since it is highly similar to one's particular instance of a Chihuahua. A pug will be categorized as a dog despite the fact that it does not share many features or dimensions that correspond with one's other instances. However, if one's DOG concept is a prototype, then at first glance, it appears unlikely that the features or dimensions of a Chihuahua will make one's list of statistically frequent features that are represented by prototypes given the other more predominant experiences one has had of large athletic dogs. Thus, it appears that a pug may not be categorized as a dog on the prototype view because one's prototype may not represent the Chihuahua features or dimensions toward which the pug may feature match.[2] However, due to using a non-linear model, it will be so categorized on the exemplar view.

If moral concepts are exemplars, then an exemplar of, for example, RIGHT ACTION for an individual may be a representation of a grouping of particular cases that one has experienced or heard about that are right acts. For instance, one's exemplars for RIGHT ACTION may be WORKING IN THAT SOUP KITCHEN LAST THANKSGIVING, BREAKING UP THAT FIGHT AT SCHOOL SOPHOMORE YEAR, and MY UNCLE, THE FIREMAN, RUSHING INTO THE TWIN TOWERS ON 9/11. These exemplars themselves have constituent components that are about the features of the extension of the exemplars. For example, WORKING IN THE SOUP KITCEN LAST THANKSGIVING may be constituted by HELPING THOSE IN NEED, VOLUNTEERISM,

JUST, and SACRIFICE. BREAKING UP THAT FIGHT AT SCHOOL SOPHOMORE YEAR may be constituted by NON-VIOLENCE, GOOD, COURAGE, and PEACE. MY UNCLE, THE FIREMAN, RUSHING INTO THE TWIN TOWERS ON 9/11 may share similar constituent components with one's exemplar BREAKING UP THAT FIGHT AT SCHOOL SOPHOMORE YEAR. Thus, when one witnesses a policeman intervening in a robbery and assault, since it closely matches the particular instance of breaking up that fight at school sophomore year and one's uncle rushing into the Twin Towers on 9/11, one will categorize this as a right act.

Real life examples of the possible use of exemplars are when precedents are cited in an argument by analogy in order to determine whether an act should be classified as right or wrong. Such precedents may be gathered consciously or subconsciously from personal experience, books, fables, fairytales, history, current events, hypothetical theorizing, etc. In childhood, particular stories of myths and legends can be the bedrock for one's subconscious perception of good versus evil. As an example of the use of exemplars, when a minority athlete may physically confront a spectator because the spectator made racial slurs against the particular athlete during a game, some would denounce the athlete's physical assault by citing the particular precedents established by Jackie Robinson, who broke the color barrier in baseball. There were many particular instances where Robinson was verbally attacked by spectators and by players with racial slurs, but he never physically confronted anyone during those games. He always maintained his composure and never got violent. Likewise, many argue that today, based on purportedly drawing analogies to such particular precedents, minority athletes should not attack spectators during games when racially provoked.

A second possibility of exemplar theory for moral concepts is that one's concept of GOOD PERSON may be constituted by exemplars that are about individuals who are moral exemplars. In other words, one's moral concept is constituted by bodies of knowledge that are about particular individual persons who one takes to be exemplary models of ethical human beings. For example, one's concept GOOD PERSON may be constituted by MY MOTHER, MY BROTHER, JESUS, and MOTHER THERESA. These exemplars that are about moral exemplars in turn each are constituted by components that represent a cluster of features. For example, MOTHER THERESA and JESUS may have the components KIND, MORAL, HELPFUL, LOVING, and BRAVE. When one comes across an instance of a doctor medically helping the poor in a third world country pro bono, since this case is highly similar to one's moral exemplars of Mother Theresa and Jesus, one classifies this person as a good individual. In this instance, one's concept GOOD PERSON may be constituted by JESUS, in which individuals are categorized under *good person* if they match the features contained by Jesus. Other such examples are when individuals such as social activists and politicians cite and use particular moral exemplars such as

Martin Luther King, Jr. or George Washington when determining which individuals they categorize under *good person*. Furthermore, one may rely on particular exemplars of virtuous agents to determine what action one should perform. For instance, one may question, "What would Jesus do?" The represented virtues in one's JESUS concept then can be used to categorize whether an act is morally praiseworthy or not.

2.4 The Theory View

The theory view or the theory-theory is a position that emerged out of psychology in the 1980s that became established based on its power to explain categorization as well as on its capacity to provide a detailed account of concept acquisition. Yet, like all of the other theories of concepts, it has its roots in philosophy. Locke (1689/1996) claims that there is a real essence to things; an essence that is responsible for making an object what it is. The real essence that we can mentally represent for a physical object is also the underlying cause of the object's superficial observable characteristics. For example, the real essence of gold is the collection of submicroscopic particles of gold that gives gold its particular properties of color, malleability, weight, etc. Darwin, in *On the Origin of Species*, argues that the classification of biological species should not be based on theory-neutral superficial similarities but should be grounded in the causal explanations that underlie the similarities among organisms. Quine (1977) in "Natural Kinds" states that an individual's psychological development and the development of society in regard to distinguishing and characterizing natural kinds is first based on perceptual superficial similarities. However, through continual development and maturation, more sophisticated scientific theories are used by the individual and society to draw such distinctions. Along the lines of these thinkers, although not necessarily agreeing with everything they say in their works, the theory-theory of concepts states that concepts are themselves theories or mini-theories. Theories contain hidden essence, explanatory, causal, functional, and general or generic background knowledge about the extension of a concept and can explain such things as categorization in standard concrete concepts (Carey 1985, Murphy & Medin 1985, Keil 1989, Gopnik & Meltzoff 1997). This knowledge occupies an empirically defeasible placeholder position and does not refer to necessary and sufficient conditions.

A major shortcoming of similarity theories is their inability to account for the additional knowledge that appears to be stored in concepts that accounts for some cases of classification. The theory-theory attempts to address this issue by claiming that background knowledge of the world rather than prototypes that are about superficial properties plays a role in such a process. For example, Frank Keil (1989) ran a study where participants were asked whether the animal in a given scenario is a horse or a cow (p. 162). In the situation, there is an animal that is called a 'horse,' makes horse sounds, looks like a horse, is strapped with a saddle so people can ride on it, and eats oats and hay. However, scientists run blood tests and X-rays on it, and they discover that its insides are actually the insides of a cow. In this experiment, Keil found that older children and adults perceived the scientists' discoveries as relevant for determining natural kind membership. These subjects relied not on superficial similarities but on folk biological theories of hidden essences to decide that the animal was really a cow despite its superficial horse appearances.

As an example of the importance and use of folk causal law knowledge in cognition, *being curved* is an equally typical feature in bananas and boomerangs. However, subjects give more weight to this attribute in boomerangs rather than bananas because it is falsely believed that curvature is causally related to the boomerang's property of *if thrown, it will return back to the thrower* (Medin & Shoben 1988). Due to this relationship between the two features, it is thought that *being curved* is more required for a boomerang rather than a banana. Theories may provide other causal explanatory relations between superficial features of an object. As an example that is an oversimplification for the point of illustration, FISH in part is constituted by my prototypes: HAS FINS, HAS A TAIL, and SWIMS (Murphy & Medin 1985). Theoretical knowledge of fish provides the explanation of the relation between fish attributes since in order to properly swim, a fish needs fins and a tail. Furthermore, participants believe that the hidden essence of a natural kind is generally causally responsible for the superficial features of the kind. For instance, many believe that the hidden essence of human beings is responsible for why we have the typical observable properties that we do. Here, theory-theorists usually do not necessarily deny that one may have in mind superficial features when representing a class, but they do emphasize the importance of causal law knowledge or theories in providing the underlying explanation to such features as well as in deciding what weight such features may possess.

Theory-theorists also hold that there are domain differences for types of knowledge where different ontological domains contain different types of central beliefs. For example, while natural kinds are believed to have hidden essences, the analog for artifact kinds generally is intended function. For example, Lin and Murphy (1997) ran an experiment where they first described and showed pictures of certain artifacts from foreign countries. One such item is a *tuk.* A tuk is a hunting tool that is a stick with a special handle on one end that protects the wielder's hand from animal bites. On the other end of the stick is a noose that goes around the head of the animal. The function of the tuk is to be able to control an animal by placing the noose over its head. After informing participants about what a tuk is and the function it performs, the experimenters showed participants a picture of what looks like a tuk minus only the special handle. When asked to categorize the item, participants categorized it as a tuk. When shown a picture of what looks like a tuk minus only the noose, subjects did not categorize it as a tuk. This suggests that functional knowledge plays a role in categorization, where participants did not categorize the latter item as a tuk because it could not perform the tuk's function. This contrasts with natural kinds where, for example, so long as an animal still has cow innards or a cow essence, it is still a cow in spite of its superficial appearances of being a horse.

Moreover, theory knowledge may not only contain knowledge of hidden essences, theoretical entities, and causal laws, but they may also contain explanatory general background knowledge. Theory knowledge need not be restricted to those kinds of knowledge that are of properties that are related to the structure of scientific theories: properties such as causal laws and essences. For example, Murphy and Medin (1985) claim that most people think the feature of *flammable* is a quality of wood rather than paper money even though both wood and paper money are flammable. The reason behind this is that we have general background knowledge about the world concerning human activity where wood is used for burning fires and paper money is mostly used for economic purposes in which its flammability plays no role. On their view, this knowledge still counts as a theory that influences feature attribution for classes even though it may not be about a causal law or hidden essence. For, such general background knowledge about human activity in principle still does provide an explanation of why we may attribute certain features to certain classes.

For moral concepts, they may be constituted by theories that have as components such things as knowledge about master moral principles from which other moral principles are inferred and explained. For example, the concept RIGHT ACTION may be constituted by a normative theoretical belief akin to divine command theory. The theory ACT IN ACCORDANCE WITH THE PRINCIPLES MANDATED BY GOD is a component of RIGHT ACTION. The theory-theory is a cognitivist view of moral concepts. Moreover, theory knowledge may be considered to occupy defeasible placeholder positions, where such knowledge does not refer to necessary and sufficient conditions.

As previously stated, prototypes are about features that may be moral principles, reasons for action, and virtues, among other things. One may derive such principles, reasons, and virtues as general or summary representations from particular moral situations or individuals. However, certain theory-theory components are more about master or top moral principles from which those middle moral principles, reasons, and virtues may be thought to be inferred and explained. For example, from divine command theory, where one must obey those laws mandated by God, one may arrive upon middle principles such as *do not lie* and *do not steal*. One may adhere to these middle moral principles based on one's background belief in the ethical theory of divine command theory. Moreover, divine command theory explains why we must not lie and steal. Also, the act utilitarian Greatest Happiness Principle, where one must perform that action that leads to the greatest happiness for the greatest number, initially appears to be only about generating verdicts on acts rather than middle principles. However, act utilitarianism may not produce formal pithy rules or principles, but it still relies on reasons for action to arrive upon its act-based conclusions. As an act utilitarian, in self-defense one may believe that one ought to take the life of a murderous assailant. However, this may be based on the specified reason that in regard to overall happiness, killing others is wrong, but in acts of self-defense, killing others is justifiable. Such a reason may be thought to stem from and be explained by act utilitarianism in that it is under the eye of the Greatest Happiness Principle that such a reason or justification is formed and used to determine what act one should follow. Thus, act utilitarianism may also be thought to be theory knowledge or a top principle from which reasons or considerations that count in favor of something are based.

While the theory-theory is a distinct view from the others due to the specific kind of knowledge it posits concepts as containing, as we can see, there is an intimate link between the theory-theory and the prototype theory for moral concepts. This is just like the intimate link between both concept theories in the standard concrete concept realm, where as shown in our previous example, general background explanatory knowledge is the reason why the folk attribute the prototypical property of flammable to wood but not paper money. Also, recall that theory knowledge need not be restricted to those kinds of knowledge that are of properties related to the structure of scientific theories. Furthermore, it is a central aspect of the theory view that different domains, such as natural versus artifact kind concepts, can store different kinds of theory knowledge. The moral concept domain is no exception. Thus, the domain of moral concepts contains theory knowledge of master moral principles, among others.

It is knowledge about these top principles that constitute the theory-theory of moral concepts, while the middle moral principles, reasons, and virtues belong more in the domain of the prototype view. The reason why this is the case is that such top principles are those that ostensibly underlie the middle principles, virtues, and reasons for action at a deeper level of theoretical abstraction just as, for example, biological theories underlie the superficial features of a biological natural kind. Second, and a related point, is that just as biological theories may be about explanatory relations between superficial features, top moral principle knowledge may provide an explanatory link between middle principles, virtues, or reasons. In this respect, middle principles, reasons, and virtues may be thought of as being superficial. Meanwhile, top principles are more theoretical and lie at the deepest explanatory level. For example, the middle principle, *do not kill*, may be ultimately explained by divine command theory. What I have provided thus far for an explanation of the structure of the theory-theory for moral concepts may not exactly parallel the structural components of the theory-theory for standard concrete concepts given the differences between the moral and standard concrete domains. However, in allying theories with knowledge of top moral principles, we can see that several important similarities as just discussed exist between the given moral and standard concrete theory-theory structures to warrant drawing the distinction between moral concept prototype and theory structural components in this manner.

Also, causal moral law knowledge about an agent's intentions for action may be theory components of moral concepts in that they may take part in the higher cognitive competences related to ethical matters. Just as natural kind concepts may contain causal law knowledge, moral concepts also may be constituted by causal moral law knowledge. For instance, in moral cognition, one may have a representation of a causal moral law or principle such as IF AN AGENT'S CAUSAL MOTIVATIONS ARE BAD, THEN THE AGENT'S PERFORMANCE IS BAD. This may constitute one's WRONG ACTION concept and influence one to judge that an agent's action is still wrong when this agent performed an act with cruel intentions but failed to bring about the intended cruel consequences. It also may be responsible for the prototype constituent of one's WRONG ACTION concept, LACKS MORAL WORTH, to carry significant weight and importance. If one does not perform an action with the proper motivations and intentions, then the act lacks moral worth, and this may lead to the greater chance that the act is classified as a wrong act. Given the above causal moral law knowledge, LACKS MORAL WORTH may be held to contain significant weight and importance in one's WRONG ACTION concept. This is somewhat analogous to the theory-theory for standard concrete concepts in which one's BOOMERANG concept may be constituted by theory knowledge of the causal principle IF THROWN, IT WILL RETURN BACK TO THE THROWER. Recall that this theory knowledge likewise impacts the weight carried by the prototype constituent of one's BOOMERANG concept, BEING CURVED. BEING CURVED is a more heavily weighted prototype component for BOOMERANG rather than BANANA because the causal principle contained in participants' BOOMERANG concept confers such additional weight.

Theory knowledge for moral concepts also can include knowledge of the ontological nature of moral properties, such as perhaps SOCIALLY CONSTRUCTED or PLATONIC ABSTRACT OBJECT. Such knowledge may vary depending on the person. This is like how natural kind concepts can contain theory knowledge of essences. Moreover, moral concepts may contain general background knowledge just as with standard concrete concepts. For instance, MORALITY in part may be constituted by represented metaethical background knowledge, such as BEING TRUE ONLY RELATIVE TO CULTURES or BEING KNOWN BY WAY OF INTUITIONS. Also, similar to how artifact kind concepts contain theory representations of functions, moral concepts may as well regarding the function of morality. For instance, MORALITY in part may be constituted by FOR COOPERATION AND DISPUTE RESOLUTION.

2.5 The Conative View

While there are numerous theories of concepts, comparatively less attention in the concepts literature in cognitive science has been paid to the view that such mental states may be constituted by sentiments, emotions, desires, and/or non-representational attitudes. This theory at hand will be called the *conative theory*. It claims that moral concepts are constituted by conative states. I use the term "conation" as it is commonly used in metaethics, where conative states include sentiments, emotions, desires, and non-representational attitudes. As there is comparatively less work done on this view in cognitive science, I leave it open to future empirical investigation as to whether conative components are weighted. Despite receiving less attention in cognitive science, this theory is commonplace in metaethics. It has its roots in the likes of Hume and Adam Smith, who all claimed that moral concepts are constituted by emotions. This view differs from the others previously discussed, since here concepts are actually constituted by conative states. While other views such as the prototype theory may mention, for example, emotions by claiming that RIGHT ACTION is constituted by ELICITS APPROBATION and ELICITS JOY, the conative theory may be thought to *use* rather than *mention* emotions since moral concepts are actually constituted by them rather than being constituted by further concepts that refer to them. Conative theory structured concepts sharply differ from the others in that they contain different mental states as well as in the fact that they rely on conative-based processing.

Many metaethicists who adopt the conative theory are metaethical non-cognitivists, although as we shall later see, one necessarily need not be a metaethical non-cognitivist if one espouses the conative view. Although I will discuss all the various metaethical theories in greater detail later in the book, non-cognitivists in part generally claim that since all moral concepts are constituted merely by one's own conative states, they do not refer to genuine moral properties. In this respect, for metaethical non-cognitivists generally understood, moral concepts are somewhat similar to non-referential concepts such as UNICORN, TROLL, and MINOTAUR.

Conative states are taken to be motivating states. Also, in metaethics, it is common to distinguish cognitive beliefs from conative states based on the notion of "direction of fit" (Smith 1994, Ridge 2014). If one believes that p and p is not true of the world, then one's belief of the world needs to change. Beliefs have a mind-to-world direction of fit. On the other hand, if one desires that *p* but *p* is not true of the world, then the world needs to be changed. Conative states have world-to-mind direction of fit. Here, moral beliefs can have moral propositional content but conative states internally do not refer to genuine moral properties.[3]

Let us now draw the distinction between sentiments and emotions (Prinz 2007). Sentiments are standing dispositions stored in long term memory to feel emotions. Emotions are occurrent manifestations in working memory of dispositional sentiments. Thus, if a moral concept is at least constituted by a sentiment, at times one may make a moral judgment without feeling any emotions, but one is still disposed to feel such emotions. Thus, in such cases of judgment, we may say that our moral concepts are themselves constituted by our sentiments, which are dispositions to feel emotions of approbation and disapprobation even though one does not presently experience any emotions. In other cases where one does feel emotions when making a moral judgment, we may say that one's moral concept in the moral judgment when activated occurrently in working memory is constituted by emotions. For an emotion-based theory, moral concepts which are stored in long term memory are constituted by sentiments, but when a moral judgment is actively rendered in working memory, the moral concept in the judgment in many but not all cases is constituted by emotions.

2.6 Summary of Moral Concept Theories

The candidate theories for moral concepts are: (1) *The Classical View* – Moral concepts are representations of necessary and sufficient conditions. This is the only theory that claims that moral concepts are representations of strict definitions. (2) *The Prototype View* – Moral concepts are representations of statistically frequent basic rules, virtues, reasons for action, and features of moral situations. (3) *The Exemplar View* – Moral concepts are representations of particular moral precedents, acts, and/or agents. These in turn are constituted by representations of features of those precedents, acts, and/or agents, respectively. (4) *The Theory View* – Moral concepts are constituted by representations of normative ethical theories, causal moral laws of an agent's intentions, the essence of moral properties, functions, and/or general background knowledge. These first four theories are cognitivist ones and claim that moral judgments express beliefs. (5) *The Conative View* – Moral concepts are sentiments, emotions, desires, and/or attitudes.

Notes

1 For Berkeley, concepts are modal rather than amodal symbols.
2 I say, "it appears," because the conclusion drawn here may be dependent upon how such things as size and athleticism are weighted.

3 Despite the general assumption in metaethics that I am using that emotions are non-cognitive and are constituted by non-cognitive states such as perhaps qualia and an action tendency or motivation for action, what emotions are is a controversial issue, and it is currently an unsettled matter in the philosophy of mind and in the mind sciences as to whether emotions are in part constituted by cognitive appraisal judgments (normative beliefs) related to one's well-being or not, *inter alia.* Nevertheless, even if an emotion-based theory of moral concepts is viable and emotions may be in part constituted by cognitive states, I do not believe this will have alternate ramifications for the metaethical implications I draw from my theory of moral concepts, such as on the metaethical cognitivism/non-cognitivism debate. This is because I also adopt three cognitivist theories of moral concepts: the prototype, exemplar, and theory views. I already incorporate cognitive states into the structure of moral concepts, so whether or not emotions also contain cognitive states is a moot issue for my ultimate metaethical aims. To note, if emotions are a complex conjunction of cognitive and non-cognitive states, emotions are still different from solely cognitive prototypes, exemplars, and theories. Emotions also are different from mere pure beliefs. Also, it could be the case that some emotions have moral propositional content not by being internally in part constituted by moral beliefs that refer to moral propositions but by standing in the proper causal relation to an external natural property (Prinz 2004, 2007), such as via a causal theory of reference. However, even if this is the case, emotions still differ from pure beliefs given the different constituent components they have. Finally, just as exemplar moral concepts are constituted by exemplars which are in turn constituted by representations of features of the exemplars, emotion-based moral concepts are constituted by emotions which are in turn constituted by such things as qualia and action tendencies.

References

Armstrong, S., Gleitman, L., and Gleitman, H. 1983. "What Some Concepts Might Not Be." *Cognition* 13, 263–308.

Berkeley, George. 1710/1982. *A Treatise Concerning the Principles of Human Knowledge.* Ed. by Kenneth Winkler. Indianapolis, IN: Hackett Publishing Company.

Brooks, L. 1978. "Nonanalytic Concept Formation and Memory for Instances." In *Cognition and Categorization.* Ed. by E. Rosch and B.B. Lloyd. Hillsdale, NJ: Lawrence Erlbaum Associates.

Carey, Susan. 1985. *Conceptual Change In Childhood.* Cambridge, MA: The MIT Press.

Gopnik, Alison and Meltzoff, Andrew N. 1997. *Words, Thoughts, and Theories.* Cambridge, MA: The MIT Press.

Hampton, James. 1979. "Polymorphous Concepts in Semantic Memory." *Journal of Verbal Learning and Verbal Behavior* 18, 441–461.

Keil, Frank C. 1989. *Concepts, Kinds, and Cognitive Development.* Cambridge, MA: The MIT Press.

Lin, E. and Murphy, G. 1997. "The Effects of Background Knowledge on Object Categorization and Part Detection." *Journal of Experimental Psychology* 50A, 25–48.

Locke, John. 1689/1996. *An Essay Concerning Human Understanding.* Ed Kenneth P. Winkler. Indianapolis, IN: Hackett Publishing Company.

Machery, Edouard. 2009. *Doing Without Concepts*. Oxford: Oxford University Press.

Medin, D.L. and Schaffer, M.M. 1978. "Context Theory of Classification Learning." *Psychological Review* 85, 207.

Medin, D. and Schwanenfluegel, P. 1981. "Linear Separability in Classification Learning." *Journal of Experimental Psychology: Human Learning and Memory* 7, 355–368.

Medin, D. and Shoben, E. 1988. "Context and Structure in Conceptual Combination." *Cognitive Psychology* 20, 158–190.

Murphy, Gregory. 2002. *The Big Book of Concepts*. Cambridge, MA: The MIT Press.

Murphy, G. and Medin, D. 1985. "The Role of Theories in Conceptual Coherence." *Psychological Review* 92, 289.

Prinz, Jesse. 2002. *Furnishing the Mind*. Cambridge, MA: The MIT Press.

Prinz, Jesse. 2004. *Gut Reactions*. Oxford: Oxford University Press.

Prinz, Jesse. 2007. *The Emotional Construction of Morals*. Oxford: Oxford University Press.

Quine, W.V.O. 1977. "Natural Kinds." *Naming, Necessity, and Natural Kinds*. Ed. S.P. Schwarz. Ithaca, NY: Cornell University Press, 155–175.

Ridge, Michael. 2014. *Impassioned Belief*. Oxford: Oxford University Press.

Rosch, Eleanor. 1973. "Natural Categories." *Cognitive Psychology* 4, 328–350.

Rosch, Eleanor and Mervis, Caroline. 1975. "Family Resemblances: Studies in the Internal Structure of Categories." *Cognitive Psychology* 7, 573–605.

Smith, Edward and Medin, Douglas. 1981. *Categories and Concepts*. Cambridge, MA: Harvard University Press.

Smith, Michael. 1994. *The Moral Problem*. Oxford: Blackwell Publishers.

Smith, E., Shoben, E., and Rips, L. 1974. "Structure and Process in Semantic Memory: A Featural Model for Semantic Decisions." *Psychological Review* 81, 214–241.

Weiskopf, Daniel. 2009. "The Plurality of Concepts." *Synthese* 169, 145–173.

Wittgenstein, L. 1953. *Philosophical Investigations*. Trans by G. Anscombe. New York: Prentice-Hall.

3 From Causal Studies in Moral Psychology to Moral Concepts

Before being able to assess the various contemporary theories of concepts in light of moral concepts, we need to clarify an important methodological point of how I will go about doing this at many times. Aside from the prototype studies explicitly on moral concepts, the evidence I will present for moral mental representations largely will rely on studies from moral psychology that do not explicitly attempt to draw constitution claims on moral concepts. However, they show that certain mental states play a causal role in moral cognition. The purpose of this chapter is to analyze how one can use such causal studies that are not explicitly on the nature of moral concepts in order to draw relevant constitution claims. I contend that by relying on a functionalist identification, we may use the relevant causal studies in order to draw constitution claims in certain cases. Then, I discuss when the use of such causal studies in order to make moral concept constitution claims is appropriate and inappropriate.

As we will see in later chapters, there are many experiments, such as on the trolley problems, showing the use of cognitive and conative states in moral cognition in the causal moral judgment literature, where psychologists and philosophers rely on experimental evidence to see what mental states influence decision-making. In this literature, Fiery Cushman, Liane Young, and Joshua Greene (2010) in "Multi-system Moral Psychology" observe that there is a general consensus in moral psychology that moral judgments are products of the interaction and competition between two distinct psychological processes: affective processes and cognitive reasoning processes. Similarly, Jonathan Haidt's social intuitionist model is also a dual process view, where affectively valenced intuitions in many cases influence moral judgments, but Haidt (2001, 2012) also acknowledges that sometimes reasoning can influence judgments. Shaun Nichols (2004) also puts forth a dual process theory he calls the sentimental rules view. He believes we have what he calls a 'Normative theory' or a set of rules that prohibit certain behaviors. To be clear, by 'Normative theory,' Nichols is not intending to refer to the theory-theory of moral concepts. For, Nichols allows basic rules that are not ethical theories to count as a 'Normative theory.' Nichols also states that we have an emotional system that can influence moral judgments. Although both of these aspects for Nichols of 'Normative theory' and of an emotional system are at times dissociable, sentimental rules involve both of these mechanisms, where 'Normative theories' become "affect-backed" when adjoined with the emotional system. Nichols maintains that in most cases, the dual processes of 'Normative theory' and emotions causally influence moral judgments.[1]

However, there is a relevant question as to what philosophical implication these kinds of experiments and findings have on moral concepts, if any. I will show in this and the next few chapters that they can be used to draw constitution claims on moral concepts, which will have a later effect on a variety of issues such as the metaethical cognitivism/non-cognitivism debate as to whether our moral judgments and concepts express beliefs, conative states, or perhaps both. Those in the causal moral judgment literature, such as the above, who examine what mental states influence moral decision-making largely do not make the connection in their writings between their findings and the moral concepts literature.[2] The causal judgment literature in moral psychology generally does not discuss the main player in moral cognition and moral decision-making in the psychological domain; namely, moral concepts. Hence, this particular route for connecting such causal experiments to the cognitivism/non-cognitivism debate is not yet open to such moral psychologists. Rather, they generally attempt to draw other ethical implications more in the domain of normative ethical theory. For instance, Greene (2003, 2008, 2013) and Peter Singer (2005) argue that since cognitive reasoning influences utilitarian judgments and emotions influence deontological ones, we should be utilitarians rather than deontologists because emotions are unreliable.

Moreover, since much of the causal moral judgment literature has yet to fully incorporate the concepts literature, it is not surprising that certain views on moral cognition by moral psychologists like Haidt, Greene, and Nichols as of yet lack certain advantages such concept theories can bring to the table in explaining decision-making. For example, Haidt, Greene, and Nichols generally do not focus on the influence of exemplars of highly virtuous agents or prototypes of virtue traits in moral cognition. My pluralistic theory of moral concepts will attempt to bring such views on moral cognition more up to speed *mutatis mutandis* with the standard concrete concepts literature that is able to a great extent explain decision-making on standard concrete entities, such as on household objects.

However, if our moral judgments are influenced by cognitive and conative states, how can it then follow that our moral concepts are constituted by and, therefore, express them? If, for example, emotions influence my categorization of stealing as being unethical, then how can it be the case that UNETHICAL in my STEALING IS UNETHICAL judgment is constituted by an emotion? We will now focus on illustrating the philosophical machinery that will allow us to newly use many of the above kinds of causal studies not explicitly on the structure of moral concepts to draw constitution conclusions on them.

3.1 How to Use Causal Moral Psychology Studies to Draw Conclusions on Moral Concepts

As previously mentioned in the first chapter, concepts are functionally defined as mental representations stored in long-term memory that play a default causal role in at least most of the higher cognitive competences of the mind, such as in categorization, induction, deduction, and analogical reasoning. The representations that constitute a concept causally influence decision-making consciously or subconsciously. In arguing for the viability of the prototype, exemplar, theory, and conative theories for moral concepts, such conclusions are in significant part motivated by the issue of categorization since given the evidence in moral psychology, at times the relevant mental states play a qualified kind of causal role in determining when *a* is categorized as an *F*. In this and many other respects, empirical data can be used to show that prototype, exemplar, and theory knowledge as well as conative states can play an important qualified role in the relevant higher competences.

However, if I causally influence a rubber ball to roll by pushing it with my fingers, then it certainly does not follow that the ball is constituted by my fingers. Rather, it is constituted by rubber, but it is causally influenced to move in its present direction in significant part by my fingers. Causation does not necessarily lead to a proper constitution inference in all cases. Likewise, it may seem to many that what psychologically influences one to form a moral judgment is one thing. However, by no means does it then follow that my moral judgment is in part constituted by the relevant influence. One cannot infer constitution claims that invoke the "is" of identity from causal evidence. However, I believe this is false. For, making moral judgments are acts of categorization where, for instance, an act is classified as being right or wrong. As previously illustrated in Machery's definition of concepts and as also pointed out by Weiskopf, in psychology, concepts are thought to play a functional or causal role in categorization and in other relevant higher competences. Based on the functional definability of concepts, they are constituted by those mental representations or structure(s) that best fill or realize the specified kind of causal role. This is the underlying metaphysics in the concepts literature. Thus, for example, if certain judgments are caused by theories, then the relevant concepts in the judgments are constituted by theories since theories best realize the specified kind of causal role. Likewise, in some cases, if certain judgments are caused by conative states, then the relevant moral concepts in the judgments are constituted by them since conative states realize the specified kind of causal role (Park 2013, 2018).

Mental representations of the statistically frequent features of members of a class and mental representations of particular instances of a class causally explain how we may classify certain three-dimensional objects. Thus, the prototype and exemplar theory, respectively, are spawned for relevant standard concrete concepts since prototypes and exemplars best fill the specified causal roles. Theoretical beliefs of biological hidden essences and causal laws in a specified way influence categorization of whether a biological object falls within a certain natural kind. Thus, the theory-theory of concepts is a viable view and some biological natural kind concepts may be constituted by beliefs about hidden essences and causal laws. Theory knowledge can causally influence some classifications in the moral domain. What realize the specified causal role in these relevant cases of these acts of classification are theories, and thus, the relevant concepts are constituted by theories. Likewise, conative states also can influence moral judgments in an appropriate way, so in such cases, the relevant moral concepts are constituted by conative states.

Notice that it is not the case that in the above circumstances, prototypes, exemplars, theories, and conative states somehow directly guide the construction of certain concepts but do not end up constituting them. Nor is it the case that in the above circumstances, prototypes, exemplars, theories, and conative states only modulate behavior in some way but do not constitute the relevant concepts. For, to make such claims and the like would be to fundamentally misunderstand the functional definition of concepts and their functional identification. Although certain qualifications will be discussed shortly, in virtue of realizing the causal role and fulfilling the job description that concepts have, the relevant concepts just are prototypes, exemplars, theories, or conative states.

Here, different structures also can work together in cognition. For example, when seeing Jay mistreat a waitress, this event may be a similarity match for my prototypes MISTREATMENT and DO NOT DISRESPECT OTHERS constituting my UNETHICAL concept. Such prototypes may be activated and used at the front end of the moral categorization process to then elicit anger, where anger next causes me to judge JAY IS UNETHICAL. Anger is a compounding factor that puts the final nail in the coffin for drawing my conclusion. In this case, the prototypes and anger conjointly influence my judgment at different points of the deliberative process, but they both are moral concept constituents since they realize the causal role. Furthermore, that different structures can work together allows for the use of coherentist or reflective equilibrium justificatory thought processes that attempt to attain coherence and a web of mutually supporting judgments among one's ethical theories, prototypes, exemplars, and affect-backed intuitions in order to attempt to justify one's moral judgments.

The above functional handling of concepts is analogous to what takes place with artifacts and many biological properties. An engine is functionally defined as playing a causal role in transforming various forms of energy into mechanical force or motion, where an engine just *is* that which realizes the causal role. Thus, the thing under the hood of my car and in my lawnmower, in virtue of realizing the specified causal role of transforming energy into mechanical force, is an engine. A heart is functionally defined as an organ that plays a causal role in pumping blood. Thus, whatever realizes or plays the causal role such as my heart, a lizard's heart, or an artificial heart is a heart because it fulfills the causal role. Once we have functionally defined what a heart is and we have determined that what I call 'my heart' realizes the causal role of pumping blood, then what I call 'my heart' is indeed a heart. Likewise, concepts are also functionally defined, with an eye toward explaining behavior, as being those psychological structures which play a specified causal role in categorization *inter alia.* Hence, once we determine what best realizes the specified causal role, such as a prototype, a concept may be the relevant realizer. While many philosophers and scientists of the mind are well aware of the causal moral judgment studies that are not explicitly moral concept studies that I will use at times in the ensuing chapters, to the best of my knowledge, no one has been able to see the implications of such studies in light of the functionalist metaphysics of drawing constitution claims on moral concepts. Even though there are no studies explicitly on the exemplar, theory, and conative views for moral concepts and many experiments in the causal moral judgment literature that we will discuss in the following chapters are not explicitly on moral concepts, these studies provide a ripe picking ground for supporting constitution claims on moral mental representations (Park 2013). Unbeknownst to those in the causal judgment literature, such researchers have been sitting on a goldmine. With a functionalist identification, such causal studies may be used to draw conclusions in the metaethical cognitivism/non-cognitivism debate.

3.2 Appropriate and Inappropriate Causal Evidence

However, not any psychological causal influence in the higher competences can be said to constitute the relevant concept. For, this would allow too many different things to constitute one's concept; some mental representations that we ordinarily would not think are relevant conceptual components. For instance, an experimenter may give participants drugs before a natural kind categorization task that makes them feel the emotion of sadness. This sadness may act as an influence at the front end of the categorization process temporarily biasing subjects' responses to be significantly different than if they had not been given the drug. Here, it seems that we would not say that subjects' LION concept is constituted by sadness even though sadness plays a causal role, especially since sadness may not be a default influence. Recall from the first chapter that a default influence is generally one that is used preferentially and presumptively in cognition.

Moral psychology has produced a wealth of studies showing the influence of emotions on some moral judgments in which we likewise would not say that emotions then truly constitute the relevant moral concepts. For instance, Thalia Wheatley and Jonathan Haidt (2005) hypnotized participants to feel the emotion of disgust when presented with a neutral word such as 'take' and 'often'. They then presented participants with situations where they must morally evaluate the protagonist in the story. When neutral studies that contained the word 'take' or 'often' were presented, many subjects still judged the protagonist to be wrong. For example, the following scenario was outlined:

> Dan is a student council representative at his school. This semester he is in charge of scheduling discussions about academic issues. He [tries to *take/often* picks] topics that appeal to both professors and students in order to stimulate discussion.
>
> (2005, p. 782)[3]

For this scenario, hypnotized patients were induced to feel disgust and many judged Dan's actions to be morally wrong even though his actions are, if anything, respectable rather than wrong. This study suggests that emotions can causally influence moral judgments, but it appears mistaken to strongly conclude that our moral concepts are constituted by disgust in this instance in the same way it appears to be wrong to do so in the above LION example.

Additionally, Schnall et al. (2008b) have performed a battery of tests to see if the emotion of disgust affects moral judgments. The first experiment had participants fill out moral questionnaires in an area that was permeated with a flatulent odor. The second test had subjects make moral judgments on vignettes in a dirty setting where there was trash and leftover food on the sticky table that was to be used to fill out the questionnaire, pizza boxes and old tissues were on the floor at their feet, and the chair was worn and had torn cushions. In the third study, subjects were asked to write about and relive a physically disgusting event in their lives. After writing about their event, participants then answered moral questions. The final study induced disgust in participants by showing them a brief film clip of a disgusting scene. Upon viewing this scene, subjects were asked to provide moral judgments for given situations. In all four studies, test participants generally made more severe moral judgments as compared to the control subjects in their respective experiments. Likewise, Schnall et al. (2008a) have shown that if you let participants wash their hands after viewing the disgusting film clip, which may have reduced their feeling of disgust, they generally make less severe moral judgments as compared to those subjects who do not wash their hands. Eskine et al. (2011) have demonstrated that participants given a bitter drink that extraneously induces disgust then generally make more severe moral judgments than control subjects. Seidel and Prinz (2013a, 2013b) have shown that inducing anger in participants by having them listen to the irritating sounds of Japanese noise music leads to such subjects generally then making more severe moral judgments on questionnaires.

These outcomes suggest that emotions can causally influence some moral judgments, but it likewise seems odd to then conclude that our moral concepts express and are constituted by such emotions, especially since such studies do not show that such emotions are used by default in moral cognition as the emotions generally were induced in participants before they even received the categorization tasks. The emotions generally were not initially elicited by subjects' contemplation of the moral dilemmas alone but extraneously by cognitive scientists before participants even entertained the questions. Such emotions may not even arise and generally be used preferentially and presumptively in moral decision-making. To be fair, however, experimenters in the causal moral judgment literature generally do not attempt to use such studies to directly draw constitution claims on moral concepts in the manner I have outlined. Hence, I am not attempting to criticize the likes of Wheatley, Haidt, and Schnall for erroneously drawing moral concept constitution claims from their tests because they make no such claims and do not discuss moral concepts. I am merely pointing out that we cannot use such studies on their own to draw strong constitution claims on moral concepts utilizing my functionalist methodology; although Prinz (2015) points out that it can provide only partial support for the conative view in that if the conative theory is correct, then it predicts that extraneously induced emotions will influence participants' ethical judgments. I will discuss this point further and criticize Prinz's contention for the conative view in chapter seven.

I will now introduce and state an important qualification concerning the fact that a causal influence can lead to a constitution claim on concepts. As I will explain, there are several characteristics that will allow us to determine when an influence is or is not constitutive of a concept, and a positive account of this will now be offered. To note, there also is not much discussion of this topic in the standard concrete concepts realm, and I understand that my theory on this matter also may help to advance our knowledge in the standard concrete concepts domain. We may claim that a causal influence generally leads to a concept constitution claim for concept *x* when the influence is knowledge that (1) is shown to be used by default in cognition when thinking or deliberating about the extension of *x* and (2) is at least in part inferable, deductively or inductively, from the concept in question's inferential base. So long as a mentally represented influence is shown in the relevant experiments to be default knowledge that is at least in part inferable from the concept in question's inferential base, then this generally leads to a constitution claim on concepts. To note, I use the term 'generally' in the previous sentence because when it comes to conative states being in part inferable from the inferential base, an alteration to the above rule of when an influence actually constitutes a concept must be made. This alteration will be discussed later in this section.

The influence must be used by default since, as discussed in the first chapter, concepts are constituted by default knowledge. An inferential base is a theory-theory body of knowledge from which other cognitive influences may be thought to be explained. As fully illustrated in the second chapter (§2.4), it is theory knowledge of normative ethical theories that can explain and systematize other more specific kinds of cognitive moral knowledge. Insofar as ethical theory knowledge provides an explanation for why we hold, for example, the moral prototype knowledge that we do, such ethical theory knowledge falls within the confines of the theory-theory. Furthermore, the inferential base is the most firmly held ethical theory belief(s), such that it would be the last theory belief to go in case one's system of knowledge required revision. The inferential base is specifically a theory belief(s) of an ethical theory master moral principle that occupies a defeasible placeholder position and is not a representation of a necessary and sufficient condition, where this theory belief(s) precisely is the most firmly held out of the set of theory beliefs one may have. The inferential base contains the most firmly held theory belief(s) because we want to be sure that the causal influence can lead to a constitution claim for the relevant concept. If whether an influence constitutes a concept generally and in part turns on whether it may be in part inferable from theory knowledge since the specified theory knowledge systematizes and explains other kinds of cognitive knowledge, it generally should be in part inferable from the most firmly held and stable theory belief(s) of a master moral principle in order to be certain that the influence may be said to constitute the concept. This is why the inferential base only contains the most firmly held theory belief(s). That the influence is in part inferable from the most stable theory belief provides auspicious support that the influence is itself a stable default concept constituent. The theoretical work that the inferential base performs is that if a default influence in the process of deliberation is in part inferable from the base, then the influence constitutes the relevant concept.

I make the qualification that the influence generally must be at least in part inferable rather than just merely inferable from the inferential base because there may be many subsidiary premises needed along with the inferential base in order to draw the relevant inferences. If one claims that in order to constitute a moral concept, one criterion is that an influence needs to be inferable from the inferential base, then this means that the inferential base must also contain all of these subsidiary premises, which may lead to the inferential base having to contain an overwhelming amount of one's knowledge. We obviously do not want the inferential base to contain all of this knowledge, so we must find a way to delimit what knowledge is in the inferential base. This specifically is a variation of the holism problem for the theory-theory in that the theory knowledge that constitutes one's relevant concept unreasonably may balloon out to inevitably include all of one's total knowledge. The claim that an influence must be inferable from the inferential base will run into the problem of holism. However, we may escape this holism problem by claiming that the inferential base contains only theory knowledge that is the last to go in case one's system of knowledge requires revision. It does not contain all of one's knowledge. Moreover, an influence need not be inferable from only what is contained in the inferential base in order to constitute the relevant moral concept, but rather, an influence generally need only be *in part* inferable from the inferential base, where subsidiary premises also may play a role in the relevant inference. However, such ancillary premises need not themselves constitute the inferential base. This is due to the qualification that one criterion for constituting a concept is that an influence generally need be only in part inferable from the inferential base. Only when an influence is default knowledge and generally is in part inferable from the inferential base can we then say that the influence constitutes the concept.

As an example of an inferential base, let us assume there is an agent named Christian whose inferential base belief is OBEY THE COMMANDS OF GOD. This is theory-theory knowledge of divine command theory, where his moral prototype and exemplar knowledge, such as DO NOT STEAL, JESUS HELPING THE BLIND MAN AT BETHSAIDA, and DO NOT LIE, may be thought to be in part inferred from this inferential base. To be sure, there are subsidiary premises needed along with the inferential base in order to reach the inferences that, for instance, one should not steal and lie. For example, one may need premises like "Moses led his people out of Egypt and came upon a burning bush," "the burning bush was God," "God spoke to Moses through divine revelation," and "God gave Moses the Ten Commandments." However, such subsidiary premises need not be represented in Christian's inferential base for his theory-theory MORAL concept since inferential base knowledge only contains the most firmly held ethical theory knowledge and generally, in order to constitute the relevant moral concept, one criterion is that inferences such as DO NOT STEAL need not be inferred solely from what is contained in the inferential base. Rather, in order to constitute the concept, an influence used by default need only be at least in part inferable from the inferential base. Here, the above subsidiary premises regarding the story of Moses can be mentally represented constituents of Christian's BOOK OF EXODUS or STORY OF MOSES AND GOD compound concepts rather than being a part of his firmly held theory knowledge contained in his MORAL concept. This is how one may handle the holism problem for the inferential base.

We will now address what it takes for a conative influence to constitute the relevant moral concept. It will be demonstrated in subsequent chapters that emotions also can constitute our moral concepts. As examples of how certain emotions may be thought to be in part inferred from the inferential base, feeling joy when given the opportunity to help others and feeling guilt when one has done something unethical may be thought to all be in part inferable from the inferential base OBEY THE COMMANDS OF GOD. However, one must be careful here in that in our above examples, it may be something like mentally represented prototype rules that merely talk about emotions rather than actually being an experience of an emotion, such as ONE POTENTIAL FACTOR FOR SEEING SOMETHING AS A WRONG ACT WOULD BE IF THE PERFORMING OF THE ACT ELICITS GUILT, that is in part inferable from the inferential base since the Bible at least implicitly says that the feeling of guilt in many cases influences people to make judgments that their act in a situation is wrong. If this is the case, it has not been shown yet that the emotion itself is in part inferable from the base.

Moreover, strictly speaking, conative states that play a causal role are not in part inferable from the inferential base. As conative states are non-cognitive, then strictly speaking, they are not in part inferable from the base. Rather, strictly speaking, only cognitive states can be logically inferred from a cognitive base. For example, the prototype BE PATIENT may be in part inferable from the inferential base EXEMPLIFY THE VIRTUES THAT LEAD TO A FLOURISHING LIFE. However, a non-representational pro-attitude in-and-of-itself is not logically inferable from the base, although cognitive states that merely talk about the attitude may be.

In order to resolve this issue of when a conative influence is a correct or appropriate influence that actually constitutes the relevant moral concept, we may state that only for conative influences, such an influence constitutes a concept when (1) the conative state is shown to be used by default in the relevant studies for the conative view and (2) the cognitive state that accompanies the influencing conative state is in part inferable from the inferential base. Notice that the above conditions for when a cognitive and conative state constitute a concept share (1) in common but not (2). With (2) for conative constituents, we may avoid the worry that conative states are not in part inferable from the inferential base by shifting the emphasis to the cognitive state that is in harmony with and that accompanies the conative state. We cannot directly test whether the conative state is in part inferable from the inferential base, but we can have an indirect link between conative states and the inferential base by focusing on the cognitive state that accompanies a moral conative state. Such a cognitive state must be in part inferable from the inferential base to draw a moral concept constitution claim with the given conative state. I will argue in more detail in the eighth chapter on the conative view that all influencing moral conative states in moral cognition are also accompanied by moral cognitive states that are in harmony with the conative state in order to make the conative state a moral one, among other things. Conative states always work conjointly with cognitive states and intimately depend on them. Conative states can override certain reasons, but when doing so, it works in conjunction and in harmony with other cognitive moral reasons to help make the conative state itself a moral one. For instance, I may be influenced by the exact same feeling of anger when making certain decisions in moral, conventional, and legal affairs. However, it then will be difficult to distinguish in my mind which is moral anger versus non-moral anger. In order to make such distinctions especially in regard to the moral domain, there must be a moral cognitive state, such as IS UNJUST, which accompanies and is in harmony with the relevant conative state that makes the conative state be a moral one. This cognitive state must be in part inferable from the inferential base, *inter alia*, for the relevant conative state to constitute the moral concept. In what follows, purely for ease of linguistic expression, when referencing the overall general conditions for when an influence actually constitutes a concept, I will state the above original conditions for when cognitive influences constitute a concept. However, this is not meant to in any way abnegate the special conditions just discussed particularly for conative states.

3.3 Tests for Concept Constitution

Now that we have stated the characterizations of when an influence does constitute the relevant concept, we now will discuss several tests that may be used to help us make stronger inferences as to whether an influence actually constitutes the concept. These additional tests may be run after one has already conducted initial studies determining that a particular influence(s) may constitute the concept in question. For example, these tests may be conducted after a theory-theory study is run in which a particular ethical theory knowledge is initially shown to influence a categorization judgment. One such additional test is seeing whether an agent does not retract a judgment that was issued from a particular influence. If the judgment is retracted, then this suggests that the influence is not a default one and/or it is not in part inferable from the inferential base. If the judgment is not retracted, then this suggests that the relevant influence may constitute the concept. Call this the *retraction test*. Here, it is vital that the retraction test be conducted in normal conditions when the experimenters are not attempting to in some way manipulate the participant by trying to get the agent to make a mental error during the test. For instance, the participants should not be hypnotized or be induced with mood altering drugs. Based on the retraction test, if the influence is later retracted, then it is suggestive that the influence does not constitute the relevant concept. It is important to emphasize that the retraction test is not meant to be a decisive method for determining whether a particular influence is in fact the constituent of a concept or not. It is only a test that provides suggestive evidence that an influence may be a constituent of a concept. Notice that it may not necessarily be the case that if the retraction test is passed, then the influence must be a constituent of the relevant concept. For, it may be the case that an individual is frequently prone to some kind of mental error and never retracts a judgment or mostly does not retract a judgment that issues from an influence that does not really constitute the relevant concept. One may wonder how to tell the difference between whether an unretracted judgment or a mostly unretracted judgment is a reflection of mental error or is a reflection of being influenced by a mental representation that is legitimately a constituent of the relevant concept. An unretracted or mostly unretracted judgment may be a result of mental error if there is a plausible causal explanation for why the judgment may be an error, such as when a doctor states that a patient is constantly making delusional judgments because the patient is under the influence of medication.

It is also important to see whether or not the influence in question or even judgment itself is actually part of the inferential base. For, if the influence is a part of the inferential base, then we may understand the ensuing judgment to not be a result of mental error because such a judgment was influenced by the inferential base knowledge. Also, if in the appropriate moral context, a judgment itself is merely a statement of one's most firmly held theory belief, then it also is not a result of mental error. One may determine whether a mental representation is a part of the inferential base or not by uncovering what someone's inferential base is. One may run theory-theory studies, which will be discussed in chapter five, to see what ethical theory knowledge an individual possesses and then also see what theory knowledge will be the last to go in case the individual's system of beliefs requires revision. If an individual maintains more than one ethical theory, then objections or tests can be presented against these various theories and against the rules, reasons, virtues, etc. that may be in part inferred from these theories in order to see which ethical theory knowledge will be most firmly held when the subject's set of beliefs may require revision. It still may be possible that after this, a subject legitimately holds several ethical theories in their inferential base or maintains a hybrid view that fuses several representations of normative ethical theories together, such as consequentialism and deontological theory. Upon finding out what the inferential base is, one may then see whether or not the influence or judgment is a part of the base. All in all, even though the passing of the retraction test may not prove to be definitive, the passing of this test may be said to still provide a degree of suggestive evidence for an influence constituting a concept.

Some factors that may be at play for why an influence is still used in cognition even though, for example, it is not in part inferable from the concept in question's inferential base are various kinds of mental error or various causal routes to mental error such as being hit on the head, mistaken reasoning, mental fatigue, being under the influence of drugs, etc. This appears to be a grab bag of factors, but they are all grounded in the fact that they are at many times various forms of mental error or causal routes to such error. Moreover, such factors may potentially lead one to use a particular mentally represented influence that is really not a part of one's relevant concept.

As an example of a retraction, Christian may be momentarily influenced by the thought PROTECT MY LIFE AT ALL COSTS when deciding to retaliate against a random murderer who has intruded his home. However, Christian is Amish and believes in a life of non-violence. Given Christian's fundamentally held theory beliefs such as OBEY THE COMMANDS OF GOD, we can understand why Christian later retracts his judgment to retaliate against the murderer because his inferential base or fundamental beliefs from which some of his other beliefs may be in part inferred and explained indicate that PROTECT MY LIFE AT ALL COSTS is not supported by them. This provides a deeper explanation for why retractions occur. For instance, Christian's later thought ALWAYS ABSTAIN FROM VIOLENCE influences his judgment to actually not physically defend himself against the intruder. Since this principle is at least in part inferentially supported by OBEY THE COMMANDS OF GOD and by hypothesis, it is default knowledge, this means that it in part constitutes Christian's concept MORALLY OUGHT.

As a qualification, when dealing with the retraction or unretraction of judgments for constitution claims for only prototype, exemplar, and conative theory knowledge,[4] we must state that the test for retraction is based on what constitutes Christian's relevant moral concept(s) as the inferential base at the time period the judgment is made t_1, where there is no change or additions to his inferential base for his relevant moral concept(s) during time periods. For, it is always possible that at a later time period t_2, Christian may receive some kind of new moral education or go through some kind of radical moral conversion that changes what constitutes his relevant inferential base, even though the inferential base knowledge was previously the most firmly held theory knowledge. For example, at t_2, Christian is influenced by an atheist book he reads and becomes an atheist. This effectively changes his inferential base for his concept MORALLY OUGHT. At t_2, he has the principle USE FORCE TO DEFEND ONE'S OWN LIFE which leads him to retract the relevant previous judgments made in t_1 in which he decides not to protect himself against violent intruders. Due to the event that kicks off t_2, many previous moral judgments would be retracted, but it seems odd to say that during t_1, Christian's concept MORALLY OUGHT is not constituted by ALWAYS ABSTAIN FROM VIOLENCE. For, this influence leads to continuous unretracted judgments until his moral conversion decades later such that there is suggestive evidence that it was in part inferable from the inferential base and it was used by default. So long as Christian's concept MORALLY OUGHT has the same inferential base constitution during a time period, his moral concept, generally speaking, is constituted by influences that are supported, explained, and systematized at least in part by the inferential base and that are used by default within that period of time but not outside that time period. Once there are additions or alterations to the inferential base of Christian's concept MORALLY OUGHT at the later period of time t_2, this does not impugn the concept constitution claims that were made during t_1.

Furthermore, a second possible test for figuring out whether a stronger constitution claim may be made in these types of cases is to see what a subject's inferential base is. Recall that I already have described above one possible way for determining what one's inferential base is. In finding what the fundamental and most firmly held systematizing theory belief(s) is, we may examine whether or not a given influence is in part inferable from it and whether it potentially constitutes the concept. If it is in part inferable from the inferential base, then this provides some suggestive evidence that the influence in question may constitute the relevant moral concept. Call this the *inferential base test.* This second test may show whether an influence in question, generally speaking, is at least in part inferable from an inferential base by first discovering what the inferential base is, but notice that it does not necessarily demonstrate that an influence in moral deliberation is used by default. The inferential base test is not meant to provide definitive evidence that an influence in fact constitutes a moral concept. Rather, it is merely a suggestive test for concept constitution. Although not definitive, the inferential base test still lends some defeasible support for drawing a stronger conclusion for when an influence actually constitutes a concept.

Knowledge of an agent's inferential base can also at times eliminate contradictory judgments. Let us return to Christian being attacked by the murderer before his conversion to atheism. Christian may at one point judge both that he should defend himself against the murderer and it is not the case that he should do so. However, the fact that one of his fundamental and most strongly held thoughts is OBEY THE

COMMANDS OF GOD provides reason to believe that he does not really hold contradictory judgments in this particular case because the influence PROTECT MY LIFE AT ALL COSTS is not at least in part inferable from the inferential base. Rather, he really believes that he should not defend himself against his assailant.

Nevertheless, as one example of how an agent may really maintain contradictory beliefs, sometimes it may be possible that an agent maintains two opposing beliefs in his inferential base that are held with equally strong conviction. For instance, Christian* sincerely holds OBEY THE COMMANDS OF GOD as well as a kind of virtue ethical theory, in which one must exemplify the virtues that lead to a flourishing life or perform those actions virtuous agents would perform. Let us say that the primary virtuous agent for Christian* is Malcolm X. Both theories for Christian* are equally important fundamentally basic beliefs. Due to this fact, Christian* judges that he should defend himself against the murderer, and he also judges that it is not the case that he should do so. Beliefs that are held with the same strong conviction within the inferential base leave open the possibility for contradictions in that what directly influence his contradictory judgment are the equally weighted principles ALWAYS ABSTAIN FROM VIOLENCE and USE FORCE TO DEFEND ONE'S OWN LIFE. Here, we may say that Christian's concept MORALLY OUGHT is constituted by both of these equally weighted mentally represented principles since they are in part inferable by the equally firmly held inferential base beliefs and by hypothesis, they are used by default.

Moreover, a third test is to see whether the ensuing judgment from an influence still holds after the influence or the influence's informational value is made aware to the agent. If the judgment does not hold, then this provides suggestive evidence that the relevant influence is not used by default and/or is not in part inferable from the inferential base. Call this the *informational value test*. For example, in a study with eighty-four participants, most test subjects will give lower life satisfaction ratings when there is rainy weather, reflecting the impact of the weather on their current moods (Schwarz & Clore 1983). However, the negative effect of mood on life satisfaction ratings is generally eliminated when experimenters inquire about the weather to participants, which draws respondents' attention to this extraneous source of their mood. In these kinds of cases, the informational value test is a further suggestive way to see whether the influence actually constitutes the concept, although it may not necessarily show that this is the case. For example, a participant in the above study may still be influenced by the weather even when made aware of the weather by the experimenter. In a completely different example in which the informational value test also does not work, one may have a subconscious influence that does not really constitute the concept at hand, but this subconscious influence still persists and plays the relevant functional role even when the subject is made aware of the informational value of this faulty subconscious influence. As we can see, the informational value test is a mere test that may provide stronger suggestive evidence as to whether an influence may constitute the relevant concept. It is not meant to be a definitive means for determining whether an influence in fact constitutes the relevant moral concept. Rather, as can be seen in some instances of the above life satisfaction/rainy weather experiment, it provides defeasible suggestive evidence regarding concept constitution.

Finally, so long as a participant in a study is not initially thought to be experiencing a possible state – such as being hypnotized, being in stormy weather, being extraneously induced with mood altering drugs, etc. – that significantly increases the odds of leading to mental error and the use of an influence that is not really a part of the relevant concept, a successful causal influence experiment provides a degree of support that the influence in question does constitute the relevant concept. When in a state like being hypnotized or given a bitter drink to feel disgust before reading moral questionnaires, the possibility is significantly raised that the given mental influence for a judgment is not a default one and/or is not in part inferable from the inferential base. Let us call this the *possible mental error test.* Like the other tests, this is not definitive for concluding that an influence constitutes the relevant concept, although it provides significant support. For example, I may not be under any kind of relevant mental duress that is an indication of the strong possibility of making a mental error, but I make a rare subconscious mental mistake in moral deliberation on a case. This subconscious influence does not really constitute my moral concept even though the possible mental error test is passed.

Hence, we can see that there are several suggestive ways to test for and make a stronger claim that an influence constitutes a concept. The actual running of the above tests provides the additional support for making a stronger claim that the influence in question makes up the relevant concept. While the passing of the inferential base test provides the most certainty, the four tests along with the other possible various combinations of them can provide more support for making a stronger constitution claim. Induction comes in matters of degree. If more tests are run, the degree of likelihood that an influence is a relevant concept constituent will increase.

While the fact that a mental representation is shown to be an influence in decision-making provides initial support for a concept constitution claim, at minimum, the possible mental error test additionally needs to come into play. For, it could be the case that experimenters hypnotized a participant to experience such an influence, but the influence is not at all inferable from the subject's inferential base and/or it is not a default influence.[5] Running the possible mental error test will highlight those experiments that we immediately should be weary of since they include conditions that likely can lead to making mental errors. Furthermore, such mental conditions may likely lead one to later retract one's judgment, especially if the informational value is provided. Once we have on the table positive and replicated empirical confirmation from well-designed experiments that a given structure(s) influences decision-making and such studies pass the possible mental error test such that they do not raise any immediate red flags, then this allows one to draw a moderate concept constitution conclusion, where running even more of the above tests will allow one to draw even stronger conclusions. It will be understood that successful causal studies that pass the possible mental error test will allow for drawing concept constitution claims or, in other words, claims about what mental states our moral judgments express. This may be the case even though the retraction, inferential base, and informational value tests have not been conducted on the influence and corresponding judgment in question. So long as the possible mental error test is passed, we can charitably interpret subjects responding to decision-making questions from studies that are, in-and-of-themselves, well designed as using thought processes and influences that are consistent with their relevant inferential base, unless suggested otherwise by the presence of things like relevant psychological biases, which will be discussed later in this book. For example, when asking participants in a manner that passes the possible mental error test whether a beagle is a dog in a prototype test, we defeasibly and charitably may presume that their answers are influenced by thought processes consistent with their inferential base, unless suggested otherwise. Therefore, for the DOG prototype study, we can claim that since they were relevantly influenced by default by HAS FOUR LEGS, BARKS, PLAYS FETCH, etc., these constitute their DOG concept. To note, many to most concept constitution conclusions drawn from experiments in the standard concrete concepts domain are moderate claims, and the constitution claims I make on moral concepts also should be understood as being moderate claims that pass the possible mental error test.

Notes

1 Joshua May (2018) also claims that both reason and emotions influence judgment, but reason is the main driver. He writes, "Our dual process minds afford both kinds of influence on moral thinking" (79). However, he does not attempt to draw constitution claims on moral concepts from such causal data.

2 A notable exception who attempts to draw concept constitution claims from such evidence is Prinz. However, his methods will be criticized in chapter seven.

3 My italics.

4 The theory-theory is excluded because if inserted, it would lead to a circular statement: We apply the retraction test to determine what is part of the inferential base, but here we appeal to what is in the inferential base to decide how to apply the test.

5 The possibility is left open that along with other premises, perhaps such an inference with such studies may be drawn. However, one cannot *only* use studies that extraneously induce mental states in subjects to draw concept constitution claims.

References

Cushman, F., Young, L., and Greene, J. 2010. "Our Multi-system Moral Psychology: Towards a Consensus View." *The Oxford Handbook of Moral Psychology*. Ed. by Doris, J., Harman, G., Nichols, S. Oxford: Oxford University Press.

Eskine, K., Kacinik, N., and Prinz, J. 2011. "A Bad Taste in the Mouth: Gustatory Disgust Influences Moral Judgment." *Psychological Science* 23, 295–299.

Greene, Joshua. 2003. "From Neural 'Is' to Moral 'Ought': What Are the Moral Implications of Neuroscientific Moral Psychology?" *Nature Review Neuroscience* 4, 847–850.

Greene, Joshua. 2008. "The Secret Joke of Kant's Soul." *Moral Psychology Volume* 3. Ed. by Walter Sinnott-Armstrong. Cambridge, MA: The MIT Press.

Greene, Joshua. 2013. *Moral Tribes*. New York: The Penguin Press.

Haidt, Johnathan. 2001. "The Emotional Dog and Its Rational Tail: A Social Intuitionist Approach to Moral Judgment." *Psychological Review* 108, 814–834.

Haidt, Jonathan. 2012. *The Righteous Mind*. New York: Vintage Books.

May, Joshua. 2018. *Regard for Reason in the Moral Mind*. Oxford: Oxford University Press.

Nichols, Shaun. 2004. *Sentimental Rules*. Oxford: Oxford University Press.

Park, John. 2013. "Theories of Moral Concepts." In *Truth Matters*. Ed. by L. Zuidervaart, A. Carr, M. Klaassen, and R. Shuker. Montreal, Quebec: McGill-Queens University Press, 211–224.

Park, John. 2018. "The Emotion Theory of Concepts." *Journal of Consciousness Studies* 25, 162–180.

Prinz, Jesse. 2015. "An Empirical Case for Motivational Internalism." *Motivational Internalism*. Ed. by G. Bjornsson, C. Strandberg, R.F. Olinder, J. Eriksson. Oxford: Oxford University Press, 61–84.

Schnall, S., Benton, J., and Harvey, S. 2008a. "With a Clean Conscience: Cleanliness Reduces the Severity of Moral Judgments." *Psychological Science* 19, 1219–1222.

Schnall, S., Haidt, J., Clore, G., and Jordan, A. 2008b. "Disgust as Embodied Moral Judgment." *Personality and Social Psychology Bulletin* 34, 1096–1109.

Schwarz, Norbert and Clore, Gerald. 1983. "Mood, Misattribution, and Judgments of Well-Being." *Journal of Personality and Social Psychology* 45, 513.

Seidel, Angelika and Prinz, Jesse. 2013a. "Sound Morality: Irritating and Icky Noises Amplify Judgments in Divergent Moral Domains." *Cognition* 127, 1–5.

Seidel, A. and Prinz, J. 2013b. "Mad and Glad: Musically Induced Emotions Have Divergent Impact on Morals." *Motivation and Emotion* 37, 629–637.

Singer, Peter. 2005. "Ethics and Intuitions." *The Journal of Ethics* 9, 331–352.

Wheatley, Thalia and Haidt, Jonathan. 2005. "Hypnotic Disgust Makes Moral Judgments More Severe." *Psychological Science* 16, 780–784.

4 The Prototype, Exemplar, and Classical Views

We will now assess the viability of the prototype, exemplar, and classical theories for moral concepts in light of categorization, cognitive content, and concept acquisition. An examination of these theories in light of other desiderata, such as concept combination, will be discussed in chapter nine. I will first criticize several attempts in the literature that contend for the viability of the prototype view for moral concepts, and I subsequently in part will provide my own contention for the prototype theory. Next, I will argue for the viability of the exemplar theory of moral concepts. Finally, I will contend that the classical view is not psychologically real for ethical concepts and discuss what implications this has for normative ethics.

4.1 Previous Arguments for the Prototype Theory

Recall that for moral concepts, prototypes are representations of statistically frequent basic rules, reasons for action, virtues, and features of moral situations. A few philosophers have adopted the cognitivist prototype theory as a viable view for moral concepts. Paul Churchland (1989), Stephen Stich (1993), Alvin Goldman (1993), Andy Clark (1996), David Wong (2006), Kim Sterelny (2010), and Gilbert Harman et al. (2012) are examples of philosophers who have espoused this view. For instance, Churchland, in *A Neurocomputational Perspective*, can be read as providing an account of moral concept acquisition by positing the existence of moral prototypes. Churchland argues that learning about morality is more about learning *how* rather than a matter of learning *that*. In other words, moral concept acquisition is about learning how to recognize various complex situations and how to appropriately respond to them by way of an at times long and painful process of social learning rather than by applying moral principles. On this view, certain moral situations will activate prototypes given the situation's similarity to one's previous experiences and training in other moral scenarios. Through social experience and further development, a child's moral prototypes and practical wisdom can change and expand by being impacted by factors such as how society expects them to react to certain circumstances. For instance, a child may be guided in life primarily by self-interest. However, later the child comes to realize that her society generally expects her to take into consideration others' feelings and interests in certain moral scenarios. Fully taking into account other people's considerations leads to a change in her moral prototypes.

While the enthusiasm and insight of applying the prototype theory to moral concepts is duly noted, Churchland and the other above-mentioned philosophers do not support the claim that moral concepts have prototype structure with the appropriate evidence. James Hampton (1981) ran tests on eight different concepts, such as BELIEF, SCIENCE, and CRIME, which are not standard concrete concepts, in order to determine whether they had prototype structure similar to the successful results of finding prototype structure in standard concrete concepts like DOG and APPLE. In Hampton's study, the results were a mixed bag where some concepts did show prototype structure, but others did not. For example, SCIENCE and CRIME showed prototype structure while concepts such as A BELIEF and AN INSTINCT, which may intuitively be thought to have prototype structure, as a matter of fact do not have such structure. This study demonstrates that when experimentally examining concepts, one may find that a concept or class of concepts does not have the psychological structure that one might expect. Just because certain structures are viable for standard concrete concepts, this does not mean that they are viable for concepts that are not standard concrete concepts. Hence, one cannot rely on experimental work on standard concrete concepts alone to sufficiently draw constitution claims on concepts that are not standard concrete concepts. Hence, without some experimental basis and justification specifically on moral concepts, it may be the case that such concepts also lack prototype structure. Without appropriate evidence specifically on the class of concepts at hand, a concept constitution claim on such a class is too speculative and thus is unjustified. As we shall see below as well as in the following chapters, there are many moral concept constitution claims in the literature that are problematically speculative and unjustified. Therefore, in light of Hampton's study, we must take precaution and make sure to support structural claims for moral concepts at least in part with experimental work on moral mental representations rather than just quickly relying on studies on standard concrete concepts. For moral concepts, experimental evidence on such concepts at least is required to appropriately conclude that a moral concept has such and such a concept structure.

What are further required in order to make conclusions about a moral concept's structure may be experimental studies on moral concepts, or they may be such studies coupled with philosophical or theoretical arguments. As stated, it is also important to note that this does not necessarily deny that the empirical findings on standard concrete concepts can be used to draw conclusions concerning moral concepts. Such empirical findings may be used to make inferences only in conjunction with specific experimental work that is focused on moral concepts. However, what is denied is that standard concrete concept empirical work can by itself be sufficient to establish a concept structural conclusion for ethical concepts. Given the above, no experimental studies on moral concepts are cited in Churchland's work or in any of the other above-mentioned philosophers' writings to warrant the claim that moral concepts have prototype structure. Thus, their prototype conclusions are speculative and unjustified.

While most experimental work on the prototype theory has generally focused on standard concrete concepts, there are a handful of studies on certain concepts that do not appear to be straightforwardly moral concepts but may be somehow related to them. For example, Linda Coleman and Paul Kay (1981) have run a study that illustrates prototype structure for the concept LIE. The issue with LIE is that it appears to be a concept that has components that are in some way or another merely about descriptive acts. Therefore, LIE may not itself be a normative concept. There does not appear to be any explicit rightness or wrongness associated with the concept LIE, as opposed to if LIE is a constituent in the judgment, ONE OUGHT NOT LIE, where this entire thought itself is about a normative principle. It will be important to keep this potential problem in mind while we examine Coleman and Kay's studies. This initial test is replicated and supported by two further experiments on the concept by Eve Sweetser (1989) on the one hand and Abigail Strichartz and Roger Burton (1990) on the other. In the Coleman and Kay experiment, they ran a study to see if the following features that are represented by the constituent components of LIE are defining necessary and sufficient conditions or whether they are a summary representation of features for folk in determining when a particular act is a lie:

(1) P is false.
(2) S believes P to be false.
(3) In uttering P, S intends to deceive A.

Thus, in essence, they tested for falsehood, deliberate falsehood, and intent to deceive. They provided participants with a host of situations that contained eight various combinations of the three given features; features that may be present or absent in the various combinations, where subjects were asked to circle whether the situation is a lie, is not a lie, or unknown. They were also questioned on the typicality of each situation as an instance of lying or not lying. Coleman and Kay found that the more of the three features of lying that a situation contained, the more typical or better instance of a lie the situation is deemed to be.

Moreover, they discovered weighted features, where (2) is the most heavily weighted and (3) is next in importance. Strichartz and Burton (1990), who were able to successfully replicate this study, also discovered that the weight placed on each of the features differs based on age or maturity. Also, situations that contained any variation of two of the features tended to have a mean score where such situations are still considered as lies. Recall that typicality effects, weighted features, and the fact that the three given qualities are not used as necessary and sufficient conditions for determining category membership help lead to the conclusion that LIE has prototype structure.

Another study in which the concept in question may or may not be a moral concept is Hampton's (1981) aforementioned study on concepts that examined the concept CRIME. This too, like LIE, initially appears to have components that are only about a descriptive kind of act. He was able to produce typicality effects and reach the conclusion that CRIME has prototype structure. By way of a standard feature-listing task experiment, as fully illustrated in the second chapter (§2.2), where participants in part list what features they think belong to a category, he was able to discover that participants associated features such as *an act, adverse effect on victim,* and *is done deliberately* with the category *crime,* where such features have different weights and account for typicality effects. Furthermore, such features are not necessary and sufficient conditions for determining category membership based on the fact that some situations are deemed to be crimes, but they do not satisfy all of the perceived features of crime.

The question now is whether the perceivably descriptive prototype concepts LIE and CRIME are in fact normative moral concepts that have prototype structure. For, if they are, then this shows that in some cases prototype theory is a viable theory of moral concepts. Mark Johnson (1993) argues that specifically LIE is in fact a moral concept that has prototype structure. He makes this claim based on Sweetser's insight that the prototype structure of LIE is dependent on one's background knowledge or what George Lakoff calls an idealized cognitive model. As Lakoff (1987) contends, "category structures and prototype effects are by-products of [idealized cognitive models]" (p. 68). Idealized cognitive models are structural organizations of our background knowledge, where such models are themselves exercised in the higher cognitive competences. They are similar to a complex version of the theory-theory for standard concrete concepts in that they associate general background knowledge and beliefs with a concept. Idealized cognitive models or organized abstracted background beliefs and information we have acquired through our experience with the world become selected during cognition based on the context or situation we find ourselves in. Such knowledge may be in the form of imaginative structures that help us make order and sense out of the world by aiding us in such things as categorization and concept combination. Moreover, such knowledge provides a way for us to evaluate certain circumstances and judgments based on our previous social experiences. Lakoff claims that idealized cognitive models underwrite the prototype structure of concepts.

Johnson claims that LIE is dependent on the idealized cognitive model of "ordinary communication." Thus, such a cognitive model provides the requisite background information when we converse with others, such that we have the proper expectations that in normal conversations we may assume such things as that the truth will normally be told. This cognitive model may account for the fact that communication is even possible among human beings given that we do not always have to worry that any and every person we talk to could very well be lying to us. Thus, we have:

The Idealized Cognitive Model of "Ordinary Communication"

(1) People intend to help rather than harm one another.
(2) Truthful information is helpful.
(3) The speaker intends to help the hearer by sharing information.
(4) A speaker who knowingly communicates false information intends to harm the hearer (Lakoff 1987).

Since the cognitive model of "ordinary communication" accounts for the background beliefs (1)–(4) that most people have with respect to *lie* and the prototype effects for LIE are grounded in this cognitive model as well, Johnson claims that LIE is a moral normative concept.

> [W]e need only remind ourselves why lying is usually considered to be a bad thing to do. The answer is that lying is typically *harmful* to others. But notice that the relevant notion of harm is partially specified by the idealized cognitive model of ORDINARY COMMUNICATION. A notion of helping and harming is *built into* that model. Therefore, to the extent that our determination of what counts as a lie in a particular situation depends on the idealized cognitive model of ORDINARY COMMUNICATION, our understanding of *lie* is inextricably tied up with an evaluative notion of help and harm.
>
> (Johnson 1993, pp. 95–96)

Johnson may be on the right track here in that he appears to want to bring in the notion of the moral wrongness of harming others as part of "ordinary communication." Insofar as there is some connection between the prototype of LIE and the idealized cognitive model, LIE may then be considered to be a normative moral concept that has prototype structure. However, the first problem is that if we closely examine the four beliefs in the idealized cognitive model for "ordinary communication," we still do not see anything explicitly normative. The concepts HELPING and HARMING, by themselves, may be thought of as merely being about a descriptive class of acts that have to do with alleviating or instigating physical or psychological harm from or to another human being, respectively. Therefore, since there is no explicit notion of moral wrongness in (1)–(4), it still may not be the case that LIE is a moral concept.

Second and what is even more problematic is that since the idealized cognitive model is claimed to be one of the fundamental structures of the concept LIE, no experimental evidence is given to indicate that LIE has such a structure. Idealized cognitive models such as "ordinary communication" are purported structural aspects of LIE, but no experimental data on this potential moral concept has been collected to warrant this assertion. Rather, such a conclusion is given based on studies on standard concrete concepts. Therefore, Johnson's claim that idealized cognitive models underwrite the prototype structure of moral concepts and supposedly allow LIE to be a moral concept is too speculative and is unjustified.

4.2 Thick Moral Concepts

The question still remains as to whether LIE may be shown to be a moral concept in a manner where the concept has prototype structure. In this way, we may conclude that the prototype theory is a viable theory for some moral concepts. In order to accomplish this, we will need to bring in the aid of Bernard Williams (1985) and his discussion of thin and thick moral concepts; a view which is influenced by John McDowell (1978). Williams argues that there are thin moral concepts which appear to be purely normative such as RIGHT, GOOD, BAD, and OUGHT. On the other hand, there exist thick concepts that have both a normative and descriptive component to them; components that are not separable and are culturally formed. Williams (1985) explicitly lists LIE as a thick concept among others such as PROMISE, BRUTALITY, COURAGE, and GRATITUDE (p. 140). For example, LIE has a descriptive or factual component in that such a component is typically about a particular kind of verbal act of deception and members of a particular community who have this concept can point out when an instance of lying has occurred. However, it also has a normative or value component that is about "oughtness" which seemingly provides reasons for action that generally one ought not to lie. It is contended that these features the two components represent are necessarily intertwined and inseparable in that they are represented by the components of culturally conditioned concepts, where, as McDowell argues, an outside observer of a community cannot fully pick up and understand the features represented by the descriptive component of a community's thick moral concepts without also imaginatively grasping the features represented by the normative evaluative component of the concept. Thus, Williams and McDowell argue that the fact/value distinction has not been found or discovered in the concepts and language of ethics, but rather, it has been artificially brought there by the minds of philosophers such as R.M. Hare. What we can see here is that even though *lie* first appears to have features pertaining to descriptive acts, it generally is thought to have a negative normative feature attached to it in the United States, where there is an initial defeasible presumption that acts of lying are wrong. Something similar to this may be at work for *promise* as well, albeit in a positive normative sense. It is this normative aspect that is represented by the components of LIE that allows LIE to be a proper thick moral concept.

Given that it has been determined that LIE has a prototype structure and that it may be a thick moral concept where members of a community who acquire the concept understand it to have components that are about descriptive and normative features, we should expect that experimentally, at least one of the components of the prototype for LIE will be about a moral normative feature. However, the three prototype studies for LIE are not feature-listing tasks where participants list what features they believe belong to the category a concept represents. Rather, the possible features for the class are already preconceived by the experimenters and given to the participants with no room for expansion. The predetermined features for *lie* are not explicitly normative features. Thus, we cannot know for certain whether participants attributed a normative moral feature to the class. However, Hampton's feature-listing task study for CRIME, which was run in the United States, did show that the corresponding concept had prototype structure in which one of the features for *crime* frequently listed by participants appears to be morally normative: *breaks the moral and social code.*

While MORAL is typically understood to be a normative concept which would mean that CRIME must itself then be a normative concept since it is in part constituted by MORAL, one may object that perhaps BREAKS THE MORAL CODE is being understood in an anthropological sense where it is merely a neutral descriptive thought had by participants of what a culture thinks about a crime. While this is a possibility, we will later examine a study on HIGHLY MORAL PERSON. While this compound concept also contains the concept MORAL, albeit in a different context as compared to the case we are presently examining, what constitutes this compound concept may help us to infer whether the folk generally understand BREAKS THE MORAL CODE to be a normative rather than an anthropological component of CRIME. The study on HIGHLY MORAL PERSON found that most participants' concepts contained what are usually thought to be normative virtue concepts such as HAS INTEGRITY and HONORABLE. It also contained concepts such as EXEMPLARY and RESPECTED that imply that one ought to imitate highly moral individuals because they are praiseworthy. Moreover, if subjects viewed morality to be anthropologically descriptive rather than prescriptive, then we should expect their components of HIGHLY MORAL PERSON to contain complex concepts such as FOR OUR CULTURE, FOR THIS SOCIETY, or something to this effect that qualifies the components this concept may have. However, no such anthropological qualifiers were found. Based on the fact that most participants' HIGHLY MORAL PERSON concept is constituted by what are typically thought to be normative concepts, concepts of or related to ought-to-be-pursuedness, and that there are no relevant anthropological qualifications to the components of the compound, it appears that a reasonable inference may be made that when simply moving from thoughts concerning MORAL PERSONS to MORAL CODES, the thought BREAKS THE MORAL CODE may likely be understood to also have like normative components *mutatis mutandis* rather than anthropologically descriptive ones. Naturally, a stronger inference may be made if the same subjects used in Hampton's CRIME study also were used in the HIGHLY MORAL PERSON experiment or if Hampton's study directly questioned the nature of BREAKS THE MORAL CODE. While such studies have not been conducted, given the present circumstances, a moderate inference still may be made that allows us to conclude that it is likely that participants in Hampton's study for CRIME think of BREAKS THE MORAL CODE in a normative rather than anthropological light.

Therefore, in this fashion, since CRIME may now be shown to be a thick moral concept, Williams' contention for dual components to thick concepts is to a certain extent empirically vindicated. Given that CRIME is a thick culturally formed moral concept with a component that represents a moral normative feature and that it has prototype structure, we may conclude that this moral concept has prototype structure (Park 2013), although it has not been proven nor need it be proven for our purposes that the dual components are inextricably linked. All that needs to be shown is that there is a normative component to CRIME which then qualifies it as a thick moral concept in the United States and most likely in other cultures as well that view crimes in a negative normative light. Nothing need be said here about whether the normative component is in principle separable from the descriptive component. Furthermore, a predictive inference may be drawn that if a feature-listing task for *lie* is actually conducted, a statistically frequent moral normative feature may be given by subjects since it is the case that such a feature has been discovered to exist for *crime.*

Also, notice that the given conclusion that the prototype theory is a viable theory of moral concepts is not speculative. By using experimental data on certain specific thick concepts that initially appear to refer to only a descriptive class of acts along with the application of philosophical argumentation regarding such concepts, we have discovered that CRIME has prototype structure.

4.3 Moral Prototype Experiments

At this juncture, I will introduce several experiments on specific concepts that are more clearly within the moral domain. These following experiments largely are not cited by philosophers who have written on the prototype theory of moral concepts. Such studies also rely on the standard feature-listing task prototype experimental design (§2.2). Jennifer Frei and Phillip Shaver (2002) have run a study on the concept RESPECTFUL TO A PARTNER, which may be considered to be more directly a moral concept in that it is a compound virtue concept. This study found that this compound concept is constituted by such things as SENSITIVE TO FEELINGS, FOSTERS EQUALITY, CARING, HAVING MORAL QUALITIES, and LISTENS TO MY VIEWPOINT. Typicality effects were discovered for this complex concept. Furthermore, the list of features was not used by participants as being necessary and sufficient conditions for determining whether a potential member belonged to the category. Hence, insofar as RESPECTFUL TO A PARTNER is a moral virtue concept with prototype structure, this provides further evidence that prototype theory is a viable theory for moral concepts.[1]

In a separate study, Lawrence Walker and Karl Hennig (2004) discovered prototype structure for compound concepts that contained representations of virtues. Specifically, they discovered prototype structure for JUST PERSON, BRAVE PERSON, and CARING PERSON. For instance, for JUST PERSON, they found that some of the statistically frequent components were LISTENS TO ALL SIDES, FAIR, MORAL, and TRUTHFUL. For BRAVE PERSON, some of the statistically frequent components were HEROIC, FACES DANGER, STANDS UP FOR BELIEFS, and GALLANT. For CARING PERSON, some of those components that passed the production frequency measure to be summary representation components were SYMPATHETIC, MORAL, GOOD-HEARTED, LOVING, and NURTURING. Common to many prototype theories, for all three compound concepts, they discovered that some of the components were weighted as more important than others. Thus, a potential member will be categorized in a class if she matches the features represented by the heavily weighted components and passes the calculated similarity threshold even though she may not match the features represented by the lower weighted components. Furthermore, members that match many components and more heavily weighted ones can be considered more typical members than those members that have less of such matching. Given that components of the compounds are weighted and are not used as necessary and sufficient features, this lends evidence to the conclusion that such moral concepts have prototype structure.

Lawrence Walker and Russell Pitts (1998) were able to discover prototype structure for a complex concept that contains a thin moral concept. The complex concept in question is the aforementioned HIGHLY MORAL PERSON. They asked participants to freely list any attributes members of such a category may have. Through a production frequency measure, they found that some of the statistically frequent features subjects listed were: *has clear values, self-disciplined, principled, exemplary, maintains high standards*, and *has integrity*. Moreover, they also discovered that of the statistically frequent qualities, certain ones were deemed to be more heavily weighted than others. Moreover, the qualities were not used as necessary and sufficient conditions in categorization tasks. Given that the statistically frequent features are weighted and are not used as necessary and sufficient conditions, this provides evidence that HIGHLY MORAL PERSON has prototype structure. What also is interesting here is that while many philosophers believe thin moral concepts like MORAL only have an evaluative component, this study shows that thin moral concepts also have descriptive components in that they are in part constituted by thick concepts, such as HAS INTEGRITY which, as we have seen, do have a descriptive component. This along with other studies examined in this section on thin concepts helps to eliminate the traditional distinction between thin and thick concepts.

Finally, Kyle Smith et al. (2007), in a cross-cultural study, have determined that there is prototype structure for GOOD PERSON. This feature-listing task experiment spanned seven different cultures including Chamorro, Filipino, Taiwanese, Turkish, United States, Venezuelan, and Palauan participants in which weighted statistically frequent features that are represented by prototypes and that are not used as necessary and sufficient conditions were discovered in all of the cultures. Here, our experimenters claim that cultures varied substantially in terms of which features they have in mind when representing GOOD PERSON. For example, a couple of heavily weighted components generally held for people in the United States are CARING and HONEST. These components were not contained within the set of heavily weighted components for the GOOD PERSON concept for the Taiwanese. Rather, their respective concept was constituted by heavily weighted components such as INDEPENDENT and TOLERANT; components not contained within the set of heavily weighted components for the GOOD PERSON concept for people from the United States.

Given all of the above studies that in part contained concepts such as GOOD, MORAL, CARING, RESPECTFUL, JUST, CRIME, and BRAVE, we now may inductively infer that moral concepts generally do have prototype structure in light of categorization. To further buttress this conclusion, in the eighth chapter on the conative view, I will argue that the presence of conative states as conceptual constituents will itself provide evidence for cognitivist theories of moral concepts like the prototype theory.

Concerning the sense desideratum, the prototype view provides a plausible account of the cognitive content or sense of our moral concepts. We in part psychologically understand ethics and the moral world in terms of prototypes. Moreover, prototypes can account for how we may understand two compound concepts differently even though they are co-referential. For example, I may not know that my good friend is really a sensible knave since he is so sensible, but others have warned me that I have a sensible knave in my life without telling me who it is. I understand MY GOOD FRIEND in part as KIND, HONEST, and TRUSTWORTHY. I understand THE SENSIBLE KNAVE IN MY LIFE in part as MEAN, DISHONEST, and UNTRUSTWORTHY. Such prototype constituents of my moral concepts can in part account for my different thoughts or senses I have for the two compound concepts even though both compounds are co-referential.[2]

The viability of the prototype theory for moral concepts sits well with the concept acquisition desideratum, which, as discussed in the first chapter, is the capacity for a theory of concepts to lend itself to theories of how concepts are acquired. Concept theories do not necessarily have to put forth a comprehensive theory of how we acquire concepts, but it must at minimum put forth a conceptual structure that plausibly can be acquired in a manner consistent with dominant views on concept acquisition. The concept acquisition and categorization desiderata can be thought of as two sides of the same psychological phenomenon – our disposition to put individual items into classes. If we have acquired a concept, then we can attempt to categorize items as supposedly being members of the extension of the concept.[3] Likewise, if we can use a concept to categorize, then we have acquired the concept in some fashion.[4] We have already discussed numerous prototype categorization studies that show that various moral concepts are constituted by prototypes, some of which were even in part run on children (Strichartz and Burton 1990, Smith et al. 2007). Such studies may also be used to demonstrate that we acquire prototype knowledge at some point in moral education. The previously discussed prototype categorization studies show that we acquire moral prototypes.

As mentioned in the second chapter regarding the illustration of the prototype view, with the possible acquisition of things such as basic rules, one's prototype MORALLY WRONG concept through moral education may be constituted by representations like DO NOT HARM OTHERS and DO NOT LIE. Here, on the prototype view, components will be weighted where there will be graded membership. For example, DO NOT HARM OTHERS may weigh more in terms of importance for a child than DO NOT LIE because, for example, the child receives more punishment for hitting others than lying or the child's parents and teachers more strongly emphasize that hitting others is bad. Therefore, in this case, the child will judge acts of striking others as more seriously wrong than acts of being dishonest.

One of the most natural ways to acquire prototypes is by ostension and inferring them by viewing particular members of a category that are mentally represented by exemplars. For example, when an anthropologist visiting the Korowai of Southwestern East Papua sees several particular acts of cannibalism and on each occasion is told by them that such acts are morally permissible, the anthropologist may infer that a prototype feature of morally permissible acts among others for the Korowai is being able to kill certain criminals and eat them. The anthropologist's MORALLY PERMISSIBLE FOR THE KOROWAI compound concept is in part constituted by the abstracted prototype KILLING CERTAIN CRIMINALS AND EATING THEM. This prototype knowledge was extrapolated from her experiences of particular culturally understood morally permissible acts of cannibalism that are mentally represented by exemplars. Also, parents may point out to a child particular acts that the child has done that are wrong, such as when the child did not share with her sibling, hit a classmate, and stole a cookie from the cookie jar. From these particular instances represented by exemplars, the child can form summary representation prototypes of wrong acts. Prototypes are well-fit to handle this kind of concept acquisition, since prototypes are representations of statistical frequencies and saliencies. Moreover, some prototypes readily can be explicitly taught to others rather than extrapolating them from exemplars. For instance, school teachers may instruct students of some of the basic moral rules of behavior that are represented as prototypes. Also, prototypes have a structure that easily lends itself to being directly learned by being read in, for example, a dictionary, religious text, or philosophy book.

4.4 The Imitation and the Prototype-Exemplar Chain Arguments for the Exemplar Theory

A host of philosophers have claimed that moral concepts have exemplar structure. For example, Goldman (1993), Stich (1993), Clark (1996), Wong (2006), Sterelny (2010), and Harman et al. (2012) have done so. However, the problem with the above thinkers is that none have provided evidence that at least has some basis on experiments run particularly on moral concepts. However, I will establish the viability of this cognitivist view for moral mental representations. Remember that the exemplar view generally claims that concepts are constituted by representations of particular members of a category, and for moral concepts, it claims that our ethical concepts are constituted by relevant representations of particular people or particular acts. There are no psychology studies explicitly on the exemplar theory for moral concepts on psychologically normal subjects. Thus, initially it appears that there is doubt as to whether it may be shown that exemplar theory is a viable theory of moral concepts. Nevertheless, it may still be shown that exemplar theory is a viable theory of moral concepts without explicit exemplar studies. For example, in the imitation literature, there are countless relevant causal studies familiar to many psychologists and even philosophers (Zagzebski 2017). Yet, none have been able to see the connection to a functionalist identification of moral concepts to sufficiently draw a conclusion that moral concepts at least in part express cognitive exemplar representations. The first contention for the moral exemplar theory is *the argument from imitation.*

Human beings are the most cognitively flexible animals. Although compared to many other species, human infants appear to be helpless and cognitively underdeveloped, our prolonged state of infantile immaturity confers the benefit of being able to learn and adapt to a wide range of environments and cultural conditions rather than being more hardwired to have fixed reflexes to a narrow ecological niche. We are born to learn and adapt such that we can live across the globe in diverse climates as well as in different cultures with diverse religions, morals, and ways of life.

While there are various methods of learning, such as by trial and error or by independent discovery, one major form of learning is by imitation. Infants imitate their mothers' facial expressions soon after birth, and as we tend to drop anything we are doing in order to rush to answer a phone, Western babies generally like to imitate talking on a phone when playing (Meltzoff 1999). An important action our species is found to imitate is moral behavior in our parents, siblings, peers, and even in media (Bandura et al. 1961, Gopnik & Meltzoff 1993, Forman et al. 2004, Hurley 2004). Younger brothers can imitate older brothers; friends can have a prestige bias and imitate the moral mannerisms of their group leader; citizens can imitate their president; and despite avowing against growing up to be like one's parents, many find themselves imitating and agreeing with them as they grow older. Thus, despite their passing, we still may see our own parents in observing ourselves and see ourselves reflected back to us in observing our children. Imitation plays a significant role in our ability to adapt to the cultural moral values of the society one is raised in and in shaping one's moral worldview at an important and impressionable early stage of moral development. While this imitation literature is not commonly tied to the moral concepts literature, it does show that we store particular precedents or events of moral actions that we observe. We also use such mental representations in decision-making and imitate or act upon them. In other words, such studies provide evidence that our moral concepts store exemplars.

In a classic study, Bandura et al. screened for aggression and had certain children up to six years old go one-by-one in a play room with various toys. They observed an adult punching and kicking a five-foot inflatable doll of a clown (1961, Bandura 1962). Then the adult would hit the doll in the head with a toy mallet and throw the doll into the air. The adult would yell at the doll saying things like, "Pow, right in the nose, boom, boom," and "Throw him in the air." Children in the control group would witness an adult who was not violent to the doll. When left alone in the play room, male children who were exposed to the aggressive adult were much more likely to be aggressive to the doll than control subjects. Such children largely interacted with the doll eerily in the same way as the adult model by punching, kicking, using the mallet on, and throwing the doll into the air. They also were much more prone than controls to utter verbatim the same yet at times idiosyncratic above phrases the adult model voiced.

In a variant, Bandura and company showed children a video of a woman punching and kicking a real life clown. When children then were led into a room with a real life clown, they immediately began punching and kicking him. Children were not instructed with prototype rules for behavior in these tests and children do not witness several different occurrences of the adult model's actions such that they can generate and rely on summary representation prototype rules. Rather, these studies suggest that from a single observation of an adult, children may acquire an exemplar that is used in normative decision-making and action. Moreover, these studies suggest there is similarity feature matching of their stored exemplars with the relevant situations being presented to them, such as being in the presence of the live clown, in order to trigger the reaction.

In support of Bandura's tests, the American Psychological Association along with numerous other groups, such as the American Medical Association, issued a joint statement proclaiming that based on over 1,000 experiments, there is overwhelming confirmation that media violence causally influences more aggressive behavior in many children (Bushman & Anderson 2001, p. 480, Hurley 2004). Despite political controversy over the issue, it is uncontroversial among expert researchers that given the data, many children imitate the particular acts of violence they see in media and understand many of such acts to be morally acceptable behavior. In other words, representations of particular events we experience in life at many times are stored in our moral concepts. The big picture take-away point from all the above replicated evidence is that children in any culture experience particular acts that can be stored as exemplar representations in their moral concepts, which then helps to shape their moral worldview. Such exemplars at many times consciously or subconsciously influence moral decision-making and behavior. Children in the relevant times and locations can store particular observed instances of, for example, how slaves are to be treated in the Antebellum South, how to treat people that are to be conquered such as in Ancient Greece and Rome, glorified urban gang violence portrayed in music videos and videogames, how their parents may use bad words indiscriminately, and how their fathers may beat their mothers in countries like Ethiopia and Mali, where most women in these cultures judge such harms to be morally permissible (Rani et al. 2004). It is well known that the data shows that children who are born in homes of violence are significantly more likely to live in such homes themselves when they are adults (Osofsky 1995).

Although individuals later may compute statistically frequent prototype rules from one's exemplars of experienced particular moral events and precedents that one imitates, the imitation literature still shows that the moral exemplar view is applicable to the human mind, especially at an earlier stage of moral development. It does verify the perhaps common sense view that particular events we experience in life in-and-of-themselves directly can have an impact on us and our moral decision-making. Also, when one has had enough experiences with exemplars to form a summary representation, it is highly unlikely that all of one's exemplars of a moral category will simply then disappear. There is empirical evidence suggesting that our memory may store an astounding number of exemplars. For example, one experiment showed participants 10,000 different pictures for five seconds each. Subjects were later able to remember a vast majority of them (Standing 1973). When looking through a high school year book from days long gone, we remember persons and events we forgot that we even knew about. When a prototype is formed from exemplars, it is highly likely the case that we consciously or subconsciously still will have retained many of the exemplars as well. With prototypes and exemplars, they may be used individually or conjointly with other kinds of structures in moral cognition depending on the circumstances. Also, recall that my pluralistic theory of moral concepts is a general claim where there may be certain exceptions and anomalies to my view. For instance, studies suggest that those with autism may not have exemplar structure to their moral concepts (Stout 2016), and such aberrations are perfectly acceptable on my theory.

As a second contention for the exemplar view for moral concepts, we will need to discuss a style of argument in the concepts literature that I call *chain arguments*. Chain arguments are claims that if one structure of concepts is already established as being viable, then based on this fact, a different concept structure may be established as being viable. It is called a chain argument because the established concept structure is linked or chained to another concept structure such that this latter concept structure can represent a viable theory of concepts based on the viable existence of the first established concept structure. The argument at hand is the *prototype-exemplar chain argument* (Park 2013).

This non-deductive argument begins by acknowledging that as previously stated, a prototype is an abstracted *summary* representation of features for a category, and it has been shown in the previous section that through empirical tests and philosophical reasoning, moral concepts do have prototype structure. As discussed in the first chapter on concept acquisition, although some prototypes can be directly taught, a prevalent form of prototype acquisition generally for concepts is to infer them from experiences with particular members of a class (Murphy 2002, Machery 2009). With this in mind, given that a prototype is a summary representation of features of particular members of a class and prototype theory is a viable view of moral concepts, it is likely that in some to many cases, one subconsciously or consciously abstracts prototypes from several experiences with particular instances of moral actions, cases, or encounters with moral agents represented by exemplars. Put simply, it is likely that we at times infer summary prototypes from particular experiences we have had in life. For instance, at times in early childhood we may not have enough experiences to form a summary representation. If we do not have a prototype for GOOD PERSONS yet in early childhood but we will at a later point by drawing relevant inferences, then at a prior time we have exemplars stored in our relevant concept of GOOD PERSONS from which such inferences can be drawn. For example, perhaps we may have exemplars at this prior time because our parents pointed out to us particular persons who are *good persons.*

This chain argument also can apply for acquiring prototypes of advanced ethical concepts as an adult, such as with JUST DISTRIBUTION OF TAX DOLLARS. In adolescence, I have had particular experiences of when the use of tax dollars seemingly has been just, such as receiving natural disaster relief one time from a hurricane and receiving an education from public schools. As an adult, when I finally ruminate about the overarching principles or rules of distributive justice for tax dollars, I happen to draw on my exemplars of my concept to form my prototypes. In this fashion, we can see that there is at many times a chain linking prototype theory to exemplar theory because if moral concepts have prototype structure, then it is likely that at times at some earlier stage, some moral concepts have exemplar structure.[5] Thus, prototype theory, by way of concept acquisition, implicates exemplar structure at many times at some earlier stage. This chain argument has a basis in experimental work on moral concepts since we are using experimental prototype studies specifically on moral concepts along with philosophical reasoning in order to establish our claim.

The above chain argument has its roots in the likes of Berkeley (1710/1982). For example, Berkeley contended that we gain abstracted knowledge of a category, such as that a triangle has three angles that equal 180 degrees, from particular instances of triangles.[6] In more modern terminology, Berkeley claimed that such general knowledge is abstracted from our exemplar mental representations. If through personal direct insight, we have drawn relevant inferences and gained some kind of knowledge of general features shared by members of a category, then we already have exemplars for this concept from which such general knowledge has been abstracted. In other words, we previously had acquired exemplar knowledge for our relevant concept.

The exemplar theory provides a plausible view concerning the sense of our moral concepts. We in part understand and have thoughts about ethics in terms of particular acts and persons, and this can also in part account for different understandings of co-referential concepts. For instance, all of my friends who I think are good people really are sensible knaves. My GOOD FRIENDS concept contains exemplars such as representations of my particular friends. Yet, my SENSIBLE KNAVES IN MY LIFE concept does not. Even though both compounds are co-referential, differences in exemplar constituents in part can account for my different understandings or senses of these two compound concepts. On top of this, exemplar theory fits well with concept acquisition since exemplars readily can be learned by observation in the process of imitation learning, ostension, and being explicitly instructed that this particular act, such as when a child participates in a case of name-calling, is wrong or that person is a bad man. They also may be acquired more easily than prototypes since the central tendencies do not have to be computed. The above provides evidence that our moral concepts generally contain at least cognitive prototypes and exemplars in light of the categorization, sense, and concept acquisition desiderata.

4.5 The Armstrong, Gleitman, and Gleitman Objection

We now will entertain an objection to the prototype and exemplar theories in light of the categorization desideratum for theories of moral concepts. This well-known objection against the prototype and exemplar views attacks the typicality effects that these theories are built to account for. Armstrong, Gleitman, and Gleitman (1983) have run experiments on mathematical concepts such as EVEN NUMBER that are thought to have classical structure. Remember that the classical or definitionist view maintains that concepts may be constituted by definitions that are representations of necessary and sufficient conditions. However, our experimenters found that such concepts also showed typicality effects, where participants believed that numbers such as 4 and 8 are more typical of the class *even number* than 34 and 106. They argue that since there are typicality effects for concepts that people do have definitions for, such effects do not provide evidence concerning the structure of concepts. In other words, as discussed in the second chapter, prototypes and exemplars are posited, in part, to account for typicality effects. The classical view is unable to explain these effects. For, the classical view predicts that there should be no typicality effects since all the members of a category must equally satisfy the same necessary and sufficient conditions for membership. All the members should be considered to be equally good members of the class. Due to typicality effects, prototype and exemplar theorists, in part, have drawn structural conclusions regarding concepts. Yet, since EVEN NUMBER has classical structure and is constituted by

DIVISIBLE BY TWO WITHOUT REMAINDER rather than having prototype or exemplar structure and it also shows typicality effects, such effects are not an indication or pertinent to the determination of the structure of concepts. Therefore, typicality effects do not show that concepts have prototype or exemplar structure. This argument attacks one means for showing that the prototype and exemplar theory are viable views of concepts.

The first response is that typicality effects are an experimental psychological categorization phenomenon that must be explained by a theory of concepts since, as discussed in the first chapter, concepts are theoretical psychological entities that are meant to explain higher acts of cognition, such as categorization. Since the classical theory cannot explain typicality effects, in the interest of scientific explanation, there must be something else in our minds in relation to the structure of our mathematical concepts that can explain it. What theory of concepts can explain such categorization judgments? This demands an answer, and the classical view is explanatorily impotent. Views such as the exemplar theory can explain typicality effects, so perhaps there is a pluralism regarding mathematical concepts, and such concepts can be constituted by classical knowledge as well as other kinds of knowledge.

Another problem with this objection against the prototype and exemplar views, which is a related point, is that Armstrong et al. have not tested for whether EVEN NUMBER indeed does have classical structure or not. If eternal correct mathematical concepts rather than psychological conceptions are really platonic abstract objects, it is the case that the platonic correct concept has a definition.[7] Nevertheless, is it the case that the psychological conception of EVEN NUMBER in the minds of fallible human beings has classical structure? They have assumed without experimental evidence that it does. However, this is speculative as they have not provided evidence with a basis on experimental support for mathematical concepts that it does have such a structure, nor have they provided relevant data that it only has such a constitution. Therefore, we cannot confidently state that it does, and their objection is inconclusive barring further evidence.

For, it very well could be the case that there is a mathematical concept pluralism, where mathematical concepts have several viable structures open to them. It may be the case that there is no one grand theory of concepts in the mathematical domain and several concept theories are viable in this realm as well. For example, it may be the case that our concept EVEN NUMBER may have classical, prototype, exemplar, and theory structure. When given tasks that test for typicality effects, perhaps our exemplar knowledge of particular members of a class is used. My limited default exemplars stored in my EVEN NUMBER concept are only TWO, FOUR, SIX, and EIGHT.[8] Thus, I understand the numbers four and eight to be more typical of an even number than thirty-two since such numbers exactly match my default exemplar representations. However, when asked to actually categorize a given number as being an even number or not, I primarily may use my classical concept knowledge. Furthermore, I may use other kinds of knowledge in different competences such as in concept combination and in induction judgments. Much of all of the above is mere speculation that is not based on proper experimental evidence, but since Armstrong et al. have not shown that EVEN NUMBER has classical structure nor that it only has such a structure, I am illustrating a possibility of how an overall pluralistic theory of mathematical concepts can account for Armstrong et al.'s particular typicality findings. The bottom line is that in order for their objection to work, they need to provide evidence with some experimental backing specifically on mathematical concepts that such concepts such as EVEN NUMBER have definitional structure and that such concepts also do not have prototype or exemplar structure. So long as this has not been done, their objection cannot come to fruition, and there is always the possibility that a mathematical pluralism may account for their findings and that typicality effects are indeed an indication of prototype or exemplar structure. Therefore, their contention against the prototype and exemplar theories and typicality effects is to date unfounded.

In response, they may claim that in their third series of experiments, they found that a different group of participants believed that EVEN NUMBER does have a strict definitional structure. They asked these new participants: "Does it make sense to rate items in this category for *degree of membership* in the category (Armstrong et al. 1983, p. 242)?" The experimenters then defined what 'degree of membership' means:

> It makes sense to rate items for degree of membership in a category if the items meet the criteria required for membership to a *different degree*. It does *not* make sense to rate items for degree of membership in a category if all the items meet the criteria required for membership to the *same degree*; that is, if the items are literally either in or out of the category.
>
> (Armstrong et al. 1983, p. 242)

They found that most subjects believed that items that are fruits, vegetables, and vehicles can be rated by degree of membership, but all participants believed that members of the class *even number* cannot be rated by degree. This may suggest that all participants believed that their concept EVEN NUMBER only has classical structure. Armstrong and company may argue that since subjects believe that EVEN NUMBER only has a definition, it must be the case that it does in fact only have a definitional structure. The problem with this is that this third study does not test for whether EVEN NUMBER only has classical structure. For, one can believe that one's concept only has a particular structure, but it does not then follow that one's concept actually only does have this structure. Empirical tests concretely may show that one's concept really does not have this structure but rather has some other constitution. For example, I can believe my concept of BELIEF has prototype structure, but Hampton's aforementioned test indicates that I am mistaken and that my BELIEF concept does not have such a constitution. Thus, at most, all their third experiment shows is that participants have the conscious belief that their concept EVEN NUMBER only has definitional structure. This third experiment does not provide evidence that EVEN NUMBER actually only has classical structure.

4.6 Arguments Against the Classical Theory

Stephen Stich (1993), Alvin Goldman (1993), and Mark Johnson (1993) have argued against the classical view of moral concepts by claiming the viability of the prototype theory along with its concomitant typicality effects. While all three attempt to rely on typicality effects found in prototype studies to make their arguments against the classical view for moral concepts, as previously mentioned, Stich and Goldman provide no experimental evidence specifically on moral concepts for the viability of the prototype theory. Thus, this conclusion against the classical view is too speculative. Moreover, as we have just discussed, Johnson also fails to establish the viability of the prototype view for moral concepts. Therefore, his conclusion against definitionism for moral concepts is also speculative and unjustified. However, I have shown in this chapter that many moral concepts do have prototype structure which, as we shall see, allows me to sufficiently argue against the classical view.

For standard concrete concepts, it is uncontroversial in the literature that such concepts do not have classical structure. There exist several general arguments against the classical view for non-mathematical and non-logical concepts. One objection is made by Wittgenstein (1953) in his analysis of GAME. He claims that the features used to classify things as games are not necessary for membership. For instance, *involving the use of a ball* is not a feature because chess and poker are games that do not include the use of a ball. *Involving two or more people* is not a necessary characteristic due to games, such as solitaire, that are played by oneself. Rather than having a definition, Wittgenstein suggests that we classify things as games based on his aforementioned family resemblance, which, as previously stated, is the main philosophical influence for the prototype view.

Another objection is that for over two thousand years, philosophers have attempted to arrive upon definitions for concepts such as JUSTICE and RIGHT ACTION without sufficient success. There is still no consensus on such definitions, and if there is a definition for them, it should have been had by now. Notice that there is no consensus even within certain ethical schools of thought, such as utilitarianism. For example, there are act utilitarians who claim that we should perform that act that leads to the greatest happiness for the greatest number, and there are rule utilitarians who conclude that we should obey that rule that leads to the greatest happiness for the greatest number. We in particular should expect a consensus over time within the utilitarianism school of thought, since they have general shared values, if our moral concepts have classical structure, but there is no such consensus. Overall, given that we have no such successful definitions for our moral concepts, this provides reason to believe that many of our concepts generally do not have classical structure. For, if our concept of, for instance, JUSTICE might embody definitional structured knowledge, then it is reasonable to expect that we should have come upon a successful definition by now. The fact that for well over two thousand years we have not arrived upon a successful definition of necessary and sufficient conditions for JUSTICE even relative to Western culture lends significant support to the inference that perhaps our JUSTICE concept does not have classical structure.

Another counter against the classical view is related to the typicality effects in prototype studies. While philosophers, like Plato and Aristotle, and psychologists, such as Piaget, have assumed definitionism to be true, typicality effects have put this theory in serious jeopardy. In positing that we have in mind necessary and sufficient features when representing a category, the classical view predicts that the members of a category should be considered as equal tokens, where no member is considered to be a better or more typical instance of the class. After all, in order to be a member, all must equally satisfy the strict definition. However, as previously discussed, cognitive scientists have discovered that there are such typicality effects or graded membership for a variety of moral concepts, where members do stand in a graded relationship with each other. This is not predicted by definitionism, and such effects actually stand as contrary to the equal membership definitionism predicts. Moreover, the inability of definitionism to explain typicality effects also includes its inability to explain how typical members are categorized more quickly than atypical ones. As discussed in the second chapter, while theories such as the prototype, exemplar, and theory views can provide an explanation for such phenomena, the classical theory cannot.

Moreover, researchers have discovered through prototype studies that human beings do not use definitions in the higher cognitive competences for standard concrete concepts. Recall that numerous moral prototype studies also have shown that subjects do not use representations of necessary and sufficient qualities when making moral judgments. Given that the mental representations attributed to members of a class are not used as necessary and sufficient conditions and that there is no experimental evidence for the classical view, cognitive science has shown that humans do not use definitions in the higher cognitive competences for moral concepts.

The above psychology-based arguments lead to the conclusion that definitions most likely are not psychologically real for moral concepts. Some may claim that humans still do have definitional knowledge as well as some other kind of knowledge such as prototypes. For example, Osherson and Smith (1981) make such a claim for standard concrete concepts. However, for moral concepts, from a psychological standpoint, it has been shown that the classical view does not partake in the scientific explanation of experimental concept phenomena such as categorization and typicality effects. Moreover, psychology studies have been successfully conducted in which opposite predictions from that of definitionism are born out. The claim that a combined theory of moral concepts that contains definitionism and some other concept theory (-ies) may be correct and that we still have definitional knowledge is empty in that there currently is no experimental evidence for the psychological reality of classical structure. Some philosophers such as Georges Rey (1983) escape this psychological reality objection by claiming that the classical view is in regards to correct concepts that are abstract objects rather than conceptions that are mental representations. However, as mentioned in the first chapter, our primary concern at the moment is only in regard to conception theories that are about mental representations that are in the head. Therefore, such a move by Rey is not immediately relevant here, although later in this book, I will contend that there are no universally correct abstract platonic moral concepts or properties.

If the classical view is not viable for moral concepts due to the above related reasons, some may argue that through further reflection upon our moral beliefs we psychologically may be able to arrive upon components that represent necessary and sufficient conditions. While this remains a possibility, as it also does with standard concrete concepts, given the above numerous moral prototype studies, there is no scientific evidence to justify the expectation that this may be so. The classical view currently plays no role in scientific explanation and prediction of experimental phenomena, and even though it may be possible that future studies will demonstrate the viability of definitionism, a sufficient level of doubt may be established against this theory such that we are warranted through inference to the best explanation in concluding that a classical structure for moral concepts is not psychologically real. This conclusion is further supported by the previously mentioned fact that for over two thousand years, we have not yet reached a consensus upon a set of necessary and sufficient conditions for moral concepts like JUSTICE and RIGHT ACTION.

One also may object that moral philosophers actually do not posit necessary and sufficient conditions for classifying something under a moral category. They do not claim or implicitly assume that they themselves or anyone else has in mind representations of necessary and sufficient conditions. However, this is simply false, as many normative philosophers do presume the existence of classical structure. As we will discuss below, Rosalind Hursthouse's virtue ethical theory and Thomas Nagel's political philosophy view on the boundaries of distributive justice clearly presuppose that we can have definitions in mind of key moral concepts such as RIGHT ACTION and BOUNDARIES OF DISTRIBUTIVE JUSTICE.

An immediate counter then may be that if philosophers believe that they have strict definitions for moral concepts and they apparently write out their thoughts that are of definitions, then do they not actually have mental representations with classical structure? In response, one must again make the distinction between what one thinks is the structure of one's concept and what actually is the structure of one's concept. They need not necessarily coincide. In many cases, we do not have full access to the workings of our minds. For example, we have a subconscious that may contain hidden intentions for a particular action or subconscious cognitive states stored in some of our concepts; intentions and cognitive states that we are not consciously aware of. At many times, these hidden mental states stand in stark contrast to the conscious mental states that we falsely think are at play in cognition. Likewise, in all cases we do not have complete access to the structure and nature of our moral concepts. Since one does not have experimental evidence on moral concepts that helps demonstrate that one has in mind a definition for one's moral concepts, one cannot justifiably claim that one has a definition for one's moral concept even though one utters what one takes to be a supposed definition from one's very mouth of what virtue or justice is. One needs to run the relevant intricate, subtle, and nuanced experiments to determine the structure of one's concepts, where in these studies, it is not immediately obvious to the subject what is being tested. The definitional view does not explain or predict any experimental psychological phenomena such as typicality effects and categorization. Recall that there are studies by Hampton showing that what we might introspectively think is the structure of certain concepts may not actually turn out to be correct. Hence, to draw a conclusion that one's moral concepts do have classical structure merely based on one's own introspection is too speculative and lacks appropriate empirical support.

Given all the evidence, we may non-deductively infer that our moral concepts do not have classical structure because (1) there is no experimental evidence demonstrating that this is so. The classical theory does not have any explanatory power and predictive success for experimental phenomena, such as in regards to typicality effects and whether concept constituents are used as representations of necessary and sufficient conditions in categorization tasks, and (2) professional philosophers and the folk have not arrived upon a successful consensus definition on moral terms like 'justice' and 'morality' for well over two thousand years. Thus, classical structure for moral concepts is not psychologically real.

4.7 Implications the Demise of the Classical View has for Normative Ethical Theory and Applied Ethics

While establishing my theory of moral concepts is primarily put forth to help lead to metaethical conclusions regarding issues like the cognitivism and non-cognitivism debate and the motivational judgment internalism and externalism debate, as an aside, let us now explore what implications the demise of the classical view has on normative ethical theory and applied ethics. To note, in a later chapter I will discuss the metaethical ramifications the demise of the classical view has on G.E. Moore's open question argument.

Although Stich, Goldman, and Johnson fail to discredit the classical theory, they do mention further normative implications the demise of the classical theory may have on ethical theory and applied ethics. These three philosophers argue against normative theories that require us to have mental representations with definitional structure. If a normative theory claims that terms such as 'justice' and 'personhood' have necessary and sufficient conditions and that we may arrive upon knowledge of such a definition, such a theory is fundamentally wrong in that our very concepts JUSTICE and PERSONHOOD do not have definitional structure. Given that many ethical and political philosophies presuppose that we can fully mentally represent their respective normative categories, they need to take into account the findings in cognitive science in order to construct a view that is at least psychologically plausible in the sense that such normative theories are required to presume that we can have moral ideas and have moral thoughts, such as what virtue is, in a manner that matches at least one of the psychologically real concept structures. If one claims that normative theories can be mentally represented completely as such, then there must be a structural match.

Some contemporary moral philosophers are immune from this criticism in that, for example, John Rawls (1971), Richard Boyd (1988), and Peter Railton (1989) do not posit necessary and sufficient conditions to their respective normative theories. For instance, Boyd claims that there are a homeostatic cluster of properties for correct moral categories. A homeostatic cluster of properties are a set of properties that are relevant to scientific induction and explanation and that are not necessary and sufficient conditions. Here, the presence of one or some properties is likely to lead to the presence of others within the set. While Boyd's view explicitly is one about correct moral categories, his theory implicitly maintains that we can mentally represent such categories. Although he does not discuss theories of concepts at all nor provide any appropriate evidence for a moral concept theory, his ethical theory is consistent with a psychologically plausible view of moral concepts.

In what he calls his 'Homeostatic Consequentialism,' he believes that moral goodness is a natural category that is defined by a cluster of mutually reinforcing properties such as the need for friendship, cooperation, and intellectual expression. What properties are human needs is a complex theoretical question that requires empirical evidence such as socio-political experimentation. For instance, we would not have understood the role political democracies play in the homeostasis of moral goodness without having the appropriate conditions that allowed for the first forms of limited democracy.

While Boyd believes the correct moral category of *moral goodness* is constituted by a cluster of properties concerning human need and the normative theory of consequentialism, when we mentally represent this moral category, it appears that we will do so using prototype, exemplar, and theory-theory structures. To note, although the folk also may have prototype, exemplar, and theory moral knowledge, such knowledge need not coincide with the perhaps more complex forms of prototype, exemplar, and theory knowledge had by the likes of Boyd. The cluster of properties of human need related to such things as friendship, cooperation, and intellectual expression will be mentally represented by prototypes, and consequentialism will be tokened by theory knowledge. As we empirically experience or gather data on particular moral cases such as on limited democracies, represented by exemplars, we then extrapolate summary representation moral prototypes from them. This kind of psychological concept acquisition is no different than, for example, empirically discovering a new natural kind such as a new species of animal and mentally representing this natural kind with new and developing prototypes as we encounter more particular instances of the class that are represented by exemplars. As we learn more about the new species, our concept of the new species likewise evolves to reflect the new knowledge gained. As we can see, this Homeostatic Consequentialism allows Boyd to escape the present criticism.

To note, I read into Boyd that his ethical theory assumes such conceptual structures. He does not discuss theories of moral concepts at all and does not provide appropriate evidence that all of such structures are viable. Boyd does not present in his writings that his ethical theory involves three different concept structures. Remember that in order to really demonstrate that such structures are viable, appropriate causal experimental data is required to actually prove that such structures influence moral decision-making and realize the functional role of concepts. Boyd at many times would have to have knowledge of the experimental moral psychology literature concerning what mental states influence decision-making and foresee using such studies along with the functionalist identification of concepts if he wanted to actually show that our moral concepts have many of these structures; an insight that, other than from myself, has yet to be explicitly made. Also, he would have to reinterpret the various theories of concepts for standard concrete concepts on how they would apply to moral concepts. Moreover, he would have to assess such structures in light of all the many moral concept desiderata. Furthermore, if he were to posit these three structures as his own view of moral concepts, it would be deficient in explanatory power and predictive success since it lacks a conative structure. As I will argue, inclusion of a conative theory along with the other three structures best explains the moral concept desiderata. I merely discuss Boyd here to show that not every normative ethical theory assumes the classical view.

Returning, Plato (or Plato's Socrates), on the other hand, appears to be guilty of requiring us to have moral concepts with classical structure. Plato appears to hold that we can fully mentally represent the platonic form of the Good; a form that has necessary and sufficient conditions. Through examining and studying the nature of the Good, it is thought that we can somehow grasp implicit and largely tacit knowledge of what the Good entails in various moral circumstances. When a definition of the Good has been rejected by way of counterexample, we then continue on our quest for uncovering and specifying necessary and sufficient conditions by articulating new solutions that may avoid previous pitfalls.

For example, in the beginning of *The Republic*, Socrates argues with Cephalus and Polemarchus about what the definition of 'justice' or 'doing what is right' is. While Cephalus and Polemarchus lay out their definitions of 'doing what is right,' through the Socratic method, Socrates provides counterexamples to their definitions and thus, convinces them to alter their definitions as a result of the counters. This has the strong appearance that Socrates is presupposing that we can mentally represent *justice* or *doing what is right* with classical structure.

"That's fair enough, Cephalus," I [(Socrates)] said. "But are we really to say that doing right, consists simply and solely in truthfulness and returning anything we have borrowed? Are those not actions that can be sometimes right and sometimes wrong? For instance, if one borrowed a weapon from a friend who subsequently went out of his mind and then asked for it back, surely it would be generally agreed that one ought not to return it, and that it would not be right to do so, nor to consent to tell the strict truth to a madman?"

"That is true," he [(Cephalus)] replied.

'Well then,' I said, "telling the truth and returning what we have borrowed is not the definition of doing right" (Plato 380 B.C./1974, p. 7).

Many normative ethical theories claim that moral categories have necessary and sufficient conditions and that we may mentally represent such categories. For instance, Kant, with his deontological theory, appears to presuppose the viability of the classical view by claiming that the grounding of all our moral duties is based upon the categorical imperative, where the first formulation is a decision procedure to act only in accordance with that maxim through which you can at the same time will that it become a universal law. Being allowed by a principle that one could rationally will to hold as a universal law is a necessary and sufficient condition for an act to be moral. Mill appears to lay out necessary and sufficient conditions to utilitarianism by claiming that an action is right so long as it maximizes overall happiness or pleasure. Rosalind Hursthouse (1999), a modern day virtue ethicist, claims that "[a]n action is right iff it is what a virtuous agent would characteristically (i.e. acting in character) do in the circumstances" (p. 28).[9] It also seems like Thomas Scanlon (1998), a contractualist, argues that a necessary and sufficient condition for determining if an act is right is if it could be justified to others on grounds that they could not reasonably reject.[10]

David Miller (2009) discusses numerous contemporary political philosophers' views, such as those by Ronald Dworkin and Thomas Nagel, concerning the boundaries within which the principles of distributive justice apply. These views presuppose that there are necessary and sufficient conditions to such boundaries of justice and that we may mentally represent them, and Miller criticizes these views in that they are not successful necessary and sufficient conditions. For instance, Miller labels Dworkin and Nagel's view as the political coercion theory. This theory claims that the boundaries of justice are the boundaries of systems of legitimate political coercion. A system of legitimate political coercion is a system where individuals have certain freedoms restricted by laws and are subject to punishment if breaking such coercive laws. Moreover, there must be a legitimate justification for such laws, and the justification that succeeds is that the overall political system is distributively just. On this view, being the boundaries of a system of legitimate political coercion is a necessary and sufficient condition for being the boundaries of distributive justice, where an individual who falls outside such boundaries is an individual in which the full extent of the principles of distributive justice does not apply.

Miller objects to the political coercion view on several accounts. As one objection, he argues that there are non-coercive settings, such as in clubs and churches, in which the principles of distributive justice do apply. For example, principles of equality for holding a certain office may come into play in some non-coercive groups. Hence, the boundaries of justice are not defined by the boundaries of systems of legitimate political coercion. Miller writes,

> So although questions of distributive justice may become especially pressing between people whose relationships to one another involve routinely applied coercion, it seems that such relationships are neither strictly necessary nor sufficient to bring principles of distributive justice into play.
>
> (2009, p. 301)

Regardless of whether Miller's objection is right that the principles of justice also apply in non-coercive settings, we may specifically criticize the likes of Miller, Dworkin, and Nagel for presupposing that there may be classical structure to our moral concepts. The primary purpose of putting forth this example is to waylay this particular criticism against the above philosophers.

Joel Feinberg claims that the personhood debate of determining what entities have moral status, rights, and duties is one of finding necessary and sufficient conditions for being a person. He writes, "A proposed criterion for moral personhood is a statement of a characteristic (or set of characteristics) that its advocate deems both necessary and (jointly) sufficient for being a person in the moral sense" (1980, p. 45). This issue of personhood has strong implications in several applied ethical issues such as the abortion debate and animal rights. On his theory of personhood, he believes that persons have the individually necessary and jointly sufficient properties of: consciousness, possession of a sense of a self-concept, the ability to experience emotions, the capacity to feel pain and pleasure, self-awareness, and the ability to plan ahead and act on the plan. Feinberg believes that we can mentally represent the necessary and sufficient conditions for personhood, so he implicitly and erroneously maintains that our moral concept PERSONHOOD can have classical structure.

Thus, while this ethical ramification at hand concerning normative ethical theory, political philosophy, applied ethics, and the demise of the classical view fundamentally implicates many if not most normative work, philosophers must take alternative routes, such as Boyd, when constructing their views.

The Plato example points to a further normative implication in that we should expect there to be counterexamples to our moral concepts given a lack of classical structure. This point is not stated by Stich, Goldman, or Johnson. Especially if we are assuming that correct moral categories (that are only relativistically correct) must psychologically or structurally be able to be mentally represented completely as such by human minds, then simply denying someone else's moral conception based on one counterexample is too simplistic a move in attempting to refute this person's conception of, for example, JUSTICE.[11] The widespread view in normative ethics that coming up with one counterexample is sufficient to refute someone's moral conception is misguided. What would be an adequate refutation of someone's moral conception will be dependent on the exact structure of a correct category. For example, one way to argue against Boyd's view would be to have a good number of counterexamples that precisely show that the homeostatic cluster of properties can come apart.

At this point we will explore some cases of why a lack of classical structure will lead to the expectation of there being counterexamples. First, let us examine a concept that is thought to have classical structure: EVEN NUMBER = A NUMBER DIVISIBLE BY TWO WITHOUT REMAINDER. If I have this concept, in order for me to categorize a number as being even, it is necessary and sufficient for the number in question to be a number divisible by two without remainder. Without exception, only numbers that satisfy this condition can be classified as even numbers. There is a strict definition here with no room for counterexamples given the supposed classical structure of my concept.

Recall how we have seen a glimmer of why the demise of the classical view will allow for counterexamples when we examined Wittgenstein's prototype or family resemblance analysis of GAME in this chapter. For moral concepts, a lack of classical structure also will inevitably lead to the existence of counterexamples to analyses presenting necessary and sufficient conditions for those concepts. As a toy example, my prototype of MORAL ACT may be in part constituted by DO NOT HIT OTHERS and DO NOT MAKE OTHERS FEEL BAD. Although these components play a role in influencing me to categorize certain acts, such as peaceful protests when people abstain from violence, as being moral acts, such constituents are not necessary conditions for me. For, I categorize acts where one physically defends oneself from an intruder in one's home as being morally permissible even though one strikes and harms the intruder. Moreover, they are not sufficient conditions for me because even if they are jointly satisfied, I still may not classify a particular act as being a moral one. For instance, if a couple did not even attempt to physically defend the lives of their children from a violent intruder in their home because they are radical pacifists, I would not categorize this to be a moral act even though the couple did not attempt to strike the intruder and make the intruder feel bad. Rather, I personally perceive that there is some kind of moral failing in this circumstance. To note, this example as well as those below are meant to be just a reminder to the reader from earlier in this chapter and from the second chapter of how prototype structured concepts *inter alia* may look like and operate. Remember that the primary refutation in this chapter of the classical structured view of moral concepts does not come primarily by way of analyzing such hypothetical cases but in significant part by way of experimentally based typicality effects and by empirical evidence concerning scientific explanation and prediction.

A normative theorist may claim that a necessary condition for categorizing an act as being moral may be that the act must match one of the features represented by the components of one's MORAL ACT concept. Therefore, when a child witnesses an act of another classmate not retaliating against a playmate who hit him, the child may categorize it as an instance of being a moral act since the act matches the features *do not hit others* and *do not make others feel bad.* This satisfies the necessary condition. However, even if this is the case since a lack of classical structure still allows for necessary but not sufficient conditions,[12] by hypothesis, these features are not taken to also be sufficient conditions in that the child knows that in certain circumstances it is permissible to hit others, such as when being kidnapped by a stranger. There are still counterexamples to one's concept because our moral concepts do not have definitional structure. For, to claim that the child has a definition in mind is to claim that the child has a psychologically unreal mental state.

Continuing with toy examples, my MORAL ACT concept may be in part constituted by the exemplars: MY FRIEND NOT LYING TO THE POLICE OFFICER LAST YEAR and OBEYING THE LAW LAST NEW YEAR'S EVE. Recall from the second chapter that such exemplar representations are themselves constituted by concepts that are about the generalizable moral attributes of the extension of the exemplars. For instance, MY FRIEND NOT LYING TO THE POLICE OFFICER LAST YEAR may be in part made up of TELL THE TRUTH. OBEYING THE LAW LAST NEW YEAR'S EVE may be in part constituted by BE A MODEL CITIZEN. TELL THE TRUTH and BE A MODEL CITIZEN may be generalizable and relevant to other different moral scenarios, such as when one takes the stand in a trial. However, TELL THE TRUTH and BE A MODEL CITIZEN are not necessary conditions for me because I would classify a person hiding Jewish persons up in his attic and lying to the Gestapo as being moral even though he lies to Nazi police officers and disobeys Nazi law by telling them that he is not hiding Jewish persons up in his attic. Furthermore, such components are not sufficient because even though particular situations may satisfy these represented conditions, I still may not categorize them as being moral acts. For instance, even though Albert did not lie to the officer and he was a model citizen by obeying the law and telling the truth to a Nazi officer that he is hiding Jewish persons up in his attic, I still do not classify his act as being moral. Rather, I deem it to be an immoral act even though he did not lie to the officer and he obeyed the Nazi law.

As stated in the second chapter, the theory-theory for moral concepts claims that theories do not represent necessary and sufficient conditions, and they occupy defeasible placeholder positions. By occupying such a position, theory knowledge can be understood as being generalizations that are taken to be defeasible based on, for example, the possibility of being defeated by new evidence or moral learning in the future. They do not represent a strict definition. Insofar as this is the case, the theory-theory is very open to the possibility of there being counterexamples to ethical theories and master moral principles about what is morally right or wrong.

In expecting counterexamples, we should adhere to those theories or views that are best protected against many to most counters, especially against the most serious objections. With all of the above in mind, as examples, if one is a rule-based deontologist, then one should construct a list of rules that are mentally represented by prototypes that can best handle the most objections and the most serious counters. Concerning the prototype view, successful counterexamples are not ones that show that the represented prototypical features simply fail to be effective necessary and sufficient conditions because such features are not even taken to be such definitions in the first place. Rather, successful counterexamples for the prototype theory, for example, will be a group of important and central cases of good acts (relative to a group) that do not match most of the prototypes of one's GOOD ACT concept and that do not match the heavily weighted prototypes either.

Moving on to the exemplar theory, if one, for instance, is a virtue ethicist who believes that we should act as the virtuous agent would act, then one should focus on particular individuals, who are mentally represented by exemplars, who can best withstand a thorough scrutiny of character. While such individuals we have in mind will not be able to remain unscathed from all scrutiny given the nature of our moral concepts and how we psychologically think about ethics, in one's normative ethical theory, one should focus on those individuals who are best able to handle the important objections and most of the objections. Recall that such exemplars themselves will be constituted by concepts that refer to things like more generalizable virtues such as *honesty* and *benevolence*. In deciding which individuals can best withstand a thorough scrutiny of character, one must look for individuals with certain generalizable attributes; attributes that can best handle the most relevant objections and the most serious counters.

While keeping in mind that theory knowledge is defeasible, normative ethical theory knowledge likewise should be adopted that presently is thought to withstand most of the objections, especially the most central or damaging ones. If there are more than one of such candidates, then we should espouse that theory knowledge that has more virtues as compared to its competitors, where this theory knowledge itself may be a hybridized view of more than one normative ethical theory. Upon learning about the demise of the classical view, it is in this fashion that we generally must proceed with normative ethical inquiry since having classical structure to our moral concepts is not psychologically real.

The history of normative moral philosophy generally is in significant part a history of thinkers providing counterexamples upon counterexamples to show that a proposed definition for a moral concept is not a flawless set of necessary and sufficient conditions. It is seemingly an endless cycle. Yet, given the human condition, we should expect and even predict there to be counterexamples to our moral concepts, and the mere existence of a counterexample alone does not necessarily demonstrate that our conception of morality or justice is incorrect (relative to a group). Previous objections one may have against a particular construal of a moral concept need to be reevaluated under a different light and a different set of more lenient standards that allow for counterexamples. For many of us, we generally must fundamentally change the way we theorize about ethics given the nature of our moral concepts. For, to then continually presuppose that our moral ideas have definitional structure and that one simple counterexample is sufficient to refute someone's moral conception is to presuppose we have psychologically unreal mental states, and it is to be a member of something akin to the Flat Earth Society.

Notes

1 On an aside, since virtues have been found to have prototype structure, such a structure may be able to explain why Aristotle believes that some mean virtues appear to lean closer to one extreme rather than another. In providing the doctrine of the mean in the *Nichomachean Ethics,* Aristotle claims that virtues are means that lie between two vices of deficiency and excess. For example, courage lies between the two extremes of cowardice and rashness. However, some virtues appear to be closer to one extreme rather than the other. For instance, courage appears to be closer to rashness than cowardice. "E.g., since rashness is thought liker and nearer to courage, and cowardice more unlike, we oppose rather the latter to courage; for things that are further from the intermediate are thought more contrary to it." Aristotle contends that the mean is difficult to hit, so at times we should aim for the excess vice that appears closer to the mean. Prototype structure for virtues may explain why one extreme for a particular virtue appears closer to it rather than the other extreme because the closer extreme shares more prototypical and more heavily weighted features and is more similar to the mean as compared to the opposing extreme. Whether this is or is not the case will be left for others to decide and empirically examine.

2 Here, the compounds are significantly in part co-referential in virtue of the extension of the non-moral conceptual components of the compounds.

3 Recall from the first chapter that the moral knowledge we acquire for a concept may be incorrect (relative to a group), and thus, our categorizations may be incorrect as well.

4 I will object to prominent nativist arguments for moral concepts in the sixth chapter.

5 This point that prototype theory acknowledges the viability of the exemplar view in more modern times has been anticipated by the likes of Murphy (2002) and Wong (2006). However, neither has shown that moral concepts have exemplar structure in a non-speculative fashion.

6 In Berekely's particular example with abstract mathematical concepts, the abstracted knowledge may be classically structured. However, this point about the reliance of abstracted knowledge on particular instances or exemplars also applies at many times to prototype abstracted knowledge.

7 Recall the concept/conception distinction from chapter one that is being invoked in this paragraph (§1.1).

8 Recall from the first chapter that concepts only store limited default knowledge that is preferentially and presumptively used in higher acts of cognition (§1.2).

9 Her notion of "acting in character" is to act based on a firm, reliable, and stable disposition that leads toward moral excellence. Even if her theory relied on a definition that in some way deferred to prototypes or exemplars, she still in part posits a definitional structure which is not psychologically real.

10 To note, the necessary and sufficient condition of reasonable rejection for Scanlon is stated here in a simplified form.
11 Moral relativism allows for talk of correct moral categories such as of *goodness*, however, categories are only relativistically correct.
12 For a study that shows that standard concrete concepts can have necessary but not sufficient conditions, see Malt (1994).

References

Armstrong, S., Gleitman, L., and Gleitman, H. 1983. "What Some Concepts Might Not Be." *Cognition*, 13, 263–308.

Bandura, A., Ross, D., and Ross, S. 1961. "Transmission of Aggression Through Imitation of Aggressive Models." *Journal of Abnormal and Social Psychology* 63, 575–582.

Bandura, A. 1962. *Social Learning Through Imitation*. Lincoln, NE: University of Nebraska Press.

Berkeley, George. 1710/1982. *A Treatise Concerning the Principles of Human Knowledge*. Ed. by Kenneth Winkler. Indianapolis, IN: Hackett Publishing Company.

Boyd, Richard. 1988. "How To Be a Moral Realist." *Essays on Moral Realism*. Ed. by Geoffrey Sayre-Mccord. Ithaca, NY: Cornell University Press.

Bushman, B. and Anderson, C. 2001. "Media Violence and the American Public: Scientific facts vs. media misinformation." *American Psychologist* 56, 477–489.

Churchland, Paul. 1989. *A Neurocomputational Perspective*. Cambridge, MA: The MIT Press.

Clark, Andy. 1996. "Connectionism, Moral Cognition, and Collaborative Problem Solving." *Mind and Morals*. Ed. by L. May, M. Friedman, A. Clark. Cambridge, MA: The MIT Press.

Coleman, Linda and Kay, Paul. 1981. "Prototype Semantics: The English Word Lie." *Language* 57, 26–44.

Feinberg, Joel. 1980. "Abortion." *Matters of Life and Death*. Ed. by Regan, Tom. New York: Random House, 185–202.

Forman, D., Askan, N., and Kochanska, D. 2004. "Toddlers' Responsive Imitation Predicts Preschool-age Conscious." *Psychological Science* 15, 699–704.

Frei, Jennifer and Shaver, Phillip. 2002. "Respect in Close Relationships: Prototype Definition, Self-report Assessment, and Initial Correlates." *Personal Relationships* 9, 121–139.

Goldman, Alvin. 1993. "Ethics and Cognitive Science." *Ethics* 103, 337–360.

Gopnik, Alison and Meltzoff, Andrew. 1993. "Imitation, Cultural Learning and the Origins of 'Theory of Mind'." *Behavioral and Brain Sciences* 16, 521–523.

Hampton, James A. 1981. "An Investigation of the Nature of Abstract Concepts." *Memory and Cognition* 9, 149–156.

Harman, G., Mason, K., and Sinnott-Armstrong, W. 2012. "*Moral Reasoning*." In *The Moral Psychology Handbook*. Ed. by John Dorris and the Moral Psychology Research Group. Oxford: Oxford University Press.

Hurley, Susan. 2004. "Imitation, Media Violence, and Freedom of Speech." *Philosophical Studies* 117, 165–218.

Hursthouse, Rosalind. 1999. *On Virtue Ethics*. Oxford: Oxford University Press.

Johnson, Mark. 1993. *Moral Imagination.* Chicago: The University of Chicago Press.

Lakoff, George. *Women, Fire, and Dangerous Things.* Chicago: The Chicago University Press, 1987.

Machery, Edouard. 2009. *Doing Without Concepts.* Oxford: Oxford University Press.

Malt, Barbara. 1994. "Water is not H2O." *Cognitive Psychology* 27, 41–70.

Meltzoff, Andrew. 1999. "Born to Learn: What infants learn from watching us." In *The Role of Early Experience in Infant Development.* Ed. by N. Fox and J.G. Worhol. Skillman, NJ: Pediatric Institute Publications, 1–10.

McDowell, John. 1978. "Are Moral Requirements Hypothetical Imperatives?" *Proceedings of the Aristotelian Society* suppl. 52, 13–42.

Miller, David. 2009. "Justice and Boundaries." *Politics, Philosophy & Economics* 8, 291–309.

Murphy, Gregory. 2002. *The Big Book of Concepts.* Cambridge, MA: The MIT Press.

Osherson, D. and Smith, E. 1981. "On the Adequacy of Prototype Theory as a Theory of Concepts." *Cognition* 9, 35–58.

Osofsky, Joy. 1995. "Children Who Witness Domestic Violence: The Invisible Victims." *Social Policy Report* 9, 1–20.

Park, John. 2013. "Prototypes, Exemplars, and Theoretical & Applied Ethics." *Neuroethics* 6, 237–247.

Plato. 380 B.C./1974. *The Republic*, 2nd edition. Trans. by Lee, Desmond. London: Penguin Books, 18–19.

Railton, Peter. 1989. "Naturalism and Prescriptivity." *Social Philosophy and Policy* 7, 151–174.

Rani, M., Bonu, S., and Diop-Sidibe, N. 2004. "An Empirical Investigation of Attitudes Towards Wife-beating of Men and Women in Seven Sub-Saharan African Countries." *African Journal of Reproductive Health* 8, 116–136.

Rawls, John. 1971. *A Theory of Justice*, 2nd edition. Cambridge, MA: Belknap Press.

Rey, Georges. 1983. "Concepts and Stereotypes." *Cognition* 19, 237–262.

Scanlon, Thomas. 1998. *What We Owe to Each Other.* Cambridge, MA: Harvard University Press.

Smith, K., Smith, S., and Christopher, J. 2007. "What Defines the Good Person?" *Journal of Cross-Cultural Psychology* 38, 333–360.

Standing, L. 1973. Learning 10000 pictures. *Quarterly Journal of Experimental Psycholoy*, 25, 207–222.

Sterelny, Kim. 2010. "Moral Nativism: A Sceptical Response." *Mind & Language* 25, 279–297.

Stich, Stephen. 1993. "Moral Philosophy and Mental Representation." In *The Origin of Values.* Ed. by Hechter, M., Nadel, L., and Michod, R. New York: Aldine de Gruyer, 215–228.

Strichartz, Abigail and Burton, Roger. 1990. "Lies and Truth: A Study of the Development of the Concept." *Child Development* 61, 211–220.

Stout, Nathan. 2016. "Autism, Episodic Memory, and Moral Exemplars." *Philosophical Psychology* 29, 858–870.

Sweetser, Eve. 1989. "The definition of Lie: An examination of the folk models underlying a semantic prototype." *Cultural Models in Language and Thought.* Ed. by D. Holland and N. Quinn. Cambridge: Cambridge University Press, 43–66.

Walker, Lawrence and Pitts, Russell. 1998. "Naturalistic Conceptions of Moral Maturity." *Developmental Psychology* 34, 403–418.

Walker, Lawrence and Hennig, Karl. 2004. "Differing Conceptions of Moral Exemplarity: Just, Brave, and Caring." *Journal of Personality and Social Psychology* 86, 629–647.

Williams, Bernard. 1985. *Ethics and the Limits of Philosophy*. Cambridge, MA: Harvard University Press.

Wittgenstein, L. *Philosophical Investigations.* Trans by G. Anscombe. New York: Prentice-Hall, 1953.

Wong, David B. 2006. *Natural Moralities.* Oxford: Oxford University Press.

Zagzebski, Linda. 2017. *Exemplarist Moral Theory.* Oxford: Oxford University Press.

5 The Theory View

As I have clarified when we may rely on appropriate causal studies to draw constitution claims on moral concepts, we will use relevant causal evidence in order to demonstrate that the theory view is a viable theory of moral concepts. Recall that moral concepts just are those relevant mental states that appropriately realize the functional role of concepts of influencing moral decision-making. Using this methodology will help establish that our moral concepts and judgments in part have a certain cognitive component. Remember that on the theory view, moral concepts are constituted by representations of normative ethical theories and causal moral laws of an agent's intentions, among other things. As previously stated, there are no explicit studies on this cognitivist theory for moral concepts in the concepts literature or in moral psychology. However, there are numerous experiments in moral psychology that provide evidence for the theory view even though the relevant literature does not at all discuss how such studies can be used to draw structural conclusions on moral concepts (Park 2015). As we shall see, the use of theory knowledge in moral cognition is just like how in Keil's previously discussed study in the second chapter, participants used theory knowledge of hidden essences in order to make their categorization judgment that the given animal that externally looks like a horse but has cow innards is really a cow instead of a horse. Although when asked, standard concrete concept theorists likely will not deny the possibility that moral concepts might have theory structure, it has yet to be stated and proven in a non-speculative manner that moral concepts indeed do have theory structure. This is due in part to the fact that, as noted in the second chapter, I am the first to articulate what theory knowledge even is for moral concepts. Moreover, no one else in the literature has foreseen the functionalist identification of concepts for moral concepts. As we have already examined the prototype and exemplar views in light of categorization, sense, and concept acquisition, I will explore the theory view in light of the first two desiderata in this chapter. Discussion of the theory view in light of the concept acquisition desiderata will occupy the next chapter.

5.1 Arguments for the Theory View

Kohlberg's (1981) stage theory of moral development provides certain correlational support for the use of disparate normative ethical theories across time that many individuals may mentally represent. For Kohlberg, the first and second stage of pre-conventional morality is where children are egoistically concerned with and influenced by rules in relation to punishment and self-interest. This provides evidence for a link between moral judgments and a kind of ethical egoism theory knowledge. The third stage is where individuals are concerned about other people and their feelings. Moreover, agents are motivated to follow rules and expectations. Stage four of development is a consequentialism stage and is described as where the right is upholding the social order and maintaining the overall welfare of society or the group. Here, what duties and rules one must obey are determined by what the best overall consequences are for the group and by what upholds the social order, where each member's welfare is counted equally. The fifth stage implements social contract theory, where it is right to uphold the basic tenets and obligations stemming from a social contract. In the last stage, people are Kantians utilizing deontological normative theory and are guided by ethical principles and individual rights that hold in all cases and that are universal laws. Kohlberg's stage theory has been heavily criticized, where, for example, studies by the likes of Shweder et al. (1987) have shown that the fourth stage is the highest and most prevalent stage that most adults supposedly reach across cultures. Most do not reach the fifth or sixth stage. Although I won't discuss all of the many objections against Kohlberg, another objection is that contrary to his beliefs, Kohlberg really fails to show that knowledge of the various ethical theories influences moral decision-making. Such studies provide only correlational support because Kohlberg gathered his evidence by interviewing his participants and asking them what justified their moral judgments when given hypothetical scenarios. Such purported justifications only may be post hoc rationalizations, where the supposed justifications only are formed after final moral decisions have been made rather than causing participants to make judgments. Further studies need to be conducted in order to ascertain whether actual causation in the right direction is involved. We need studies that demonstrate that theory knowledge appropriately influences the reaching of a moral conclusion, not the other way around.

For example, Jonathan Haidt (2001), who was influential in overturning Kohlberg's moral stage theory paradigm, has run a study asking participants if it is morally permissible for a brother and sister to secretly have protected sex on a one-time basis. While some participants stated that it was morally permissible, most claimed that it was morally wrong. When the relevant subjects were asked for the justification for their negative response, some said that it would lead to a deformed child. However, experimenters then reminded them that they used sufficient protection. Some said that it may cause problems in their family, but experimenters reminded them that the sexual encounter was kept as a secret and the siblings even grew closer together as a result of the act even though they never had sex again. Haidt found that most of those who said the act was morally impermissible still held on to their judgment even though all the false non-moral facts they held regarding the case were corrected. This study as well as others indicates that at many times reasons and justifications for belief may be post hoc. They do not influence decision-making but only arise after the decision has been made. Haidt further hypothesizes that this demonstrates that emotions are what really influence our moral judgments at many times, where such judgments are emotion-based intuitions. However, against Haidt, his move is too quick just based on these studies since other possibilities are still available that have yet to be ruled out, such as that subconscious reasoning influences judgment in such cases. Nevertheless, the take home message for our purposes is that if a philosopher or folk subject verbally claims or thinks that a mental state influenced their judgment, this only establishes correlation, where appropriate experiments need to be run to establish actual causation. Hence, Kohlberg's stage theory does not yet establish that the relevant represented ethical theories influence moral decision-making, but it may establish correlation. Such correlational evidence needs to be coupled with relevant causal studies in order to make a sufficient claim for the viability of the theory view. It is important to note that Haidt's study shows that appropriate experimental evidence that establishes that a mental state causally influences judgment is required, and mere introspection that a mental state influences one's judgment is insufficient. Not only is experimental data on moral concepts required to help establish that a moral concept has a particular structure, but when using a functionalist metaphysics to determine what constitutes a concept, appropriate causal experiments also are required.

As stronger support for the theory view, Liane Young et al. (2010) discovered that causal moral law knowledge of an agent's causal intentions to act can influence moral categorization. In other words, an agent's causal intentions which influence the agent's behavior affect one's moral judgment of the agent. In this study, the experimenters used transcranial magnetic stimulation (TMS) in order to disrupt the neural activity in the right temporoparietal junction (RTPJ) before and during moral judgment. There has previously been shown to be a correlation between activation in the RTPJ and when a participant reads about an agent's causal intentions for action in certain moral contexts (Young et al., 2007). Moreover, the RTPJ is not understood as being a brain structure related to emotions. What they found was that in attempted harm cases, where the agent causally intends to do harm but fails to bring about the negative consequences, TMS to the RTPJ causes subjects to judge the agent's attempted harm as being less morally forbidden and more morally permissible as compared to participants who received TMS to a control site. Due to the nature of attempted harm cases, this suggests that TMS to the RTPJ affects the ability of subjects to fully account for the agent's causal intentions in making moral judgments and that assessing an agent's causal intentions does play a default role in influencing typical normal moral judgments in relevant cases. This study demonstrates that in making many normal moral judgments for normal subjects who are not receiving TMS to the RTPJ, such participants take into account causal knowledge about an agent's intentions and what causally motivates the agent to perform a given action. Normal participants have cognitive causal moral law knowledge to the effect that if an agent's causal motivations for action are wrong, then the agent's action still is wrong even though the agent fails to bring about the bad consequences. This moral principle knowledge impacts their moral decision-making at times. As further support, Electroencephalogram (EEG) studies suggest that processing intent in the RTPJ occurs 62 milliseconds after being presented with a moral case but before a decision has been made (Decety & Cacioppo 2012). Given that the causal knowledge of an agent's intentions for action affects the gravity of moral judgments, this provides evidence for the viability of the theory-theory for moral concepts in light of categorization.[1]

There are experiments that may support the appropriate causal influence of consequentialism knowledge; knowledge that one should bring about the greater overall consequences. Joshua Greene et al. (2009) ran a cognitive load study where subjects were filling out moral questionnaires on a computer. They were presented with "high conflict" moral dilemmas in which subjects were asked whether it is appropriate to harm another individual in order to save several lives or to bring about less overall harm. Cases ranged from bioethics to environmental ethics to business ethics, among others. One example of such a dilemma is the crying baby case:

> Enemy soldiers have taken over your village. They have orders to kill all remaining civilians. You and some of your townspeople have sought refuge in the cellar of a large house. Outside you hear the voices of soldiers who have come to search the house for valuables.
>
> Your baby begins to cry loudly. You cover his mouth to block the sound. If you remove your hand from his mouth his crying will summon the attention of the soldiers who will kill you, your child, and the others hiding out in the cellar. To save yourself and the others you must smother your child to death.
>
> Is it appropriate for you to smother your child in order to save yourself and the other townspeople?
>
> (2009, pp. 4–5)

While answering such questions on moral dilemmas, numbers continually stream across the bottom of the screen and participants have to press a button when they see the number five. The result is that subjects selectively had a longer reaction time when making apparent folk consequentialism judgments under the cognitive load as opposed to having no cognitive load, but there was no increase in reaction time for supposed non-consequentialism-like judgments under cognitive load. This study provides causal rather than correlational support that purported folk consequentialism knowledge influences some moral judgments for some people because the longer reaction time suggests that the cognitive load of having to press a button when seeing the number five interferes with a controlled cognitive process, such as perhaps some kind of cost–benefit analysis reasoning process, whereas the cognitive load should have no effect on a fast automatic process, such as on an emotion-based process. This conclusion is further buttressed by neuroimaging studies that show a strong correlation between the making of supposed folk consequentialism judgments and activation in the dorsolateral prefrontal cortex (DLPC) (Greene et al. 2004). This brain region is known for such things as complex planning, working memory, deductive/inductive reasoning, and long-term economic decision-making.

Jeurissen et al. (2014) used TMS on normal patients when they were filling out the moral questionnaires also used in the above studies. They used TMS in order to disrupt the neural activity in the DLPFC for normal agents. They found that TMS to the DLPFC led to moral judgments that were less consequentialist in normal participants in dilemmas like the crying baby case, where one person may be killed to save many others. If activation in the DLPFC is causally responsible in the appropriate way for making consequentialist-like judgments in certain cases, then we should expect that TMS to the DLPFC should lead subjects to make less consequentialist judgments on these cases. The fact that this prediction is borne out in experimental tests provides further confirmation that supposed folk consequentialist-like representations influence decision-making in the appropriate way, and such cognitive knowledge constitutes some of our moral concepts.

For more causal evidence, we can turn to the trolley problems (Greene et al. 2001, 2004, Hauser 2006, Hauser et al. 2007, Greene 2008, 2013, Mikhail 2013); cases that were also used in the cognitive load study and at times in conjunction with sixty other moral scenarios in questionnaires first used by Greene et al. (2001, 2004). In the trolley cases, imagine there is a *lever case* in which a train is about to run over five people, but you may pull a lever to divert the train on a side track in order to save the five people. However, it just so happens that there is one person who is on the side track who will be killed if you pull the lever to save the five. 89% of participants agree that one ought to pull the lever in this scenario. In the *footbridge case,* imagine that the same train is heading toward the same five people, but now you are on a footbridge that hovers over the track. In your company is a heavyset man whose body mass is large enough to stop the train if you kill him by pushing him over the bridge on to the track in order to save the five. In this case, 89% of participants state that one should not push the heavyset man. Greene interprets the trolley cases as a matter between utilitarianism and deontology. Hauser et al. (2007) have replicated these results in a variety of cultures, such as in the United States, India, and Brazil.

Studies may indicate that the lever case is one in which most participants make supposed folk consequentialist judgments to bring about the greater consequences, where it is permissible to pull the lever in order to save a greater number of lives while the footbridge case is one in which most subjects make supposed Kantian deontological judgments that focus on rules and individual rights, where the heavyset man has an individual right not to be pushed regardless of the greater consequences that will arise in pushing him. In these trolley studies, when stating that subjects supposedly make deontological or consequentialist judgments, what is meant is that they draw conclusions that would be thought to be made by deontological or consequentialist normative theory, respectively. At this point, it is not meant to necessarily mean that deontological or consequentialist reasoning is actually used to arrive upon a moral conclusion. However, concerning folk consequentialist reasoning, it later will be argued that such cognitive reasoning is being used by normal subjects at times in the trolley problems and their ilk. It is not yet decisive in our current assessment of the trolley problems that subjects are truly making folk consequentialist or, for that matter, deontological judgments, but as a matter of convenience, we shall abide by these classifications for the two different types of judgments for now, and objections to the use of these two normative categories will be addressed in the following section.

We may understand the possible use of this consequentialism ethical theory knowledge as being one of *folk* consequentialism in that philosophers who are consequentialists tend to view this theory as a criterion of rightness rather than being a decision procedure that actually must be used in everyday circumstances. In other words, a consequentialist calculation is for determining which acts actually are right or wrong, but it should not be used to make everyday decisions in all cases. For example, consequentialists generally believe that one should visit one's mother in the hospital not for the reason that it leads to the best overall consequences but because one love's one's mother. A consequentialist calculation is a criterion for determining that visiting one's mother is ethically right, but in real life, one must justify such an action by using alternative reasons. One must have the proper moral motivation for action. However, *folk* consequentialism will be understood as where the folk actually do use a consequentialist calculation as a decision procedure. Moreover, this folk consequentialism at this point is a bare kind of consequentialism and cost/benefit analysis, where the best consequences are choosing those options that save more lives and lead to less overall physical harms. I leave it open that future empirical research may show that this theory knowledge is a more complex kind of consequentialist theory knowledge that, for example, also takes into account what it is to live a flourishing life or perhaps has other provisions.

Mendez et al. (2005a) have run trolley studies on patients with frontotemporal dementia (FTD), which involves a deterioration of the ventromedial prefrontal cortex (VMPFC) and anterior temporal emotion areas of the brain. Such patients show no deficits in cognitive moral semantic memory and basic moral knowledge for simple ethical dilemmas compared to psychologically normal patients as they can make judgments on the Moral Behavior Inventory consistent with the socially understood correct answers to basic moral questions, such as whether it is morally permissible to break a promise, cut people in line, and take credit for others' work (Mendez 2006).[2] They fully can describe the real life moral situations they find themselves in as well as the consequences and wrongness of their actions in the real world. When they do perform transgressions, they report that right before performing such acts they fully know that what they are about to do is unethical but just lack motivation to act accordingly (Mendez et al. 2005b). Any cognitive functions that may be relevant to moral thinking for the above cases appear to be intact. However, these patients have been found to not only show diminished concern for others but they also exhibit emotional blunting or severely diminished emotions such as having a lack of empathy. Due to emotional blunting, such patients are prone to committing transgressions such as stealing and inducing violent physical harm to others. They have a tendency to not respond to the needs of others, and they also can exhibit pedophilia. At many times they appear to lack sufficient motivation to act upon their moral judgments.

Mendez, et al.'s study has been successfully replicated by Koenigs et al. (2007) and Ciaramelli et al. (2007) on patients that have lesions to the VMPFC. In *Descartes' Error*, Antonio Damasio (1994) has similarly concluded that his patients with lesions to the VMPFC have intact reasoning capacities but have deficiencies in affect. For instance, Damasio describes the case of one of his patients who scores normally and at times above normal on intelligence and reasoning tests but exhibits diminished emotions. When discussing the many tragic hardships of his life, the subject displays an unusual emotional detachment from such events with no sign of frustration or sadness. Moreover, when shown visually stimulating and emotionally charged pictures of people drowning and individuals being in gory accidents, the patient showed no emotional response and remained emotionally neutral. This patient's everyday life was generally characterized as one of disaffection, which is opposite from the time period in his life before he suffered damage to the VMPFC.

In these three studies, patients were given the lever and footbridge cases. In the lever case, patients' responses matched the general reaction of normal subjects. For example, in the lever scenario most patients stated that it is permissible to pull the lever. However, in the footbridge case, patients significantly diverged from the answers generally made by normal subjects by allowing for the pushing of the heavyset man onto the track. With blunted emotions, the patients were more inclined to consistently make apparent folk consequentialist judgments in this situation, while those with normal emotions tended to believe that pushing the heavyset man is not permissible. Ciaramelli et al. replicated this finding with VMPFC patients using Greene's sixty moral scenarios that include cases that pit harming one life in order to bring about greater overall consequences in a wide variety of applied ethical domains. These studies provide causal evidence that in certain cases such as the lever case, some kind of folk consequentialist reasoning generally influences moral judgments for normal subjects and the patients. After all, the patients who have blunted emotions and VMPFC patients who do not have a skin conductance response (SCR), which measures for emotional arousal, when making folk consequentialist judgments (Moretto et al. 2010), drew the same conclusions as normal subjects in such cases. The theory view is implicated for moral concepts related to core moral areas such as killing, helping the poor, and biomedical ethics. The possibility is left open that emotions simultaneously still can have some influence on the relevant judgments, but regardless of whether this is so, from these studies we still may infer that a kind of supposed folk consequentialism theory knowledge plays the relevant causal role for psychologically normal individuals in a wide variety of moral cases.

However, since the emotionally blunted patients diverged in judgments from normal participants in the footbridge case by making apparent folk consequentialist rather than deontological categorizations, this and other studies demonstrate that negative emotions from the thought of pushing the man generally do play a causal role in making judgments for normal subjects in the footbridge case. In that emotionally blunted patients consistently make folk consequentialist judgments and generally did not reach the same decisions as normal subjects did in the footbridge case, this shows that normal participants generally are influenced by emotions when making such categorizations. Likewise, some kind of cognitive reasoning also can play a role alongside emotions in footbridge case categorizations for normal subjects as Greene et al. (2001, 2004) also did find a correlation between making such judgments and activation in "cognitive" brain regions. Regardless, we still may infer that emotions at least in part play the specified causal role, and for our purposes, this is important. As we will discuss in a later chapter on the conative view, this replicated study provides evidence that the conative theory is a viable view of moral concepts.

However, there may be an objection. There is an apparently contradictory ultimatum game study run by Koenigs & Tranel (2007). In typical ultimatum games, two players can split a sum of money, where the first player makes an offer, and the second can either accept or reject the offer. If the offer is rejected, no one gets any money. For example, a fair offer would be to split $10 equally, and an unfair offer would be an $8/$2 split. A convergence of studies suggests that rejections of unjust offers are influenced by emotional reactions of frustration and anger. However, Koenigs and Tramel discovered that VMPFC patients had a higher rejection rate of the most unfair offers ($7/$3, $8/$2, $9/$1) as compared to normal subjects. They conclude that VMPFC subjects experience anger and frustration which causes them to have a higher rejection rate of unfair offers and that damage to the VMPFC disrupts the ability to regulate the emotions such that one may harness one's anger and accept unfair offers in order to "rationally" attain at least some financial gain for one's self-interest. This particular study apparently contradicts the above VMPFC studies in that VMPFC subjects, despite generally having blunted emotions, are known to experience emotions such as anger and irritability in certain situations, and such emotions influence judgment. However, when they do so, the outburst is swift, and patients quickly return to their calm detached states without bearing any grudges. This seems to put into question or to contradict the fact that in the trolley dilemmas, it is thought that for VMPFC patients, emotions play little to no role in affecting such moral categorizations.

However, Koenigs et al. (2007) note that the emotional effects of VMPFC damage are context dependent. VMPFC subjects may exhibit emotions such as anger and frustration when being directly and personally provoked such as in the ultimatum game when frustration is triggered due to unfair take-it-or-leave-it offers that also involve an element of self-interest and direct involvement. On the other hand, such subjects are generally characterized as having severely diminished social emotions related to such feelings as empathy and a concern for others, where such an emotionally detached state is manifested, inter alia, in hypothetical scenarios such as in the trolley dilemmas where the patient is not directly and personally involved in a real life situation. Hence, we still can use such VMPFC studies on the trolley problems to draw the given concept constitution claims. Also, recall that VMPFC patients do not produce a SCR when faced with the trolley problems.

The replicated evidence from the trolley problems along with the data presented in this section concerning Greene et al.'s cognitive load study, neuroimaging studies, Jeurissen et al.'s TMS study, and correlational evidence from work on Kohlberg's stage theory on the fourth stage, show that folk consequentialism knowledge may be used at many times by default to influence moral decision-making.[3] This is where participants generally perform a kind of cost/benefit analysis and take into account the greater consequences of having more overall lives saved or not harmed versus lives lost or harmed. They largely decide in the relevant cases that one should bring about the greater consequences even if it means violating others' individual rights. Such theory knowledge at many times may be used by default, and the relevant studies pass the possible mental error test. Here, I leave open the possibility that further testing can modify the specifics of this theory knowledge. Combining all the evidence that are not explicitly designed to draw conclusions on moral concepts appears to allow us to make a novel claim that since theory knowledge appropriately influences moral categorization, the theory-theory is a viable view for moral concepts in light of categorization. Using the functionalist metaphysics of concepts, some moral concepts and judgments for many people seem to be constituted by and to express cognitive folk consequentialist theory knowledge.

5.2 The Doctrine of Double Effect

One might raise a potential objection against my theory concept conclusion as some interpret this set of trolley problems as a matter concerning the Doctrine of Double Effect (DDE) (Hauser 2006, Hauser et al. 2008, Mikhail 2011). DDE generally states that sometimes it is permissible to harm a person as a foreseen unintended side-effect of bringing about some good end even though it would not be permissible to cause such a harm when it is intended as part of one's means to attaining the same good end. DDE is a moral principle that, in order to reach a verdict, takes into consideration causal knowledge of intentions for harming someone as a means or not, so when mentally represented, DDE is a causal moral law theory knowledge.

Some moral psychologists, like Mikhail, believe that the participants in the trolley experiments generally have subconscious innate knowledge of DDE and are using it in the two cases. For, it is permissible to pull the lever in the lever case because the one person on the side track who dies will die as an unintended side effect in attaining the greater consequences. This person's body is not intentionally used as a means to stop the trolley from running over the five. Yet, taking the obese man's life in the footbridge case is not permissible since the obese man is being intentionally used as a means to physically stop the trolley and attain the same greater consequences.

As a first response, recall that the purpose of this chapter is to establish the viability of the theory-theory for moral concepts in light of the categorization and sense desiderata. Even if DDE is really being used by most participants in order to make their moral categorizations rather than, for example, folk consequentialism knowledge, then this still will show the viability of the theory-theory in light of categorization. A main aim of this chapter still will be accomplished. In other words, the potential objection currently being addressed in this entire section is a moot point. Although what follows is moot, I will contend that at least folk consequentialism knowledge is being used by many people at times in these trolley problems and their ilk. In other words, despite being moot, I continue discussion on this topic in order to more precisely specify what particular kind of theory knowledge can be shown at this point in time to constitute many moral concepts in light of categorization.

I by no means deny the possibility that DDE can be used to reason in certain moral scenarios by certain people as studies show that for those subjects on the trolley problems who make judgments consistent with DDE, about one third of them provide correlational evidence for its use in that they verbally can articulate DDE and readily claim that it supposedly is influencing their decision-making (Cushman et al. 2006). Nevertheless, there is evidence against the fact that DDE, completely as such, is being used by itself in the lever and footbridge circumstances by *most* of the trolley study participants because there are several variants of the trolley problems that strongly suggest that DDE is not being so used. For example, in the *remote footbridge case* (Cushman et al. 2006), the scenario is exactly the same as the footbridge case. However, you can press a button to release a trap door on the footbridge under the obese man. You do not push him. Pressing the button will cause the man to drop down on to the track and stop the trolley. Regardless of whether one is standing right next to the obese man or far away, most participants believe that one ought to press the button. However, if most subjects are mainly using DDE in these trolley experiments, then we should expect the majority to state that one should not press the button to kill the obese individual just as one should not push the obese man in the *footbridge case* because one should not intentionally harm him as a means toward attaining the greater consequential end. Pressing the button violates DDE.

In yet another trolley problem variant that we will call the *loop case*, there are five people on the main track with a trolley heading toward them (Greene et al. 2001, Hauser 2006, Hauser et al. 2008, Mikhail 2011). However, if you pull a lever, the trolley will go on to a sidetrack that loops around back onto the main track in front of the five people strapped to the main track. Thus, pulling the lever seems like it will be ineffective since this will just cause the trolley to go on the side track that eventually loops back to the main track. Once returned to the main track, the trolley again will be moving toward the five people. However, on the side track is a man that when hit, will stop the trolley and save the five. Some versions of this loop case analogize the man to a heavy inanimate object (Hauser 2006, Hauser et al. 2008, Mikhail 2011). This problematically highlights his function as being merely an inanimate stopping device and perhaps makes his possible death seem crueler to test subjects. When correcting for this possibility in the vignette and eliminating the analogy, a strong majority of participants believe that one should pull the lever in the loop case and intentionally use the man's life as a means to save the five (Waldmann & Dieterich 2007, Greene 2013). The DDE thesis fails to predict this phenomenon.

Meanwhile, in the disparate *loop weight case*, the scenario is exactly like the loop scenario except the person's body on the loop track cannot stop the trolley, but the large weight immediately behind him can (Hauser 2006, Hauser et al. 2008, Mikhail 2011). If one pulls the lever, the trolley will move onto the loop track and kill the lone victim, but the trolley will be stopped by the heavy weight behind him. This will save the five. Notice that the person in front of the weight in this scenario is not used as a means to stop the trolley as in the loop case. In the loop weight case, a strong majority of participants roughly matching that in the loop case agree that it is morally permissible to pull the lever (Zimmerman 2013). However, if DDE mainly was being used, then most participants would have stated that it is impermissible to pull the lever in the loop case because one should not intentionally use a man's life as a means to attain the greater consequences, but it is permissible to pull the lever in the loop weight case. The prediction of DDE is not borne out in the above experiments.

Moreover, the use of DDE does not explain why replicated data shows that most people judge that it is permissible to push the obese man onto the track when many more than five lives are at stake if you fail to push the man, such as twenty, millions, or even billions of lives (Nichols and Mallon 2006, Greene 2013). For example, Shaun Nichols and Ron Mallon (2006) found that most choose to push the obese man when told that billions will die from a virus released into the atmosphere if he is not pushed. Let us call these *the high consequences cases*. Most judge that someone intentionally can be harmed as a means by using personal force, such as physically pushing someone with one's hands or a stick, to attain a good result when the consequences are extremely severe and reach a certain body count threshold. The use of folk consequentialism can help to explain these phenomena, but DDE cannot. Given the relevant above studies, such as on VMPFC patients, we know that cognitive reasoning is at work when participants make judgments consistent with folk consequentialism. At minimum, even if DDE or some other principle is at work for most people in most of the trolley problems, the high consequences cases demonstrate that most people at least have folk consequentialism knowledge stored in their moral concepts. Here, once a certain threshold value is passed when a more severe number of lives are at stake, then for most people, folk consequentialism trumps all including the negative emotional reaction from the thought of pushing the obese man in the footbridge case. This demonstrates that the theory-theory is a viable view of moral concepts, where different contexts can trigger the use of different concept constituents. Different concept constituents can be used individually or conjointly depending on the situation.

To note, most subjects on the footbridge and remote footbridge cases explain their different judgments on both situations by claiming that they were influenced by the moral principle that harm involving physical contact with a victim is worse than harm involving no physical contact. An overwhelming majority of such participants believed that this is morally relevant (Cushman et al. 2006). Later, it was discovered that pushing someone using a stick in one's hand is also considered by many to be as bad as making physical contact with a victim (Greene et al. 2009). Greene et al. have hypothesized that instead of DDE, the *Doctrine of Personal Force* is in play, which is consistent with the general judgments made in the lever, footbridge, remote footbridge, loop, and loop weight cases (Greene et al. 2009, Greene 2013). For the footbridge case, this Doctrine says that if you intentionally harm someone as a means *and* you use personal force, such as physically pushing someone or pushing them with a stick, then the action is wrong. It can be hypothesized that this causal moral law is in play in the footbridge case for most people, which causes them to judge that one should not push the obese man. Meanwhile, for the lever, remote footbridge, loop, and loop weight cases, sacrificing one life to save many more is permissible in light of the Doctrine of Personal Force because at minimum, personal force is not being used.

However, even if the Doctrine of Personal Force is in use, it still will provide evidence for the viability of the theory view in that this Doctrine is causal moral law knowledge. A main aim of this chapter will have been attained. Moreover, we still can infer that folk consequentialism is in play given the high consequences cases since this Doctrine of Personal Force cannot explain them. Rather, the Doctrine of Personal Force makes opposite predictions. Also, there is good reason based even on Greene et al.'s own studies to believe that this Doctrine of Personal Force cannot explain all the trolley phenomena. In an experiment, Joe is on a footbridge and needs to pull a switch in order to save the five lives from the trolley (Greene et al. 2009, Greene 2013). However, in order to get to the switch, Joe needs to push a victim out of the way and off the bridge, hurling the victim to his death. This involves intentionally harming someone as a means and using personal force. However, most subjects claim that it is permissible to push the victim. Yet, this runs contrary to the Doctrine of Personal Force.

Overall, instead of maintaining that there is some single overarching moral principle that neatly governs judgments on trolley-like dilemmas, it appears that different mental states can be used individually or conjointly in moral cognition depending on the context or situation, and there are no necessary and sufficient conditions. This is consistent with my pluralistic theory of moral concepts and with my prior established conclusion that classical structure to our moral concepts is not psychologically real.

It is important to keep in mind that the results of the trolley studies are not universal where, for example, everyone agrees to pull the lever in the lever case. Some people differ, and they may be using different theory knowledge than most test subjects. However, from a big picture perspective regarding the use of theory knowledge, come what may, the theory view for moral concepts can handle new discovered theory knowledge.

5.3 Utilitarianism Over Deontology?

Based on some of the above studies such as the lever and footbridge cases, Greene at times claims that deontological judgments only are generated by affective automatic processes while, in contrast, utilitarian judgments are generated by cognitive controlled processes. Greene and others like Peter Singer (2005) contend that this shows that we should not rely on deontological theory since such decision-making is based on unreliable processes. I do not agree with this strong thesis for several reasons. First, there are prototype studies discussed in the fourth chapter that demonstrate that we do store basic cognitive rule-like or deontological representations in our moral concepts. Also, in a later chapter, I will provide the conative-prototype/exemplar/theory chain argument. This contention claims that if non-cognitive conative states influence moral decision-making, then cognitive moral prototype, exemplar, and/or theory knowledge must also be used in conjunction with the conative state. The conative states that influence moral decision-making that seemingly are consistent with deontological theory are accompanied by cognitive normative concept constituents that also are consistent with deontological theory. Greene readily argues that emotions influence judgments when people make decisions consistent with deontological theory, but I will contend that when they do so, non-utilitarian cognitive moral representations must also be used conjointly in moral cognition. Such representations may be deontological in nature. Furthermore, we already have discussed positive evidence for the use of a deontological causal moral law knowledge from Young et al.'s TMS study to the RTPJ. Hence, judgments consistent with deontological theory also are impacted by cognitive moral mental states.

Moreover, given that deontological thought does not exclude cognitive rational processes, one may place rational constraints on emotions to help justify moral judgments in order to object against the likes of Greene and Singer. Using emotions with rational constraints may justify moral judgments, and the presence of emotions does not automatically disqualify relevant judgments as being unreliable. For instance, the neosentimentalist, John McDowell (1985), emotionally justifies moral judgments based on those emotional reactions that are merited in particular circumstances. A negative or positive emotional reaction on a moral case is merited if it is backed by good reasons. Thus, for McDowell, if one feels disapprobation regarding a person's action and such disapprobation is merited, then one's judgment that the action is wrong is justified. Although I do not necessarily endorse McDowell's view, it is important to keep in mind that emotions may reliably justify moral judgments when rational constraints are placed on them, such as has been argued by sentimentalist philosophers like Hume and Adam Smith.[4]

5.4 Objections Against the Theory-Theory Claim

As a possible objection to my theory-theory conclusion, in an earlier work, Prinz (2007) speculates that it is really the emotions driving judgments in the lever case rather than some kind of folk consequentialist rational calculation since there is a small activation of emotion regions of the brain when subjects make folk consequentialist categorizations (Greene et al. 2001). The activation of emotional regions is small and not as robust as the activation in the DLPFC, but it is still there. For folk consequentialist categorizations, there is a greater emotional response present than in decision-making for non-moral cases. Perhaps emotions are really what is at work when making apparent folk consequentialist judgments. However, Prinz problematically uses only correlational fMRI data on the lever case to draw a causal conclusion on it. Such brain scans only provide correlational evidence, and without further support on the lever scenario, it could be the case that the moral judgment causes one to experience emotions rather than emotions causing one to make a particular judgment on it. Prinz's objection fails. On the other hand, there is causal evidence in numerous above discussed studies that show cognitive reasoning processes are influencing judgments on the lever case, among many other cases. I do leave open the possibility that it later may be shown that emotions are working conjointly with such consequentialist representations in the lever case, but even if this is so, my pluralistic theory of moral concepts that includes the conative theory has the resources to handle this. In a later chapter, Prinz's point about the correlation between moral judgments and emotional regions of the brain, among other reasons, will resurface when discussing one of his more recent works, and although criticizing his use of such findings here, I eventually will use such evidence in a suitable fashion along with appropriate causal evidence of the influence of emotions in certain situations to sufficiently support the conative view.

One may object that there are psychological biases associated with the trolley problems and their ilk. For example, experimenters like Eric Schwitzgebel and Fiery Cushman (2012, 2015) have found order effects on them, where a participant's judgment on a case in a group of questions may potentially vary depending on what order the items are presented. People may give different answers on the lever and footbridge cases depending on which of the situations is presented first to them.

Schwitzgebel and Cushman (2015) have found that professional philosophers with PhDs working at top research institutes are equally susceptible to order effects than the folk. Furthermore, this susceptibility does not decline even when the philosopher is forced to think longer about the cases and told to contemplate alternative phrasings of them, is already familiar with the trolley problems, claims to have expertise on such problems, or reported beforehand that they already have prior stable views on the issues. Also, Petrinovich and O'Neill (1996) found framing effects in the trolley problems. Our experimenters found that what moral decision is made in the scenarios can depend on the wording that is used. They presented the cases to some subjects using the word 'save' rather than 'death.' For example, the lever case to some would be described as where pulling the lever will *save* five lives. However, to the other group of subjects, they framed the situation differently and used the word 'death' rather than 'save.' For instance, the lever case would be described to the other group as where pulling the lever will lead to the *death* of one life. They write,

> Once again, a tendency was found for a number of individual to shift from disagree to agree when the answer was in the Save compared with the Kill wording, and this tendency was evident for 39 of the 40 questions.
>
> (1996, p. 152)

Nadelhoffer and Feltz (2008) have found that there is an actor-observer bias in the trolley problems, where the people or actors involved in an action view things differently than those observers that are not a part of the action. Our experimenters ran tests on the lever case trolley problem. Some subjects received the *actor lever case*, where the vignette stated that the subjects themselves were the person who had the option of pulling the lever. The other participants were given the *observer lever case*, where the vignette stated that someone else was at the lever and had the option of pulling it. In this setup, the subject filling out the moral questionnaire is merely an observer. When asked about the moral permissibility of pulling the lever, subjects were more likely to allow for the permissibility of pulling the lever in the observer lever case rather than the actor lever case. This study suggests that whether one is an actor or an observer in a moral situation can have a significant impact on what moral judgment one makes. However, the morally correct answer for the lever scenario should not be dependent on whether you are the actor or the observer. Whether one is the actor or the observer in this case is morally irrelevant. Professional philosophers also have been shown to be more susceptible to the actor-observer bias than folk subjects (Tobia et al. 2013).

The above studies suggest that morally irrelevant factors can affect one's moral judgment and may lead one to make an inconsistent judgment at times depending upon how a moral scenario is framed or ordered. Although I discussed in the third chapter how it is possible for someone to make genuinely inconsistent judgments, these studies on psychological biases lead to the threat that for the relevant participants, their judgments on the trolley problem-like scenarios will not pass the informational value test. As the objection goes, when told the informational value that their judgments were influenced by such biases and irrelevant factors, in an effort to maintain consistency, it is possible that they may then lay down firm final decisions on the cases; decisions that are no longer susceptible to biases, where none of such judgments may be influenced by folk consequentialism knowledge. Their later performance on the tests may then mirror their competence or their true and ideal nature of their moral concepts. Hence, folk consequentialism knowledge may not really constitute the relevant moral concepts.

The response to this objection is that it is correct. Such biases do put into doubt concept constitution claims for the relevant subjects in light of the heightened threat that the relevant claims may not pass the informational value test. However, notice that the big picture aim of this chapter of establishing the viability of the theory-theory for moral concepts is still reached. There are plenty of participants who are not susceptible to such cognitive biases, where the relevant theory-theory claim for such individuals carries sufficient support. For instance, on a scale of 1–7 from "extremely morally good" (1), to "neither good nor bad" (4), to "extremely morally bad" (7), Schwitzgebel and Cushman (2012) found the mean rating for all groups combined, including folk and the novel test group of expert philosophers. For pulling the lever in the lever case, where this case is presented before the footbridge scenario, the average rating is 3.38. The mean for the lever case when presented after the footbridge situation is 3.88. The discrepancy between the average ratings for the footbridge case when given first and second is likewise similar. This data allows a lot of leeway in these studies for many, if not most, participants to maintain consistent judgments and not be susceptible to order effects. At one point they write, "The effect sizes we report, though large, are consistent with the possibility that a majority of philosophers adhere consistently to principles" (Schwitzgebel & Cushman 2012, p. 150).

The results of the study on framing effects by Petrinovich and O'Neill likewise permit for many to most participants to be unmoved by how a scenario is framed and to give consistent judgments as to whether an act is generally good or bad. Nadelhoffer and Feltz (2012) note that in both actor versus observer circumstances, most participants still judge that it is morally permissible to pull the lever, but still "... [twenty-five percent] of the participants' intuitions were affected by the actor-observer difference" (p. 140). In other words, seventy-five percent of the subjects' judgments were not so affected. In fact, a meta-analysis of framing effects studies shows that about 80% of people's moral judgments are not susceptible to framing effects (Demaree-Cotton 2016). All in all, even though the above biases do cast doubt on drawing concept constitution claims for the relevant participants for cases like the trolley problems, many to most people are not susceptible to such biases on these kinds of moral scenarios, so those who are not susceptible do provide evidence for the viability of the theory view for the relevant moral concepts for the relevant people.

Guy Kahane (2012) has argued in the trolley problems that the supposed evidence for the use of act utilitarian knowledge is really support for the use of deontological theory knowledge. Greene does initially describe the kind of knowledge being used in relevant cases as being one of utilitarianism rather than my specified brand of folk consequentialism. As a general category, consequentialism is the view that an act being morally correct is determined by whether it brings about the best consequences. Even if the means to bring about the best consequences require violating someone's individual rights, one ought to bring about the best consequences. The ends justify the means. Consequentialism is an umbrella category in that more specified tokens of the type can cash out what the best consequences are in different ways. For example, John Stuart Mill's utilitarianism generally claims that bringing about the greatest happiness for the greatest number is what brings about the best consequences, where happiness gets further cashed out in terms of qualitative and quantitative pleasure and the absence of pain.[5] For Mill, we should take into account the *quantity* of overall pleasure produced in our minds but should also take into account the *quality* of pleasure. For example, pleasures of the intellect are of a higher quality of pleasure than living a wanton life merely satisfying one's base desires even though living a wanton life may bring about a higher quantitative feeling of pleasure. Meanwhile, folk consequentialism, as defined here, does not necessarily rely on the more intricate notions of qualitative and quantitative pleasure and pain, but the best consequences are choosing those options that save more lives and lead to less overall physical harms. Once again, given further or future empirical research, I do allow for alterations to my notion of folk consequentialism, where it could be the case that folk consequentialism in people's minds is discovered to also include many ideas from act utilitarianism.

Kahane criticizes Greene et al.'s act utilitarian interpretation in that there is no evidence showing that participants fully are taking into account qualitative happiness. While participants are taking into account the happiness of a person's life being saved, there is no evidence that subjects are taking into account other kinds of happiness that are of a high quality, such as pursuing personal goals, which would help lead to living a flourishing life rather than merely just being alive. Hence, Kahane objects that there is insufficient evidence for the general use of a full-blown act utilitarianism representation in subjects. Notice, that I avoid this objection in that I do not posit that people have robust act utilitarian knowledge in mind, but rather, they have my more limited and specific folk consequentialism.

Kahane also contends that if participants really held act utilitarianism knowledge, then they should always be making judgments consistent with act utilitarianism since the greatest happiness principle is supposed to be a necessary and sufficient condition for moral categorization. Yet, participants in the trolley studies do not always do so. However, since I showed in the fourth chapter that such classical structure to our moral concepts is not psychologically real and I posit that folk consequentialism is theory knowledge, this mental state does not represent necessary and sufficient conditions. Thus, my view perfectly allows for reaching non-folk consequentialist conclusions at times, and it is not always required that one will draw conclusions consistent with such folk consequentialism.

Kahane then suggests that a deontological rule that we have a reason to reduce overall harm is really what could be influencing decisions when subjects seemingly make act utilitarian judgments. We have prima facie individual rights such as to be free from torture and from being murdered, but when a threshold of harm is surpassed, such as when a given number of lives are at stake, such rights are cast to the side, and we must reduce the overall harm.

Kahane interprets the principle of reducing overall harm as being deontological in nature, citing the prominent deontologist W.D. Ross in promulgating it. However, it can be viewed as being a folk consequentialist principle in that in the right situation, one should violate prima facie core individual rights in order to bring about the best consequences of choosing the option that saves more lives. Indeed, some view this overall scheme from Ross as inevitably melting into a mixed normative ethical theory called *threshold deontology* that fuses deontology and consequentialism (Moore 1997). Deontology and individual rights govern despite the adverse consequences up to a point, but once the consequences become so calamitous that they cross a certain threshold, then consequentialism overrides.

Kahane's reducing harm principle mirrors folk consequentialism in that folk consequentialism also comes into play in the studies when a certain threshold of lives is at stake. Kahane's suggestion of the use of the reducing harm principle in the relevant cases of moral cognition is basically the same suggestion I have put forth regarding the use of folk consequentialism. However, I interpret his principle of reducing overall harm as being consequentialist rather than deontological in nature since it matches a traditional conception of consequentialism of being able to override core individual rights, like the right to life, in order to bring about the greater consequences of reducing harm and overall loss of human life. Individual rights can be violated. The principle of reducing harm essentially states that in the right circumstances, what is morally important is the consequences, not the means of achieving those consequences. If we are going to draw any distinction between deontological and consequentialist thought, the line must be drawn here. The reducing harm principle is a consequentialist principle. Hence, I maintain my conclusion that folk consequentialism influences judgments in the relevant cases. Therefore, in light of categorization and the functionalist identification of concepts, there is evidence that some of our moral concepts may be constituted by cognitive folk consequentialism theory knowledge.[6] This knowledge may or may not be used depending on the circumstances.

5.5 The Prototype-Theory Chain Argument

There is a prototype-theory chain argument. Recall from the previous chapter that a chain argument attempts to establish the viability of one theory of concepts based on the viable existence of a different concept structure. The chain argument at hand attempts to establish the viability of the theory view for moral concepts based on the existence of prototype knowledge in our moral concepts. So far, we have only established the viability of the theory-theory for many people for moral concepts like MORALLY RIGHT and MORALLY WRONG. However, recall from the previous chapter that there are a variety of different kinds of moral concepts, such as virtue trait concepts. Since we drew the conclusion in the previous chapter that there is strong support that moral concepts as a class generally have prototype structure in light of categorization, sense, and concept acquisition, the present chain argument will help to allow us to draw a broader conclusion concerning the possible viability of the theory view generally for the wide spectrum of moral concepts.

Nelson Goodman (1972) points out that to say that two things are similar is to roughly say that they share a certain number of features in common. However, the problem with this is that any two objects can have many properties in common. For instance, two apparently dissimilar things like a hammer and a laptop computer both weigh less than ten million pounds, weigh less than nine and a half million pounds did not exist ten billion years ago, did not exist nine billion years ago, take up space, both have functions, both can be dropped, both can fit in my trunk, both can fit in my house, both can fit in a garbage bag, etc. Due to this fact, Goodman points out that to say that two things are similar requires a theoretical frame of reference in order to delimit and specify what kinds of properties are relevant for determining similarity in a particular instance.

Likewise, as suggested by Murphy and Medin (1985), some of our concepts may contain similarity-based knowledge like prototypes, but there must be at least implicit theoretical constraints on what kinds of similarity-based knowledge gets stored in our relevant concepts such that certain of our mental representations can be said to be similar to objects and things in the world. There must be some kind of mentally represented frame of reference for why constituents like HAS KEYS, HAS A SCREEN, and HAS A HARD DRIVE are similarity-based knowledge I associate with the category *laptop* rather than WEIGHS LESS THAN TEN MILLION POUNDS and DID NOT EXIST TEN BILLION YEARS AGO. Murphy and Medin claim that it is theory knowledge, such as the knowledge of what a computer's function is, which provides the requisite theoretical constraints.

Likewise, for moral concepts, why do I have similarity-based prototype knowledge such as HONEST, KIND, and JUST that I associate with the class *good person* rather than A QUALITY HELD BY SOME PEOPLE IN IRELAND, IS NOT EXEMPLIFIED ON SATURN, and IS NOT EXEMPLIFIED ON VENUS? The answer is that there are theoretical constraints that reign in what kinds of similarity-based knowledge get stored in our relevant concepts. More precisely, it is theory knowledge, such as possibly of virtue ethical theory, which provides the reference point for what kinds of similarity-based knowledge is relevant and irrelevant. It is knowledge of this ethical theory that for me may constrain my similarity-based knowledge for GOOD PERSON such that my GOOD PERSON concept is in part constituted by the prototypes HONEST, KIND, and JUST rather than by A QUALITY HELD BY SOME PEOPLE IN IRELAND, IS NOT EXEMPLIFIED ON SATURN, and IS NOT EXEMPLIFIED ON VENUS. For, I believe that being honest, kind, and just are virtues that will lead one to live a flourishing life. Therefore, we have on our hands a prototype-theory chain argument that if one has prototypes of a moral category, then it follows that one has a theory (-ies) of the moral category as well. Theories are shepherds and in part play the relevant causal role in moral deliberation of helping to determine what kinds of prototype rules, reasons, virtues, and/or features of moral situations one maintains. The previously detailed argument for the prototype theory for the class of moral concepts also provides relevant evidence for the existence of theory knowledge generally for the class of moral concepts. This chain argument for the viability of the theory-theory of moral concepts is non-speculative in that it is in part reliant on prototype experimental studies on moral concepts.

5.6 Sense Desideratum

Recall that the aim of this chapter is to show how the theory view can account for the categorization and sense desiderata. While we have just finished discussing how theory representations can help to explain moral categorization, the theory-theory also does well in being able to account for the sense of our moral concepts, where how we understand ethics is in part based on theory knowledge. The theory view can account for certain times when an individual may understand two co-referential phrases differently, although for my pluralistic theory of moral concepts, different kinds of structures can fulfill this role individually or conjointly depending on the circumstances. For example, Christian's irresponsible next door neighbor who forgets to return any tools he borrows from Christian and the resident who Christian's community regards as the metaphorical patron saint and protector of the neighborhood is the same person. Yet, Christian may not be aware that his concepts MY IRRESPONSIBLE NEXT DOOR NEIGHBOR and THE PATRON SAINT OF THE NEIGHBORHOOD refer to the same person. However, the sense of his moral concepts that is based on theory knowledge can in part account for his different understandings of the co-referential compound concepts. He may understand IRRESPONSIBLE in part in virtue ethical theory terms in that this is not a character trait that should be exemplified since it is not a quality of a virtuous person, and he understands PATRON SAINT, where SAINT is a so-called thick moral concept, in part in divine command theory terms as someone who devoutly obeys the commands of God.

Especially in light of drawing the connection between the causal moral judgment literature and my functionalist identification of concepts, we now see that there is strong evidence for this cognitivist theory view on moral concepts. While I have shown how the prototype and exemplar theories satisfy the categorization, sense, and concept acquisition desiderata for theories of moral concepts, I only have demonstrated that the theory-theory satisfies the categorization and sense desiderata. In the following chapter, we will assess the theory view in light of the concept acquisition desideratum, and in so doing, we will explore issues in evolutionary ethics and whether moral concepts are innate.

Notes

1 Curiously enough, there have been studies showing that in certain other cases and moral situations, one's moral judgment itself influences one's causal knowledge of whether an agent intends to perform an action or not (Knobe 2003). This is known as the Knobe effect.

2 Although such patients generally make the same *kinds* of verdicts as normal subjects on this questionnaire, their answers may differ in degree from each other, such as in the degree of wrongness of an act (Carr et al. 2015).

3 Greene and company have other studies that might be used to support the theory-theory. One such study implements the Cognitive Reflection Test and has participants try to solve tricky math problems, in which the correct answer is counterintuitive, before answering moral questions (Paxton et al. 2011). This could influence participants to give more counterintuitive consequentialist responses to certain moral questions. However, this study is controversial due to replication problems (Royzman et al. 2015).

4 Hume and Smith's views will be discussed in the final chapter.

5 Mill at times can be interpreted as an act utilitarian, but at other times can be interpreted as a rule utilitarian.

6 Kahane also attempts to use experimental evidence to claim that intuitive judgments generally are associated with automatic processing and counter-intuitive judgments are associated with controlled processing regardless of the possible utilitarian or deontological content of such judgments (Kahane 2012). However, they received mixed results, and Paxton et al. (2012) have run a response study that contradicts their findings.

References

Carr, A.R., Paholpak, P., Daianu, M., Fong, S.S., Mather, M., Jimenez, E.E., Thompson, P., and Mendez, M.F. 2015. "An Investigation of Care-based vs. Rule-based Morality in Frontotemporal Dementia, Alzheimer's Disease, and Healthy Controls." *Neuropsychologia* 78, 73–79.

Ciaramelli, E., Muccioli, M., Ladavas, E., and di Pellgrino, G. 2007. "Selective Deficit in Personal Moral Judgment Following Damage to Ventromedial Prefrontal Cortex." *Social Cognitive and Affective Neuroscience* 2, 84–92.

Cushman, F., Young, L., and Hauser, M. 2006. "The Role of Conscious Reasoning and Intuition in Moral Judgment: Testing Three Principles of Harm." *Psychological Science* 17, 1082–1089.

Damasio, Antonio. 1994. *Descartes' Error.* New York: Penguin.

Decety, J. and Cacioppo, S. 2012. "The Speed of Morality: A High-Density Electrical Neuroimaging Study." *Journal of Neurophysicology* 108, 3068–3072.

Demaree-Cotton, J. 2016. "Do Framing Effects Make Moral Intuitions Unreliable?" *Philosophical Psychology* 29, 1–22.

Goodman, Nelson. 1972. *Problems and Projects.* Indianapolis: Bobbs-Merrill.

Greene, Joshua. 2008. "The Secret Joke of Kant's Soul." *Moral Psychology Volume* 3. Ed. by Walter Sinnott-Armstrong. Cambridge, MA: The MIT Press.

Greene, Joshua. 2013. *Moral Tribes.* New York: The Penguin Press.

Greene, J., Nystrom, L.E., Engell, A.D., Darley, J.M., and Cohen, J.D. 2004. "The Neural Bases of Cognitive Conflict and Control in Moral Judgment." *Neuron* 44, 387–400.

Greene, J., Sommerville, R.B., Nystrom, L.E., Darley, J.M., and Cohen, J.D. 2001. "An fMRI Investigation of Emotional Engagement in Moral Judgment." *Science* 293, 2105–2108.

Greene, J., Cushman, F., Stewart, L., Lowenberg, K., Nystrom, L., and Cohen, J. 2009. "Pushing Moral Buttons: The Interaction Between Personal Force and Intention in Moral Judgment." *Cognition* 111, 364–371.

Haidt, Johnathan. 2001. "The Emotional Dog and its Rational Tail: A Social Intuitionist Approach to Moral Judgment." *Psychological Review* 108, 814–834.

Hauser, Marc D. 2006. *Moral Minds.* New York: Harper Collins Publishers.

Hauser, M., Cushman, F., Young, L., Kang-Xing Jin, R., and Mikhail, J. 2007. "A Dissociation Between Moral Judgments and Justifications." *Mind and Language* 22, 1–21.

Hauser, M., Young, L., and Cushman, F. 2008. "Reviving Rawls Linguistic Analogy: Operative Principles and the Causal Structure of Moral Actions." *Moral Psychology Volume* 2. Ed. by Walter Sinnott-Armstrong. Cambridge, MA: The MIT Press, 107–144.

Jeurissen, D., Sack, A., Roebroek, A., Russ, B., and Pascual-Leone, A. 2014. "TMS Affects Moral Judgment, Showing the Role of DLPFC and TPJ in Cognitive and Emotional Processing." *Frontiers in Neuroscience* 8, 1–9.

Kahane, Guy. 2012. "On the Wrong Track: Process and Content in Moral Psychology." *Mind & Language* 27, 519–545.

Kohlberg, Lawrence. 1981. *Essays on Moral Development, Vol.* 1, *The Philosophy of Moral Development.* New York: Harper & Row.

Knobe, Joshua. 2003. "Intentional Action and Side Effects in Ordinary Language." *Analysis* 63, 190–193.

Koenigs, M. and Tranel, D. 2007. "Irrational Economic Decision-making After Ventromedial Prefrontal Damage: Evidence from the Ultimatum Game." *Journal of Neuroscience* 27, 951–956.

Koenigs, M., Young, L., Adolphs, R., Tranel, D., Cushman, F., Hauser, M., and Damasio, A. 2007. "Damage to the Prefrontal Cortex Increases Utilitarian Moral Judgments." *Nature* 446, 908–911.

McDowell, John. 1985. "Values and Secondary Qualities." *Morality and Objectivity: A Tribute to J.L. Mackie.* Ed. by Honderich, Ted. London: Routledge & Kegan Paul.

Mendez, Mario. 2006. "What Frontotemporal Dementia Reveals About the Neurobiological Basis of Morality." *Medical Hypothesis* 67, 411–418.

Mendez, M.F., Anderson, E., and Shapria, J.S. 2005a. "An Investigation of Moral Judgment in Frontotemporal Dementia." *Cognitive and Behavioral Neurology* 18, 193–197.

Mendez, M.F., Chen, A., Shapira, J., and Miller, B. 2005b. "Acquired Sociopathy and Frontotemporal Dementia." *Dementia and Geriatric Cognitive Disorders* 20, 99–104.

Mikhail, John. 2011. *Elements of Moral Cognition.* Cambridge: Cambridge University Press.

Mikhail, John. 2013. *Elements of Moral Cognition.* Cambridge: Cambridge University Press.

Moore, Michael. 1997. *Placing Blame: A General Theory of the Criminal Law.* Oxford: Oxford University Press.

Moretto, G., Làdavas, E., Mattioli, F., and Di Pellegrino, G. 2010. "A Psychophysiological Investigation of Moral Judgment After Ventromedial Prefrontal Damage." *Journal of Cognitive Neuroscience* 22, 1888–1899.

Murphy, G. and Medin, D. 1985. "The Role of Theories in Conceptual Coherence." *Psychological Review* 92, 289.

Nadelhoffer, T. and Feltz, A. 2008. "The Actor–observer Bias and Moral Intuitions: Adding Fuel to Sinnott-Armstrong's Fire." *Neuroethics* 1, 133–144.

Nichols, Shaun and Mallon, Ron. 2006. "Moral Dilemmas and Moral Rules." *Cognition* 100, 530–542.

Park, John. 2015. "The Theory-theory of Moral Concepts." *Journal of Cognition and Neuroethics*, 3, 117–138.

Paxton, J., Unger, L., and Greene, J. 2011. "Reflection and Reasoning in Moral Judgment." *Cognitive Science*, 36, 1–15.

Petrinovich, L. and O'Neill, P. 1996. "Influence of Wording and Framing Effects on Moral Intuitions." *Ethology and Sociobiology* 17(3), 145–171.

Prinz, Jesse. 2007. *The Emotional Construction of Morals.* Oxford: Oxford University Press.

Royzman, E.B., Landy, J.F., and Leeman, R.F. 2015. "Are Thoughtful People More Utilitarian? CRT as a Unique Predictor of Moral Minimalism in the Dilemmatic Context." *Cognitive Science* 39, 325–352.

Shweder, R.A., Mahapatra, M., and Miller, J.G. 1987. "Culture and Moral Development." *The Emergence of Morality in Young Children*. Ed. by J. Kagan and S. Lamb. Chicago: University of Chicago Press, 1–83.

Schwitzgebel, Eric and Cushman, Fiery. 2012. "Expertise in Moral Reasoning? Order Effects on Moral Judgment in Professional Philosophers and Non-philosophers." *Mind & Language* 27, 135–153.

Schwitzgebel, Eric and Cushman, Fiery. 2015. "Philosophers' Biased Judgments Persist Despite Training, Expertise and Reflection." *Cognition* 141, 127–137.

Singer, Peter. 2005. "Ethics and Intuitions." The *Journal of Ethics* 9, 331–352.

Tobia, K., Buckwalter, W., and Stich, S. 2013. "Moral Intuitions: Are Philosophers Experts?" *Philosophical Psychology* 26, 629–638.

Waldmann, M. and Dieterich, J. 2007. "Throwing a Bomb on a Person Versus Throwing a Person on a Bomb: Intervention Myopia in Moral Intuitions." *Psychological Science* 18, 247–253.

Young, L., Cushman, F., Hauser, M., and Saxe, R. 2007. "The Neural Basis of the Interaction Between Theory of Mind and Moral Judgment." *Proceedings of the National Academy of Sciences of the United States of America* 104, 8235–8240.

Zimmerman, A. 2013. "Mikhail's Naturalized Moral Rationalism." *Jerusalem Review of Legal Studies* 8, 44–65.

6 Moral Nativism and Evolutionary Ethics

We will now discuss the concept acquisition desideratum for moral concepts in light of the theory view. This third desideratum will take us into discussion of evolutionary ethics and chimpanzees as we explore whether there is an evolutionary basis for the concept acquisition claim that we have innate moral concepts. Most contemporary moral nativist claims pertain to the theory view, and this is why I have put the discussion of moral nativism alongside the theory-theory. However, as we discuss moral nativism further, this will open the door to entertaining other moral nativist claims that promote different concept structures.

6.1 Theory-Theory Concept Acquisition

Overall, the theory-theory sits well with the concept acquisition desideratum for moral concepts. Theory structure lends itself to acquisition by ostension and inference. When particular instances of moral acts and persons are pointed out to us, represented by exemplars, we can compute statistically frequent prototypes, and we also can infer a theory that provides a frame of reference for what kinds of prototypes should be stored in our moral concepts. Theories also can be readily acquired through direct verbal instruction or from being read.

Theory knowledge also may be acquired innately. Plato claimed that we have innate moral concepts that can be awoken in us through reflection, while Aristotle differed and claimed that our moral concepts are acquired through experience and practice in the world. Most proponents of invoking DDE to explain the trolley problems claim that this knowledge as well as many other represented rules are innate principles that actually are operative in cognition but not widely expressed when interviewed (Rawls 1971, Dwyer 1999, Harman 1999, Hauser 2006, Hauser et al. 2008, Mikhail 2011). I now will address the most prominent nativist claim for moral concept acquisition, first suggested by John Rawls (1971), which is a poverty of the stimulus argument. The primary conclusion I will reach is that their thesis that we have innate moral principles is unjustified. The issue of whether moral concepts are innate or learned has roots in the rationalist versus empiricist debates made heavily popular in the Modern Era. The particular nativist claim at hand has similarities to Noam Chomsky's (1965) universal grammar thesis. Chomsky's poverty of the stimulus argument for a universal grammar is that in order to comprehend and produce novel sentences, a person must have knowledge of grammatical rules. However, children are not instructed about the complex rules of grammar when they begin picking up a language. They have a poverty of the stimulus. Yet, they largely are able to understand and speak the language in a grammatically appropriate way without such instruction and without being able to articulate the relevant rules of grammar. Therefore, the human language faculty must include innate knowledge of a universal grammar that helps guide a child in constructing grammatically proper sentences. This puts constraints on possible grammatical systems. Moreover, principles of grammar are connected to binary parameters, each of which can occupy one of two positions. Which position is occupied can be determined by cultural interaction with others without being explicitly taught. For instance, there is a parameter for whether a sentence must contain a subject, as in English, or not, as in Italian.

Moreover, Chomsky claims that a speaker's grammatical competence constitutes a modular cognitive system. A module in the brain has a neural architecture that is dedicated to processing information specific to only a particular domain and is informationally encapsulated in that it does not have access to information stored elsewhere in the mind (Fodor 1983). An example of being informationally encapsulated may be low-level visual processing. For instance, even though one is aware that an optical illusion, such as the Müller-Lyer illusion, is false, this does not prevent the illusion from persisting before one's eyes. Our belief that we are witnessing an illusion does not correct our visual experience of the illusion. Low-level visual processing of illusions is not impacted by any external influences.

Contemporary moral nativists largely do not claim that moral judgments on particular cases are innate. For, evidence abounds in fields like anthropology, history, political science, sociology, religion, and psychology that particular moral judgments can vary greatly across cultures, time, and even within cultures.[1] For instance, when looking at specific moral positions about not killing humans, as a descriptive matter, there is variance in the general social construction of morals in this regard across time and location for issues like capital punishment for murderers, infanticide, killing foreigners or people in the out-group for fun, killing a female for being raped, killing an innocent stranger because there is a natural death in one's family, stoning women for adultery, stoning mentally handicapped people for fun, taking another's life in self-defense, dueling for honor, killing based on religious affiliation, gladiatorial killing for entertainment, hunting for cannibalism, suicide, warfare for conquest and wealth, genocide, euthanasia, assisted suicide, revenge killings, religious human sacrifices, etc.

Although there is a general expectation that if a belief is innate then it widely should be found cross-culturally, cross-cultural universality of a trait does not necessarily lead to innateness, and innateness does not necessarily lead to cross-cultural universality. For, it is a general universal belief that the sun rises in the morning, but this belief is not innate. It is acquired by experience. It is biologically innate for teenagers who have reached puberty to want to have sex, but teens raised in certain conservative religious communities may not desire to have sex until they get married. However, the great diversity in moral judgments across time and location, even within the same communities such as between moral philosophers on such matters as abortion and international distributive justice, strongly suggests that judgments on particular moral cases are not innate. Such robust cross-disciplinary evidence can be said to at least place a significant level of doubt on the thesis that moral judgments on particular cases are innate in our species; a burden that most contemporary moral nativists are unwilling to take on.

Therefore, modern-day moral nativists generally avoid claiming that judgments on particular cases are innate since there is or there very well could be in the possible future significant cultural variance on judgments on specific cases, which creates a significant burden of proof. Instead, moral nativists generally go up to a higher level of abstraction and claim that there are more general principles that have parameters that can be filled in by culture, as with grammatical principles, which will allow for a degree of cultural variance in the moral principles. Such moral nativists tend to draw an analogy from universal grammar to a universal moral grammar. As a toy example, a nativist may claim that we have the innate belief KILLING X IS NOT MORALLY PERMISSIBLE UNLESS Y, where X and Y get filled in by culture. For instance, Darwin in *The Descent of Man* observes that the Fijians permit burying one's parents alive if they are old or sick. This principle can be represented in the relevant Fijians as KILLING ONE'S OWN PARENTS IS NOT MORALLY PERMISSIBLE UNLESS THEY ARE OLD OR SICK.

The analogy to linguistics can be taken as being a strong or weak one. On the strong version, language and moral thinking work in the same way. For example, just as grammatical principles have binary parameters and occupy a relevant module, so do moral principles. On the weak version, the analogy is not as tight, and there is not an exact analogical correspondence between an innate grammar and an innate moral grammar. For instance, on the weak view, the moral mind contains innate principles, but it may or may not be modular (Dwyer 2008) and/or the moral competence may or may not have binary parameters. For instance, it may have more than two parameters.

One of the main contentions for this kind of nativism is that given the poverty of the moral stimulus (POMS), where children are not taught certain complex moral principles that they use in moral cognition, the best explanation of the moral categorization phenomena is that such principles are innate. Properly explaining the many moral categorization phenomena supposedly requires the presence of certain complex and inaccessible moral principle(s) in people's minds that they have difficulty articulating, but there is a gap between the complexity of learning such a principle and the limited resources available to the moral learner. People do not learn certain complex principles that can help sufficiently explain relevant moral categorization phenomena. Hence, positing certain innate complex moral principles in our minds is the best explanation, and such principles are truly operative in moral cognition.

6.2 'Innate'

While the definition of what it is to be 'innate' is itself a controversial philosophical question, we may adopt an understanding of the term that is generally accepted in the relevant literature surrounding the universal moral grammar hypothesis. We will understand a phenotypical psychological moral capacity to be innate if its existence is dependent upon genes that have been replicated in virtue of causally facilitating the phenotype in the past. The psychological capacity must be an evolutionary adaptation that has evolved and has been maintained by natural selection. It must be selected for. The psychological capacity should be an adaptive response to survival challenges faced by our ancestors. The phenotype must be fitness-enhancing, leading to the survival of individuals and the production of viable offspring. The relevant genes and their phenotypic expression that are passed on then can provide relevant advantages to future generations and eventually can overrun a population. Also, innate psychological traits cannot be comprehensively explained solely in terms of environmental conditions under which they are acquired.

Furthermore, although it is not wholly uniform, there is a tendency to maintain that the proposed innate moral psychological capacity must be modular. It is thought by many to be acquired by psychological mechanisms that are dedicated to the moral domain, as opposed to being acquired only by mechanisms that evolved for some other purpose or for no purpose at all. For instance, Mikhail (2011) writes that his moral grammar thesis "is broadly mentalist, modular, and nativist in its basic orientation" (p. 38). Hauser et al. (2008) state, "Though we explicitly recognize the role of domain-general mechanisms, we are nonetheless committed to the existence of some cognitive mechanisms that are specific to the domain of morality" (p. 172). In cognitive science, many innate capacities are often presumed to be modular, although some are not, such as innate domain-general capacities that are not domain specific. Generally, the domain specificity of a trait provides defeasible support that the trait is an adaptation. The fact that the trait develops early in childhood and its development is distinct from the development of other traits suggests that natural selection acted on its developmental pathway, and the trait is not acquired as a byproduct or tag-along companion of another psychological capacity that is adaptive. As an example of a byproduct trait that really is not adaptive, a polar bear's coat being thick is adaptive due to the cold climate that polar bears live in, but the accompanying property of the thick coat is that it is heavy. Yet, being heavy is not adaptive. Rather, it is merely a byproduct of the coat being thick. One thing to look out for is that the moral capacity may just be a tag-along companion of other cognitive capacities that are adaptive.

On the other hand, contemporary moral empiricists generally maintain that the capacity to think of morals is the product of environmental inputs, such as culture, interacting only with more domain-general innate cognitive capacities, such as potentially the capacity to feel emotions, learn, or think about norms, generally understood. An innate normative capacity, generally understood, allows us to think about moral, pragmatic, legal, artistic, conventional norms, etc. There is no specific and distinct innate moral capacity, understood as a specific normative capacity, for the moral empiricist. It has long been known in the nativism debate that a mind that is a complete blank slate absent of any innate structures will be incapable of learning at all. There must be something innate in the mind for us to first be able to know anything about the world around us. Hence, empiricists claim there are only domain-general innate cognitive capacities while nativists contend there are more specific innate capacities along with domain-general ones.

As an example of nativism, fear of snakes in humans may be innate. This phenotype of certain genotypes may be an adaptation that has contributed to the survival of our species and has been selected for. Those who had this phobia, as a result, had increased fitness, and thus, the genetic facilitators of this fear were replicated more than other genes. This psychological trait may be modular in that it is informationally encapsulated and is dedicated specifically for arousing a fear response in the presence of snakes. However, it may be the case that one may only become snake phobic when one sees a member of one's species exhibit a fear reaction to snakes during a critical period (Mineka et al. 1984). Although this snake phobia is in part dependent upon the environment for being instantiated, it cannot be fully explained by the relevant environmental conditions. For, given a variety of phenomena, such as that other primates of which we have a common ancestor appear to have a natural fear response to snakes, an evolutionary genetic story must also be invoked. Meanwhile, despite its prevalence, fear of atomic bombs is not innate because whatever genes allow us to have this particular fear did not end up persisting in our species due to its contribution to fear of atomic bombs in our ancestral evolutionary history.

6.3 Moral Nativism and Evolutionary Ethics

As possible support for the POMS argument, the psychological capacity to make moral judgments and accept them is speculatively proposed by many to have the evolutionary function of coordination (Gibbard 1991, Joyce 2006, Wong 2006, Kitcher 2011). In other words, the capacity to make moral judgments may have the general evolutionary job description of leading to coordination, which means that this psychological capacity is perhaps adaptive. This is not a moral substantive claim that we ought always to cooperate, but it is merely an evolutionary biological claim about the function of ethics. As an example of this function, it could be that at many times the coordinated action of raping, pillaging, and plundering other groups is adaptive behavior for one's group in many environments, such as during the Age of Imperialism. Such behavior is readily found in our close cousins, the chimpanzees, and is suffused throughout human history. As we evolved the capacity to think about ethics, different groups can reach a disparate general consensus and construct their cooperative values in different advantageous ways. The function of ethics can be multiply realized. Such values then can be passed on to future generations, shaping their moral intuitions and viewpoints. Ecological factors can even play a role in how groups construct their moral norms since in evolutionary biology, what is adaptive is always relative to an environment and time. As an example of this relativity, it may be the case that when in an environment where there are no ground predators, birds may eventually lose their ability to fly, as the production of functional wings is costly to produce and more energy rather can be channeled into producing offspring and surviving. Flightless island birds such as the kakapo and penguins do not have any natural ground predators. However, relative to an environment in which there are or would be natural ground predators, it would be advantageous for flightless birds to have functional wings.

In order to claim that something is an adaptation as the moral nativist attempts to do, hard experimental data is required. As would be expected from scientific inquiry, empirical confirmation is necessary to sufficiently establish the evolutionary genealogy of morals and what the function of our moral psychology may be. In biology, any purely a priori claim about what the biological function of our moral psychology is will be relegated as being a "just-so" story that is not supported by the requisite experimental evidence (Gould & Lewontin 1979). Although the claim that our moral capacity is an adaptation and is fitness-enhancing is widely regarded as the most plausible view in the evolutionary psychology literature given the evidence (Gibbard 1991, Joyce 2006, Wong 2006,

Kitcher 2011), it is still speculative.[2] Examples of some common arguments for this claim are that all cultures have moral norms of cooperation which may be expected if the moral capacity is adaptive. This lends some inductive support. Also, this functional claim is consistent with historical evidence of the earliest books on ethics. For example, the Mesopotamian law codes, The Book of the Dead, the Gilgamesh epic, and the Code of Hammurabi have the general aims of promoting intra-social peace, stability, and cooperation. When a trait is ancient and universal, it is either because it is innate or it is easily acquired by learning, such as the belief that the sun rises every morning. However, unlike the belief that the sun rises every morning, it is more difficult to see how the psychological *capacity* to think about morals, as opposed to maintaining particular moral norms, is easily and readily acquired by each psychologically normal individual based largely on external environmental conditions. Learning certain moral norms is easy in cultural environments, but acquiring the capacity to think about moral values does not appear to be as easy. However, notice this particular contention also can be made *mutatis mutandis* for having an innate normative capacity, generally understood, rather than for having an innate moral capacity. If we have an innate normative capacity, then this allows for the possibility that the moral capacity is acquired by cultural construction and learning and is not innate but is in part dependent on an innate domain-general normative capacity.

There are also numerous "how-possibly" models of the evolution of morals that are possible models of the evolutionary genealogy of morals that attempt to establish how the thesis that moral cognition was selected for is consistent with evolutionary theory. Such models also try to show how moral cognition would have been selected for in certain plausible evolutionary situations (Henrich and Boyd 2001, Joyce 2006, Kitcher 2011, Sterelny 2012, Tomasello 2016). These are not necessarily actual models of how events occurred, but they do provide suggestive evidence.

However, if the moral psychological capacity is an adaptation, the first objection to the relevant moral nativists is that there is not enough data to determine whether the capacity to think morally is a genetic or cultural adaptation. Moral nativists claim that the moral capacity is a genetic cognitive adaptation that is genetically inherited. Hence, it is innate. For example, Mikhail writes,

> ...the argument from the poverty of the moral stimulus holds that at least part of the best explanation of how children acquire their unconscious moral knowledge is the assumption that the human genetic program includes instructions for the acquisition of a moral sense.
>
> (2011, p. 17)

However, this may not be the case, but rather, it may be a cultural adaptation that is not genetically inherited. On this picture, there are no underlying innate moral principles that can be shaped by culture. Instead, our capacity to think about ethics may be a trait constructed by culture and passed on through social learning and cultural transmission across generations, in part relying on only innate domain-general cognitive capacities like a domain-general normative capacity.[3] This moral empiricist picture could be so rather than it being passed on by genes that are selected for and that underlie a specific moral capacity. Cultural traits are subject to selection and evolution. For example, we do not have a gene specifically for creating guns, although our ability to create guns may be a byproduct of more general innate cognitive capacities, such as for learning, among other traits. However, it may be fitness-enhancing at many times for members of cultures to first produce such weapons and pass on this knowledge via cultural inheritance to future generations of one's own culture, as exemplified when the Europeans met the natives of the Americas. The production and teaching of gun-making may be a cultural adaptation in many environments. A like story may hold for moral judgment. While it is a plausible claim that the capacity to think about ethics is adaptive, it is an open question as to whether it is a genetic or cultural adaptation. More empirical data is required to draw a strong conclusion on this issue. Yet, without the requisite empirical evidence that the moral capacity is a genetic adaptation, the defenders of POMS are unjustified in their moral nativist conclusion.

In Hume's (1738/2000) genealogy of morals, he states that justice emerged with the need to extend natural sympathies to large societal groups. In a how-possibly explanation of the moral capacity that relies on cultural evolution, Boyd and Richerson, among others, argue that as human populations grow, humans start getting in contact with members that are not close friends and kin (1985, Gibbard 1991, Kitcher 2006, Prinz 2007).[4] Large-scale societies have large projects that require coordination, such as farming and constructing roads, water pipelines, buildings, and mutual trading/business relations. Proper mechanisms are required to make sure that such cooperation occurs and individuals do not fail to cooperate. If helping behaviors evolved when cooperative relationships were dyadic, then such evolved mechanisms may not be strong enough to ensure cooperative behaviors among individuals who are strangers. However, moral norms paint a plausible picture of how to ensure cooperation in large societies with individuals who may not know one another. This development of morality offers a plausible solution to how culture responded to the pressure of being able to get individuals to be nice to other members even though they are strangers. Morality generally can provide the right kind of content to the language of "oughtness" that can lead to the ultra-social cooperation found in our species, such as having a welfare state, which far surpasses even the complex cooperation found in Hymenoptera. On this picture, cultural moral traits regarding cooperation rather than genes may apparently be what is selected for at the group rather than individual level.

Some have contended that we may have an innate domain-general normative capacity, but we do not specifically have a distinct innate moral capacity with innate moral principles (Sripada & Stich 2006). While the capacity to think of morality may in part involve an innate domain-general capacity to think about norms, generally understood, the moral capacity itself is not innate. Kim Sterelny (2012) argues that the moral capacity is not prewired, although it involves innate domain-general capacities, such as the ability to feel pro-social emotions and learning in social environments, which constrain moral judgment-making. Emotions like feeling guilt when harming others and feeling love make us have stronger commitments to one another such that it enhances cooperation. It is such innate domain-general capacities that we acquired in our ancestral history before we could even think about ethics, along with rigorous cultural moral education and inculcation, that are responsible for the moral capacity. Michael Tomasello (2016) provides a how-possibly explanation that morality is not a module with an isolated evolutionary history (p. 152). He claims that the ability to think of ethics is grounded in various more domain-general innate cognitive capacities that have their own evolutionary history, such as the cognitive skill of joint intentionality. Joint intentionality is where two individuals realize they must cooperate with each other to attain the same desired end, and in this regard, they view each other as being equivalent. The moral capacity is a cultural adaptation that in significant part springs from social-cultural interactions with others and are then passed on inter-generationally. We do not have innate moral principles.

Given the current evidence, it is speculative as to whether the moral capacity is a genetic or cultural adaptation, assuming it is an adaptation. What is most important for our purposes, it is not clear from the evolutionary ethics evidence whether we have innate moral principles or not. Although they also can allow for the partial influence of domain-general capacities, moral nativists require the premise that the capacity to think of ethics is a genetic adaptation that we are prewired for. In this manner, we may have innate moral principles. If our moral principles only come from domain-general innate capacities and cultural learning, then this is the claim made by the contemporary moral empiricist. While the possibility is still left open that there may be universally held moral principles on the empiricist account, they would be more along the lines of the belief THE SUN RISES IN THE MORNING. The moral principles would not be innate. However, the genetic adaptation premise in the POMS contention is currently unjustified given the evidence, and there are how-possibly explanations for the other side. Hence, regardless of whether the nativist adopts the strong or some weak POMS contention, their conclusion is unjustified.

Regarding strictly the evolutionary ethics evidence for whether the moral capacity is innate, the right kinds of studies have not been run nor data collected, so I frame no hypothesis. Concerning this particular question on human nature and the rationalism versus empiricist debate in light of the evidence from evolutionary psychology, whatever strong conclusion is drawn absent of the appropriate empirical evidence has no place in experimental philosophy.

As a second objection against the POMS contention, if the nativist makes the claim that there is a moral module, there is good reason to believe that we do not have such a module. If we did, then recall that moral decision-making would be informationally encapsulated, which means that it would not be influenced by other domains such as by scientific and mathematical beliefs. An informationally encapsulated moral module is one in which when processing inputs, such as witnessing a crime, the module can only use information contained in the inputs and any information stored in the module itself, such as innate moral principles, when making a judgment. It cannot access any other information stored elsewhere in the mind. However, moral judgment-making is not so encapsulated from other domains. For instance, scientific and economic non-moral facts apparently are frequently taken into consideration in order to impact moral decision-making in fields such as biomedical, business, and environmental ethics. For example, I witness a couple preparing to have a child through in vitro fertilization, and I then immediately ponder about the ethics of this. The input is that a couple is about to use in vitro fertilization because they cannot conceive through natural means. When making a moral decision, my module can only use this information and the innate moral principles stored within it. However, in deliberating, I bring in external knowledge from a previous biology class I took. I learned that for every normal live birth, a woman naturally will miscarry on average one to four embryos. This in part helps me to think that it is morally permissible for couples to use in vitro fertilization to conceive a child, where the process of in vitro fertilization involves the loss of embryos. Moral cognitive processes are global rather than local and can draw on a wide variety of knowledge stored in central memory. Globality rules out encapsulation. Fodor (1983) claims that higher acts of cognition, like scientific decision-making, are not modular since they are not encapsulated from other domains, such as from mathematics. Making moral categorization judgments is also a higher act of cognition that is not informationally encapsulated from other domains.

Moreover, against the moral modularity thesis, there is good reason to believe that there is not a part of the brain that is dedicated to processing information specific to only the moral domain. There is a growing general consensus in neuroethics that many different brain regions can be part of the neural basis of moral judgment, and which region(s) is active can be context dependent on the situation. Consistent with my moral concept pluralism, many studies have found that both cognitive and affective brain regions are correlated with moral judgment-making. Moreover, such regions can have domain-general functions and also can take part in non-moral forms of decision-making or in other kinds of functions. For instance, there is support that moral evaluations can arise from the posterior superior temporal sulcus, amygdala, insula, VMPFC, DLPFC, and/or medial prefrontal cortex, among others (Buckholtz & Marois 2012, Decety & Cacioppo 2012, Fumagalli & Priori 2012). The posterior superior temporal sulcus is involved in various activities such as in perception of biological motion and theory of mind. The amygdala also is thought to be responsible for moral and non-moral emotions, among other things. The insula also is the neural basis for functions such as perception, motor control, and self-awareness. The VMPFC also is thought to be the basis of various kinds of moral and non-moral decision-making and of the processing of risk and fear in moral and non-moral settings. The DLPFC is responsible for a variety of other activities concerning moral and non-moral planning, abstract reasoning, and cognitive flexibility, and the medial prefrontal cortex is the basis for other functions such as moral and non-moral memory retention and thinking about the moral and non-moral attributes of other individuals. Hence, there is no moral module in our brains that is exclusively dedicated to moral decision-making.

Next, one piece of evidence used for the POMS contention is the moral/conventional task. Psychology studies appear to suggest that children can sufficiently distinguish between moral versus conventional norms at a very young age without the relevant moral education. Here, moral and conventional judgments are posited as natural kinds. This universal moral/conventional distinction is supposedly made along the same lines across cultures. This suggests that there is an innate moral capacity. However, I will object to the very nature of the moral/conventional task in the next chapter. I will claim that the distinction between the moral and the conventional is constructed differently by different cultures, and there is no universal natural kind moral/conventional distinction. Since this distinction really is based on cultural construction, children respond to the moral/conventional task differently based on what culture they are raised in. Hence, we may conclude that this specific argument from the nativist using the moral/conventional task is unjustified since their premise that children generally can make the universal moral/conventional distinction is false. My objection applies to both strong and weak versions of the POMS contention that rely on the moral/conventional task.

Richard Joyce (2006) has claimed that we have innate moral concepts, although such representations do not store any innate moral principles since he acknowledges that culture inculcates us with moral rules. He speculatively claims that we have innate moral concepts because they are adaptive in that having a moral sense increases the likelihood that one will perform a cooperative act. Insofar as morality has practical clout such that it has an inescapable authority over us and provides reasons for action, we generally will understand the realm of morality to be more serious and of overriding influence. For us, moral norms are conversation stoppers in that they carry the greatest weight of importance, eliminating alternate competing considerations such as pragmatic ones. This moral sense increases the likelihood of acting cooperatively and thus, was selected for. However, the problem here is that this view predicts that people generally should understand the domain of morality to be more serious than other normative domains, as Joyce is willing to agree. If a moral sense is adaptive because it increases the chance that one will act cooperatively as compared to other norms or as compared to the generic notion of normativity, then we should expect people to understand the moral realm to be most important. However, in the next chapter, when examining the moral/conventional task, we will see based on experimental evidence that people do not reliably understand moral norms to be more serious than conventional ones. Hence, Joyce's adaptationist and nativist contention for moral concepts fails.

Furthermore, while the POMS contention requires a poverty in moral education, there does not appear to be such poverty, especially when contrasted with the principles of grammar (Prinz 2008, Sterelny 2012). Children can speak grammatically perfect sentences without explicit instruction in the principles of grammar; however, children are constantly taught and corrected in matters of ethics. There is constant instruction from parents, teachers, family members, coaches, religious leaders, governmental agencies, etc. of right from wrong. Recall from prototype concept acquisition that children can be explicitly taught general principles, such as to share one's toys or to not hit one's sibling. We have examined numerous feature-listing task experiments that show that people have acquired prototype representations stored in their moral concepts that they can readily articulate and use in moral cognition. They are not inaccessible. They can be taught other principles, such as the theory principle to obey the commands of God. It is a fact that many also are instructed in the complex laws and rights of one's society in classes like government and social studies as they are growing up, which at many times mirrors the moral values of that society. Such laws and rights are further inculcated and reinforced in students' minds with historical stories of cultural heroes who have valiantly fought or died to bring about such goods. Furthermore, that the greater good is at times important is a rule that can be taught to people or that people simply can infer from moral exemplars and socialization. In many cultures, citizens are instructed about the importance of bringing about the greater consequences at times, such as regarding certain political values and overarching societal issues. Individuals can readily learn the principles, such as of folk consequentialism, which can help explain the trolley phenomena, where different weights and non-moral facts can trigger the use of different beliefs and emotions in disparate circumstances.

Moreover, from a previous chapter that discussed exemplar concept acquisition, children are taught that particular acts and persons are good or bad, such as when one cleans up after playing or when one steals from one's classmate. Recall that evidence showed that children also have a natural conformity bias where they imitate and endorse the particular ethically related actions of others, such as those of people in positions of prestige. The moral learning environment is rich. They are read stories, myths, fables, and fairytales with moral messages of particular acts of heroism and goodness that can be represented by exemplars. They can use exemplars as moral precedents and consciously or subconsciously draw analogies to them when faced with new ethical situations. Also, just as the standard concrete concepts literature shows that we can infer prototypes from exemplars, we may infer that children also take particular exemplar cases of moral actions and persons and then infer general prototype or even complex theory moral principles and rules from them. The moral mind is an active mind. Parents generally want their offspring to succeed in the world, and this, in most cases, requires raising children to adhere to the moral values of one's community. Hence, in order to shape the moral mind, the moral education of children is largely environmentally rich with instruction of right from wrong there in the waiting.

Notice also that syntax is usually acquired without the presence of negative feedback and corrections made by others. However, empirical evidence in the history of moral learning is replete with negative feedback such as being tortured, reprimanded, punished, ostracized, or corrected from the likes of parents, teachers, law enforcement agents, tyrants, or governments. The POMS contention has as a premise that there is a poverty of the moral stimulus as with the rules of grammar. However, this really does not appear to be the case. Experimental data shows that we have many consciously accessible mental representations of principles and virtues that we use in moral cognition, which stands in stark contrast to the predominantly inaccessible principles of grammar. At minimum, this at least shifts the burden of proof onto the moral nativist to demonstrate that there are inaccessible innate moral principles that influence decision-making. Moreover, they also must somehow demonstrate that such subconscious principles have not been subconsciously inferred from exemplars. This objection applies to both strong and weak versions of the POMS contention.

The POMS advocate may attempt to meet the burden and state that even if many principles are consciously accessible, there still are a certain set of complex moral principles used in cognition that are innate, inaccessible, and that may not be inferred from exemplars. Two of the most common and perhaps most promising candidates in which causal rather than correlational experiments actually have been run for them are DDE and the act/omission doctrine that a harmful act is worse than an equivalently harmful omission. As an example of the act/omission doctrine, killing a terminal patient by giving her a lethal injection is worse than doing nothing and letting this patient die from the illness. On the strong view, such principles potentially can have binary parameters that are filled in by culture. For example, DDE may have parameters appended to it regarding its possible differential application for in-group versus out-group members.

However, for DDE, there is a problem at the level of descriptive adequacy of first demonstrating that certain complex moral principles and computational processes adequately describe the decision-making phenomena.[5] Notice from our previous discussion of DDE, given all the experimental phenomena, attaining descriptive adequacy is problematic for the claim that DDE is generally used by participants in the trolley problems due to cases like the remote footbridge and loop cases. The supposed use of DDE fails to accurately describe the general decision-making phenomena. Yet, there must be evidence that such principles can adequately *describe* the diverse decision-making phenomena before one can claim that such complex innate principles *explain* the relevant moral decision-making. Upon finding the sets of candidate principles that can consistently describe moral decision-making, we must then attain explanatory adequacy by finding the one set of principles that people actually do use in moral cognition. As Chomsky notes, descriptive adequacy is a prerequisite for explanatory adequacy. However, descriptive adequacy here is the very point in question for the POMS contention for DDE. Moreover, moral nativists have yet to show that DDE is not subconsciously inferred from exemplars.

Third, even if DDE is used pervasively by some cultures, it is not found across all cultures. For instance, Tibetan Buddhist monks and lay Tibetans predominantly judge that it is permissible to push the large man in the footbridge trolley case (Xiang 2014). Bilingual Slovenian-Italians in Italy mostly make this same judgment as well (Michelin et al. 2010). Millenials are more likely to give judgments consistent with folk consequentialism on the trolley problems like the footbridge case than those in the older baby-boomer generation (Hannikainen et al. 2018). Such judgments run contrary to the use of DDE. *If* DDE is widely used in the trolley problems in certain cultures, it seemingly is not universal as people can give different answers to exactly the same trolley problems depending on culture, which conflicts with the consistent use of DDE on them. This variance creates a significant level of doubt against DDE as being an innate principle for humankind.

Moreover, if such innate principles are inaccessible and operating subconsciously, it must be demonstrated that participants do not already have the relevant principles consciously in mind. However, experiments have shown that subjects generally can readily articulate the act/omission doctrine as supposedly influencing their decision-making (Cushman et al. 2006), although it is currently questionable whether such knowledge plays the relevant causal role in moral cognition.[6] It may be the case that participants can articulate this doctrine by first inferring it based on previous experiences of receiving more severe reprimands for actively causing harm to another as compared to harmful omissions. Also, there is cultural variance in adherence to the act/omission doctrine, which creates a significant burden of proof. For instance, Mayans living in Chiapas generally do not judge harms to be worse than omissions (Abarbanell & Hauser 2010). Therefore, moral nativists fall severely short of meeting the burden of proof. Hence, given the evidence, we may conclude that moral nativism is unjustified. The above objections apply to both strong and weak versions of the POMS contention.

Also, J. Kiley Hamlin (2015) contends that several studies on human infants can be used to construct a POMS argument; the most prominent of which shows that infants prefer helpful cooperators rather than anti-social entities. In this study, infants witness seeing a protagonist puppet attempt to climb a steep hill (Kuhlmeier et al. 2003). On one iteration, there is a distinct hinderer puppet that pushes the protagonist back down to the bottom of the hill. On another iteration, infants see a helper puppet that pushes the protagonist up to the top of the hill. After viewing the events, both the hinderer and helper puppets are placed before the infants. 88% of ten-month-olds and 100% of six-month-olds choose the helper puppet. Hamlin interprets infants as making moral judgments when they pick a puppet and contends that there is a poverty of the moral stimulus in that such infants are too young to have been taught to give a positive evaluation for such cooperative acts. Thus, infants have innate moral principles such as BLOCKING OTHERS' GOALS IS BAD that influences their moral categorizations.

In response, it may be the case that we have an innate non-cognitive desire to cooperate or be with cooperators rather than having an innate cognitive moral principle. I would be surprised if we did not have such an innate general desire regarding cooperation. Cooperation runs deep in our evolutionary history, and as discussed above, humans have partaken in the advantages of cooperation in a variety of different ways. These studies on infants could alternately be suggesting that we have an innate COOPERATION concept that is at least constituted by an innate non-cognitive desire to cooperate or be with cooperators. This desire becomes activated generally in many cooperation contexts and can explain the infants' puppet choices. Yet, this does not mean that we come prepackaged with an innate cognitive moral principle. Possessing this concept that is at least constituted by a non-cognitive desire does not mean that one's COOPERATION concept is a moral concept. First, there are many kinds of cooperation that in many cultures is not necessarily moral cooperation, such as being helpful by participating in a group cheer at a sports game. The desire for cooperation can be a domain-general desire rather than specifically a moral desire. Potential innate cognitive constituents to an infant's COOPERATION concept also can be generic domain-general cognitive states about cooperation rather than specifically moral ones. Therefore, if my alternate possible interpretation is correct that the studies may show that infants at least have an innate domain-general desire to cooperate or be with cooperators without having an accompanying innate cognitive moral principle, such an interpretation does not demonstrate that we have innate moral concepts. Hamlin's contention is invalid, and she must eliminate this alternate possible and plausible interpretation of these infant studies in order to help reach her conclusion. Therefore, thus far, I conclude that strong or weak versions of the POMS contention are unjustified.[7]

6.4 Chimpanzee Moral Concept Possession

There is another possible moral nativist contention regarding concept acquisition. One may begin by arguing that chimpanzees have moral concepts (Bekoff & Pierce 2009, Rowlands 2012).[8] Chimpanzees share about 99% of our DNA, and we have a common ancestor with them about 5–7 million years ago. It is thought that our ancestors had behavioral similarities to chimpanzees, bonobos, and the like (de Waal 1996). Chimpanzees and bonobos are thought to have changed the least over time since our common ancestors with them because they have encountered the least or little selection pressures to change. Hence, they look and act most like the forest ape from which humans descend. Thus, examination of chimpanzees and bonobos provide a window into our evolutionary history and human nature.

Chimpanzees appear to live according to codes of conduct that prohibit certain kinds of behavior and that generate social expectations. Such codes at many times are backed up by punishment or negative reactions. For instance, being overly rough during play can lead to a look of surprise and an end to the encounter, where other group members even will avoid playing with the deviant as well (Bekoff & Pierce 2009). Harming an infant chimpanzee is to be avoided and is backed by punishment from the mother and alpha male as well as by receiving vocalizations of disapproval ("waa" barking) from the group that can lead to group punishment if not heeded (Goodall 1971, de Waal 1982, 1996). They live in hierarchical societies that provide general structure and stability with norms pertaining to the pecking order that are known to all, such as regarding having access to sex (de Waal 1982, von Rohr et al. 2011). Chimpanzees generally demonstrate having obedience norms to the hierarchy and restrain their impulses accordingly. When breaking such norms, they at many times attempt to do so in stealth. For example, at times, low-ranking males will sneak off from sight of the alpha male to copulate with a female, where the female can even muffle her screams at climax to not draw attention from the alpha male. She does not muffle her screams when mating with the alpha. When a chimpanzee has acquired specifically meat, the chimp appears to have rights to that meat that are respected no matter how low ranking the chimp is and even when an alpha desires this food, although chimpanzees frequently distribute meat especially with those who helped in the hunt and with females with swollen genitals (Goodall 1971). A chimpanzee group in the Arnhem Zoo in the Netherlands receives their food at the end of the day only after all the chimpanzees have entered their cages (de Waal 1982). Chimpanzees who come to their cages excessively late are later punished by the group and are the first to enter their cages the next day. Dominant males do not use their canines, which can crack bones, against females (de Waal 1982). Outside of more rare extreme escalation that can lead to death in male-to-male conflict, they restrain themselves and use them only against male rivals in extremities such as a finger or foot. There are norms of reciprocity, where chimpanzees seem to form political coalitions for dominance in the hierarchy (de Waal 1982, Nishida 1983). If a coalition partner fails to come to a chimpanzee's aid when attacked, the chimpanzee who was assailed will attack this coalition partner. Furthermore, alpha male chimpanzees show policing behavior or third-party interventions of trying to resolve disputes and keep the general peace, where they generally favor siding with the weaker party (de Waal 1982, Boehm 1994).

One who maintains that chimpanzees have moral concepts need not claim they are innate concepts. Chimps are cultural beings who pass on things, such as group hunting techniques and tool use, via cultural transmission (Whiten et al. 1999, van Schaik 2003). Different chimpanzee groups have disparate relevant practices. It could be the case that if chimpanzees have moral concepts, they do so only through cultural transmission. Moral concepts are not innate. For example, the above norm of coming home to one's cage on time to eat dinner is likely a cultural norm held by those chimpanzees at Arnhem as such a setup is not found in the wild. However, one might maintain that at least some moral concepts are innate. For example, other norms, such as reciprocity grooming norms, are widely found in chimpanzee communities. Due to its pervasiveness, perhaps this at least provides some evidence that the trait is innate. While culture can shape the specifics of such norms differently, perhaps the above provides at least initial evidence that chimpanzees have innate moral concepts and principles as certain general moral norms may not be mere cultural products. If our common ancestor had innate moral concepts, then it is likely that we do too.

However, the mere pervasiveness of a trait alone, such as fire-making for humans, does not necessarily mean that the trait is innate rather than being passed on and learned through culture. Nevertheless, the nativist then may respond that such evidence for the pervasiveness of certain norms at least can create a burden of proof. In response, I now will object to this possible nativist claim by contending that chimpanzees, bonobos, and the like do not have moral concepts to begin with, so it is not possible for such species to provide evidence for moral nativism along the above line of argumentation.

Due to a lack of speech, Descartes viewed animals as being like mindless machines or automatons without thought, reason, and emotions. Like much of his philosophy of mind, this held court for centuries. Even in the mid-20th century, philosophers and scientists largely held the Cartesian view of the animal mind. This philosophy has since been overturned and replaced by a view in which animals, like dogs, now are attributed with having a richer mental life where they can reason and feel emotions like pain and joy. However, the question of whether chimpanzees and potentially other non-human animals have moral concepts is a much narrower question of the mind.

Hume, Darwin, and noted contemporary primatologist, Frans de Waal (1996, 2013), claim that higher forms of non-human animals, like chimpanzees, have a proto-morality. They do not have moral concepts but they have the beginnings and foundations of moral thought. Darwin stressed that we have an evolutionary continuity in anatomical and psychological traits with other social mammals. All three view emotions as the beginning bedrock of morality, and they hold that non-human animals have them along with limited forms of rational thought. Yet, they maintain that non-human animals fail to have moral concepts due to certain deficiencies in rational processing, such as being able to assess situations from another's perspective for Hume, being able to compare past and future events in deliberation for Darwin, and being able to wholly and abstractly think about the community good over the individual good for de Waal. Aristotle argued against non-human animal moral minds because they lack the ability to reflect on their own character traits and realize that relevant ones are virtues. A similar point is raised by Joyce (2006). Moreover, Aristotle claimed that in order to possess moral concepts, one must have *phronesis* or practical wisdom and be able to act because one knows that the action is virtuous. These are things animals like chimpanzees seem to lack. The modern-day Kantian, Christine Korsgaard (2006), argues that chimpanzees fail to have moral concepts because they lack sufficient rational complexity to reflect on their decision-making and ask themselves whether an act is the right thing to do. Being a moral agent requires the right kind of consciousness or self-awareness. There must be cognitive control or governance over one's actions so that one may choose one's ends rather than merely decide how to best satisfy one's pre-existing ends. One must have autonomy in order to be a moral agent.

On the other hand, many have argued that chimpanzees do have moral concepts. They emphasize that the difference between chimpanzees and humans in moral thought is a difference in degrees rather than in kind. They can think ethically, but their moral cognitive capacities are not as sophisticated as human moral cognition. Non-human primates were once universally thought to not have the capacity to use tools or have the capacity for language. These were heralded as qualities that make humans unique and that separate us from the animal kingdom. New discoveries have shown the above is false as some apes can use tools such as in extracting insects to eat or in cracking open nuts and learn sign language. They can use tools and have language just as humans but with a difference in degree of complexity. Perhaps chimpanzees and bonobos likewise have moral concepts but not ones that are as sophisticated as ours. Overall, we should be leery of having too high standards against non-human animals for possessing moral concepts. There can be differences in degree but not of kind especially given our shared evolutionary history. Moreover, to have moral thoughts, one need not be able to maintain some complex ethical theory that one personally favors, such as utilitarianism and looking out for the community good over individual interests or to arrive upon categorical imperatives where one can assess one's own end. If they are to store ethical theory knowledge, a simpler view such as a particular brand of ethical egoism, where one ought to act to satisfy one's pre-existing self-interests and ends, may be held.

In order to possess a moral concept, there are several conditions. To note, the below conditions may not be exhaustive as a completed list may be vast, and for our purposes of criticizing the nativist contention at hand, we also will not need a complete list. Also, the conditions are not about possessing a *correct* moral concept but for possessing a moral concept simpliciter, whether correct or incorrect.[9] First, one needs a notion of normativity or "oughtness." Other features on the list can be tying such notions of normativity to social expectations, having or being disposed to having negative reactions when certain norms are violated, having emotional capacities such as empathy, possessing a rudimentary theory of mind where one ascribes mental states to others and uses such ascriptions to explain and predict others' behavior, the ability to regulate immediate behavioral drives and act against them, having personal norms of expectations of how one should be treated, having in mind social norms that others have expectations of how they ought to be treated, etc.

Chimpanzees have been shown to seemingly satisfy all of the features in the above list (Goodall 1971, de Waal 1982, 1996, Tomasello et al. 2003, von Rohr et al. 2011). To note, the above is not a set of necessary and sufficient conditions for possessing a moral concept as MORAL CONCEPT POSSESSION does not have classical structure. As lack of classical structure still allows for necessary but not sufficient conditions, some of these conditions may be necessary, such as having a notion of normativity. Others are not, such as having the capacity to feel emotions. Possible alien life forms and future AI, such as perhaps certain automatically driving cars, may have moral concepts without having the ability to feel emotions.

However, a condition for moral concept possession that is of significant importance for our limited purposes here regarding chimpanzee moral concept possession is the condition of having an understanding of the moral domain as contrasted with other normative realms. What chimpanzees have not been shown to have is the capacity to distinguish moral norms from other norms, such as conventional or pragmatic norms. On the other hand, if all norms are moral norms for them, it appears that they do not understand that all their norms are *moral* norms as opposed to being other kinds of norms. There are a variety of different kinds of norms, so in order to possess specifically *moral* concepts, one condition is to understand that one's relevant norms are specifically moral ones rather than being different kinds of norms. As in the next chapter, I contend that the moral/conventional distinction is constructed and is correct only relative to a culture, more precisely, one condition is to understand the moral domain as distinct from other normative domains relative to one's own cultural distinction. However, if one's culture does not have any alternative norms at all but only moral ones, then one must fully understand that this is so. It is this condition that has yet to be found in chimpanzees and other non-human primates, and it appears they do not have the cognitive sophistication to have such a complex understanding, consciously or subconsciously. They appear to only have the general notion of normativity. This seeming lack of comprehension provides a strong yet defeasible reason to believe that chimpanzees and other non-human primates do not have moral mental representations. Hence, it appears false that humans have innate moral concepts based on the premise that our common ancestor with chimpanzees had innate moral concepts.

6.4.1 Bekoff and Pierce

Bekoff and Pierce claim that chimpanzees and other primates' abilities to perform moral acts of cooperation, empathy, and justice demonstrate that they have moral concepts. The mere performance of such acts is sufficient as acts that fall within such categories are moral ones. For example, for cooperation, chimpanzees will help conspecifics in a different room get food by initiating a relevant mechanism even though they have no access to the food themselves (Melis et al. 2011). They will not initiate the mechanism if they do not see a fellow chimpanzee in this other room to get the food. They also form political coalitions with each other (de Waal 1982, 1996), hunt together (Boesch 1994), cooperate during play (Bekoff 2007), try to rescue each other from drowning (de Waal 2013), and work together to defend the territory (Wilson et al. 2001). For empathy, chimpanzees are well known to empathize with fellow chimps and humans. They will console other chimps who have been in an altercation by grooming them (De Waal 1982, 1996) and console bedridden and non-kin chimps dying of cancer (de Waal 2013). They also appear to empathize with the disabled. When an elderly chimp has arthritis and has great difficulty in walking a long distance to get water, other chimpanzees will recognize when she is thirsty and race to put water in their own mouths, run back, and then spit the water into the elderly chimp's mouth (de Waal 2013).

For fairness or justice, studies show that brown capuchin monkeys can be trained to exchange a token to get food, such as a cucumber or a better tasting grape (Brosnan & de Waal 2003). However, when a monkey who receives a cucumber sees that a partner monkey receives a grape for the same task, the monkey receiving the cucumber will refuse to continue with the experiment and may even throw a temper tantrum shaking the chamber and hurling away the cucumber. Moreover, the monkey's protest is not due to the mere sight of a better reward. For, the monkey will not protest when merely shown a grape but given a cucumber. Monkeys also will not protest when they merely are fed unequally and there is no work involved to get the food. Rather, the monkey will protest only when the monkey sees that another monkey receives a better reward for performing the same task or work. Also, in some other experiments, they are given different colored "prosocial" tokens, where turning this token in gives both them and their partner food (de Waal 2013). They quickly favor using this token. It is not out of fear of retribution from one's partner that primates use this token and distribute goods because dominants are found to use this token the most.

Bekoff and Pierce contend that since many non-human primates perform moral acts, they have moral concepts. However, the problem here, among possible others, is that in order to have specifically moral concepts that are distinct from etiquette or other normative concepts, it seems like the relevant primates should be able to distinguish the moral from the non-moral normative domain. Chimpanzees must grasp that their relevant concepts are not about other normative realms but only about the moral domain. This is an important yet defeasible condition to possess moral concepts. However, it appears that they do not have such notions but only have the generic notion NORMATIVITY. Hence, one can't use chimpanzees to contend that humans have innate moral concepts.

6.4.2 Rowlands

Mark Rowlands (2012) claims that chimpanzees and bonobos have moral concepts in that they are moral *subjects* rather than moral *agents.* They lack the autonomy, responsibility, free will, critical reflective capacities, and complex rational capacities to be full moral agents, but they are still moral subjects with moral concepts insofar as they act based on moral reasons. The relevant moral reasons are moral emotions with moral content. It is uncontroversial that chimpanzees and the like have emotions like sympathy, care, anger, fear, etc. Being motivated by moral emotions, which are moral reasons for Rowlands, is a sufficient but not necessary condition for being a moral subject for him.[10] An emotion is a moral one rather than some other normative emotion if it reliably tracks a true moral proposition. Rowlands can respond to my above objection to Bekoff and Pierce in that the non-human primate need not have any internal mental thoughts about moral normativity as being differentiated from other kinds of normativity. Being able to make such a differentiation is not a necessary condition for moral concept possession, and it is defeasible. So long as the emotion is being causally influenced by an external natural moral property or fact that has causal efficacy, then the emotion has moral content or reference. The emotion refers to the corresponding natural moral fact. This is to presume the causal theory of reference for moral concepts without argument. As Rowlands claims that chimpanzees' relevant emotions that supposedly constitute their relevant concepts are causally regulated by apparent objective natural moral facts such that appropriate chimpanzee emotional reactions will reliably or stably align at most times with the moral facts, their relevant concepts refer to moral facts. Since their relevant concepts refer to moral properties or facts, such concepts are moral ones for chimpanzees, and therefore, chimpanzees have moral concepts and are moral subjects. This supposedly is true even though chimpanzees fail to have an understanding of the distinction between moral and conventional norms and are not even aware of the supposed given causal connection. If Rowlands is right, this opens the door for chimpanzees to have innate moral concepts, and then perhaps humans have innate moral concepts too.

One problem is that Rowlands presumes the predominance of the causal theory of reference for moral concepts without argument. As will be discussed in a later chapter, this presumption is too controversial, and it requires proper support. Hence, his contention is unjustified. Second, Rowlands claims that chimpanzees' apparent moral concepts are supposed to be *reliably* regulated by objective natural moral facts such that they motivate the chimpanzee to make decisions and act in accordance with the moral facts. Although in later chapters I contend that there are no objective moral facts, let us disregard this issue for the moment and assume there are such facts. For Rowlands, there may be exceptions to the rule of chimpanzees not acting in accordance with the moral facts, but they should be minority cases, and we should expect such exceptions to diminish over time given the reliable causal influence of the moral facts on chimpanzee emotions and moral concepts like RIGHT ACTION.

However, in many cases this has not been so. For instance, recall that chimpanzees work together to defend their territory and boundaries. This also involves pillaging other communities. They depart in raiding groups raping, killing, and plundering other chimpanzee groups. Moreover, alpha males reliably will perform bluff displays among members of their own group by going on a rampage and making swift charging motions in order to exhibit their dominance and power (de Waal 1982). This causes significant fear in other chimpanzees and can lead to physical harm if a fellow chimp is in the way. Also, alpha male chimpanzees reliably limit the sexual activities of other males in the group and monopolize access to the females even though the females may want to mate with others. We have previously discussed how chimpanzees can perform many "admirable" acts from a Western perspective, but they can perform many "despicable" acts as well. Hobbes claimed that human nature is fundamentally self-interested and belligerent; Hume stated that we are mostly self-interested while having only limited sympathy; and Rousseau maintained that we are by nature peaceful. However, at first glance, our evolutionary roots appear to point to a more even picture that we have a robust duality that tends to manifest itself across a wide variety of different environments for having the capacity of being self-interested, altruistic, angry, joyful, fearful, empathic, vengeful, caring, violent, cooperative, etc.[11] As nature and nurture always work together,[12] it appears that human nature and the environment are a prism, refracting light into a multiplicity of colors.

Returning to Rowlands, if there is a reliable causal connection between supposed objective moral facts and the tokening of RIGHT ACTION or WRONG ACTION moral concepts in chimpanzees, then these transgressions should be found in only exceptional cases rather than being discovered throughout chimpanzee communities. Furthermore, chimpanzees and their ancestors have likely displayed such behavior for millions and millions of years. Yet, if there is a reliable causal connection between supposed objective moral facts and chimpanzee emotions, then this predicts that over such an extensive period of time, the chimpanzee emotions that lead them to go against objective morality should not be elicited in the relevant contexts in a vast majority of chimpanzee groups. There should be change for the good over time in such instances. However, this prediction is false. There is no reliable causal connection for supposed moral concepts for chimpanzees in such cases, unlike how a chimpanzee's MONKEY or MEAT concept is reliably tokened when in the presence of a colobus monkey. Hence, Rowlands' argument that chimpanzees have moral concepts and moral emotions fails based on the absence of a reliable causal connection between supposed natural objective moral facts and relevant chimpanzee emotions in the above cases, among other reasons. Therefore, the above relevant studies and line of argumentation on chimpanzees and the like do not demonstrate that humans have innate moral concepts that have their roots in our evolutionary history since such non-human species do not even have moral concepts to begin with.

Rowlands may respond that there are chimpanzee culturally constructed moral facts relative to a chimpanzee culture that reliably influence their decision-making. Hence, their relevant concepts refer to relative moral facts rather than objective ones. However, such concepts still are moral ones insofar as they have moral content. In response, it is not apparent that chimpanzees have socially constructed a domain of moral facts that their culture differentiates as being distinctly moral. In the next chapter, I will show that the moral/conventional distinction is socially constructed and is relative to a culture. If there are culturally constructed moral facts that influence judgment, the culture at issue must construct uniquely *moral* facts as distinct from other normative domains. Yet, this does not appear to be so for chimps. It appears chimpanzees at least at times have constructed normative rules that they understand to be generically normative, but their relevant cultures explicitly do not differentiate them as being distinctly moral rules as contrasted with, for example, conventional rules. Hence, as chimpanzee troops do not appear to have constructed distinctly moral facts, this counter-objection fails. As relying on a causal theory of reference will not save Rowlands' conclusion that chimpanzees have moral concepts and chimps cannot differentiate the moral domain from the non-moral normative realm, they do not possess distinctly moral concepts. Thus, one cannot use chimpanzees to argue for moral nativism in humans.

The main purpose of this chapter is to newly establish the viability of the theory-theory for moral concepts in light of the concept acquisition desideratum. In so doing, we have had to explore at a general level the issues of moral nativism and evolutionary ethics, where I have argued that moral nativism is unjustified. Thus far, we have seen positive evidence for the cognitivist prototype, exemplar, and theory views in that they help to explain the moral concept desiderata of categorization, sense, and concept acquisition. In the next two chapters, we will turn to assessing the conative view in light of these three desiderata.

Notes

1 To note, cultural anthropology, as a field, assumes moral relativism is true.
2 Wong (2006) also claims that the function of the moral capacity may be to resolve intrapersonal conflict.
3 However, this in turn may lead to genetic level selection that favors psychological traits, such as the experiencing of certain emotions, that are made to enhance one's success in a pro-social environment. Overall, this may create a feedback loop between genetic and cultural evolution, where ultra-social human beings are produced, and the moral capacity may be in part genetically encoded perhaps in more domain-general capacities like the capacity to feel emotions (Henrich and Boyd 2001).
4 At times, Prinz may be read as claiming that morality is not adaptive, but it is a byproduct. I read him as claiming that morality may be adaptive at the cultural rather than genetic level in that he clearly maintains that cultural moral values are likely fitness-enhancing in allowing for wide-scale cooperation in large societies. Whether he realizes it or not, this allows one to read Prinz as believing that morality may be a cultural adaptation.
5 This problem also applies to the Doctrine of Personal Force.
6 There is suggestive evidence that many people may use the act/omission doctrine in moral cognition (Ritov & Baron 1990). However, such evidence is being contended by findings in neuroscience (Cushman et al. 2012). More empirical studies need to be run to draw a more decisive conclusion one way or the other. If the representation of this doctrine does appropriately influence decision-making, it is causal moral law theory knowledge and would help to show the viability of the theory view for moral concepts.
7 There are numerous other objections in the literature against different versions of the POMS contention, strong or weak, that I do not go into more detail here. For instance, many moral rules do not contain binary parameters like in the rules of grammar that cultures can toggle on or off (Dupoux & Jacob 2007, Prinz 2008). Rather, many moral rules are open ended. For example, the rule of not harming others can apply to a variety of different things depending upon one's culture, such as applying or not applying to animals, criminals, those in the out-group, women, those who attack you, infants, etc. Furthermore, in many cases, situations do not involve the application of a single principle with a binary switch, but they implicate competing principles, where different groups can place different weights of importance on each principle (Dupoux & Jacob 2007, Prinz 2008). For example, whether one should blow the whistle on one's company can involve the competing principles of loyalty to one's company versus being honest to the public. Moreover, the rules of grammar are generated quickly, automatically, and effortlessly. However, in ethics, there are moral dilemmas that at many times involve slow deliberation in reaching a conclusion that can last for days. There is no counterpart to the length of time at many times used in moral dilemmas as compared to making grammatical sentences (Dupoux & Jacob 2007). Finally, once the parameters are set, rules of grammar are fixed. The same should hold in the case of a moral grammar if the linguistic analogy is a strong one. However, there are moral conversions where people at times can significantly overturn their adopted moral system (Sterelny 2012). For instance, a deontologist who previously adopted DDE may convert to becoming a utilitarian. Yet, if DDE is supposedly an innate principle, this is very unlike the linguistic grammar case. DDE should not be able to be overturned like this.

8 This literature has close ties to AI in assessing when robots may have moral concepts. I anticipate that much of this work on animal cognition may be helpful in the field of AI, *mutatis mutandis.*

9 Recall that in a later chapter, I will argue that there are no objectively correct moral concepts.

10 Although we are examining Rowlands here regarding concept acquisition and moral nativism, he appears to adopt a conative theory of moral concepts for many non-human primates. However, he does not support this concept constitution claim with appropriate causal evidence or with any rigorous experimental support. Thus, I do not explore his conative theory of moral concepts in the chapters on the conative view as not much evidence is given to support it such that it should be taken seriously.

11 I do not pretend to provide and defend a complete theory of human nature here as that would require its own book. This point on human nature is only meant to be a prima facie claim, a quick aside, or a brief initial observation point that has no ramifications on my present argument against moral nativism.

12 For example, even though it may be in a normal human zygote's genes to generally develop into a complexly rational being, this still requires a healthy environment, such as a healthy womb, to develop. If a woman drinks alcohol while pregnant, this fetus may not develop to have complex rational capacities.

References

Abarbanell, L. and Hauser, M.D. 2010. "Mayan Morality: An Exploration of Permissible Harms. *Cognition* 115, 207–224.

Bekoff, Mark. 2007. *The Emotional Lives of Animals.* Novato, CA: New World Library.

Bekoff, Mark and Pierce, Jessica. 2009. *Wild Justice: The Moral Lives of Animals.* Chicago: The University of Chicago Press.

Boehm, C. 1994. "Pacifying Interventions at Arnhem Zoo and Gombe." In *Chimpanzee Cultures.* Ed. By R.W. Wrangham, W.C. McGrew, F.B.M. de Waal, P.G. Heltne. Cambridge, MA: Harvard University Press, 211–226.

Boesch, C. 1994. "Cooperative Hunting in Wild Chimpanzees." *Animal Behavior* 48, 653–667.

Boyd, R. and Richerson, P. 1985. *Culture and the Evolutionary Process.* Chicago: University of Chicago Press.

Brosnan, S.F. and De Waal, F.B. 2003. "Monkeys Reject Unequal Pay." *Nature* 425, 297.

Buckholtz, J.W. and Marois, R. 2012. "The Roots of Modern Justice: Cognitive and Neural Foundations of Social Norms and Their Enforcement." *Nature Neuroscience* 15, 655–661.

Chomsky, Noam. 1965. *Aspects of the Theory of Syntax.* Cambridge, MA: MIT Press.

Cushman, F., Murray, D., Gordon-McKeon, S., Wharton, S., and Greene, J.D. 2012. "Judgment Before Principle: Engagement of the Frontoparietal Control Network in Condemning Harms of Omission." *Social Cognitive and Affective Neuroscience* 7, 888–895.

Cushman, F., Young, L., and Hauser, M. 2006. "The Role of Conscious Reasoning and Intuition in Moral Judgment: Testing Three Principles of Harm." *Psychological Science* 17, 1082–1089.

Decety, J. and Cacioppo, S. 2012. "The Speed of Morality: A High-Density Electrical Neuroimaging Study." *Journal of Neurophysicology* 108, 3068–3072.

de Waal, Frans. 1982. *Chimpanzee Politics.* Baltimore: The Johns Hopkins University Press.

de Waal, Frans. 1996. *Good Natured: The Origins of Right and Wrong in Humans and Other Animals.* Cambridge, MA: Harvard University Press.

de Waal, Frans. 2013. *The Bonobo and the Atheist.* New York: W.W. Norton & Co.

Dupoux, Emmanuel and Jacob, Pierre. 2007. "Universal Moral Grammar: A Critical Appraisal." *Trends in Cognitive Sciences* 11, 373–378.

Dwyer, Susan. 1999. "Moral Competence." *Philosophy and Linguistics.* Edited by K. Murasugi and R. Stainton, New York: Routledge.

Dwyer, Susan. 2008. "How Not to Argue that Morality Isn't Innate: Comments on Prinz." In *Moral Psychology, Vol.* 1. Ed. by W. Sinnot-Armstrong. Cambridge, MA: The MIT Press, 407–418.

Fodor, Jerry. 1983. *The Modularity of Mind.* Cambridge, MA: The MIT Press.

Fumagalli, M. and Priori, A. 2012. "Functional and Clinical Neuroanatomy of Morality." *Brain* 135, 2006–2021.

Gibbard, Allan. 1991. *Wise Choices, Apt Feelings.* Oxford: Clarendon Press.

Goodall, Jane. 1971. *In the Shadow of Man.* New York: Collins.

Gould, S.J. and Lewontin, R.C. 1979. "The Spandrels of San Marco and the Panglossian Paradigm: A Critique of the Adaptationist Programme." *Proceedings of the Royal Society of London. Series B. Biological Sciences* 205, 581–598.

Hamlin, J. Kiley. 2015. "Does the Infant Possess a Moral Concept?" *The Conceptual Mind.* Ed. by E. Margolis and S. Laurence. Cambridge, MA: The MIT Press.

Hannikainen, I.R., Machery, E., and Cushman, F.A. 2018. "Is Utilitarian Sacrifice Becoming More Morally Permissible?" *Cognition* 170, 95–101.

Harman, Gilbert. 1999. "Moral Philosophy and Linguistics." *The Proceedings of the Twentieth World Congress of Philosophy* 1, 107–115.

Hauser, Marc D. 2006. *Moral Minds.* New York: Harper Collins Publishers.

Hauser, M., Young, L., and Cushman, F. 2008. "Reviving Rawls Linguistic Analogy: Operative Principles and the Causal Structure of Moral Actions." In *Moral Psychology Volume* 2. Ed. by Walter Sinnott-Armstrong. Cambridge, MA: The MIT Press, 107–144.

Henrich, J. and Boyd, R. 2001. "Why People Punish Defectors: Weak Conformist Transmission Can Stabilize Costly Enforcement of Norms in Cooperative Dilemmas." *Journal of Theoretical Biology* 208, 79–89.

Hume, David. 1738/2000. *A Treatise of Human Nature.* Ed. By D. Norton and M. Norton. Oxford: Oxford University Press.

Joyce, Richard. 2006. *The Evolution of Morality.* Cambridge, MA: The MIT Press.

Kitcher, Philip. 2006. "Biology and Ethics." *Oxford Handbook of Ethical Theory.* Ed. by Copp, D. Oxford: Oxford University Press.

Kitcher, Philip. 2011. *The Ethical Project.* Cambridge, MA: Harvard University Press.

Korsgaard, Christine. 2006. "Morality and the Distinctiveness of Human Action." *Primates and Philosophers.* Ed. by Franz de Waal. Princeton: Princeton University Press.

Kuhlmeier, V., Wynn, K., and Bloom, P. 2003. "Attribution of Dispositional States by 12-month-olds." *Psychological Science* 14, 402–408.

Melis, A., Warneken, F., Jensen, K., Schneider, A., Call, J., and Tomasello, M. 2011. "Chimpanzees Help Conspecifics to Obtain Food and Non-food Items." *Proceedings of the Royal Society of London, Series B: Biological Sciences* 28, 1405–1413.

Michelin, C., Pellizzoni, S., Tallandini, M.A., and Siegal, M. 2010. "Should More Be Saved? Diversity in Utilitarian Moral Judgment." *Journal of Cognition and Culture* 10, 153–169.

Mikhail, John. 2011. *Elements of Moral Cognition.* Cambridge: Cambridge University Press.

Mineka, S., Davidson, M., Cook, M., and Keir, R. 1984. "Observational Conditioning of Snake Fear in Rhesus Monkeys." *Journal of Abnormal Psychology* 93, 355.

Nishida, T. 1983. "Alpha Status and Agonistic Alliance in Wild Chimpanzees (Pan troglodytes schweinfurthii)." *Primates* 24, 318–336.

Prinz, Jesse. 2007. *The Emotional Construction of Morals.* Oxford: Oxford University Press.

Prinz, Jesse. 2008. "Resisting the Linguistic Analogy: A commentary on Hauser, Young, and Cushman." In *Moral Psychology Volume* 2. Ed. by Walter Sinnott-Armstrong. Cambridge, MA: The MIT Press, 157–170.

Rawls, John. 1971. *A Theory of Justice,* 2nd edition. Cambridge, MA: Belknap Press.

Ritov, I. and Baron, J. 1990. "Reluctance to Vaccinate: Omission Bias and Ambiguity." *Journal of Behavioral Decision Making* 3, 263–277.

Rowlands, Mark. 2012. *Can Animals Be Moral?* Oxford: Oxford University Press.

Sripada, Chandra Sekhar and Stich, Stephen. 2006. "A Framework for the Psychology of Norms." *The Innate Mind: Culture and Cognition.* Ed. by P. Carruthers, S. Laurence, and S. Stich. New York: Oxford University Press.

Sterelny, Kim. 2012. *The Evolved Apprentice: How Evolution Made Humans Unique.* Cambridge, MA: The MIT Press.

Tomasello, Michael. 2016. *A Natural History of Human Morality.* Cambridge, MA: Harvard University Press.

Tomasello, M., Call, J., and Hare, B. 2003. "Chimpanzees Understand the Psychological States of Others – The Question is Which Ones and To What Extent." *Trends in Cognitive Sciences* 7, 153–157.

van Schaik, C.P. 2003. "Local Traditions in Orangutans and Chimpanzees: Social Learning and Social Tolerance." In *The Biology of Traditions: Models and Evidence.* Ed. by Fragaszy, D.M., Perry, S. Cambridge: Cambridge University Press, 297–329.

von Rohr, C.R., Burkart, J.M., and Van Schaik, C.P. 2011. "Evolutionary Precursors of Social Norms in Chimpanzees: A New Approach. *Biology & Philosophy* 26, 1–30.

Whiten, A., Goodall, J., McGrew, W.C., Nishida, T., Reynolds, V., Sugiyama, Y., Tutin, C.E., Wrangham, R.W., and Boesch, C. 1999. "Cultures in Chimpanzees. *Nature* 399, 682–685.

Wilson, M.L., Hauser, M.D., and Wrangham, R.W. 2001. "Does Participation in Intergroup Conflict Depend on Numerical Assessment, Range Location, or Rank for Wild Chimpanzees?" *Animal Behaviour* 61, 1203–1216.

Wong, David B. 2006. *Natural Moralities.* Oxford: Oxford University Press.

Xiang, X. 2014. *Would the Buddha Push the Man Off the Footbridge?: Systematic variations in the moral judgment and punishment tendencies of Han Chinese, Tibetans and Americans* (Doctoral dissertation, Harvard University).

7 The Conative View and the Moral/Conventional Task

Based on empirical evidence on moral concepts, several theorists have contended for the viability of the conative theory of moral concepts, where concepts may be constituted by sentiments, emotions, desires, and/or non-representational attitudes. However, I will object that no one has yet been able to demonstrate with the requisite empirical evidence that moral concepts are constituted by conative states. This chapter will scrutinize the various empirical arguments for the conative theory and show how they fail.[1] In so doing, I also will argue that moral judgment is not a natural kind. In the next chapter, I will present my own contentions for the conative view for moral concepts in light of the categorization, sense, and concept acquisition desiderata.

While the conative theory generally is not widely discussed in the contemporary concepts literature in cognitive science, a minority of contemporary psychologists and neuroscientists have posited that concepts can be made up of emotions. Although they do not speak specifically of moral concepts, they have claimed that emotions can constitute a variety of different concepts (Barsalou 1999, Kousta et al. 2011, Paivio 2013). The above claim that a plethora of various kinds of concepts may be emotions, but this aspect of their theories linking concepts with emotions is substantially undeveloped. For, they largely use or inevitably in part rely on only correlational psychology or neuroscience data to argue that concepts may be constituted by emotions without providing the appropriate causal evidence. For example, many contend for their thesis by using neuroimaging scans to show that there is a correlation between categorization and emotional regions of the brain. With only correlational data, it is still open that emotions are only elicited after the judgment is made rather than before. Insofar as they primarily lean on correlational rather than the specified causal data to draw their conative theory claims, their conclusions are unwarranted because they do not fully realize that concepts play a causal role in categorization, *inter alia*. They do not realize that they must establish causation rather than mere correlation. They must show that emotions cause judgments rather than the other way around.

For example, Kousta et al. (2011) crucially rely on brain imaging scans done in different studies that only establish correlation even though they themselves do not run neuroimaging experiments in their particular paper. Paivio (2013) in part claims that emotions influence categorization of pictures as being pleasant because the emotion of being pleased will influence one's categorization of things as being pleasant. However, he does not account for the possibility that emotions may only come into play after the categorization rather than before. There is no establishment of an appropriate direction of causation that emotions causally influence the categorization process. Moreover, there is a huge question as to whether emotions even are experienced at all. There are a multitude of purely cognitive factors that can explain the categorization of things as being pleasant or not that need not rely on the use of emotions. Cognitive states like BRIGHTLY COLORED, SMILING FACES, and PEACEFULNESS can lead to the categorization of pictures as being pleasant or not rather than emotions. Paivio does not eliminate or account for these alternate possibilities or interpretations in his study.

In what follows, I will critically examine Gibbard's evolutionary psychology contention for the conative theory of moral concepts. Next, Prinz's two main arguments for the conative view will be scrutinized.

7.1 Gibbard's Evolutionary Psychology Arguments and Thick Moral Concepts

Gibbard (1991) bases his moral philosophy on human nature. After noting the long history of moral philosophy in failing to reach any consensus in laying down an a priori foundation to ethics, Gibbard claims that we must look to the fields of psychology and biology to do so. He states that his methods are a posteriori, relying on such means as common observation, biology, and evolutionary psychology. He writes:

> The philosophical program I develop in this book rests on a human psychology. My theory of the meaning of moral terms rests on a psychology of norms. Fundamental normative principles may, for all I can establish, be accepted or rejected on the basis of psychological considerations…I do not think either that we can develop good fundamental theory independently of empirical considerations….
>
> (1990, p. 30)

In *Wise Choices, Apt Feelings* (WCAF), Gibbard (2003) claims that moral concepts are constituted by non-cognitive attitudes of norm acceptance for when one should feel moral emotions like anger and guilt. Notice that this view does not claim that moral concepts are constituted by emotions. Rather, they are constituted by non-cognitive attitudes.

The attitude is one of accepting a norm for when to feel certain emotions. In this respect, we can view Gibbard's account as *mentioning* emotions but not *using* them. In a later work, *Thinking How to Live* (THTL), he roughly contends that normative judgments express states of planning or of contingency planning for various possible circumstances. As our present focus is only on Gibbard's evolutionary arguments for the conative view and only his earlier work contains such contentions, we will focus only on what is said in WCAF.[2]

In his earlier work, Gibbard supports this theory of moral concepts based on the fact that we are highly social animals who coordinate our actions and use language to communicate with conspecifics. He further claims that the psychological capacity to make moral judgments and accept them has the evolutionary function of coordination, although he acknowledges that this is speculative. Coordination, such as working together to grow food and defending the community from invaders, is adaptive behavior.

Before discussing Gibbard further, let me provide a little more relevant background about evolutionary ethics. Darwin points out that those groups that have moral norms to raise the alarm when the enemy approaches and to coordinate their efforts in a common defense will have a greater chance for its members to survive, reach reproductive age, and pass on their moral values to their children. Groups that do not have such moral norms will tend to die off, and thus, their values will not be passed on to future generations.

> A tribe including many members who, from possessing in a high degree the spirit of patriotism, fidelity, obedience, courage, and sympathy, were always ready to aid one another, and to sacrifice themselves for the common good, would be victorious over most other tribes; and this would be natural selection. At all times throughout the world tribes have supplanted other tribes; and as morality is one important element in their success, the standard of morality and the number of well-endowed men will thus everywhere tend to rise and increase.
>
> (Darwin 1871/2004, p. 157–158)

If the moral capacity's function is cooperation, then cultures that have many intragroup anti-cooperative norms, such as with the Dobu of Papua New Guinea or the Ik of Uganda, are a possibility. To note, the Dobu allow for the moral permissibility of such things as killing one's own family members and others within one's society. For instance, husbands and wives are constantly suspicious of each other. Perhaps due to previous years gone by of extreme famine, the Ik do not have such things as strong familial bonds and obligations between parents and children, where they freely allow for starvation and death among their family members.

The existence of such groups should be expected since biological functions can at times go awry or malfunction. For example, even though a heart has the function of pumping blood, some hearts may malfunction, which may lead to the death of the relevant organism. However, the fact that a particular heart malfunctions does not mean that a heart's function is not to pump blood. Likewise, even though some moral systems generally do not properly function in terms of coordination, this does not mean that the capacity to think morally does not have the function of coordination. Despite the function of moral judgments, culture can at times have the habit of distorting the evolutionary function of ethical judgments such that values in a particular culture may take on a life of its own. This may result in cultural factors like religion and political systems creating values that may not be fitness-enhancing. However, even in such cases where culture distorts the evolutionary function of the moral capacity and certain norms fail to properly perform their function, as with the heart example, we still may claim that the capacity to make moral judgments has the function of cooperation, but it is just the case that in relevant particular circumstances, the norm malfunctions or does not perform its evolutionary function.

Returning to Gibbard, he notes that it will be important to coordinate our emotions for dispute resolution and for forming complex plans. If I feel resentment from an offense you made against me, but you do not feel guilt for your actions, this can lead to violence and discord. Guilt makes possible restitution, apologetic acknowledgments, forgiveness, and a return to social harmony. Hence, in order to explain the evolutionary history of moral judgments and social harmony, Gibbard speculates that our moral concepts are constituted by his non-cognitive attitudes.

In response, it could be the case that beliefs about virtues, rules, or reasons for action in regard to coordination at least in part help to explain normative judgments and their evolutionary history. Our common ancestor with chimpanzees did not have the capacity to think about ethics, but likely did have the capacity to feel certain emotions and to form beliefs, such as beliefs of what is instrumentally rational to do in a particular situation and beliefs of what other conspecifics are intending to do (Tomasello 2016). When we eventually developed moral thinking, we already had the capacity to form beliefs, and moral beliefs may have played an integral role in moral-decision-making and aiding in social harmony. For example, rules about sounding the alarm when the enemy approaches, coordination rules of dispute resolution, beliefs that one ought to exemplify virtues of being dutiful and courageous in battle, etc. may at least help to account for the evolutionary function of moral judgments being coordination.

Gibbard acknowledges that his view that non-cognitive attitudes are more precisely what is adaptive is speculative and requires further empirical support. As perhaps an equally speculative theory as Gibbard's, it may be the case that cognitive representations of moral rules and virtues at least in part play the requisite functional role in leading to fitness enhancing coordinated behavior for a tribe or society. It also could be the case that backed by punishment, mentally represented moral rules of behavior concerning how to treat others, defend the tribe, and hunt together for large game and mutual advantage, among other cognitive states, in part played a causal role in cooperative decision-making. Such cognitive beliefs may help to put a significant damper on one's possible decision to perform an offensive action and may provide guidance on how to resolve interpersonal disputes that may arise. If moral judgments express and are constituted by the relevant moral beliefs, then this may have the same explanatory power as Gibbard's conative view. Since this is a legitimate possibility, it appears that Gibbard's contention is invalid, and he is not as of yet justified in reaching his conclusion.

In response to this possibility, in WCAF, Gibbard argues that our moral concepts are constituted by non-cognitive attitudes that do not refer to moral properties. Moral concepts are not at all made up of normative beliefs that do refer to moral properties. Cognitive states such as DOGS refer to or are about properties or categories in the world, like *dogs*. Likewise, if moral concepts are cognitive states, then they can refer to moral properties. For instance, if JUSTICE is a cognitive concept, it can refer to *justice*. However, if moral concepts are only conative states, then since such concepts only may express one's own non-representational attitudes, Gibbard claims that they do not refer to genuine moral properties. In fact, for Gibbard in WCAF, there are no genuine moral properties like *justice*, *goodness*, or *wrong action* at all. Rather, he is an eliminativist in that such properties are eliminated from our ontology.

Gibbard acknowledges that there can be so-called thick moral concepts. Recall from the third chapter that such concepts like LIE, COURAGEOUS, and WICKED have both a normative and descriptive component. Gibbard claims that the normative component is an attitude that does not refer to moral properties, and the descriptive component is constituted by non-normative descriptive beliefs that influence categorization of when the moral concept applies. For example, a community's COURAGE concept may be in part constituted by a pro-attitude and by descriptive representations such as ENTERS BATTLE WITHOUT HESITATION. The descriptive components of thick moral concepts play a causal role in influencing when community members label or categorize a person as being courageous, and they refer to non-normative descriptive facts of the world, such as to when someone actually enters the field of battle without hesitation. In this respect, moral judgments, such as ACHILLES IS COURAGEOUS, do not refer to moral properties since COURAGEOUS does not contain a cognitive moral component. He also claims that both components of thick concepts can in principle be separated from each other.

For, we can imagine a representationally equivalent judgment that exhausts the representational content of thick moral judgments without having their normative commitments. Using our example, ACHILLES IS COURAGEOUS and ACHILLES ENTERS BATTLE WITHOUT HESITATION are representationally equivalent for Gibbard in that they both refer to the same non-normative descriptive fact. However, Gibbard writes that neither judgment refers to a moral fact. ACHILLES IS COURAGEOUS is in part constituted by an evaluative non-cognitive attitude, but the conative state does not refer to a moral fact. ACHILLES ENTERS BATTLE WITHOUT HESITATION does not contain any moral concept such that it even possibly could refer to a moral property. Hence, Gibbard maintains a hybrid view only for so-called thick judgments in that such judgments can express both descriptive beliefs and conative states since the judgments are constituted by such states, but the beliefs are not normative ones. Gibbard can respond to my objection – that given evolutionary ethics, a cognitive moral account of judgment can at least in part help to explain the phenomena – by agreeing that given so-called thick concepts, beliefs can in part help to explain how the capacity to make moral judgments may be an adaptation. However, he will disagree with me in that he will claim that such beliefs are not normative. For example, they are not representations of moral rules of what one ought to do. They are purely descriptive rather than prescriptive. Moral beliefs cannot explain the phenomena since moral concepts are not constituted by cognitive moral mental states, where conative attitudes fully account for the evaluative component of thick judgments.

In response, I will take perhaps the most direct route. Recall the prototype studies from the fourth chapter. These experiments showed that thick concepts like CRIME, RESPECTFUL, and CARING contained the normative cognitive concept MORAL. The evaluative component in thick concepts at least in part contains moral cognitive components. This was also found for thin concepts. Hence, Gibbard's response is empirically wrong in that at minimum, it does not tell the whole story. While I allow that it may be discovered in the future through further experimentation that the evaluative component also contains Gibbard's particular attitude, as Gibbard conjectures, this is to date a speculative hypothesis of evolutionary psychology that still requires the right kinds of experiments to be run or data collected. What is not speculative is the prototype experiments which directly examine what constitutes moral concepts. They demonstrate that moral concepts are in part constituted by normative cognitive components. Regardless of whether the evaluative in principle can be separated from the descriptive in thick concepts, Gibbard's claim that the evaluative component to thick judgments only contains non-representational attitudes is empirically false. Hence, against Gibbard, moral beliefs very much can at least be part of the explanation of the evolutionary history of moral judgments and social harmony, where his conative attitudes might not be. To note, for both moral judgments with so-called thin or thick concepts, in the next chapter I will provide a chain argument that if a non-cognitive conative state constitutes a moral judgment, whether in the present or in the past, then this provides evidence that a moral cognitive state must also constitute the judgment.

However, in WCAF, Gibbard then makes a contention based on ontological parsimony. We can explain the capacity to make moral judgments without invoking moral beliefs and the potential concomitant moral properties and facts. We can invoke non-normative descriptive beliefs in thick judgments and use attitudes in so-called thin and thick judgments to explain the phenomena. Our ontology in this case will not include moral properties since non-cognitive attitudes do not refer to moral properties. There is no need to bring in moral beliefs to help explain moral judgments because if there are such beliefs, then they can refer to moral properties. This can lead to a less parsimonious ontology because now there may be the existence of moral properties perhaps in addition to other properties in the world. The normativity in the relevant judgments simply can be explained by non-cognitive attitudes and the fact that such judgments can lead to fitness-enhancing cooperation. Invoking moral beliefs and properties into the story is an unnecessary complication. Simplicity is a virtue.

However, given the advancements in the experimental investigation of moral concepts, Gibbard's argument from ontological parsimony does not work because his theory of moral concepts fails to account for the more recent replicated phenomena that our moral concepts are constituted by moral cognitive states, among other states. Hence, his theory in WCAF will not be on par with the explanatory power of a view, such as my pluralistic theory of moral concepts, which includes moral cognitive states constituting our moral concepts. Since Ockham's razor and ontological parsimony of favoring the simpler theory only comes into play for adjudicating between opposing theories when the competing views are equivalent in terms of factors like explanatory power and predictive success, Gibbard's contention from ontological parsimony cannot even come into play because his theory of moral concepts is explanatorily deficient and fails to make wholly accurate predictions of experimental data. Gibbard has yet to prove the viability of his particular conative theory of moral concepts.

Gibbard also contends that language is adaptive in that it enhances coordination to communicate plans, feelings, laws, moral norms, acceptance of negotiations, discussion of real and hypothetical scenarios, gossip of who violated norms, etc. However, such language at relevant times must motivate in order to enrich coordination in communities. If moral concepts are constituted by motivating attitudes, then moral judgments that contain moral concepts will be motivational. Since normative language seemingly has played an integral role in fitness-enhancing coordination for the survival of our species, Gibbard, therefore, non-deductively infers that our moral concepts are constituted by the relevant motivating attitudes.

At face value, there is some virtue to this point. If the ability to think about ethics is in fact adaptive, genetically or culturally, and we at times communicate fitness-enhancing values through language, the thoughts and language of ethics at least for the most part should be in-and-of-themselves motivating to some degree in order to be adaptive. If our moral judgments are expressions of certain motivating conative attitudes, then this can provide a plausible explanation of how such judgments can motivate. As this argument has as a premise a speculative yet plausible claim from evolutionary psychology about the function of the moral capacity, I leave open the possibility that it may be discovered that our moral concepts are so constituted. Nevertheless, there are other possibilities that may be equally good explanations than Gibbard's. In other words, this particular contention from Gibbard is invalid until he rules out other relevant possibilities. As one possibility, our moral concepts generally may be constituted at least in part by sentiments and emotions rather than by his non-representational attitudes. This alternate view can account for the general motivational force that will allow for normative judgments to be motivational and adaptive. In fact, I later will help prove the viability of the conative view by contending that moral concepts generally in part are constituted by sentiments or emotions. Once again, however, it still may be the case that in future experimentation, we discover that our moral concepts are also constituted by Gibbard's particular attitudes.

7.2 Prinz's Argument from Psychopaths and the Moral/ Conventional Task

We now will examine what I take to be the main argument by Prinz (2007) in *The Emotional Construction of Morals* for the conative view.[3] Prinz maintains a strong position that all genuine moral concepts only are constituted by sentiments or emotions. Recall that sentiments are dispositions to feel emotions. Prinz allows for the more plausible position that in calm and cool settings, one's moral judgment need not express emotions, but it still expresses a sentiment. Prinz provides an empirical argument based on studies on psychopaths. Prinz turns to moral psychology studies on psychopathic individuals who have severe deficiencies in emotions. Psychopaths appear to make sincere moral judgments, but they seem to lack the emotion-backed motivation to act upon their judgments. To note, in chapter ten, I will fully discuss the question of whether the making of sincere moral judgments must include a degree of motivation or not. Psychopaths are well known for their deficiencies in affect

(Cleckley 1941, Blair 1995) as well as their participation in heinous crimes. For example, they have deficiencies in feeling emotions like fear, empathy, guilt, and anxiety and are more prone to committing murder, fraud, sexual molestation, and arson. At face value, they appear intelligent and able to make sincere moral judgments, but they fail to act upon such judgments and may lack the moral motivation to so act based on their blunted emotions. To note, psychopaths differ from frontotemporal dementia patients in that although they are both emotionally shallow, psychopaths display more deliberate deceitfulness and have the need for constant stimulation (Mendez 2006).

However, Prinz (2007) as well as James Blair (1995) and Shaun Nichols (2004) have pointed out that psychopaths apparently cannot distinguish between supposed moral versus conventional norms. Thus, it does not appear to be the case that psychopaths make sincere moral judgments. Instead of making genuine judgments that an act *x* indeed is wrong, inside their minds, they really may be saying something along the lines that "our society generally believes *x* is wrong" when uttering supposed moral judgments. Numerous philosophers in the latter half of the 20th century have attempted to make the distinction between the moral and the conventional. For example, in the edited volume *The Definition of Morality* (Wallace & Walker 1970), Alasdair MacIntyre, Elizabeth Anscombe, Philippa Foot, Peter Strawson, and others attempt to draw such a distinction a priori. However, all the philosophers reach different conclusions and unsurprisingly fail to reach any consensus. Due to this general failure to reach consensus during this era, debate on this topic faded in metaethics as promising new solutions were harder to come by, so metaethicists just moved on to different topics. It was a failed project. On the other hand, Turiel (1979), Smetana (1993), Nucci and Turiel (1978), and other psychologists and philosophers have posited that there supposedly are respective properties to the moral and the conventional domains that may distinguish the two and that also are relevant to scientific induction and explanation. Such properties are psychologically real and psychologically important in today's time. In other words, psychologists have argued by drawing on empirical data rather than by relying on a priori intuitions that moral judgment is a purported natural kind and has a set of related properties in which scientific inductive generalizations may be drawn. Moral and conventional judgments carve nature at the joints and are real natural categories that mark structures of the natural world, like the elements in the periodic table, rather than mirroring merely the interests of human beings. The moral and the conventional are scientific categories, like atoms and quarks, which are discovered rather than being kinds that are invented by humans – artificial categories such as *chair*, *hammer*, and *table*. The debate as to whether moral judgment is a natural kind or not is similar to how philosophers and scientists of the mind have debated whether other psychological properties, such as emotions, are natural kinds or not.

More precisely, the claim in the literature is that moral and conventional judgments are supposed homeostatic clustered natural kinds. Recall that a homeostatic cluster is a group of properties that is not a set of necessary and sufficient conditions, where due to underlying causal homeostatic mechanisms, the presence of one or more properties is likely to lead to the presence of the others within the set (§4.7). There is very likely to be a homeostasis or equilibrium, where all the properties are present. It is important that the cluster of properties is not a set of necessary and sufficient conditions for being a member of the corresponding category because in the moral/conventional task literature, there are exceptions where a certain judgment, for example, may be a moral one but does not satisfy all the purported conditions for being a moral judgment. The homeostatic mechanism is likely to cause an equilibrium in the properties, but there can be limited exceptions.

The homeostatic cluster theory of natural kinds is the best option here among possible views on natural kinds. For, an essentialist theory on natural kinds that presumes that there is a psychological essence of necessary and sufficient conditions to moral judgment will be too rigid and will not be able to account for exception cases that may turn up in people's thoughts about the moral/conventional. Moreover, it presumes that our MORAL JUDGMENT concept has classical structure, and we can mentally represent a definition of necessary and sufficient conditions. Yet, this is not psychologically real. Furthermore, alternatively claiming that there is a neurobiological essence to moral judgment that distinguishes it from other judgments does not take into account the possibility of intelligent alien life forms or future developments in artificial intelligence where the relevant entities may have the notion of moral judgment and morality, but the neural or physical bases of such thoughts are different from human beings. Also, recall that the neurobiological bases of moral judgment are also involved in non-moral tasks. However, if such brain regions are necessary and sufficient conditions for moral judgment, then their activation means that one should be making a moral judgment. However, this is not always so. All in all, there is no set and precise physical essence to moral judgment.

On a different account of natural kinds, psychological natural kinds feature in ceteris paribus generalizations in psychology. For example, moral judgment may take part is psychological generalizations, such as morality being thought by people to be associated with serious harms. However, this account of natural kinds does not contain the important element or idea of what the causal mechanism is that underwrites the generalizations. This is an important feature that philosophers and psychologists are interested in for inductive purposes, so a proper theory of natural kinds needs to include the element of an underlying causal mechanism. On the other hand, such an element is included and plays a vital role in a homeostatic cluster theory of natural kinds. All in all, the homeostatic cluster theory of natural kinds is the most promising option for the claim that moral judgment is a natural kind.

The standard list of properties for moral judgment in the moral/conventional task literature can differ based on the theorist at hand, but we may generally understand the list to be: (1) Scope objectivity, where the norm in question has the broad scope of applying across cultures and time. (2) Authority independence, where a norm still holds even though an authority figure says otherwise. For example, it is still wrong to hit a fellow classmate even if your teacher says it is permissible. (3) Involves a victim who has been harmed at the level of being treated unfairly or having his or her individual rights violated. This can be contrasted with a mere offense or harmless offense, where only one's feelings are adversely affected, such as perhaps when one witnesses someone belch at the dinner table. (4) Serious.

Meanwhile, conventional norms are characterized by the following cluster of properties: (1) Lack of scope objectivity. (2) Authority dependence. (3) Does not involve a victim who has been harmed at the level of being treated unfairly or having his or her individual rights violated. A conventional violation can offend, but it does not harm. (4) Not serious.

To note, the categories of moral and conventional judgments are posited as psychological natural kinds. Thus, the homeostatic cluster should be about psychological properties that can be empirically discovered. Hence, we should understand the above lists of properties as being psychological thoughts of what people *think* about the moral and the conventional. For instance, the cluster of properties for the moral domain is that people *think* that morality has scope objectivity, authority independence, etc. Given the empirical findings of what people think about the moral and the conventional, psychological homeostatic properties have supposedly been discovered.

In common studies by the likes of Turiel, Smetana, and Nucci, they found at many times that school children understand harm violations, such as hitting a classmate or stealing food, to still apply even though they are told that there is no rule against committing such violations. This supposedly ties scope objectivity to harm violations. Students also state that harm transgressions are still wrong even though a teacher says that one can commit such violations. This leads to the import of authority independence for moral judgment. Moreover, students are asked whether the harm violation is very wrong, a little wrong, or perfectly OK in order to test for seriousness. Subjects are asked to justify why they perceive a transgression to be wrong in order to examine whether they give a rights-based justification or not.

However, psychopaths apparently treat both harm and non-harm norms as having scope objectivity and being authority independent. For example, even if the teacher says that one may speak out in class, psychopaths still replied that it is wrong to speak out in class. Blair (1995) hypothesizes that since he examined imprisoned psychopaths, such subjects have an interest in pleasing their interviewers in the hopes of receiving an early release. Thus, psychopaths apparently claim that all rules, moral or conventional, are inviolable at all times, which stands in opposition to normal prisoners who are able to successfully complete the supposed moral/conventional task. Psychopaths appear to be able to get a few of the questions right on the task, but they do significantly worse than normal prisoners on it. Prisoners who truly understand the ostensible moral/conventional distinction and desire to show their moral competence supposedly will be able to draw the distinction. Thus, Blair claims that psychopaths really cannot distinguish between the supposed moral and the conventional because they would have done so if asked. Rather, it apparently is the case that they really view morality as equivalent to conventional norms and merely pay lip service to morality. This hypothesis supposedly is further backed by Blair's (1997) ostensible moral/conventional task study on children with psychopathic tendencies. Due to these findings, Prinz claims that it is not the case that psychopaths have proper moral concepts and can make sincere moral judgments. Thus, Prinz argues that psychopaths cannot be used as evidential support against the conative view.

Prinz takes this a step further and adds that there appears to be a necessary link between emotions and moral competence. Psychopaths have an emotional deficit which co-occurs with the fact that they supposedly cannot make the apparent moral/conventional distinction. This suggests that one must have moral sentiments in order to comprehend morality. In other words, for Prinz, to have a correct moral conception in order to make a sincere moral judgment, one's concept must be constituted by sentiments or emotions. Thus, Prinz believes that the case of psychopaths does not provide evidence against the conative view, but rather, it actually supports it.

At this point, I will present arguments against this contention, although in the next chapter I will present a different psychopaths-based argument for the conative view. First, given Prinz's contention, it may be the case that absolutely no emotions are required at all to complete the task, and some other mental deficiency is responsible for their supposed inability to distinguish between purported moral and conventional judgments. There are several studies indicating that psychopaths have various cognitive deficiencies as well (Gorenstein 1982, Blair et al. 2005). For example, in one study, Ethan Gorenstein (1982) has shown that psychopaths do worse than controls in the Wisconsin Card Sorting Task (WCST) and the Sequential Matching Memory Task (SMMT).

The WCST asks participants to sort or categorize a stack of cards into various piles based on certain qualities that the pictures on the cards contain. The WCST then tests to see how well subjects are able to flexibly adapt to the categorization process once the rules of categorization have changed. The SMMT is a cognitive memory test in which participants are shown a series of cards one by one that either have a plus or minus sign on them. Subjects are tested as to whether they can recall the sign of the card two cards previous to the one currently displayed. While these studies suggest there are cognitive deficiencies in psychopaths related to categorization and memory, I contend that they open up the possibility that psychopaths may have deficiencies in categorization as it pertains to the moral/conventional task. If they already have cognitive deficits in general categorization tasks, then they very well may have problems in the categorization test that is the moral/conventional task due to such cognitive deficiencies. Without any evidence to the contrary presented by Prinz, this possibility remains open. I argue that Prinz's psychopaths-based argument to contend for the conative view may be put in some doubt, and given his contention, one cannot sufficiently conclude that blunted emotions are responsible for psychopaths having apparent problems with the purported task. It is possible that absolutely no emotions are required at all to complete the purported task, and it may be deficits in moral cognitive functions that really are responsible for their apparent failure in the supposed task.

Second, recent studies have shown that psychopaths can successfully draw the distinction between the moral and conventional. In order to eliminate the possible design flaw in previous experiments that incarcerated psychopaths can really distinguish between the purported moral and the conventional but they do not do so because they want to impress the parole board by inflating conventional harms to that of moral ones, Aharoni et al. (2012) gave the moral/conventional task to groups of psychopathic inmates and non-psychopathic inmates. However, before answering the sixteen questions, subjects were told in advance that eight of the acts were pre-rated to be morally wrong, or, in other words, wrong even if there were no conventions or laws against them. Moreover, they were told that eight were pre-rated to be conventionally wrong, or, in other words, not wrong if there were no conventions or laws against them. In this fashion, our experimenters attempt to eliminate the possibility that psychopaths are attempting to impress others with their answers. Participants were asked to label each violation according to whether or not the act would be wrong if there were no conventions or laws against it. Notice that the moral/conventional distinction predicts that if psychopaths cannot really distinguish between the moral and the conventional, then they should do rather poorly on this test since they do not understand that harm norms are not justified by appeal to custom but non-harm norms are so justified. The results of the experiment were that psychopaths indeed were able to distinguish between purported moral and conventional norms comparable to the non-psychopathic inmates. Hence, we now can use their tests and apply them to Prinz and his claim on moral concepts. Given that there is evidence that psychopaths do actually properly make the supposed moral/conventional distinction, it appears to not be the case that all moral concepts must be constituted by sentiments and emotions based on the psychopath studies used by Prinz. Moreover, this result has been replicated with adolescent psychopaths (Dolan and Fullam 2010). These studies at hand place enough doubt on previous conclusions that psychopaths cannot make the purported moral/conventional distinction that Prinz's possible reliance on the existence of the distinction in order to support his conative view is unjustified.

One may object to these studies in that the number of conventional versus moral harms is already given to subjects and this may provide weak cues to make it easier for participants to make the supposed distinction. This may be analogous to how color-blind persons can guess which colors are which based on the weak cues of lightness and contextual appropriateness. However, one must ask what all the weak cues may be in the apparent moral/conventional case. If there are cues, they allow for psychopaths to do just as well as non-psychopathic inmates. I see no other possibility but that it must be some features of the situations that allow psychopaths to successfully complete the ostensible task. However, if this is the case, then emotionally blunted psychopaths must be relying on some kind of conscious or subconscious knowledge of the purported moral/conventional distinction as it is certain features of the situation that are supposed to allow normal subjects to differentiate between the moral and the conventional. Unlike the color-blind case, there does not appear to be some weak or intermediate cue, such as contextual appropriateness, in the supposed moral/conventional case that allows one to tell the difference between the moral and the conventional without actually knowing the difference between the moral and the conventional. If psychopaths really do not know how to make the supposed distinction, then we should still expect them to do worse than non-psychopathic inmates. However, they do just as well as non-psychopathic inmates, and this must be due to the fact that it is based on certain features of the situations that allow them to successfully complete the study. Yet if this is the case, then it appears that they really do know how to distinguish between the purported moral and the conventional because it is thought that such a distinction is usually made based on situational features.

7.2.1 Against the Moral/Conventional Task

Third, I will now attack the natural kind moral/conventional task itself. If successful, this will show that the premise that "psychopaths cannot successfully complete the moral/conventional task" is problematic since the moral/conventional task is not itself legitimate. Given that this is the case, the requisite premise cannot be said to support Prinz's conative view, and his argument is unsound. Moreover, recall from the prior chapter that some moral nativists contend for their position by claiming that children can articulate the natural kind moral/conventional distinction while having a poverty of the moral stimulus, where they are not taught this distinction. Thus, this supposedly shows that we have an innate moral capacity. I object in that there is no such natural kind moral/conventional distinction in the first place.

A host of philosophers, anthropologists, and psychologists have run experiments in order to explicitly or implicitly challenge the moral/conventional task. I will provide a review of such studies now to give an adequate background for our inquiry. Furthermore, such studies will be part of an argument against the cluster natural kinds view in the subsequent section. Richard Shweder and colleagues (1987) have shown that Brahmin Indians believe such acts as when a widow eats fish two or three times a week and when a woman does not change her clothes after defecating and before cooking are universally wrong and wrong in an authority independent way. However, such acts, especially when done in private, do not violate anyone else's individual rights. In fact, Shweder et al. found that most norms in this culture, such as that a woman should not eat at the same table as her husband and elder brother, are held to be moral norms in the sense that they are viewed as having scope objectivity and authority independence. Stereotypical conventional norms in Western society, such as those regarding food or clothing, are understood to have scope objectivity and authority independence in Brahmin culture. In this culture, there are very few norms that lack scope objectivity and authority independence, even for norms that do not involve harming others. This provides evidence that the proposed moral/conventional distinction is not a universal natural category. Rather, what is held to be moral versus conventional is relative to cultural construction.

However, an objection against Shweder from Turiel et al. (1987) is that participants may have believed that certain violations, such as when a widow eats fish two or three times a week, still harm others. In response, Haidt et al. (1993) ran an experiment where they discovered that lower socio-economic subjects in the United States and in Brazil judged a host of non-harmful transgressions to have scope objectivity and to be harmless. For example, when such participants were asked to make judgments on a man who privately has sexual intercourse with a dead chicken before cooking and eating it or on a woman who privately cleans her toilet bowl with the national flag, they answered that these cases are moral violations in the sense that they are universally wrong even though they perceived such transgressions as not harming anyone or violating anyone else's individual rights. Shweder's suspicion that there are moral violations in which people do not think they harm others' individual rights was confirmed. On the other hand, higher socio-economic participants did not hold such cases to be universally wrong. They also generally did not understand such acts to harm others. Thus, this study indicates that perceived harmless transgressions that should elicit an opposing conventional response pattern can actually elicit the moral response pattern of scope objectivity. Moreover, whether or not one perceives certain harmless transgressions to have scope objectivity may be relative to one's socio-economic status. These studies suggest that how one reacts to the moral/conventional task may be relative to one's class.

Moreover, Shweder and Haidt are keen to point out that moral norms are not merely limited to those about harming other's individual rights or being unfair to others. Rather, there are other kinds of moral norms, such as purity or divinity norms against defiling one's body, which can be found especially in heavily religious societies. Such purity moral norms, such as refraining from masturbating with the carcass of a dead chicken, are in regard to the self and how to respect one's body. They are not necessarily about violating others' individual rights. To limit the moral domain to just harms against others' rights is to adopt a peculiar narrow-minded perspective on ethics largely from a Western secular vantage point that stands in contrast to common ethical practices in many other societies.

Shaun Nichols (2002) has run studies on disgusting and non-disgusting violations of etiquette norms. For example, a disgusting non-harm transgression is when a dinner guest snorts then spits into his water glass and drinks from it. A non-disgusting non-harm violation is when a dinner guest drinks soup directly out of his bowl. He found that children generally believed disgusting transgressions to be serious, authority independent, and as having scope objectivity. Meanwhile, adults also generally took such disgust violations to be serious and authority independent, but they generally claimed that such violations lacked scope objectivity. In this case, various stereotypical etiquette norms elicit significant aspects of a moral response pattern. Moreover, this study shows that authority independence and scope objectivity can come apart from each other.

The studies run by the likes of Turiel, Smetana, and Nucci involve transgressions that are not socially controversial ones. Instead, they were rather uncontroversial ones, such as hitting another child, stealing a classmate's apple, and name-calling. Goodwin and Darley along with many others have found that most in the United States believe that for a debate between two interlocutors from the United States, any judgments regarding prototypical moral issues that are socially controversial and that involve serious harms or possible harms, such as abortion, euthanasia, and embryonic stem cell research, will lack scope objectivity (Goodwin & Darley 2008, 2010, 2012, Wright et al. 2013, 2014, Beebe 2014, Uttich et al. 2014, Beebe & Sackris 2016).[4] For example, Goodwin and Darley (2008) provided participants with a large number of statements purporting to make claims about how things are in moral matters, such as "consciously discriminating against someone on the basis of race is morally wrong" (p. 1361). After being asked whether they agreed with these statements, participants were told that none of the statements had, in fact, elicited full consensus. Whatever judgment they happened to maintain, there were some fellow participants within their same culture who held the opposite view. Subjects basically had the options of responding to the fact that another same-culture individual held a contrary position by choosing either that only one may be mistaken while the other is correct, neither are mistaken, or the participants could choose "other" and write down and explain some other alternative option that was not presented by the experimenters.

As expected, participants did not choose "other" and write in some other alternative option like non-cognitivism or error theory. The folk generally are not non-cognitivists or error theorists. Given common experience with the folk, it would have been quite surprising if most people claimed that judgments are incapable of being substantially true/false or that both judgments are false, respectively. Rather, across all age groups in the Unites States, most believe that controversial yet stereotypical moral issues involving serious harm or possible harm simply do not have scope objectivity, where neither are mistaken and both are correct. Meanwhile, for socially uncontroversial cases in the United States, like opening gunfire on a crowd, most believed such issues have scope objectivity.

One possible objection is that perhaps subjects understood an interlocutor's different moral judgment to not be a genuine moral judgment, but an inverted commas one such as a tongue-in-cheek judgment. Also, subjects may think the other interlocutor does not fully understand the moral scenario, had somehow misconstrued it, was thinking of unnecessary extraordinary extenuating circumstances, misread the case, had not relied on conventional meanings to words, etc. There may have been many ways participants may have interpreted the study in a fashion that does not align with the intended interpretation of the experimenters. However, Goodwin and Darley also asked participants after each case an open-ended question that instructed them to explain why they thought the differences in moral judgments had arisen. In their own variant, Wright et al. (2013) asked subjects to explain why they thought their answer was the best answer. They removed any data in which the subjects did not construe the differences in moral judgments as being real and in which there was a misinterpretation of the study. They found that only a small number of participants had such issues. For example, in one study, only 2% of responses had to be relevantly removed (Goodwin & Darley 2008). Upon removing such entries, their results still held.

Moreover, many of the above cited studies replicating Goodwin and Darley's findings point out worries and problems with the original Goodwin and Darley studies. These studies run by others then made the required changes to experimental designs to account for the concerns and still were able to replicate the results. For example, they found that subjects are not confused as to erroneously believing that just because an issue is socially controversial, this means that there is no underlying objectivity to it. For, participants were found to believe there is an underlying objective answer to whether the theory of evolution is true even though they perceived this subject to be socially controversial. On the other hand, for controversial *moral* issues, people generally believe that there is no objective fact of the matter for the relevant cases.

Yet, Sarkissian, Tien, Wright, Knobe, and I have suggested in a cross-cultural study with participants in the United States and Singapore that socially uncontroversial harm violations in these societies that are serious can elicit aspects of a conventional response pattern (Sarkissian et al. 2011). For example, participants are given scenarios in which an individual finds his youngest child to be unattractive, so he kills this child based on this fact. In each scenario, the participant is told that one's classmate believes such an act of violence is morally wrong but a member of a hypothetical alien culture called the Pentars hold the opposite view. Notice that unlike the Goodwin and Darley style studies, the interlocutors are from different cultures rather than from the same culture of the United States. Moreover, studies run by the likes of Turiel, Smetana, and Nucci also lack this crucial feature of pitting interlocutors from different cultures against each other and sufficiently describing the other culture in full detail. The Pentar culture is described in detail by the experimenters as being significantly different from any human culture, where the Pentars' main goal in life is to expand the number of equilateral pentagons in the universe. In such tests, we also employed a hypothetical traditional human warrior culture called the Mamilons rather than the Pentars. Subjects are then asked about these conflicting judgments in regard to whether at least one of them must be mistaken or if both may be correct. They are asked whether they believe at least one of the disputants must be wrong. To note, insofar as this study uses the same general design as the Goodwin and Darley style studies of providing a moral issue, pitting two interlocutors against each other, and basically asking whether one is mistaken or both may be correct, we may inductively infer that the subjects at hand largely also were not misinterpreting the study in some way. Returning, if participants believe that neither of them are wrong, then this provides evidence that the folk do not believe that typical moral transgressions have scope objectivity, but rather, seemingly conflicting moral judgments both can be true relative to different cultures. This study found that when the interlocutors are one's classmate and a Mamilon, roughly half give relativist responses that deny scope objectivity and the others provide objectivist ones. Interestingly enough, when the interlocutors are one's classmate and a Pentar alien, where the cultural difference is more radical, we found that most participants deny scope objectivity. On many socially uncontroversial and serious harm transgressions, most in the relevant countries claim that there is a lack of scope objectivity when the interlocutors are from significantly different cultures.[5] These results may be somewhat like how people who are objectivists on what season of the year it currently is may become relativists after they are told that seasonal patterns are different depending upon whether one is in the Northern or Southern Hemisphere. This replicated study implies that beliefs about local customs factor into judgments about culturally uncontroversial serious harm norms and that the folk in such countries generally believe that relevant moral judgments are true and false relative to cultures.[6]

Daniel Kelly, Stephen Stich, and colleagues (2007) have run studies in the United States attempting to challenge whether serious harm violations are characterized by the moral response pattern. For example, they found that most participants believed a ship captain whipping his derelict and drunken sailor 300 years ago was acceptable, but such an act would not be acceptable today. That one should not whip another human being in this situation lacks scope objectivity. Furthermore, they found that if the Pentagon approves of simulating physically abusive enemy interrogation in military training, then most judge that such torture is morally permissible. However, if the Pentagon disapproves of such torture, then participants generally hold that such abuse is not morally permissible. In other words, judgments concerning such serious physical harms lack authority independence and scope objectivity.

Prinz objects to Kelly et al.'s experiment (2007). He states that the reason why subjects give a different response based on time periods is that they may think that sailors required more discipline in the past because they were more unruly. Hence, although there is a moral norm against whipping, it is overridden in past times by other norms, such as perhaps overriding consequentialist norms, that allow for the whipping. Given how unruly sailors used to be in the past, it would lead to the greater consequences to whip them, but this is not true in today's times with more professional sailors. Since this alternate interpretation where the folk are still moral objectivists and consequentialists is a possibility, perhaps the whipping vignette has not yet been shown to provide evidence against the moral/conventional task.

The problem with this is that others have run experiments to eliminate the confound, but Kelly et al.'s results still hold (Quintelier et al. 2012, Quintelier & Fessler 2015). For example, Quintelier and Fessler provide participants with two whipping scenarios. Both situations occur in the present day, involve U.S. sailors, and take place in international waters. In both cases, when a ship is in international waters, persons on the ship must follow the laws of the state whose flag the ship sails under. In the first case, the flag is of a state that has laws that allow for whipping derelict sailors, so sailors who fail to follow orders are whipped. In the second scenario, the flag is of a state that has laws against whipping sailors, so no sailors are whipped. When eliminating Prinz's concern by having both scenarios take place at the same era of time with sailors from the United States, the studies demonstrate that Kelly et al.'s results still hold. The folk state that whipping derelict sailors is acceptable on the ship that flies under the relevant flag but not on the other ship.

A number of studies have shown that seriousness comes apart from the cluster. For instance, the conventional transgression of a boy wearing a dress to school is considered to be more serious than if a student commits the stereotypical moral violation of stealing an eraser (Turiel 1983). Children also consider the supposed conventional violation of wearing pajamas to school as being serious (Tisak & Turiel 1988). The readiness of seriousness coming apart from the cluster has led stalwart proponents such as Turiel (Tisak & Turiel 1988) and Smetana (1993) to later deny that seriousness and lack of seriousness are part of the moral and conventional judgment clusters, respectively. Smetana (1993) writes that "the severity of the transgression is not considered to be a formal criterion for distinguishing moral and conventional rules and transgressions" (p. 117). Also, recall that Joyce argued that moral concepts are innate in that they are adaptive because morality has practical clout and is prescriptive in providing strong reasons for action to all. Thus, he states that we consistently should understand morality to be more serious than other normative domains. However, experimental evidence has shown that Joyce's claim concerning seriousness is empirically false.

The above generally are well-known studies in the literature. Yet, one may defend a truncated rendition of the homeostatic cluster for moral judgment that includes scope objectivity, authority independence, and being a harm norm from the previously discussed studies that counter it in that the feature list is not a set of necessary and sufficient conditions for being a moral judgment. A response may be that the homeostatic cluster view can allow for such exceptions. One can object to the homeostatic cluster by showing that the properties come apart, but one will need more evidence and instances showing that they do so come apart in order to provide a sufficient objection. There is already a promising list of studies against the moral/conventional task, but more evidence is still required. For, there are many studies in support of the moral/conventional task, so more evidence that the cluster can come apart at many times is needed to adequately pursue this line of objection. If there is such evidence, then one is not warranted in drawing an induction that moral judgment is a natural kind since such support for a conclusion is not sufficiently robust. To warrant the induction, the exceptions that the homeostatic property cluster theory allows for must be rather limited.

For the natural kinds view, in order to induce that the properties are really homeostatically clustered and are attributes of a real natural category, the presence of some properties in the cluster must make it very likely that all the other properties will be present as well due to an underlying causal mechanism that makes it so. Exceptions to the cluster should be rather rare. If this is not the case, then this theory fails as will Prinz's psychopaths-based contention that moral judgments are constituted by emotions.

7.2.2 The Alternate Fields of Inquiry and Psychology Argument

What is generally lost in the moral/conventional task debate is that evidence from psychology and anthropology studies is not the only form of empirical evidence that can be gathered to address the issue. Other relevant empirically drawn inferences can be garnered from alternate fields of inquiry, such as from history, religion, political science, sociology, and military science to see whether the moral/conventional distinction has held across time and location. When one stops to think about it, one may find it remarkable that such evidence generally has not found its way to the table on this debate. Indeed, natural kind theorists would have to draw inferences from history to establish that the cluster holds across time as well, but this has not even been attempted. Hence, their natural kinds view is unjustified. The additional evidence found in the alternate fields of inquiry combined with previously undiscussed psychology studies and already discussed skeptical studies will provide enough replicated support that the cluster of properties comes apart at many times such that the natural kind moral/conventional distinction is false. Let us call this *the alternate fields of inquiry and psychology argument.* It will be the general failure to take into account all the alternate fields of inquiry that examine and make claims about the various facets of ethics that significantly in part will help lead to the demise of the homeostatic cluster view. As a qualification, I do not pretend to list all the rich available evidence against the cluster in all the various alternate fields of inquiry.

First, let us discuss more support of how harming or violating the rights of another individual can come apart from the cluster. Let us look at evidence from religion. It is a general maxim of Christian Mormons today that drinking alcohol is unethical. Yet, when one drinks alcohol in private in moderation, it does not harm others or violate another's rights. Some Christian denominations have fasting moral norms. Transgressing such norms does not violate anyone else's individual rights, especially when such restrictions are contravened in private. Such evidence coupled with the above cross-cultural evidence from Haidt that a variety of violations of purity norms performed in private in predominantly Christian societies that do not harm others' rights also are not thought to harm others' rights, we can inductively infer that the given transgressions done in private in Christian societies are not thought to be harm violations. The above studies and empirical information about purity moral norms provide evidence against the scientific generalization that cross-culturally, moral transgressions are thought to violate other people's rights. In addition, there is more evidence along with Nichols' studies that prototypical etiquette norms can share significant aspects of a moral response pattern. Mongolians believe that eating noodles with your hands is objectively wrong in an authority-independent way, but they do not believe that it is a harm or fairness violation (Berniūnas et al. 2016).

Next, let us discuss evidence of how authority independence comes apart. In Ancient Egypt, during the Old Kingdom (2686 BCE–2181 BCE), a pharaoh was considered to be an earthly god, and with his divine right, it was his interpretation of ethics that determined right from wrong (Malek 1992). Egyptians during this time believed that what was moral changed depending on the mandates of the pharaoh. Morality lacked authority independence. In military history as well as in military science, in many cultures, the particular moral duties for one's country a soldier must fulfill on the battlefield, such as carrying out a certain mission or maintaining a specific troop formation, largely is dependent on the authority of the general. First and second graders judge that the prototypical conventional norm of not wearing pajamas to class still holds even though an authority figure says otherwise (Tisak & Turiel 1988).

There is more evidence that scope objectivity and/or authority independence can come apart. Traditional Arab children differed from urban Jewish children in Israel in that their justification of why harm transgressions are wrong is based on an appeal to customs rather than scope objectivity and authority independence (Nisan 1987). Moreover, Fessler et al. (2015) examined folk judgments across seven different cultures, like in the Karo Batak and Sursurunga small clan-based societies. They tested them on stereotypical harm transgressions, such as initiating a fight, raping a woman, and beating one's wife, but they were told such acts were made in the distant past or in a faraway land. Across all seven societies, most judgments were altered when faced with a particular harm transgression that had a temporal or spatial distance. Meanwhile, four of the seven cultures' stereotypical moral judgments generally showed the presence of authority dependence rather than independence in that judgments were altered when an authority figure says otherwise. Here, we can see that at times scope objectivity and authority independence together can come apart from the cluster, but both properties even can come apart from each other as well at times.

Thomas Pölzler (2018) raises ten objections that apply to many but not all studies that test for lay metaethical beliefs on moral truth and scope objectivity. For example, some studies fail to include options for the error theorist and non-cognitivist, some conflate the issue on moral truth with the cognitivism/non-cognitivism debate, some may elicit first order moral judgments of whether a particular act is right or wrong rather than second order metaethical ones about whether first order judgments are objectively true or not, and some presume that participants have a sufficient understanding of moral truth, such as objective moral truth. However, when he ran new experiments that are designed to account for all the worries along with comprehension screening tests, results showed that most overwhelmingly do not understand morality to have scope objectivity, but most maintain that moral judgments are only relativistically true (Pölzler & Wright forthcoming).

There is more proof that scope objectivity and harming others' rights comes apart. Korean children claim that the transgression of not appropriately greeting one's elders as having scope objectivity (Song et al. 1987). However, they only provide a conventional rather than rights-based justification for this norm. Vegetarian children judge that eating meat is morally wrong because it harms animals, but they do not believe their judgments are universal (Hussar & Harris 2010). Children aged three to nine view the wrongness of between-group harm as being dependent on whether there are the relevant laws (Rhodes & Chalik 2013).

Political scientists have long noted the spread of liberal democracies across many countries such as in the United States, Canada, England, South Korea, and Argentina. Inspired by Enlightenment philosophers like John Locke, it is a hallmark of liberal democracies generally to hold values such as having free and fair elections, separation of powers, equal civil rights, and *a high degree of freedom to live one's life as one so chooses so long as one does not harm others.* In liberal democracies, it is common for many people to believe that when there is a career decision to be made, at many times it is up to the subjective interests of the agent as far as which life choice he or she should make. The agent has this freedom or liberty. There is a component of ethics that is concerned with pursuing one's personal goals in life and maintaining healthy relationships with family and friends, *inter alia.* These are part of living a good or flourishing life and are serious ethical issues that all the major ethical views like utilitarianism, virtue ethics, and deontology incorporate within their respective theories. Moreover, the notions of liberty and freedom are integral in political philosophy. However, it appears that many in liberal democratic societies do not view certain norms on certain cases concerning the good life as being wholly objective, and many life decisions just boil down to subjective interests. What sort of life one should live, such as to shun certain modern technologies like the Amish or to incorporate them in everyday life, at many times is essentially based on subjective choice so long as one does not harm others. However, scope objectivity as articulated in the natural kinds debate says that a particular norm one may hold about what it is to live a good life largely should be thought of as having the broad scope of applying across cultures and time for all people. Moreover, it needs to be more rigid due to the underlying homeostatic mechanism that is supposed to make it highly likely that people attribute this kind of scope objectivity to ethics. Yet, those in a liberal democracy largely believe to each his own, and there is no one judgment about living a specific lifestyle that is objectively correct for all people across time and location. This subjectivity in a liberal democracy for the good contrasts with communitarian and hierarchical societies in which decisions about the good life is more tightly constrained by what is good for the community, family, or what conforms to the caste hierarchy. Relative to liberal democratic societies, individuals have the freedom to participate in something like John Stuart Mill's notion of "experiments in living" and have the liberty to choose their own conception of the good life so long as doing so does not harm others.

One may object that purity violations and certain issues concerning the good life such as one's career choice are not paradigmatic moral judgments, and the cluster theory is limited only for such judgments. However, even if this is so, recall that we have discussed numerous "paradigmatic" judgments above, such as on abortion, rape, murder, etc. that do not exemplify all of the relevant properties. Therefore, this view still fails. Second, what is considered to be paradigmatic can be culturally relative. The objection at hand is narrow-minded and largely peculiar to a Western secular perspective. Many non-Western cultures believe purity norms are paradigmatic. Such purity norms at many times stem from religious belief, and religion is central to a way of life, especially for people in non-secular societies. For example, the purity norm against homosexuality is so paradigmatic in certain Islamic cultures that they kill homosexuals by throwing them off roofs. Moreover, in communitarian societies such as in many Latin, African, and Asian cultures, each individuals' job is seen as an essential cog in the machine that is the community. A person's career decision is viewed as being important for the proper functioning of the community and for the greater good of society. Hence, a career choice in a communitarian society is largely perceived as being a paradigmatic moral judgment.

One also may object that the cluster only holds for social judgments on how to treat others. These are "moral" judgments and are other-regarding. Yet, they do not hold for judgments that pertain to the self, such as judgments about purity norms or pursing personal projects. Such judgments are intrapersonal "ethical" ones. Hence, one cannot use evidence about intrapersonal "ethical" judgments to criticize the claim that "moral" judgment is a realist natural kind category. However, even if this distinction can be wielded for this purpose, we have discussed numerous other-regarding judgments where an equilibrium of all the relevant properties at many times is wanting, like judgments concerning harming animals, doing violence to those in the out-group, rape, killing one's own ugly child, and beating one's wife. Hence, this view still fails.

Second, this particular distinction is itself a recent Western individualistic construct that is non-existent in many communitarian societies. In communitarian cultures, the self cannot be disentangled from the community as an individual atom. Rather, it is inextricably intertwined with the community; hence, the African proverb: "I am because we are; I exist because the community exists." Thus, what is good for the individual is what is good for the community and vice versa. The notion of Kantian individual rights in the cluster that holds regardless of the greater good for the community is non-existent in the relevant communitarian societies. Also, violations of intrapersonal "ethical" norms have an effect on others since one's self is intimately tied to the group. In principle, making a poor decision for oneself just is to make a poor decision for the group since one's self is inextricably bound to the group. Whether one chooses a career as a farmer that helps feed the people of one's community or one violates a purity norm that may offend the gods and bring wrath upon the group, breaking intrapersonal "ethical" norms is to break a "moral" norm that impacts or potentially impacts the group. Such intrapersonal "ethical" violations effect group rights and thus, are also other-regarding, but they do not violate notions of others' individual rights and equality that are contained in the cluster view. The distinction between "moral" judgments and atomistic intrapersonal "ethical" ones cannot exist in the relevant cultures and was incapable of existing in most of the history of Western civilization (MacIntyre 1984). Hence, one cannot use this distinction to posit a realist natural kind claim on moral and conventional judgments that is supposed to hold across time and location.

The proposed homeostatic cluster for the moral domain is incorrect since we have seen that there are many replicated cases where the cluster comes apart in various ways such that one is not warranted in drawing the induction that moral judgment is a natural kind. As the cluster can change based on cultural influence, the evidence strongly supports the positive descriptive point that intuitions concerning the confines of the moral domain differ at many points based on culture, and the moral realm is at many times constructed differently by disparate cultures or groups in a fashion that cannot be captured by a realist a posteriori analysis of the categories. Moral judgment does not carve nature at the joints. If anything, moral judgment is a social kind that is based on human social construction, as with certain other properties studied in the social sciences, rather than being a natural kind.

Notice also that in some cultures, there may not be a principled distinction between the moral and the conventional, understood as socially constructed kinds, in which one may lay out general distinguishing properties pertaining to each disparate realm. Rather, an extensional definition may be more appropriate, where one can only define moral and conventional judgment by providing a list of particular kinds of acts or cases, such as abortion and table manners, that are either in the moral or conventional domain based on one's culture or even subculture.

All in all, any conative theory conclusion that is grounded on the truth of the natural kind moral/conventional distinction, where psychopaths cannot make this distinction, is false. Given that this is the case along with the other two previously given objections, Prinz's psychopaths-based argument that all moral concepts are constituted by sentiments or emotions fails.

7.2.3 The Persistence Argument

There is an additional independent argument against the claim that moral judgment is a natural kind that we will call *the persistence argument.* If moral and conventional judgments are homeostatic natural kinds, then there is supposed to be an underlying causal mechanism, where the predominant view in the literature is that the proximate psychological homeostatic mechanism is an affective one (Nichols 2004). However, one can view the ultimate evolutionary explanation underlying the affective mechanism as involving a biological or cultural evolutionary history that causally explains why today, the presence of some properties likely will lead to the presence of the other properties in the cluster (Joyce 2006). There is an underlying natural reason as to why the properties cluster together, and it is not by chance. There is likely to be a homeostasis of the cluster of properties where all properties are present today because such an equilibrium and each of the properties are supposed to confer a survival advantage and be fitness-enhancing by enhancing cooperation. Exceptions can occur, but their continued persistence across generations should be rather limited since the homeostatic mechanism should cause all the properties to re-cluster together again or at least make it highly likely that such re-clustering will occur. Moreover, while members of a natural kind may have countless possible properties in common with each other that can be candidates for being a part of the cluster, only those properties that are underwritten by the homeostatic mechanism are part of the cluster. For example, members of the class of *human beings* largely share the properties of having hair, two eyes, being shorter than eight feet tall, being able to punch keys on a keyboard, being able to hum a tune, etc. Obviously, not all the properties that human beings widely have in common are part of the homeostatic cluster of properties for being human.

At least one underlying mechanism for the class of *human beings* is their genes and their exchange within a population. Given human genes, it will be rare for a human being to be greater than eight feet tall. There can be exceptions due to genetic mutations, but we should expect such exceptions to be rare and to diminish over generations. This is because gigantism and acromegaly is usually accompanied by serious disorders that can lead to premature death before one reproduces. Being under eight feet tall is part of the cluster of properties for human beings because it is underwritten by a human gene-based causal mechanism where the presence of other properties in the cluster that are grounded in human genes likely will lead to the presence of the property of being less than eight feet tall. It is likely because if one is more than eight feet tall, then one's chance to reproduce and pass on the gene for such extreme height are significantly diminished, diminishing the likelihood that others are greater than eight feet tall in future generations.

The *Uroplatus* or leaf-tailed gecko is camouflaged against predation such that when it is on tree bark, it is extremely difficult for human eyes and predators to detect. Lacking this camouflage in such geckos will lead to decreased fitness and will be selected against. This property of being so camouflaged is part of the homeostatic cluster for the *Uroplatus* due to underlying evolutionary mechanisms. The presence of other properties of the *Uroplatus* that are underwritten by the evolutionary homeostatic mechanisms means that it is likely that the particular gecko also will have the property of being camouflaged because if it is not camouflaged due to a genetic mutation, then it is unlikely to survive and reach reproductive age to pass on its genes for not being camouflaged. We should expect a decrease in the persistence of leaf-tailed geckos that lack camouflage due to the underlying evolutionary mechanisms. Such geckos and their persistence in the same relevant ecological niche should be very rare if not non-existent.

Likewise, moral judgment is thought to have an underlying homeostatic mechanism. Therefore, we should expect that cases where all three properties are not present should not persist or be very unlikely to persist. Such cases should be rather rare and anomalous. There should be a general trend toward homeostasis and equilibrium, where all three properties will be present. The persistence argument contends that there are moral situations where it is persistent that one or more properties from the cluster are missing. Such situations are not rare within the particular populations. Therefore, the proposed cluster is not part of a homeostatic natural kind.

For the property of authority independence, as previously mentioned, empirical evidence from military history and military science shows that soldiers in many cultures and in much of history believe that what one ought to do on the battlefield is authority dependent on the dictates of the general. Noted political scientist, Samuel Huntington (1957), relies on reports from those in the military along with civilians to conclude that the mind of the soldier is generally rigid and disciplined. "When the military man receives a legal order from an authorized superior, he does not argue, he does not hesitate, he does not substitute his own views; he obeys instantly" (p. 73).

There is a moral duty for many soldiers to perform certain actions on the field of battle to, for example, save human societies, fulfill an oath, do one's duty for country, or exemplify virtues like courage, honor, and loyalty. However, the specific morally required strategic act that soldiers must perform on the battlefield in many cases is subject to the authority of the general. Even if a soldier thinks the army strategically should do something else, was previously told to do something else, or a given command flies in the face of orthodox military strategy, there is a chain of command where particular moves on the battlefield, such as specific troop formations and strategies as well as their alterations in real time, are authority dependent on the general. The military may carry out complex operations, where different units must coordinate by performing different tasks. If one unit fails to obey orders, it can lead to the death of fellow soldiers. Moreover, many soldiers are drilled into accepting the necessity of this chain of command and how what one ought to do in many cases is authority dependent. Indeed, in order to be admitted, all military personnel in the United States must swear by a morally binding oath that they have a duty to follow all lawful orders given to them by superiors. Turiel, Smetana, and Nucci claim that in various circumstances, many children and people act based on reasons of not harming others rights, and they still purportedly claim that harm violations are authority independent. Likewise, soldiers may have various reasons for their actions on the field of battle as well, such as to help one's fellow soldiers or to serve one's country, but what is important for our purposes, when asked whether the military strategy is authority dependent or not, most will say that it is so dependent.

Particular judgments on troop movements on the battlefield being understood as being authority dependent have persisted for millennia in many cultures, and there is no empirical evidence in many cultures, such as in the United States, that this going away any time soon. There is no support that soldiers who believe that military commands are authority dependent are rare. The fact that this has persisted for so long across diverse cultures should be alarming to the natural kind theorists. If the properties are homeostatically clustered, then the underlying causal mechanism should have caused a homeostasis or near homeostasis of all three properties on many of such military situations by now in various cultures. Yet, this is not the case.

Moreover, the relevant soldiers believe that many military commands lack scope objectivity. For, if one has a new commander that replaces the previous one and this leader changes the strategy, then what one morally ought to do on the battlefield changes. Such mandates are not universal across time. This lack of scope objectivity for such judgments has persisted for millennia in many cultures, and there is no current indication in many of such societies that those who break from homeostasis are rare. Also, if the properties are homeostatically clustered, then the underlying causal mechanism should have caused a homeostasis or near homeostasis of all properties on many of such military situations by now in various cultures. Yet, this is not so. Hence, this case of persistence stands against the property of scope objectivity. Of course, there are other examples of persistence regarding the lack of scope objectivity, such as concerning conceptions of the good life in liberal democracies that has lasted for centuries.

Furthermore, in Haidt's above study, a man who masturbates in private with the carcass of a dead chicken does not commit a harm transgression of violating someone else's individual rights. This has been so for centuries. Moreover, subjects generally do not understand such acts to be harm violations, and presumably, given that a second agent is not even involved in the situation for this second agent's individual rights to be harmed, this has persisted for quite some time. Yet, if moral judgment is a homeostatic natural kind, then a homeostasis at least should have nearly been reached by now on this purity moral violation, where most should believe that someone else's individual rights are harmed in this case. Most in the relevant cultures should have reached an equilibrium, and any breaks from homeostasis should be rare. Yet, this is not so.

Given the above, we see examples where the absence of some of the properties at times have persisted for centuries or millennia, and there is no indication that breaks from an equilibrium are rare, where most of the relevant populations have reached an equilibrium. However, this should not be the case if the properties are homeostatically clustered. Hence, moral judgment is not a set of homeostatic properties that are underwritten by a causal mechanism. Therefore, given all of the above, the proposed cluster is not part of a natural kind.

It is plausible that there is an evolutionary history to our ability to make moral judgments, which really may be a history about the capacity to think about norms, generally understood, rather than being specifically about moral decision-making; in which case the underlying evolutionary moral mechanism may be a cultural one. Nevertheless, the moral natural kind theorists must provide causal empirical evidence that today, this evolutionary mechanism likely will bring a homeostasis of the relevant properties that we think the domain of morality may have for each and every subdomain of moral judgment. They must be hooked up in such a way that the homeostatic mechanism will cause us to believe that morality has the relevant properties. If we do not believe all of such properties are present, the supposed evolutionary moral mechanism should make it very likely that a homeostasis will be attained, where it is very likely that we will believe that all properties are present on each and every kind of moral issue. However, it is just such a connection that I believe is lacking in certain cases, where in such situations that at times have persisted for centuries or even millennia, there is no indication that breaks from homeostasis are rare. My approach of critically assessing the connection between the homeostatic mechanism and the cluster of properties is a novel contribution to the moral/conventional task literature.

The most promising account that moral judgment is a natural kind is one that utilizes the homeostatic property cluster theory. Yet, if moral judgment is a homeostatic natural kind, it should not allow for my above counterexamples in the persistence argument. Hence, for this and other reasons, this natural kinds theory is incorrect, and moral judgment is a constructed social kind. Being a constructed social kind, where our intuitions on the moral/conventional distinction vary based on factors such as culture, also beneficially helps explain why the a priori project on the moral/conventional judgment distinction in metaethics in the latter half of the 20th century that largely attempted to capture the intuitions of ordinary competent speakers of a language failed and why no consensus was attained. Moreover, Prinz's contention for the conative theory based on psychopaths and their performance on the natural kinds moral/conventional task fails based on this reason, among many others.

One may object that Prinz makes this psychopaths-based argument in *The Emotional Construction of Morals* for the conative view by using the above discussed moral/conventional distinction. Let us call this distinction *the original distinction.* However, later in the book, he posits his own different truncated list of properties for the moral/conventional. Morality is characterized with scope objectivity and being about harm norms. Conventionality is attributed with lacking scope objectivity and not being about harm norms. This is a subset of the original distinction. Perhaps my objections against the claim that moral judgment is a natural kind can be deflected if we replace the original distinction with Prinz's view. Yet, my contentions against the original distinction at many times will also still apply *mutatis mutandis* to Prinz's moral/conventional task if he were to rely on it rather than the original distinction in his psychopaths-based argument. For instance, there is much evidence demonstrating that the property of scope objectivity and being a harm transgression get separated from each other, and such separation is prevalent across many cultures, which should not be the case. Moreover, as noted above, scope objectivity does not escape the persistence contention.

Likewise, Victor Kumar (2015) may object that he has his own different natural kind theory for moral judgment that may help Prinz's psychopaths-based argument. He contends that the cluster of properties are: (1) Serious, (2) General, (3) Authority-independent, and (4) Objective. However, like other natural kind views, he does not even attempt to justify it across time and history, where he must show that people across time attribute his homeostatic properties to morality. Hence, his view is unjustified and commits the biased sample fallacy of basing his conclusion on an unrepresentative sample. Moreover, his cluster includes the property of authority independence, which is not immune from my persistence contention against it. Also, recall that the property of seriousness has been abandoned even by the likes of Turiel and Smetana for stereotypical moral judgments. Therefore, Kumar's overall theory is false.

7.3 Prinz's Inference to the Best Explanation

In this section, our focus specifically will be on Prinz's (2015) latest and different argument for the conative theory that is based on drawing an inference to the best explanation.[7] This hinges on three phenomena that he claims the conative view predicts. Given the apparent confirmation of the predictions, Prinz claims that his conative view is the best explanation of the phenomena. The first phenomenon is that there is a correlation between making moral judgments and activation in emotion regions of the brain from brains scans. If our moral judgments are constituted by sentiment or emotions, we should expect this to be the case since emotions and moral judgments must co-occur on this view. In a wide variety of experiments, this prediction is borne out. For instance, Heekeren et al. (2003) have discovered this prediction is confirmed when subjects read morally significant cases, and recall from the fifth chapter that Greene et al. (2001, 2004) confirmed this prediction when participants make judgments on a variety of cases such as on trolley dilemmas. Greene and his colleagues also found such emotional correlation with decision-making in regard to straightforward cases about donating money to the poor, lying on a resume, cheating on one's taxes, and making an environmental policy decision, among other scenarios. Even in several of Greene's studies discussed in the fifth chapter that show that cognitive reasoning is at least in part responsible for participants' moral decision-making, emotional regions of the brain are still activated (Greene et al. 2001, Greene 2013).

However, as Prinz rightly points out in this later work, the above correlational data from brain scans is insufficient to establish his view.[8] For, given the correlational evidence, it still could be the case that emotions only become activated only after one makes one's moral judgments. If this is the case, emotions will not be constitutive of moral judgments. Although this correlational evidence is an important prediction that should be the case if Prinz's conative theory is true, Prinz leans on two other predictions to combine them all together to non-deductively infer that his conative view is the best explanation of all the relevant psychological phenomena. Prinz believes that the following two predictions, if confirmed, will help to show that emotions are not post hoc.

The second prediction is that if sentiments or emotions constitute moral judgments, then we should expect that if relevant emotions are extraneously induced in test subjects by experimenters, then this should alter their moral judgments. If this prediction is confirmed, then this may help to show that emotions are not post hoc effects of moral judgments. It may show that emotions influence normal moral judgments. This prediction has been borne out numerous times. Recall the many studies discussed in the third chapter showing how emotions extraneously induced by experimenters in test subjects influence moral decision-making. For instance, Seidel and Prinz have found that induced disgust by listening to a recording of a person continually vomit generally augments the perceived wrongness of violations against nature, such as on sexual transgressions and cannibalism. Meanwhile, induced anger from listening to the irritating sounds of Japanese noise music generally has the same effect when making judgments on crimes against persons, such as on battery and unfairness (Seidel and Prinz 2013a). They also found that induced happiness generally increases positive judgments of moral praiseworthiness, but it has no impact on negative judgments. Induced anger generally leads to subjects making more severe negative judgments of moral wrongness as well as reducing the tendency of making positive moral judgments (Seidel and Prinz 2013b).

Yet, the second prediction is inconclusive. Prinz is aware that induced emotions can influence almost any kind of judgment-making, let alone moral decision-making, so this by itself does not establish that emotions influence moral decision-making in normal conditions when participants are not being purposefully manipulated by experimenters. It may be the case that cognitive reasoning is what normally influences our moral decision-making, but as with generally any kind of decision-making, emotions can interfere when they are extraneously induced, such as when being hypnotized to feel emotions. If this is the case, all moral judgments do not express sentiments or emotions. Also, such studies do not pass the possible mental error test as the participants have been mentally manipulated by the experimenters before they even receive the moral questions, so they alone cannot be used to draw constitution claims on moral concepts. The possibility is left open that along with other premises, perhaps such an inference with such studies may be drawn, but Prinz's burden is to provide such additional premises. Hence, even if the second prediction is confirmed, it does not alone significantly help the conative view.

However, Prinz attempts to meet the burden and claims that since certain extraneously induced emotions have been shown to exclusively influence only particular kinds of moral cases and other emotions exclusively impact other respective moral subdomains, this suggests that emotions do normally influence our decision-making in the relevant circumstances. For instance, he writes that since induced disgust is the only emotion that affects harms against nature without impacting other subdomains and induced anger is the only emotion that affects harms against persons without impacting other subdomains (Seidel & Prinz 2013a), this indicates that disgust and anger normally do impact the respective subdomains of decision-making even when experimenters are not attempting to manipulate the participants.

One problem with this is that there is conflicting data. For instance, Wheatley and Haidt (2005) found that hypnotized subjects induced with disgust also made more severe judgments in regard to harms against persons, such as for a congressman taking bribes and for an ambulance chasing lawyer. Likewise, Schnall et al. (2008) found that induced disgust made subjects make more severe moral judgments as compared to control subjects against a film documentary company that releases a film in which the interviewees do not know that they are being filmed. Induced disgust influences judgments on both harms against nature and persons. Moreover, induced anger does not exclusively impact judgments on harms against persons. Furthermore, recall that in another experiment in part run by Prinz himself, induced anger is not restricted to a single moral realm as it has an effect on both positive and negative moral judgments (Seidel & Prinz 2013b). Also, induced happiness is not the only emotion that can positively influence judgments of praiseworthiness as the induced feelings of gratitude and awe also can have such an impact (Horberg et al. 2011). All in all, the second prediction fails to help establish the pervasive influence of emotions in moral categorizations.

The third prediction is that differences in the emotional makeup of certain subjects, such as having diminished emotions, should lead to differences in moral categorizations. Prinz states that the confirmation of this prediction will show that emotions play a crucial role in decision-making especially for psychologically normal people, and he further contends that this prediction is confirmed in a variety of studies. A case he mentions is that it has been found that subjects who are prone to disgust have less tolerance for crimes against nature (Horberg et al. 2011). The other two cases Prinz explicitly discusses are Huntington's disease patients and psychopaths. Huntington's disease patients who have deficits in disgust display patterns of sexual deviancy and a penchant for committing a variety of crimes (Schmidt and Bonelli 2008). Moreover, psychopaths with blunted emotions display a multiplicity of anti-social criminal behavior.

The third phenomenon attempts to basically show that emotions influence moral decision-making for psychologically normal people. For instance, since certain patients with diminished emotions generally make very different judgments than psychologically normal subjects, Prinz claims that this supposedly shows that emotions must be playing a causal role in deliberation for normal subjects but not for the relevant patients. This is why such patients generally make divergent judgments in the relevant scenarios. Moreover, such emotions are not mere causal influences but are important influences because their absence actually leads to deficits in moral decision-making. Hence, moral concepts in psychologically normal individuals are constituted by sentiments or emotions.

However, recall from above that psychopaths also have cognitive deficiencies that also could be responsible for their criminal behavior and perhaps, moral judgment-making. More argumentation on psychopaths is needed to draw a strong conclusion one way or the other. To note, I will provide such argumentation in the next chapter. Moreover, Huntington's disease patients also have cognitive deficiencies in things like planning, abstract thinking, rule acquisition, and memory (Montoya et al. 2006) that could be responsible for their misbehavior rather than emotions. Further work is required to demonstrate that it is the diminished emotions rather than impaired cognitive functions in Huntington's disease patients that are responsible for their actions, which then may demonstrate that psychologically normal agents generally may be relying on emotions in many cases of moral decision-making.

Prinz's move also is highly questionable in light of the issue of how it can be the case that when supposedly discovering that emotions influence moral decision-making, the best explanation of this phenomenon is that emotions constitute the moral concept in the judgment. Why is it the case that the conative theory of moral concepts predicts that emotions will influence judgment? Prinz attempts to draw a concept constitution claim based on an inference to the best explanation, but there needs to be a theoretical bridge as to how it can be the case that what mental state influences decision-making is what constitutes the relevant concept in the judgment based on an inference to the best explanation. Just because the push of my fingers causes the rubber ball to roll does not necessarily mean that via an inference to the best explanation, the ball is constituted by my fingers. For his third prediction, he is somehow trying to use causal evidence to draw a moral concept constitution conclusion without fully stating how this can be done. Yet, without a theoretical bridge that allows him to show the relevance of utilizing an inference to the best explanation in this case for drawing a constitution claim, this third prediction is questionable and incomplete. From his perspective, it is highly mysterious how one can draw a moral concept constitution claim based on causal evidence. There is a major theoretical gap in Prinz's argument, and he cannot handwave his way to a concept constitution claim.

He may respond that the influences are important in that their absence leads to deficits in judgment-making. Hence, the influences constitute the concept. However, my fingers are extremely important for causing the stationary rubber ball to roll as it did, but it does not necessarily follow that therefore, the rubber ball is constituted by my fingers. An adequate theoretical bridge linking causation to constitution still is required. Insofar as the second prediction also is about how emotions influence decision-making, this worry here also applies to it. Prinz fails to explain how one can use causal evidence to draw a moral concept constitution claim. I have provided the requisite philosophical and functionalist framework for drawing constitution claims based on causal evidence that is missing from Prinz's contention. Given my objections to the second and third phenomena, Prinz is not warranted in drawing his inference to the best explanation in favor of the conative view based on his own arguments. As we have seen in this chapter, no one has empirically established the viability of the conative view in a non-speculative fashion. In the ensuing chapter, I will present my own case for the conative theory.

Notes

1 Recall that in chapter ten and afterward, I will explore a priori approaches to the nature of moral concepts.

2 In THTL, Gibbard offers a position that blurs the distinction between cognitivism and non-cognitivism. He is silent as to whether moral judgments express cognitive beliefs or non-cognitive states. Whether he is aware of it or not, this silence could put in jeopardy his evolutionary arguments and their specifically stated conclusions in WCAF. It is open as to whether Gibbard even espouses the conative theory of moral concepts given what is said in THTL. However, as we are only focusing on a posteriori arguments for the conative view in this chapter, in addressing Gibbard's evolutionary contentions for the conative view in WCAF, I assume from here forward the theoretical commitments contained in WCAF. For instance, we will presume that Gibbard argues for the conative theory and that he is an eliminativist, where genuine moral properties do not exist. These are commitments he may no longer endorse. If anything, even if one reads Gibbard as later changing his mind on them, we can think of such contentions for the conative view as being ones that a conative theorist may potentially make. We can view our entertaining of Gibbard's contentions for the conative view with his particular theoretical commitments in WCAF as being instructive for anticipating moves that a particular conative theorist might make.

3 Prinz provides a host of arguments for the viability of the conative theory in this book. For instance, he attempts to use Haidt's aforementioned dumbfounding findings, where participants in experiments were found to use post hoc rationalizations for their moral judgments. As moral judgments apparently are not grounded in reasoning, Prinz concludes that all moral concepts must then be constituted by sentiments or emotions. However, recall my criticism of these studies in that they do not alone eliminate the possibility that subconscious reasoning may be the grounding of moral judgments. Prinz also claims that Kohlberg's stage theory of moral development is consistent with the conative view. For instance, recall that in the first two stages of preconventional morality, children, based on interviews, are supposedly influenced by self-interest and fear of punishment when making moral decisions. This is consistent with the picture that moral judgments are constituted by emotions. In response, it is important to keep in mind that Kohlberg's studies only provide correlational data. Therefore, one cannot draw constitution claims on moral concepts based on only correlational results.

4 Goodwin and Darley mischaracterize their study as testing whether moral judgments are true independent of human minds versus being mind dependently true. They essentially ask that when two interlocutors from the U.S. give different answers to a moral issue, is one mistaken or are both correct? Notice that Kant believed that moral truth is universal and mind dependent, where one will be mistaken. Someone who maintains that moral truth is mind independent also can maintain that one is mistaken. Hence, these questions are not testing between mind independence versus mind dependence. We see that their questions are in fact testing for scope objectivity versus the lack of it. The numerous other cited studies in this area also test for scope objectivity.

5 It will be interesting to test whether participants maintain something like the argument for moral relativism which generally states that there is interminable discourse on many moral issues. Such unyielding debates on many moral issues across cultures separates ethics from other fields such as science, math, and logic, where in these latter fields, there generally is a much greater degree of consensus on issues, and debates usually get resolved. What supposedly best explains this empirical phenomenon of interminable and fundamental moral conflict is that there are no objective moral facts. This argument in metaethics is commonly called 'the argument from disagreement.' It may be the case that participants consciously or subconsciously may implicitly be using this argument or perhaps a loose version of it to judge that the seemingly unyielding moral issues between cultures have no objective answers. They may be using this kind of argument to conclude for moral relativism. For, recall that the folk do not deny moral objectivity merely based on the fact that something is controversial. The finding by Goodwin and Darley (2008) that the folk believe science is more objective than ethics may provide additional support for this.

6 In a later chapter, I will elaborate upon the varieties of moral relativism.

7 Prinz also provides several other contentions in this article. However, he admits that these other arguments are incomplete and require further investigation. Here, I only examine his main new argument.

8 Recall from the fifth chapter that in his earlier work, he speculates the truth of a causal claim based on correlational neuroimaging data.

References

Aharoni, E., Sinnott-Armstrong, W., and Kiehl, K.A. 2012. "Can Psychopathic Offenders Discern Moral Wrongs? A New Look at the Moral/Conventional Distinction." *Journal of Abnormal Psychology* 121, 484.

Barsalou, Lawrence. 1999. "Perceptual Symbol Systems." *Behavioral Brain Sciences* 22, 577–660.

Beebe, J. 2014. "How Different Kinds of Disagreement Impact Folk Metaethical Judgments." In *Advances in Experimental Moral Psychology*. Ed. by H. Sarkissian and J. Wright. London: Bloomsbury Academic, 167–187.

Beebe, J. and Sackris, D. 2016. "Moral Objectivism Across the Lifespan." *Philosophical Psychology* 29, 912–929.

Berniūnas, R., Dranseika, V., and Sousa, P. 2016. "Are There Different Moral Domains? Evidence from Mongolia." *Asian Journal of Social Psychology* 19, 275–282.

Blair, R. 1995. "A Cognitive Developmental Approach to Morality: Investigating the Psychopath." *Cognition* 57, 1–29.

Blair, R. 1997. "Moral Reasoning and the Child with Psychopathic Tendencies." *Personality and Individual Differences* 25, 731–739.

Blair, R., Mitchell, D., and Blair, K. 2005. *Psychopath: Emotion and the Brain.* New York: Wiley-Blackwell.

Cleckley, H.M. 1941. *The Mask of Sanity: An Attempt to Reinterpret the so-called Psychopathic Personality*, St. Louis, MO: The C.V. Mosby Company.

Darwin, Charles. 1871/2004. *The Descent of Man.* London: Penguin Books.

Dolan, M.C. and Fullam, R.S. 2010. "Moral/Conventional Transgression Distinction and Psychopathy in Conduct Disordered Adolescent Offenders." *Personality and Individual Differences* 49, 995–1000.

Fessler, D.M., Barrett, H.C., Kanovsky, M., Stich, S., Holbrook, C., Henrich, J., Bolyanatz, A.H., Gervais, M.M., Gurven, M., Kushnick, G., and Pisor, A.C. 2015. "Moral Parochialism and Contextual Contingency Across Seven Societies." *Proceedings of the Royal Society B* 282, 20150907.

Gibbard, Allan. 1991. *Wise Choices, Apt Feelings.* Oxford: Clarendon Press.

Gibbard, Allan. 2003. *Thinking How to Live.* Cambridge, MA: Harvard University Press.

Goodwin, G. and Darley, J. 2008. "The Psychology of Meta-ethics: Exploring Objectivism. *Cognition* 106, 1339–1366.

Goodwin, G. and Darley, J. 2010. "The Perceived Objectivity of Ethical Beliefs: Psychological Findings and Implications for Public Policy." *Review of Philosophy and Psychology* 1, 1–28.

Goodwin, G. and Darley, J. 2012. "Why are Some Moral Beliefs Seen as More Objective than Others?" *Journal of Experimental Social Psychology* 48, 250–256.

Gorenstein, E. E. 1982. "Frontal Lobe Functions in Psychopaths." *Journal of Abnormal Psychology* 91, 368–379.

Greene, Joshua. 2013. *Moral Tribes.* New York: The Penguin Press.

Greene, J., Sommerville, R.B., Nystrom, L.E., Darley, J.M., and Cohen, J.D. 2001. "An fmri Investigation of Emotional Engagement in Moral Judgment." *Science* 293, 2105–2108.

Greene, J., Nystrom, L.E., Engell, A.D., Darley, J.M., and Cohen, J.D. 2004. "The Neural Bases of Cognitive Conflict and Control in Moral Judgment." *Neuron* 44, 387–400.

Haidt, J., Koller, S., and Dias, M. 1993. "Affect, Culture and Morality, or Is it Wrong to Eat Your Dog?" *Journal of Personality and Social Psychology* 65, 613–628.

Heekeren, H., Wartenburger, I., Schmidt, H., Schwintowski, H., and Villringeeer, A. 2003. "An fMRI Study of Simple Ethical Decision-making." *Neuroreport* 14, 1215–1219.

Horberg, E.J., Oveis, C., and Keltner, D. 2011. "Emotions as Moral Amplifiers: An Appraisal Endency Approach to the Influences of Distinct Emotions Upon Moral Judgment." *Emotion Review* 3, 237–244.

Huntington, Samuel P. 1957. *The Soldier and the State.* Cambridge, MA: The Belknap Press of Harvard University.

Hussar, K.M. and Harris, P.L. 2010. "Children Who Choose Not to Eat Meat: A Study of Early Moral Decision-Making." *Social Development* 19, 627–641.

Joyce, Richard. 2006. *The Evolution of Morality.* Cambridge, MA: The MIT Press.

Kelly, D., Stich, S., Haley, K., Eng, S., and Fessler, D. 2007. "Harm, Affect, and the Moral/Conventional Distinction." *Mind and Language* 22, 117–131.

Kousta, S., Vigliocco, G., Vinson, D., Andrews, M., and Del Campo, E. 2011. "Representations of Abstract Words: Why Emotion Matters." *Journal of Experimental Psychology, General* 140, 14–34.

Kumar, Victor. 2015. "Moral Judgment as a Natural Kind." *Philosophical Studies* 172, 2887–2910.

MacIntyre, Alasdaire. 1984. *After Virtue*, 2nd edition. Notre Dame, IN: Notre Dame Press.

Malek, Jaromir. 1992. *In the Shadow of the Pyramids.* London: Little Brown and Company Ltd.

Mendez, Mario. 2006. "What Frontotemporal Dementia Reveals About the Neurobiological Basis of Morality." *Medical Hypothesis* 67, 411–418.

Montoya, A., Price, B., Menear, M., and Lepage, M. 2006. "Brain Imaging and Cognitive Dysfunctions in Huntington's Disease." *Journal of Psychiatry and Neuroscience* 31, 21–29.

Nichols, Shaun. 2002. "Norms with Feeling: Toward a Psychological Account of Moral Judgment." *Cognition* 84, 223–236.

Nichols, Shaun. 2004. *Sentimental Rules.* Oxford: Oxford University Press.

Nisan, M. 1987. "Moral Norms and Social Conventions: A Cross-Cultural Comparison." *Developmental Psychology* 23, 719–725.

Nucci, Larry and Turiel, Elliot. 1978. "Social Interactions and the Development of Social Concepts in Preschool Children." *Child Development* 49, 400–407.

Paivio, A. 2013. "Dual Coding Theory, Word Abstractness, and Emotion: A Critical Review of Kousta et al. (2011)." *Journal of Experimental Psychology General* 142, 282–287.

Pölzler, Thomas. 2018. "How to Measure Moral Realism." *Review of Philosophy and Psychology* 9, 647–670.

Pölzler, Thomas and Wright, Jen. Forthcoming. *The Psychology and Philosophy of Folk Moral Objectivism.* London: Routledge Press.

Prinz, Jesse. 2007. *The Emotional Construction of Morals.* Oxford: Oxford University Press.

Prinz, Jesse. 2015. "An Empirical Case for Motivational Internalism." In *Motivational Internalism.* Ed. by G. Bjornsson, C. Strandberg, R.F. Olinder, J. Eriksson. Oxford: Oxford University Press, 61–84.

Quintelier, K.J. and Fessler, D.M. 2015. "Confounds in Moral/Conventional Studies." *Philosophical Explorations* 18, 58–67.

Quintelier, K.J., Fessler, D.M., and De Smet, D. 2012. "The Case of the Drunken Sailor: On the Generalisable Wrongness of Harmful Transgressions." *Thinking & Reasoning* 18, 183–195.

Rhodes, M. and Chalik, L. 2013. "Social Categories as Markers of Intrinsic Interpersonal Obligations." *Psychological Science* 24, 999–1006.

Sarkissian, H., Park, J., Tien, D., Wright, J., and Knobe, J. 2011. "Folk Moral Relativism." *Mind & Language* 26, 482–505.

Schmidt, E.Z. and Bonelli, R.M. 2008. "Sexuality in Huntington's Disease. *Wiener Medizinische Wochenschrift* 158, 78–83.

Schnall, S., Haidt, J., Clore, G., and Jordan, A. 2008. "Disgust as Embodied Moral Judgment." *Personality and Social Psychology Bulletin* 34, 1096–1109.

Seidel, A. and Prinz, J. 2013a. "Sound Morality: Irritating and Icky Noises Amplify Judgments in Divergent Moral Domains." *Cognition* 127, 1–5.

Seidel, A. and Prinz, J. 2013b. "Mad and Glad: Musically Induced Emotions have Divergent Impact on Morals." *Motivation and Emotion* 37, 629–637.

Shweder, R.A., Mahapatra, M., and Miller, J.G. 1987. "Culture and Moral Development." In *The Emergence of Morality in Young Children*. Ed. by J. Kagan & S. Lamb. Chicago: University of Chicago Press, 1–83.

Smetana, J. 1993. "Understanding of Social Rules." *The Development of Social Cognition: The Child as Psychologist*. Ed. by M. Bennett. New York: Guilford Press.

Song, M., Smetana, J., and Kim, S. 1987. "Korean Children's Conceptions of Moral Conventional Transgressions." *Developmental Psychology* 23, 577–582.

Tisak, M.S. and Turiel, E. 1988. "Variation in Seriousness of Transgressions and Children's Moral and Conventional Concepts." *Developmental Psychology* 24, 352.

Tomasello, Michael. 2016. *A Natural History of Human Morality*. Cambridge, MA: Harvard University Press.

Turiel, E. 1979. "Distinct Conceptual and Developmental Domains: Social Convention and Morality." *Nebraska Symposium on Motivation*. Ed. by H. Howe and C. Keasey. Lincoln: University of Nebraska Press.

Turiel, E. 1983. *The Development of Social Knowledge*. Cambridge: Cambridge University Press.

Turiel, E., Killen, M., and Helwig, C. 1987. "Morality: It's Structure, Functions, and Vagaries." *The Emergence of Morality in Young Children*. Chicago: The University of Chicago Press.

Uttich, K., Tsai, G., and Lombrozo, T. 2014. "*Exploring Metaethical Commitments: Moral Objectivity and Moral Progress*." In *Advances in Experimental Moral Psychology*. Ed. by H. Sarkissian and J. Wright. London: Bloomsbury Academic, 188–208.

Wallace, G. and Walker, A. (eds.) 1970. *The Definition of Morality*. London: Methuen & Co.

Wheatley, Thalia and Haidt, Jonathan. 2005. "Hypnotic Disgust Makes Moral Judgments More Severe." *Psychological Science* 16, 780–784.

Wright, J., Grandjean, P., and McWhite, C. 2013. "The Metaethical Grounding of our Moral Beliefs: Evidence for Metaethical Pluralism. *Philosophical Psychology* 26, 336–361.

Wright, J., McWhite, C., and Grandjean, P. 2014. "The Cognitive Mechanisms of Intolerance: Do Our Metaethical Commitments Matter?" *Oxford Studies in Experimental Philosophy*. Ed. by T. Lambrozo and J. Knobe. Oxford: Oxford University Press, 28–61.

8 The Conative View Established

I will now address a possible objection from Adina Roskies (2003), where she may be read as arguing against the conative theory for moral concepts. In so doing, we will see initial successful evidence for the conative view. Next, I will provide more of my own arguments for the conative theory and will assess the viability of this structure for moral concepts in light of the categorization, sense, and concept acquisition desiderata.

8.1 VMPFC Patients and Roskies' Objection

Although Roskies does not directly address the conative theory, we may read her as attempting to make an argument that not all moral concepts in moral judgments are constituted by sentiments or emotions by relying on experimental evidence from studies on those with lesions to the VMPFC; studies most notably conducted by Antonio Damasio. Recall that Damasio has concluded that patients with lesions to the VMPFC have intact reasoning capacities but are considered to have deficiencies in affect. In regard to one patient, when he is in the real world, the subject generally fails to reliably act in ethical scenarios regarding certain issues concerning the good life as psychologically normal subjects generally do or as the subject previously acted before the injury, although such patients generally do not commit violent crimes like psychopaths and they generally treat strangers well. For example, after suffering the lesion, the patient subsequently lacks focus and direction at work and constantly gets fired from his jobs. The subject is unable to maintain a healthy relationship with his long-time wife and gets divorced. He also chooses to remarry with a woman who his family completely disapproves of only to again get divorced shortly thereafter. He uses his life savings to enter in business deals and personal projects with men of shady characteristics only to lose all of his money. In speaking of such patients with lesions to the VMPFC, Eslinger and Damasio state:

> In highly structured tasks with standardized verbal instructions delineating the extent of the problem and expected response

> patterns,... he was highly effective. In real-life situations, with no overt external guidance and greater freedom to choose from behavioral options, he often conceived inappropriate plans of actions, which he both *verbalized* and carried out.
>
> (Eslinger & Damasio 1985, p. 1738)[1]

Thus, such patients appear to be able to make sincere moral judgments in the laboratory, but in the real world, when personally faced with ethical choices regarding personal projects and relationships, they appear to lack the appropriate motivating emotional response to act. Therefore, Roskies takes VMPFC patients to be prime examples of individuals who make sincere ethical judgments in the laboratory but many of such judgments are not expressions of sentiments and emotions because they have blunted affect and are unable to act in the real world upon the relevant judgments they made in the laboratory. While motivation to act from emotions can be overridden at times, if the moral concepts in their judgments are constituted by emotions, then they should be motivated at least to an extent to act upon such judgments in the real world such that there should at minimum be many cases where VMPFC patients act consistently with their laboratory-made ethical decisions on particular issues concerning the good life. However, this is not so. Given their blunted affect, VMPFC patients are a class of subjects that are not even disposed to feeling emotions when making such judgments.

In response, first let me reiterate from the first chapter that my pluralistic theory of moral concepts is a general empirical claim regarding moral psychology. As many contemporary claims about human beings are general empirical claims about Homo sapiens in which there can be aberrations and counterexamples, my claim is no different. Just as it may be generally part of the human condition for us to be social animals, speak a language, or even experience a wide variety of emotions, there can be exceptions to this, such as for those who are hermits, severely mentally handicapped, or born with alexithymia with blunted affect, respectively. If it is the case that certain psychologically abnormal patients with lesions to the VMPFC or even frontotemporal dementia patients can make moral judgments without even expressing a disposition to feel an emotion, then so be it, and this does not necessarily impugn my theory of moral concepts. My view perfectly allows for aberrations, especially for patients in abnormal psychology. Hence, Roskies' possible objection is averted.

Second, we may use such patients to argue for the conative view. In laboratory settings, VMPFC patients have no problems making first person moral judgments, but once they step outside of the laboratory into the real world, they have enormous problems making first personal judgments in regard to the relevant situations. Recall in the above quote that the experimenters mention that the patient verbalizes his plans for inappropriate actions. Roskies does not fully take into account that the VMPFC patients make judgments inside the laboratory, *but* they also make contrary judgments in regard to the particular issues on the good life outside the laboratory in the real world under real circumstances. There are two sets of judgments here. Roskies problematically only focuses on the judgments made in the laboratory. With less external guidance and a greater range of options in the real world, VMPFC patients make certain inappropriate life decisions with disastrous consequences. The contrast between the kinds of judgments made in the laboratory as compared to those made in the real world is so stark that we may seriously question whether any of their ethical judgments in regard to the given issues on the good life in the laboratory are legitimate or sincere ones. As there are serious inconsistencies in the two sets of judgments and the ones made in the laboratory obviously have less ecological validity than those made in the real world, we may inductively infer that the set of judgments made in the laboratory on personal projects and relationships likely are not their real judgments, but those made under real world conditions with a greater variety of options likely are their actual judgments. In psychology, test subjects generally can provide different responses to experiments on the same subject matter depending on how similar the testing condition is to the real world, where findings from testing conditions that are more ecologically valid carry greater support. One may seriously question whether VMPFC patients make their real ethical judgments on the particular issues on the good life in the laboratory given their contrary judgments made in the real world. Due to the inconsistencies in judgments corresponding to differences in ecological validity, we may infer that VMPFC patients' real judgments on the pursuit of personal projects and maintaining personal relationships are those made in the real world.

If the real judgments for the patients are those made in the actual world and in the real world they largely make disastrous judgments in regard to many situations concerning the good life, then we may non-deductively infer that emotions appropriately influence by default many psychologically normal people's decision-making concerning particular aspects of the good, which includes the pursuit of personal projects, having financial stability,[2] and beginning or maintaining healthy relationships with loved ones. This is further supported by Bechara et al. (1996) who found through using a SCR test that normal subjects were influenced by emotions when making certain long-term financial decisions, but VMPFC patients were not and made disastrous judgments compared to normal participants. To note, I am not using Damasio's studies to draw constitution claims for his patients' concepts. Rather, I am relying on his work to first infer what psychological factors influence normal subjects' timely decision-making processes when various options are presented to them. From Damasio's work we may infer that when normal subjects make relevant decisions, they at least are in part influenced by emotions by default although cognitive states can jointly play a role. Given my insight of the functionalist metaphysics of moral concepts, this then provides evidence that the conative view is a viable theory of moral concepts regarding certain intrapersonal and interpersonal norms concerning living a flourishing life because emotions appropriately realize the functional role of the relevant moral concepts (Park 2013, 2018). Relevant moral concepts, such as GOOD, KIND, PERSEVERENCE, PREPARED, PRUDENT, CARING, and LOVING, are in part constituted by sentiments and emotions for the relevant psychologically normal individuals. Also, since VMPFC patients' laboratory judgments on cases involving potentially harming strangers, such as the trolley problems or whether one should drive out the homeless, generally are consistent with their judgments made outside the laboratory when relevant, these kinds of laboratory judgments that are not about personal projects and personal relationships may be taken to be their actual judgments.

However, there have been several objections to Damasio's general thesis that emotions influence judgments in psychologically normal people. Gerrans (2007) contends that VMPFC patients have a "myopia of the future" and cannot imagine themselves in future scenarios. Being able to project to the future is crucial for making decisions in the real world. Damasio does not take this into account. However, Gerrans still concludes that emotions at many times play the relevant causal role in normal decision-making, and hence, for our purposes, we still get our conclusion for the conative theory. Gerrans (2007) writes, "I have endorsed the general idea that the VMPFC does play a role in coordinating the retrieval and manipulation of information, including affective information, required for decision-making…" (p. 472).

Linquist and Bartol (2013) claim there are various stages in an act of deliberation. They argue against Damasio that emotions are not relevant to all stages of deliberation, but they do acknowledge that emotions likely play a role in eliminating the indecisiveness that VMPFC patients usually portray. For our purposes, this still demonstrates that emotions play the requisite causal role in normal decision-making in crucially impacting the final decision made between competing options at the end of the deliberation process, and hence, the conative theory still is a viable view. Recall that my pluralistic theory of moral concepts allows for different kinds of knowledge to work together during different stages of the deliberative process. At times, decision-making is complex, and concept constituents are designed such that they must help to explain this complexity once subjects are given a functional task and the deliberation process begins. For instance, Keil and company (1998) found that prototype and theory knowledge frequently can work together in cognition. For example, when given a newly learned animal to categorize, a participant may begin the deliberative process by using theory knowledge to decide what weight of importance is possessed by certain prototype features of the animal. Then the more heavily weighted prototype components kick in at the end of the deliberative process to lead to the final decision. These studies show that both prototypes and theories jointly constitute the relevant natural kind concept. It likewise can be the case at many times for moral decision-making that, for instance, prototypes are used early in the deliberative process, but emotions crucially come in to play at the end of this process to make the actual final decision.

8.2 More Arguments for the Conative View

I will now continue to posit my own arguments for the conative view, although much of the heavy lifting for this already has been done in previous chapters. Remember that concepts are functionally defined as playing a causal role in decision-making, *inter alia.* Thus, they are constituted by those psychological structures that appropriately realize the causal role. As I continue to lay down new arguments for the conative view, recall that no one in the causal moral judgment literature has been able to draw this functionalist connection in their writings. Nor has anyone yet empirically confirmed that the conative theory is viable. By relying on appropriate causal evidence from the causal judgment literature and from correlational neuroimaging studies, I will finally empirically establish the viability of the conative view in light of the categorization desideratum in a non-speculative manner.

Remember the trolley problems and their ilk from the chapter on the theory view. It was demonstrated from various studies on frontotemporal dementia patients and those with lesions to the VMPFC that emotions appropriately influence judgments in psychologically normal subjects at many times on the footbridge case and in other like situations such as some of those on Greene's sixty moral questions. Since such patients' relevant cognitive reasoning capacities are intact but they have diminished emotions, the fact that they largely make different folk consequentialist judgments on the footbridge case and other relevant situations than psychologically normal subjects mean that normal participants are being at least in part influenced by emotions in footbridge-like cases in order to reach their different decisions as compared to the relevant patients. Emotions play a vital role in these cases, and they largely account for why normal participants generally made different decisions than the patients on many related and tested scenarios. This demonstrates that emotions appropriately are used at many times in moral decision-making by default, and the relevant moral concepts are constituted by sentiments or emotions.

Josh May (2018) objects that the VMPFC is responsible for many cognitive functions, like drawing calculations and learning, along with experiencing emotions. Hence, cognitive deficiencies rather than blunted emotions may be responsible for the divergent decision-making made by patients with lesions to the VMPFC. However, recall that the VMPFC patients in question passed relevant cognitive tests, so this is unlikely. Thus, we can infer that it is emotions that play an important causal role here in normal subjects.

Bryce Huebner (2015) objects to the causal influence of emotions by speculating that perhaps in these high conflict dilemmas in which you may take one life to save many others, the patients have cognitive deficits in being unable to integrate and appropriately pit the deontological value of not harming others against folk consequentialist considerations. That is why they make so many folk consequentialist judgments as compared to normal participants on such cases. However, normal subjects do not have such cognitive deficits, and this is why they do not make as many folk consequentialist decisions. It is the cognitive factor of being able to give appropriate consideration to not harming others in high conflict dilemmas, rather than a conative factor, that is influencing decision-making in normal subjects when they do not make decisions consistent with folk consequentialism. Hence, emotions do not play the relevant causal role in normal subjects for such cases.

However, there is an ad hoc nature to this objection. For example, frontotemporal dementia patients have been found to answer straightforward moral questions that are not high conflict dilemmas, where they consistently state that one should not harm others even though they have a proclivity to cause such harm (Mendez 2010). They have no problems making judgments against harming others in such cases but do not make such judgments in high conflict dilemmas. In order to save his theory that emotions play no role in moral cognition, it is all too convenient for Huebner to speculate that such patients may have cognitive problems providing due consideration for not harming others in high conflict dilemmas but curiously not in other scenarios where there may be other conflicts for such patients, such as between not harming a person versus having a self-interest in harming the person. Coupled with the fact that there is no independent confirming evidence that there are such specifically moral cognitive deficiencies in the patients that also explains why such deficiencies do not apply to low conflict dilemmas, this objection is ad hoc. FTD patients have shown the ability to significantly take into account the deontological value of not harming others. Furthermore, there is plenty of evidence that such patients have deficiencies in affect. Hence, we may conclude via inference to the best explanation that emotions are in significant part responsible for the relevant decisions made by normal subjects.

Also, there is strong evidence that negative emotions influence decisions of unfairness and distributive justice at many times in the ultimatum game. Recall that in this game, a proposer subject has to share some money with a responder subject. The responder can accept or reject the offer. If it is accepted, the money is divided accordingly. If it is rejected, then no one gets any money. It is thought from rational game theory that proposers should offer the most unfair split in their own favor while responders should accept any offer since getting one dollar is better than getting none. However, studies show that proposers tend to offer equal shares of money while responders will tend to reject highly unequal offers (Pillutla & Murnighan 1996, Sanfey et al. 2003, van't Wout et al. 2006), although this result can vary based on culture (Henrich 2000). On the other hand, rejection rates are substantially lower for highly unequal offers when the proposer is a computer rather than a human subject.

It is found that when responders reject unfair offers, there is a correlation with activation in the anterior insula, which is associated with negative emotions (Sanfey et al. 2003). Furthermore, replicated findings show that the experiencing of anger provides a better causal explanation for why responders reject an offer rather than the mere fact that there is a wide distributive disparity in the offer (Pillutla & Murnighan 1996, van't Wout et al. 2006). For instance, van't Wout et al. used a SCR test to measure when responders will feel emotions. They found that responders produced a higher SCR right before they made decisions to reject unfair offers from humans. However, they did not produce as high of a SCR right before they accepted fair offers or before they accepted a highly unequal offer from a computer. The fact that the strong emotional response is elicited after one receives an unfair offer from a human but whose activation precedes the final judgment supports the claim that negative emotions appropriately causally influence by default many judgments that contain concepts like UNFAIR or UNJUST. They play an important role in leading to certain judgments regarding fairness. Moreover, the use of such negative emotions provides a better causal explanation of why there are rejections than the mere fact that there is a large discrepancy in certain offers. For, when there is a large discrepancy in an offer from a computer, there is no higher SCR and such an offer is largely accepted. However, when there is a large discrepancy in an offer from a human, there is a higher SCR and such an offer is largely rejected. We may infer that negative emotions at least in part causally explain why responders reject unfair offers in this particular setup of the ultimatum game, although cognitive states can conjointly play a causal role. What has not been foreseen in the literature is that this evidence provides support for the viability of the conative view and of the position that moral judgments express conative states.

Huebner (2015) may object that perhaps during moral deliberation, participants may make several initial judgments, kind of like forming a working hypothesis, before arriving upon their final answer, and they continually may change their initial working judgments during deliberation as they assess more of the evidence. Hence, the feeling of disapprobation may be only a byproduct of and caused by an initial negative judgment in the process of deliberation, but it is epiphenomenal and does not actually play a role in contributing to making the final judgment. After the initial judgment, perhaps one forms several other working judgments, but the judger in this case finally settles on a negative judgment. The problem with Huebner's objection is that if it is true, we should then expect to see a spike in the SCR at times when participants receive unfair offers from a computer. We should expect at least in a few cases that some participants will form working judgments that the offer is unfair such that it would then arouse a negative emotional response as a byproduct even though they later change their judgments to accept the offer. We should also expect to see at times a greater SCR when participants receive offers from humans that are on the borderline of being fair or unfair even though they eventually accept the offer. A working judgment in some of such cases in the middle of deliberation may be that the offer is unfair, which should cause a strong emotional reaction. However, we do not see these spikes. Therefore, Huebner's objection fails.

Crockett et al. (2008) demonstrate that when you diminish the amount of serotonin to the brain via acute tryptophan depletion, this causes subjects to reject more offers in the ultimatum game. As serotonin is responsible for the feeling of happiness or approbation, this shows the importance of the appropriate use of happiness in forming judgments of fairness in normal subjects under normal circumstances. The emotion of happiness in part constitutes our JUSTICE, FAIR, and EQUAL concepts.

Acute tryptophan depletion also decreases cooperation in prisoner's dilemma and public goods games (Wood et al. 2006). In the prisoner's dilemma, there are two partners who cannot communicate with one another and are about to be sentenced for a crime they jointly committed. If they both cooperate and do not testify against each other, then they both get one year in jail. If one of them cooperates and the other defects by testifying against his partner, then the defector will go free, and the cooperator will get three years in jail. If they both defect and testify against each other, then they both get two years in jail. There is a Nash equilibrium, where no player has an incentive to deviate from his or her chosen strategy after considering an opponent's choice. The equilibrium is for both to defect. Yet, if both cooperate, this will lead to a better outcome than if both defect. This study shows that happiness in part constitutes concepts like OBLIGATION TO PARTNERS and LOYALTY.

In the public goods game, subjects secretly decide how many of their own tokens they would like to put in a public pot. The tokens in the pot are then multiplied by a given factor and distributed evenly to all participants. The Nash equilibrium is to contribute nothing despite any contributions from others as this will always be to the advantage of the individual. The above study shows that happiness plays the relevant causal role for normal individuals in normal conditions and thus, in part constitutes moral concepts such as RIGHT ACTION and DISTRIBUTIVE JUSTICE.

Psychopaths also provide support for the importance of emotions in moral deliberation for normal agents. Although I have criticized Prinz's attempt to use psychopaths to support the conative view, I will now provide my own psychopaths-based argument that I believe works. Remember that psychopaths are known to have a severe lack of empathy, which is the capacity to understand and share the feelings of others. There exist strong correlations between disparities in empathic response and having differences in moral judgments. For instance, liberals generally are in favor of a welfare state that helps the poor but conservatives are not, with liberals also showing a much higher capacity for empathy than conservatives (Haidt 2012). Psychopaths have deficits in being able to process distress cues, such as the fear, sadness, and pain of others (Blair et al. 2005). This capacity is housed in the amygdala, and studies have shown that the recruitment of the amygdala is disrupted when psychopaths make moral judgments (Glenn & Raine 2008, Harenski et al. 2010). Moreover, psychopaths have been shown to make different moral judgments as compared to normal subjects in certain regards concerning care harms, such as regarding physically harming others, stealing, and fairness (Glenn et al. 2009, Koenigs et al. 2012, Young et al. 2012). Cima et al. (2010, May 2018) found from experiments on a sample size of 14 psychopaths that perhaps they do not differ from normal subjects in the care harm moral judgments they make, but they just are not motivated to act upon such judgments. However, Koenigs et al. (2012) discovered that when increasing the sample size and eliminating the lenient criteria Cima et al. relied upon to classify a subject as a psychopath, Cima et al.'s data was not replicated. Psychopaths do make different judgments from normal subjects on care harm issues on trolley-like dilemmas as they make more consequentialist judgments compared to the folk, which mirrors the consequentialist leanings certain other agents with blunted emotions have, like FTD and VMPFC patients. Given that (1) psychopaths have severe deficits in empathy, (2) differences in empathic response is correlated with differences in moral decision-making, (3) activation in the amygdala is strongly correlated with making care harm moral judgments in normal subjects (Heekeren et al. 2003, Greene et al. 2004), and (4) the recruitment of the amygdala that houses empathic response is disrupted when making care harm moral judgments in psychopaths, we may draw an inference to the best explanation that it is likely that the ability to understand and feel the emotions of pain and distress of others at least in part plays the appropriate causal role in many cases of care harm moral decision-making in normal subjects. The evidence that the recruitment of the amygdala is disrupted for care harm judgment-making is a key piece for allowing a causal inference between psychopaths' emotional deficits and their anomalous moral judgment-making – a piece that is missing from Prinz's discussion of psychopaths. The appropriate influence of emotions is at least in part why normal subjects generally make different care harm judgments as compared to psychopaths. Here, I leave open the possibility that other mental deficiencies may also contribute to psychopaths' aberrant decision-making. However, it is at least the case that having deficiencies in empathy significantly impact psychopaths' moral judgment-making for care harms, which demonstrates the importance of feeling empathy for normal subjects when forming care harm moral judgments. Tying this now in with the functionalist metaphysics of concepts, the above supports the conative theory of moral concepts.

Given all the above appropriate causal explanatory evidence of the appropriate use of emotions by default in regard to a variety of different moral concepts and a robust correlation between moral judgments and activation in emotion regions of the brain in normal subjects for a wide variety of moral judgments that are deontological, folk consequentialist, high conflict, low conflict, etc., we are now justified in extrapolating a broad induction concluding that emotions generally at least in part appropriately influence moral categorization judgments by default. Hence, based on my functionalist metaphysics I established that allows for using causal evidence to draw constitution claims on moral concepts, the conative theory of moral concepts generally applies to moral concepts and is at least in part needed to explain the moral categorization desiderata. At many, if not at all times, emotions appropriately realize the causal role of moral concepts of influencing and causally explaining decision-making. Furthermore, given the above robust evidence for the wide use of emotions, we may infer that even if some moral judgments do not express an emotion, such judgments generally express a sentiment or disposition to feel an emotion especially in agents that do not have blunted affect. The viability of the conative view is a general claim about the human condition that allows for exceptions. Although many have failed in trying to empirically prove that moral judgments express sentiments and emotions in philosophy and psychology, I have provided novel arguments that finally empirically confirm this thesis.

One may object that although emotions may be used by default in making many moral judgments, there are certain situations in psychologically normal humans in which they may not. For instance, when asked what is morally right and wrong, a Christian may dispassionately read the ten commandments straight from the Bible. Also, the Christian at the dinner table may dispassionately claim that one should not harm strangers. Recall from the previous chapter that frontotemporal dementia and VMPFC patients at times make the same judgments as normal subjects. This provided evidence for the theory view, and emotions may not be activated in normal subjects for such cases. Hence, since conative states seemingly may not be used in all cases to make moral judgments, they do not in any way constitute one's MORAL concept. However, the broad robust evidence for the emotion theory shows that most, if not all, moral judgments express emotions even when we're not consciously aware of it. Moreover, even if no conative states are so elicited, recall from above that it has been found in the concepts literature that concepts can be constituted by a variety of different kinds of psychological structures. A relevant mental state can be used by default at many times individually or conjointly with other concept constituents in cognition depending upon the situation, although I will argue in the final section of this chapter that non-cognitive conative states must always be accompanied by a moral cognitive state in moral cognition. Moreover, there can be contexts where a particular concept constituent is not used at all. Remember that concepts and their constituents are functionally defined in order to help causally explain acts like categorization once subjects are given a relevant functional task to perform. When we categorize and make decisions, experiments have shown that different contexts can bring to bear different kinds of mental states in what influences us to make a decision. Due to this context-dependent complexity of decision-making and given that concept constituents have the function of playing a causal explanatory role in how we make decisions, I have claimed and have had to claim that our moral concepts are constituted by a variety of different kinds of structures. Hence, that a conative state may not be used in all cases to make moral judgments is not an objection against my pluralistic theory of moral concepts, but rather, given the complex contextual nature of decision-making, it may be the case that it is not always so used. However, since conative states have been found to impact moral judgments in a wide variety of cases by default in studies that pass the possible mental error test and there always has been found to be a correlation between moral decision-making and activation in emotional regions of the brain in neuroimaging tests for normal subjects, sentiments and emotions generally constitute our moral concepts. To claim otherwise would be to posit a theory of moral concepts that is severely lacking in explanatory power and predictive success regarding the categorization desideratum. Moreover, given the frequency of the use of emotions, we may infer that people generally are disposed to feel emotions if there are cases where no active conative state is being expressed by a judgment. For instance, the Christian who reads off the ten commandments is disposed to feel anger at times when forming the relevant judgment if someone were to break one of the ten commandments. This disposition will be manifested in the right circumstance to impact judgment-making for this particular agent, such as if her husband were to cheat on her. Her disposition to feel disapprobation concerning harming strangers will be manifested to appropriately influence judgment if faced with the situation of potentially pushing a stranger off a footbridge in order to save five lives.

8.3 The Evolutionary Argument from Chimpanzees and Bonobos

Another new and independent argument for the conative theory is what I shall call *the argument from chimpanzees and bonobos.* The first step of this argument that concludes that the conative view is viable for human moral concepts is to show that emotions at least in part influence cooperative judgments in chimpanzees and bonobos. As previously mentioned, chimpanzees and bonobos provide a window into examining the traits of our evolutionary ancestors given our common ancestor with them only 5–7 million years ago, they have 99% of our DNA, and they have experienced relatively less or little selection pressures to change since the times of our common ancestors. Ethologists like de Waal who study animal behavior under natural or more natural living conditions rather than in a laboratory largely attribute emotions as influencing chimpanzee and bonobos' normative judgments. However, we have seen that common observation is insufficient for making psychological causal claims for human beings. Hence, it still could be the case that emotions are post hoc and only come after the judgment is made for chimpanzees and bonobos. Relevant ethology studies only demonstrate at best correlation between emotions and cooperative decision-making in our close cousins.

Some experimental psychology studies also fail to draw relevant causal claims in non-human primates. For instance, Melis et al. (2006) ran tests on chimpanzees and bonobos. They each respectively need to work in pairs with conspecifics in order to reach a fruit object from a machine, where it is not possible for an individual to get the food alone. Bonobos are more prosocial in that they share food more regularly than chimpanzees. Even though the chimpanzees had previous experience obtaining food from the mechanism and bonobos did not, bonobos were overall more successful in working cooperatively to obtain the food. Chimpanzees were more successful when they were paired with a chimp that they cofed with previously. However, chimp dyads in which there was a dominant in the pair who might monopolize the food were much less likely to cooperate even though they knew they had to work together to get the food.[3] The experimenters then contend that this shows that prosocial emotions influence cooperation in chimpanzees and bonobos. However, this is much too quick. Chimpanzees could have cognitive rules, such as COOPERATE WITH FRIENDS BUT NOT WITH DOMINANTS, while bonobos have the represented rule COOPERATE WITH WHOEVER YOU CAN TO GET FOOD. These can equally explain the phenomena for both species. Melis et al. have failed to show that emotions influence decision-making in such primates.

Chimps and bonobos do have degrees of rational cognitive processing, such as of trying to satisfy long-term self-interests. For instance, chimps can form strategic political alliances of which it may take months of dedication before any benefits from the coalition can be harvested (de Waal 1982). For instance, a clever chimpanzee past his prime can play the puppet master forming an alliance with a younger chimpanzee in his physical prime to take over power from the current alpha male. This allows the older chimp to have greater access to sex, be the de facto leader of the group, take charge of resolving disputes, and even receive more acknowledgments of submission from group members as compared with his younger counterpart who becomes the de jure alpha. Moreover, as attaining leadership status requires a general acceptance from the community since chimpanzees actively partake in conflicts between competing males, the chimp deftly can campaign and curry favor in his quest for power through a variety of one-on-one tit-for-tat exchanges with group members, outcompeting his rival in such interactions. Hence, cognitive rational processes at least in part could be influencing chimpanzee decision-making, and more definitive evidence of the influence of emotions in our cousins is needed.

However, there are more promising experiments and lines of reasoning for the influence of emotions. For example, in studying the behavior of chimpanzees, Bard et al. (2014) found that emotions are significant and unique predictors of cooperation and social cognition in chimpanzees, and this is so even when taking into consideration various possible cognitive reasoning processes as well. Also, studies have shown that when chimpanzees (Fraser et al. 2008) and bonobos (Palagi & Norscia 2013) console a fellow group member, it can help reduce anxiety and reduce the likelihood of further group aggression on the member who was attacked. It has been found at least for bonobos that the likelihood of displaying consolation behavior is greatest for one's kin, then friends, and then acquaintances. This gradient corresponds with the gradient of the degree of empathy bonobos have, where they tend to have the greatest amount of empathy for their kin, then friends, then acquaintances. Moreover, bonobos have a like gradient in yawn contagion (Demuru & Palagi 2012). They are more likely to yawn when their kin and close friends do as compared to acquaintances and strangers. Bonobos have an empathy gradient that matches the degree of probability for consoling and having yawn contagions with others. It is likely that empathy causally influences consoling behavior and yawn contagion given how the gradients match and since such an explanation is able to unify both phenomena under a single and simple explanation. It has unification power and simplicity. On the other hand, it appears unlikely that there is a single and simple cognitive principle that can explain both the consoling and disparate yawn contagion behavior. Also, empathy and cooperation psychologically develop in tandem in bonobos (Palagi & Norscia 2013). Therefore, via inference to the best explanation, empathy is likely what at least in part causally influences bonobos to console others. In addition, emotion-based algorithms and models, where emotions influence cognition, can help explain the computational processes of cooperative decision-making in our evolutionary history (Loch et al. 2006). The above causal evidence, coupled with the robust correlational data from ethology that affect co-occurs with cooperative decision-making, provides a good case that emotions at least in part influence chimpanzee and bonobo cooperative judgment-making.

If this is right that our cousins at least in part are influenced by emotions for acts of cooperation and consoling each other, then the next step in the argument from chimpanzees and bonobos is to contend that this likely means human cooperation at least in part is appropriately influenced by emotions as well. To note, interpersonal moral decision-making is largely a subset of cooperative decision-making. Also, humans may have cooperative moral obligations, such as to a spouse, to console and help those who have experienced a traumatic event.

If our cousins at least in part are relevantly influenced by emotions for cooperation, then we at least in part should be as well broadly for cooperation because we have a shared phylogeny and evolutionary descent. If closely related species act similarly, such as to cooperate, then we should expect the underlying psychological mechanisms that bring about cooperation to be similar. If not, then there would be two divergent evolutionary processes that led to chimpanzee and bonobo cooperation versus human cooperation. Two divergent evolutionary processes would have led to convergence across species in exemplifying many similar acts of cooperation, such as in political power coalitions, defending a community's boundaries, consoling those who are suffering, helping the sick, sharing food, cooperative hunting, helping those in distress, etc. However, this is highly implausible and uneconomic given that Homo sapiens and our cousins have been separated by only a few million years of separate evolution. Human cooperative decision-making being at least in part influenced by emotions is the evolutionary parsimonious explanation. Emotions at least in part influence chimpanzee and bonobo cooperative decision-making, so it is very likely that emotions, such as empathy, care, and concern, at least in part influence human cooperative decision-making. No doubt, given the unparalleled complexity of human cooperation and human moral decision-making, it is likely that several or many adaptations have been added to human cognition to account for this complexity.[4] However, this does not mean that the emotional undergirding of cooperative decision-making has disappeared in Homo sapiens. For, once again, it is highly unlikely in the short amount of evolutionary time since our common ancestors that wholly distinct non-emotional cognitive processes evolved in humans that led to cooperative behavior that includes matching much of the cooperative practices of chimpanzees and bonobos, such as those listed above.

Cognitive evolution in cooperative decision-making largely works with the ancient affective infrastructure rather than wholly supplanting it with something brand new. It builds on top of pre-existing emotional processes that already have successfully helped lead to cooperation in ancestral species, adding greater cognitive sophistication. The cognitive processes underwriting human, chimp, and bonobo cooperative decision-making are homologous and are derived from a shared ancestry. When an adult human drops a stick on the ground and tries to retrieve it, both the chimp and a human child will help by picking it up to give it back. Neuroanatomical data shows that the brain evolved with older and simpler networks generally being preserved, extended, and combined with newer capacities (Sporns & Kötter 2004, Sterelny 2012). It is very unlikely that complex structures are produced entirely anew. Emotional processes at least in part impacting our ancestor's cooperative practices means that it is likely that affective processes, like feelings of trust, empathy, and friendship, are at least in part impacting us in our cooperative decision-making, including moral decision-making, such as when one decides that one ought to console one's spouse. This non-deductive evolutionary argument shows that emotions generally at least in part appropriately influence our moral decision-making by default. Hence, given the functional identification of moral concepts, the argument from chimpanzees and bonobos demonstrates that our moral judgments at least in part express emotions or sentiments.

8.4 Sense and Concept Acquisition Desiderata for the Conative View

Conative-based moral concepts can at least in part account for the sense of moral concepts. Moreover, the conative view can account for how we may understand two compound concepts differently even though they are co-referential. Let us return to our example where I do not know that my good friend is a sensible knave because he is so sensible, but others have warned me that I have a sensible knave in my life without telling me who it is. In this case, I have a positive feeling of approbation in part constitute MY GOOD FRIEND concept. I have a negative feeling of disapprobation in part constitute my THE SENSIBLE KNAVE IN MY LIFE concept. Although other kinds of structures also can play a role in accounting for the different senses of the concepts, such conative constituents of my moral concepts can in part account for my different emotive senses I have for the two compound concepts even though both compounds are co-referential.

For the concept acquisition desideratum, many in the emotions literature understand at least the basic emotions, such as anger and happiness, to be innate.[5] Basic emotions are evolved emotions that do not contain other emotions as parts. Some reasons for why certain emotions are understood to be innate are that there are universal facial expressions for certain emotions found even in isolated cultures (Darwin 1872/1998, Ekman & Friesen 1971). It is extremely unlikely that these isolated communities just happened to invent the same emotional facial expressions as those in the West. The neural circuitry of emotions in humans also can be found in the most primitive mammals, and this circuitry plays the same dedicated role of responding to emotionally significant stimuli (LeDoux 1996). This suggests that certain emotions found in humans stem from ancestral species deep into our evolutionary history. If certain emotions are innate, then this means there is at least a partial domain-general nativist element associated with moral concept acquisition.

Moreover, even if certain emotions are innate, it is important to note that culture at many times still plays a significant role in determining when one feels a particular emotion or conative state even as early as at the age of one (Hornick & Gunnar 1988, Forman et al. 2004). For instance, culture can create unique syndromes for when one feels anxiety and fear. On the Indian subcontinent, semen is viewed as containing a man's energy. There is extreme semen loss anxiety unique to this subcontinent. Moreover, in another case, there was fear that shaking a foreigner's hand will make one's penis melt in Sudan in the early 2000s and anxiety of becoming a zombie in Haitian voodoo cultures.

For ethics, feelings and sentiments of approbation versus disapprobation for an act vary in accordance with the great cultural variability of ethics. The recent experimental findings showing the cultural variability of emotional reactions should be of no great surprise as even in antiquity, philosophers like Aristotle observed how our emotional makeup can be profoundly shaped by culture and habit. Hence, he held that moral education and training are vital in setting up our emotional makeup for proper moral motivation. As culture plays a significant role in moral concept acquisition, the conative theory of moral concepts can accommodate this cultural acquisition since the intuitive gut feeling of many moral emotions and other conative states that can be the basis of our moral intuitions is significantly in part shaped by cultural conditioning.

As possible examples, Westerners tend to feel moral disgust at the notion of cousin-marriage, but many members of certain societies today, such as in Sub-Saharan Africa, South Asia, the Middle East, and in the past, such as in Ancient Athens, do or did not.[6] While Westerners may tend to feel disapprobation at arranged marriages, such disapprobation is not found in many people in societies that have relevant arranged marriages as a cultural practice, such as in parts of India, China, and Africa. General Western moral disapprobation at polygamy, where a man can have many wives, and polyandry, where a woman can have many husbands, is generally not felt in polygamous and polyandrous societies as such marriage arrangements are cultural norms. In fact, most communities in the world across time are not monogamous when considering that for most of our existence we have lived in hunter–gatherer societies, and the recent spread of monogamy is an aberration in world history. Eskimos generally look with approbation on lending out one's wife to a guest overnight as a display of hospitality, while most in industrialized Western society do not. Fundamental Islamic societies generally feel moral disgust at homosexual marriages, while in a recent swift shift in cultural sentiments, many people in the West do not. Many of those in fundamental Islamic societies have a severe con-attitude toward pornography and depicting women as sex objects as it is seen by them as a mark of social degradation, but many in the West do not. For much of the history of Christian societies, many members felt moral anger at a female for having premarital sex. For instance, the Bible states that women who are not found to be virgins on their wedding night must be burned at the stake (Deut 22:13–21). However, as a relatively recent development, such feelings of anger for such situations in significant part have waned in contemporary industrialized Western Christian cultures. Divorces and breaking a marriage vow or promise that was made before the eyes of God and the community in Western Christian societies once tended to elicit extreme moral disapprobation and at times shunning, but such feelings for breaking such promises have significantly subsided, if not evaporated, in recent times. Moral anger and disgust is largely felt in contemporary Western society at men having sex with male adolescents. In Ancient Greece, the foundation of Western civilization, as well as for the Keraki of new Guinea, sentiments generally were or are different as such practices were or are commonplace, respectively.

8.5 The Conative – Prototype/Exemplar/Theory Chain Arguments

In this chapter, I have shown how the conative theory, like the prototype, exemplar, and theory views, can help account for the categorization, sense, and concept acquisition desiderata. In the next chapter, I will show how this concept theory along with the prototype, exemplar, and theory views can handle the remaining two desiderata of concept combination and induction. All in all, I will conclude that my pluralistic theory of moral concepts best explains the desiderata. Therefore, it's true. However, before moving on to this, I now will provide three chain arguments that if the conative theory is viable, then the prototype, exemplar, and/or theory views are viable. This contention is in part justified since it will be based on the experimentally established viability of the conative view specifically on moral concepts. I will show how we can infer the viability of the prototype, exemplar, and/or theory views of moral concepts from the conative theory.

8.5.1 First Chain Argument

The first argument is that even though conative states are used at many times in moral cognition, they require the joint use of cognitive representations of features of the situation at hand to trigger what conative state should be elicited, such as of approbation or disapprobation. Representations of features of moral situations or persons, such as TAKES A PRODUCT WITHOUT PAYING, MAXIMIZES HAPPINESS, and SAVING THE LIFE OF A LOVED ONE, can be stored as moral prototypes, theories, or as constituents of exemplars. Such representations may refer to non-normative descriptions or possibly even moral properties, such as *happiness.* They are taken to be morally relevant rather than morally irrelevant features that can influence a moral decision or even be a mitigating factor in lessening blame. If whether I feel anger or gratitude on a moral case is not completely random in the sense that it is based on no context whatsoever but rather is influenced by certain morally relevant features of the situation, then conative states respond to cognitive representations of morally relevant contextual features in order to be elicited. These representations of *morally* relevant features rather than irrelevant ones are and should be stored in *moral* concepts. It is not the case that I feel anger when a stranger takes drugs from a pharmacy without paying and then feel joy at some later date because the same event occurs with all else being held equal. What emotions influence our decision-making are not random but are responsive to certain contextual features of the situations we find ourselves in. In other words, with the proper use of conative states, cognitive representations of moral contextual features also are at work in the appropriate way at the front end of the categorization process triggering the relevant conative state. Notice that this holds both for so-called thin and thick concepts that have a conative normative component. There is also a cognitive descriptive component for both of such concepts since such cognitive representations help realize the concept's causal role of leading to moral categorization judgments. Thus, this, in effect, eliminates the traditional distinction held by most between thin and thick concepts because both kinds of moral concepts have descriptive and normative components. Furthermore, recall in the fourth chapter that I also argued against the distinction between thin and thick concepts based on contravening experimental evidence from prototype studies sufficiently showing that thin concepts have both descriptive and normative components. In the process of moral categorization, we at many times take into account morally relevant features of the situation in helping shape our decisions. I take it that this is not an outrageous claim.

Prinz (2007) contends that we may use reasoning to non-morally categorize an act as stealing. For instance, the fact that I saw a person take someone else's wallet without permission is a factor that leads me to classify the act as stealing. STEALING is then tokened in working memory. However, when next morally judging that this stealing is wrong, one is only influenced by sentiments or emotions. For Prinz, cognitive states play no role in judging that stealing is wrong. Rather, we have a sentiment such as of anger that is triggered by STEALING such that one may judge that stealing is wrong. Cognitive representations like TAKING WITHOUT PERMISSION help us realize that an act is one of stealing, but then it's only anger that influences one's moral categorization of this act as being wrong.

However, as the story goes, once we finish categorizing the act as one of stealing, which is the non-moral categorization, we then intend to draw a moral judgment on the matter, which is the moral categorization phase. Yet, when STEALING triggers anger for Prinz, this occurs after the non-moral categorization has already been made. One categorizes the act as being an instance of stealing, and *then* STEALING causes one to feel anger. In other words, Prinz fails to realize that this emotional triggering from STEALING occurs during the moral deliberation stage. Hence, against Prinz, cognitive representations of morally relevant contextual features, such as STEALING, do play the appropriate causal role during the moral categorization process. This also fits neatly with the idea that since moral emotions are not triggered based on no context whatsoever, there must be a morally relevant context to the situation that elicits my moral emotion of anger earlier in the moral decision-making process. This morally relevant rather than irrelevant feature is that of stealing, and so STEALING plays an appropriate causal role at the beginning of the moral categorization process. Hence, STEALING in part constitutes my so-called thin compound concept WRONG ACTION. Cognitive representations of moral contextual features are where they belong, stored in moral concepts.

In a variant of our example, let us say that the stranger is stealing drugs he cannot afford because he lost his job to a recession, where such medicine is required to save his wife's life. In moral deliberation when presented with this case, the prototype STEALING in my WRONG ACTION concept becomes activated in working memory to then trigger anger rather than gratitude or awe. Meanwhile, the equally weighted prototype SAVING THE LIFE OF A LOVED ONE is tokened in my RIGHT ACTION concept to elicit compassion rather than disgust or fear. That one can feel both emotions in deliberation, perhaps at different stages of the thought process, is no more problematic than analogously doing so in regard to a love and hate relationship. Both prototypes carry equal weight, but since my anger carries greater weight for me than compassion, I judge that the stranger's act is wrong. The conative state can be a compounding factor among others that together carry the requisite force to lead to the corresponding judgment.

To note, at times compounding factors are not necessary for making the judgment since the threshold for making a judgment has already been passed. For instance, my DOG concept may be constituted by BARKS, PLAYS FETCH, WAGS ITS TAIL, HAS FOUR LEGS, etc. These are prototypes that are not necessary and sufficient conditions for categorization. A dog I see may satisfy all the features, but let us say that it really only needed to satisfy the first three in order to cross the similarity threshold such that I classify it as a dog. HAS FOUR LEGS is superfluous in this instance, but it still contributes to a higher similarity score. In this respect, it still plays a causal role that can have a significant impact on decision-making. For, due to a higher score, I categorize the object as being a more typical dog as compared to other dogs with a lower score. HAS FOUR LEGS still constitutes my DOG concept. Also, it may play a greater and decisive role in different contexts of dog categorizations, such as when presented with a dog that does not play fetch. Likewise, for moral concepts, sometimes certain cognitive or conative states may be superfluous, but they still add compounding weight to the categorization process leading to a higher typicality judgment of moral rightness or wrongness, perhaps on a Likert scale, and may play a more important role in categorization in other contexts that lack certain features.

In summary, since the elicitation of particular conative states in moral deliberation is not wholly random such that no context at all is taken into consideration, this means that representations of contextual features relevant to moral decision-making are also properly used in the moral categorization process along with the conative state. This provides evidence for the moral prototype, exemplar, and/or theory views.

8.5.2 Second Chain Argument

Second, even though conative states may be appropriately used at many times in moral cognition, a cognitive *moral* representation must also conjointly play a causal role in deliberation with the conative state. In the first chain argument, I showed that moral concepts must be constituted by descriptive representations and perhaps moral cognitive ones if moral concepts are constituted by conative states. Notice that I am contending more firmly here in this second chain argument that if a moral judgment expresses a non-cognitive conative state, it must also express a moral normative cognitive state as well.

When the moral concept in a judgment expresses a conative state, a cognitive moral representation also must be contained in the judgment in order to make a decision a moral one in one's understanding rather than a non-moral one. This also is required in order to make an emotion a moral emotion rather than a non-moral one in one's understanding. Conative states can be expressed in aesthetic, legal, pragmatic, self-interested, conventional, and other normative contexts, such as when I get angry at my favorite sports team for losing and not playing well. I may express anger when judging that an act is legally wrong. Your dog may become angry at your assailant, but your dog is not understanding such anger to be moral anger and to be a distinctly moral judgment. A chimpanzee can express anger at a political rival, but the chimp is not understanding it to be a moral judgment in virtue of expressing such anger. We had the capacity to feel emotions like anger before we had our first moral thoughts (Sterelny 2012). Therefore, if my distinctly moral judgment just is, for instance, an emotional expression of anger with no moral cognitive representations constituting the moral judgment, then it is psychologically unclear that I understand my judgment in-and-of-itself to be a moral one. For, this exact same feeling of anger also constitutes so many non-moral judgments and states of mind.

Many, such as Gibbard (1991) and Simon Blackburn (1998),[7] who espouse the conative theory of concepts, tout that conative states expressed by moral judgments account for the moral normativity or evaluative component of the judgments. However, if conative states account for some kind of normativity, we still do not know what kind of normative judgment is at hand in one's understanding. A non-cognitive conative property by itself cannot account for whether the judgment is understood to contain moral normativity, legal normativity, aesthetic normativity, pragmatic normativity, normativity about how well a sports team is doing, etc. In order to make a judgment a moral one in one's mind, the judgment must at least be in part constituted by a cognitive mental state, such as MORALLY OUGHT, that is distinctly morally normative, not generically normative, in order to properly indicate that one understands the judgment *in-and-of-itself* to be a moral one. One cannot make such a moral judgment without it. After all, we are presuming in this case that one unequivocally understands oneself to have in mind a *moral* judgment.[8] We are not looking here for an abstracted principled distinction between moral and conventional judgments as was entertained in the previous chapter, but rather, we are looking for an account of what concept constituents must be in an individual's mind to account for the fact that the agent understands herself to be making a distinctly moral judgment.

One may respond with a causal theory of reference that so long as a natural moral property causally influences judgment, then the relevant concept refers to the moral property. This makes the relevant concept a moral concept given its extension, and one need not have a cognitive moral constituent to make one's concept and judgment a moral one in one's understanding. However, this presumes the causal theory of reference for moral concepts in all cases. Yet, in a later chapter when we turn to the semantic project, I will demonstrate that this theory of reference does not apply to moral concepts at all times. Second, even if the causal theory of reference applies in all cases, it cannot always account for how in one's understanding, one understands one's judgment specifically to be a moral one. There must be something in the sense of one's concept to account for this understanding since one may not understand that there is a causal connection between one's moral concepts and the relevant natural property. The causal theory of reference does not require that one have awareness of the causal connection or of even the referent of one's concept. So long as the causal connection exists even without one's awareness, it determines reference. Hence, a cognitive moral component is needed for one's moral concepts to explain why one understands or is aware that one's judgment distinctly is a moral judgment. Recall that concept constituents are responsible for the human understanding and how we understand the world. When morally judging THIS IS WRONG, there must be a personal internal psychological explanation and a mental state that constitutes the judgment that accounts for the fact that I mentally and personally understand my judgment to be one of moral wrongness rather than some other notion of wrongness. There must be a proper account of the sense of the judgment that makes it a moral one. Concerning human understanding, the sense desideratum needs to be satisfied. However, the presence of a conative property alone cannot accomplish this because the exact same feeling of this conative property constitutes so many other normative judgments that are not moral ones. In such a case, a conative property still is an important part of the moral judgment and it in part does play the functional role, but it must work in harmony with a moral cognitive component to account for the fact that one understands the judgment to be a moral one.

Furthermore, non-normative descriptive cognitive states that may in part constitute a moral judgment cannot distinctly account for the moral normativity of the judgment. For, such states are not even normative ones, and they also can constitute non-normative judgments and concepts.[9] Thus, non-normative cognitive constituents are not distinct indicators of moral normativity.

8.5.3 Third Chain Argument

The third chain-argument is that conative states are not fine-grained enough to account for how certain moral concepts are differentially used. Particular moral concepts may be constituted by the same conative states, but these conative states alone cannot account for why such concepts individually each are used at times in different circumstances. There is a plethora of different moral concepts that each can apply in unique circumstances – such as HONEST, KIND, PATIENT, BENEFICIENT, BRAVE, HUMBLE, CARING, LOVING, JUST, GOOD, RIGHTEOUS, HONORABLE, etc. – and not enough disparate conative states to differentially match them on a one-to-one basis. For instance, I may express the same feelings of pride for my judgments that ALLOWING FOR EQUAL CIVIL RIGHTS FOR HOMOSEXUALS IN MY COUNTRY IS FAIR and MY SON'S DONATION TO THE POOR IS BENEFICENT. However, the moral concepts of FAIR and BENEFICENT are different concepts that can apply to disparate situations. They both are constituted by the same feelings, but these feelings alone cannot account for why I categorize certain acts as being fair rather than beneficent and why I classify other acts as being beneficent rather than fair. If these two concepts are only constituted by the same feelings, then this will not explain differences in the application of such concepts.

The concepts in part must be constituted by different mental states, like cognitive states, in order to causally explain why I use such concepts in disparate circumstances. For instance, my FAIR concept in part may be constituted by TREATING OTHERS THE SAME while my BENEFICENT concept is not. Meanwhile, my BENEFICENT rather than FAIR concept in part is constituted by BEING VERY GENEROUS WITH ONE'S MONEY. In this fashion one can get around the problem that conative states are not fine-grained enough to account for fine-grained differences in the application of numerous moral concepts. The relevant moral concepts are used in different situations because they at times contain disparate cognitive components which help to trigger their differential use. Hence, to generally account for the phenomena of the differential and fine-grained use of moral concepts in many higher acts of cognition, if moral concepts are constituted by conative states, they are also in part constituted by cognitive ones.

Notes

1 My italics.
2 For instance, Aristotle says that having some financial stability can help fill out a good life, although a life primarily focused on making money and greed is not a good life.
3 Recall that chimps seem to have personal property rights in regard to meat that are not violated by dominants, but this does not hold for non-meat foods.
4 These are not necessarily adaptations for a specifically moral capacity but can be non-moral adaptations, such as to have a more complex theory of mind.
5 There is current debate as to whether anger and disgust constitute the same basic emotion or whether both of them are distinct basic emotions.

6 I am merely attempting to show the possible cultural variability in feeling emotions here. I am not positing a precise causal rather than correlational claim about specific emotions influencing the relevant judgments, as this would require experimental data, although the wide influence of emotions on judgment has already been sufficiently proven above.
7 Once again, I am leaning on Gibbard's WCAF here rather than his later work.
8 Even though what is a moral judgment may be culturally constructed, if this is so, there still are moral judgments as contrasted to conventional ones. It is just that such a distinction is relative to culture.
9 One can determine that such cognitive states constitute moral judgments and concepts rather than non-moral ones by the presence of a cognitive moral representation that also in part constitutes the judgment and concept.

References

Bard, K.A., Bakeman, R., Boysen, S.T., and Leavens, D.A. 2014. "Emotional Engagements Predict and Enhance Social Cognition in Young Chimpanzees." *Developmental Science* 17, 682–696.

Bechara, A., Tranel, D., Damasio, H., and Damasio, A.R. 1996. "Failure to Respond Autonomically to Anticipated Future Outcomes Following Damage to Prefrontal Cortex." *Cerebral Cortex* 6, 215–225.

Blackburn, Simon. 1998. *Ruling Passions.* Oxford: Oxford University Press.

Blair, R., Mitchell, D., and Blair, K. 2005. *Psychopath: Emotion and the Brain.* New York: Wiley-Blackwell.

Cima, M., Tonnaer, F., and Hauser, M.D. 2010. "Psychopaths Know Right From Wrong But Don't Care." *Social Cognitive and Affective Neuroscience* 5, 59–67.

Crockett, M.J., Clark, L., Tabibnia, G., Lieberman, M.D., and Robbins, T.W. 2008. "Serotonin Modulates Behavioral Reactions to Unfairness." *Science* 320, 1739–1739.

Darwin, Charles. 1872/1998. *The Expression of the Emotions in Man and Animals,* 3rd Edition. Ed. by Paul Ekman. New York: Oxford University Press.

Demuru, E. and Palagi, E. 2012. "In Bonobos Yawn Contagion Is Higher among Kin and Friends. *PLoS ONE* 7, e49613.

De Waal, Frans. 1982. *Chimpanzee Politics.* Baltimore: The Johns Hopkins University Press.

Ekman, P. and Friesen, W.V. 1971. "Constants Across Cultures in the Face and Emotion." *Journal of Personality and Social Psychology* 17, 124.

Eslinger, P. and Damasio, A. 1985. "Severe Disturbance of Higher Cognition After Bilateral Frontal Lobe Ablation." *Neurology* 35, 1731–1741.

Forman, D., Askan, N., and Kochanska, D. 2004. "Toddlers' Responsive Imitation Predicts Preschool-age Conscious." *Psychological Science* 15, 699–704.

Fraser, O.N., Stahl, D., and Aureli, F. 2008. "Stress Reduction Through Consolation in Chimpanzees." *Proceedings of the National Academy of Sciences of the United States of America* 105, 8557–8562.

Gerrans, Philip. 2007. "Mental Time Travel, Somatic Markers and Myopia for the Future." *Synthese* 159, 459–474.

Gibbard, Allan. 1991. *Wise Choices, Apt Feelings.* Oxford: Clarendon Press.

Glenn, A.L., Iyer, R., Graham, J., Koleva, S. and Haidt, J. 2009. "Are all types of morality compromised in psychopathy?" *Journal of Personality Disorders* 23(4), 384–398.

Glenn, A. and Raine, A. 2008. "The Neurobiology of Psychopathy." *Psychiatric Clinics of North America* 31, 463–476.

Greene, J., Nystrom, L.E., Engell, A.D., Darley, J.M., and Cohen, J.D. 2004. "The Neural Bases of Cognitive Conflict and Control in Moral Judgment." *Neuron* 44, 387–400.

Haidt, Jonathan. 2012. *The Righteous Mind.* New York: Vintage Books.

Harenski, C.L., Harenski, K.A., Shane, M.S., and Kiehl, K.A. 2010. "Aberrant Neural Processing of Moral Violations in Criminal Psychopaths." *Journal of Abnormal Psychology* 119, 863.

Heekeren, H., Wartenburger, I., Schmidt, H., Schwintowski, H., and Villringeeer, A. 2003. "An fMRI Study of Simple Tthical Decision-making." *Neuroreport* 14, 1215–1219.

Henrich, J. 2000. "Does Culture Matter in Economic Behavior? Ultimatum Game Bargaining among the Machiguenga of the Peruvian Amazon." *The American Economic Review* 90, 973– 979.

Hornick, R. and Gunnar, M.R. 1988. "A Descriptive Analysis of Infant Social Referencing." *Child Development* 59, 626–634.

Huebner, Bryce. 2015. "Do Emotions Play a Constitutive Role in Moral Cognition?" *Topoi* 34, 427–440.

Keil, F., Smith, W., Simons, D., and Levin, D. 1998. "Two Dogmas of Conceptual Empiricism: Implications for Hybrid Models of the Structure of Knowledge." *Cognition* 65, 103–135.

Koenigs, M., Kruepke, M., Zeier, J., and Newman, J.P. 2012. "Utilitarian Moral Judgment in Psychopathy." *Social Cognitive and Affective Neuroscience* 7, 708–714.

LeDoux, J. E. 1996. *The Emotional Brain.* New York: Simon and Schuster.

Linquist, Stefan and Bartol, Jordan. 2013. "Two Myths About Somatic Markers." *British Journal for the Philosophy of Science* 64, 455–484.

Loch, C.H., Galunic, D.C., and Schneider, S. 2006. "Balancing Cooperation and Competition in Human Groups: The Role of Emotional Algorithms and Evolution." *Managerial and Decision Economics* 27, 217–233.

May, Joshua. 2018. *Regard for Reason in the Moral Mind.* Oxford: Oxford University Press.

Melis, A., Hare, B., and Tomasello, M. 2006. "Engineering Chimpanzee Cooperation: Social Tolerance Constrains Cooperation." *Animal Behavior* 72, 275–286.

Mendez, Mario. 2010. "The Unique Predisposition to Criminal Violations in Frontotemporal Dementia." *The Journal of the American Academy of Psychiatry and the Law* 38, 318–323.

Palagi, Elisabetta and Norscia, Ivan. 2013. "Bonobos Protect and Console Friends and Kin." *PLOS One* 8, e79290.

Park, John. 2013. "Theories of Moral Concepts." In *Truth Matters.* Ed. by L. Zuidervaart, A. Carr, M. Klaassen, and R. Shuker. Montreal, Quebec: McGill-Queens University Press, 211–224.

Park, John. 2018. "The Emotion Theory of Concepts." *Journal of Consciousness Studies* 25, 162–180.

Pillutla, M. and Murnighan, J. 1996. "Unfairness, Anger, and Spite: Emotional Rejections of Ultimatum Offers." *Organizational Behavior and Human Decision Processes* 68, 208–224.

Prinz, Jesse. 2007. *The Emotional Construction of Morals.* Oxford: Oxford University Press.

Roskies, Adina. 2003. "Are Ethical Judgments Intrinsically Motivational? Lesson from 'Acquired Sociopathy.'" *Philosophical Psychology* 16, 51–66.

Sanfey, A., Rillig, J., Aronson, J., Nystrom, L., and Cohen, J. 2003. "The Neural Basis of Economic Decision-making in the Ultimatum Game." *Science* 300, 1755–1758.

Sporns, O. and Kötter, R. 2004. "Motifs in Brain Networks." *PLoS Biology* 2, e369.

Sterelny, Kim. 2012. *The Evolved Apprentice: How Evolution Made Humans Unique.* Cambridge, MA: The MIT Press.

van't Wout, M., Kahn, R., Sanfey, A., and Aleman, A. 2006. "Affective State and Decision-making in the Ultimatum Game." *Experimental Brain Resonance* 169, 564–568.

Wood, R.M., Rilling, J.K., Sanfey, A.G., Bhagwagar, Z., and Rogers, R.D. 2006. "Effects of Tryptophan Depletion on the Performance of an Iterated Prisoner's Dilemma Game in Healthy Adults." *Neuropsychopharmacology* 31, 1075–1084.

Young, L., Koenigs, M., Kruepke, M., and Newman, J.P. 2012. "Psychopathy Increases Perceived Moral Permissibility of Accidents." *Journal of Abnormal Psychology* 121, 659.

9 Induction and Concept Combination

Thus far, I have demonstrated how the prototype, exemplar, theory, and conative views satisfy the categorization, sense, and concept acquisition desiderata. In this chapter, we will tie up the loose ends to my theory of moral concepts by examining these four views in light of the remaining induction and concept combination desiderata. Next, Jerry Fodor's concept combination objections will be addressed. Fodor provides several objections primarily against the prototype theory that prototypes do not combine such that they can account for compound thoughts. I will attempt to address Fodor's objections by relying on my tetrad view of moral concepts. I finally conclude that my new pluralistic theory of moral mental representations best explains the desiderata of a theory of moral concepts.

9.1 Induction

Recall from the first chapter that the induction desideratum is where theories of concepts apparently must have a structure that allows and can explain how we make inductive inferences about the world. There are many different kinds of induction such as philosophical induction and category induction. In logic, an inductive inference is one in which the conclusion follows from true premises with probability, not necessity. As induction is a higher cognitive competence that is reliant on concepts, an ability to account for this desideratum appears to be important for any theory. Philosophical induction is where one draws a general conclusion about a class based on particular information from a subset of the class. An example of this in category-based language is drawing the conclusion that all objects within the category *crows* are black based on previous limited experiences with particular instances of objects that fall under this class. What is meant by "category induction" in the concepts literature is the broadening of information from an already known *given* category to a known but different or *target* category. This differs from philosophical induction in that the target category is not a superordinate of the given category, and vice versa. In other words, the target category is not taken to have the given class as a subset category in the way polar bears are a subset of bears. Also, the target category is not a subset of the given category. An example of this kind of induction is where if I am told that those classified under *humble person* have the property of being soft spoken, then I may induce that those under the target class *honest person* also have this property.

To the best of my knowledge, there are no studies on moral concepts specifically attempting to account for the induction desideratum. Even though this is the case, we may still mount enough evidence to infer that the prototype, exemplar, and theory views are most likely responsible in the specified way for many instances of induction. By drawing on previously discussed moral categorization studies as well as on induction test results taken from the standard concrete concepts literature, we may infer that the above views satisfy the induction desideratum for theories of moral concepts.

In the standard concrete concepts domain, similarity-based accounts have been shown to appropriately influence inductive inferences in many instances (Rips 1975, Osherson et al. 1990). In Lance Rips' (1975) classic induction studies, he used blank predicates. Blank predicates are predicates that subjects most likely will be unfamiliar with, attributes that most people will not have any strong feelings about, or qualities that are made up. Using blank predicates, such as 'sesamoid bones,' allows experimenters to test for induction without any influence of previous knowledge about the attribute. In one test, participants were asked how strong the induction is that if robins have sesamoid bones, then all birds have sesamoid bones. Another proposed induction was that if penguins have sesamoid bones then all birds have sesamoid bones. Rips found that an induction can be considered to be stronger to the extent that the given category is judged to be more similar to the target category. Since the given category of robins is more similar to the target category of birds than penguins are to birds, subjects judged that the induction from robins to birds is stronger than the induction from penguins to birds. Moreover, another factor that can influence induction in the appropriate way is typicality. If the given category is a more typical member of the target category as compared to a different given category, then this will lead to a stronger inductive inference. Since robins are more typical birds than penguins, the induction involving robins is stronger than that which involves penguins. Insofar as prototypes and exemplars can account for similarity and typicality effects, this study suggests that similarity-based views can be at work in the specified way in induction.

While demonstrating that similarity plays a role in inductions, Osherson and company (1990) have further shown that *coverage* also can appropriately influence induction judgments. The notion of coverage is dependent on how well the objects in the premises cover the smallest category that includes all the items in the induction problem. If there is a greater level of coverage of the smallest inclusive category, then the induction will be perceived to be stronger. Take for example:

(1) Foxes have sesamoid bones.
Pigs have sesamoid bones
Gorillas have sesamoid bones
(2) Foxes have sesamoid bones.
Pigs have sesamoid bones
Wolves have sesamoid bones.
Gorillas have sesamoid bones.

In both (1) and (2), the smallest inclusive category is mammals. (2) has a larger coverage of the mammal category than (1), so this explains why participants generally understand (2) to be a stronger category induction than (1).

Osherson et al. have tested participants on the philosophical induction problem:

Grizzly bears love onions.
Polar bears love onions.
All bears love onions.

Since grizzly and polar bears have a high degree of similarity to bears, generally understood, they are typical of bears, and they provide a strong coverage over the class of bears, participants judge the induction to be a likely one. Similarity, typicality, and coverage have been shown to explain many cases of both kinds of induction.

Regarding the theory-theory, Lopez et al. (1997) have demonstrated that at times underlying causal explanatory knowledge relevantly may be responsible for inductions rather than superficial similarity, typicality, or coverage. For instance, tree experts were told that a blank predicate disease A affects a tree species *x*, while disease B affects a different tree species *y*. The experts then were asked which of the two diseases would most likely affect the other kinds of trees found in their local area. Our experimenters discovered that tree experts were more likely to base their judgments on knowledge of causal explanations rather than superficial similarity, typicality, or coverage. Experts would draw conclusions that at times went counter to the conclusions that would be drawn if participants were relying on superficial similarity, typicality, or coverage. Rather, they would base their inductions on theory knowledge. For example, tree experts would appropriately use knowledge of the root systems of trees and whether certain trees had root systems that were more likely to spread diseases. This supports the theory-theory regarding induction.

Numerous studies have established that similarity-based accounts and theory knowledge are at work in the specified way at various times in the higher competence of drawing inductions for standard concrete concepts. Previous chapters of this book also have established that in order to explain moral categorization, there is sufficient empirical evidence that moral concepts generally have prototype, exemplar, and theory structures, among others. When human beings make moral inductions, the knowledge stored in our moral concepts must be doing the work in these cases. As it has been shown that similarity-based views and theories do the work for standard concrete concepts in induction cases and there is sufficient evidence that moral concepts, in order to explain categorization, have prototype, exemplar, and theory structures, we may draw an inference based on explanatory simplicity that at least prototypes, exemplars, and theories in various circumstances also do the specified work for moral concepts in moral inductions. Given the available evidence that such structures are responsible for induction for standard concrete concepts, there is no reason to complicate the explanatory story by supposing that things are different for the moral concepts cases. Notice that this inference from simplicity is based on empirical evidence from moral and standard concrete concepts. Since such structures do the induction work in the appropriate way for standard concrete concepts and there is evidence for such structures in moral concepts, this presents the case that such structures at least in part are also appropriately responsible for moral inductions individually or conjointly depending on the situation. Due to this simplicity and that such structures can explain the phenomenon, this pluralistic account of moral induction is the best explanation of the phenomenon.

For example, using blank predicates like 'property x,' one may be presented with the problem of judging on a scale how strong the induction is from 'Brave people have property x, so therefore, good people have property x.' Another case may be 'Just people have property x, so therefore, good people have property x.' When presented with these problems, a subject may judge the second to be a stronger induction, and the explanation for this may be that the participant was in large part using similarity-based knowledge, such as prototypes. For, just people are more similar to, typical of, and have a greater degree of coverage of good people as compared to brave people for this participant. On the other hand, another subject may draw the same conclusion, but he or she may have used folk consequentialism theory knowledge. When given the vignette, this participant may have reasoned that just people will bring about better consequences for society than persons who are only brave. Due to this inference and the fact that this participant maintains that good people bring about the best consequences for society, this participant judges that the induction involving just people is stronger than the one involving brave people.

Although there are no tests on conative states and induction, conative states may participate in this act of cognition as well. For example, it may be that I have stronger positive emotions in my JUST concept than my BRAVE concept. This is why I judge that it is more likely that a good person has property x when a just person does, where I have a positive affect stored in my GOOD PERSON concept. Yet, since there are no studies on conative states and induction in the standard concrete and moral concepts literature, it could be that the conative view may not be able to handle the induction desideratum. As we shall see in the next section, a similar potential problem also may hold for the conative view in relation to the desideratum of concept combination. The response to these worries is that we should relax the desiderata for theories of moral and standard concrete concepts. The idea that a single concept structure needs to satisfy all the desiderata of a theory of concepts is a by-product of the days when philosophers and psychologists thought that there could only be one viable theory of concepts. As discussed in previous chapters, now that there is strong empirical evidence that there may be a multiplicity of viable conceptual structures in the moral and standard concrete domains that may be used in different circumstances and times, we no longer have to perceive the concept theory desiderata as being inert edifices marking the guidelines for determining what single theory of concepts is correct. Decision-making is complex. Some concept structures may be responsible in the specified way for competences such as induction while different structures may be appropriately at work in different higher competences and in different situations. Relaxing the desiderata where a particular psychological structure within a pluralistic view of concepts need only satisfy some rather than all of the desiderata is more appropriate, and, in light of the empirical evidence, where there is a multiplicity of conceptual structures at work in the proper way in higher cognition in different circumstances and times, it brings a coherence to our metatheory of how we should theorize about theories of moral and standard concrete concepts. Even if the conative theory cannot handle the induction or combination desiderata, this does not necessarily mean the demise of this view. Conative states still participate in moral categorization and in potentially other competences, while prototypes, exemplars, and theories are responsible for moral inductions, among other competences. In these respects, my overall theory of moral concepts still stands. As concepts are mental representations that play a qualified functional role in some of the higher competences, it has already been shown that conative states do play such a role in making moral categorizations. To contrarily conclude that the conative theory for moral concepts is not viable because it potentially cannot handle the induction or combination desiderata would be to conclude that none of our moral concepts are constituted by such states and therefore, such states do not partake in moral cognition at all; a gross misrepresentation of the empirical facts.

9.2 Concept Combination

Recall from the first chapter that concepts supposedly must respect productivity and systematicity (Fodor 1975). Productivity is where with a finite set of concepts and rules of combination, we can have an infinite amount of new thoughts. For example, if we have concepts of the ten digits of the Arabic numerals, we can have the thoughts 1, 7, 12, 215, 9060045621, etc. ad infinitum. Systematicity is where if one understands the given concepts and combination rules, one can understand variations on a thought. An example of this is where if one can understand JACK LIED TO JILL, then one may also understand the idea JILL LIED TO JACK.

Concept combination is the desideratum that attempts to explain how lexical (one word) or even compound concepts at many times combine with each other in order to form even more complex concepts or ideas. It examines how certain mental representations in many cases play the appropriate causal role in how we are able to understand at times new compound thoughts. Combination apparently must respect the productivity and systematicity of thought. If the constituent thoughts of a compound concept come from the constituent thoughts of the lexical concepts that make up the compound, then, along with the rules of combination, productivity and systematicity will be respected. Concept combination apparently must also account for emergent features or supposed new components of a compound concept that represent features that apparently "emerge" from a complex class that are not ordinarily thought to be contained within the constituent classes.

As an example of prototype concepts accounting for concept combination, in Smith and Osherson's (1984) classic selective modification model for concept combination as well as in some of the other more advanced models that actually can account for many emergent features, prototype components of the constituent concepts combine in certain cases to account for the components of the complex concept (Hampton 1987, Medin & Shoben 1988, Murphy 1988). For instance, in the adjective-noun phrase SMOOTH APPLE, the prototype components of SMOOTH and APPLE combine with each other to account for the components that make up the compound SMOOTH APPLE. In order to account for concept combination, most lexical concepts apparently should have a structure of being constituted by further concepts so that the structures of lexical concepts combine with each other when their respective lexical concepts are joined together to form a compound. This allows us in certain cases to understand new compound thoughts. As an example of concept combination, since SMOOTH is made up of SURFACE and NO ROUGH SPOTS while APPLE is constituted by FRUIT, RED, MEDIUM SIZED, and PICKED FROM TREES, the components of SMOOTH and APPLE causally combine in the appropriate way in order to account for the compound thought

SMOOTH APPLE. To the best of my knowledge, there are no direct studies on concept combination and moral concepts. However, a like argument will be made as with the above induction desideratum in order to show that at least some of the viable theories of moral concepts can account for this desideratum. The first step in being able to show this is to examine standard concrete concepts and concept combination.

Hampton (1987) found that the typical features of the members of the individual categories that are represented by the constituent concepts in a compound are also the typical features found in the members of the compound category that are represented by the compound concept itself. For instance, the typical feature of *no rough spots* for *smooth* and the typical features *fruit*, *red*, and *picked from trees* for *apple* for me are also the typical features of what I think belong to *smooth apple.* Hampton's study provides evidence that prototypes are responsible for concept combination.

There are studies showing the appropriate influence of exemplars in concept combination in order to account for emergent features, such as by Hampton (1987) and Medin and Shoben (1988). For example, PET FISH for many people has the component TROPICAL COLORED. However, based on the prototype view, this component may not appear to be a constituent of PET or FISH when taken individually. The feature may not be in a summary or general representation of features for me for *pet* or *fish.* It may not be thought that typical examples of pets, such as a dog or a cat, and typical examples of fish, such as bass and catfish, have *tropical colored* as a general property. *Tropical colored* somehow appears to mysteriously emerge from the combination of the concepts, but this cannot be the case if concepts combine through strict compositionality. Nevertheless, the exemplar theory can account for the apparent emergent feature. For, one has stored exemplars of pets or of fish that are of tropical colored fish. For instance, I've seen a tropical colored fish in a fish tank at the dentist's office. I have not seen enough tropical colored fish for TROPICAL COLORED to be a part of a relevant summary representation of features, but I still have a stored exemplar of such a fish or of such a pet. The corresponding representation of this particular instance is stored as an exemplar of a particular pet or of a particular fish. Since the exemplar itself is constituted by representations of features such as TROPICAL COLORED, the apparent emergent component of the compound concept does actually come from the relevant constituent concepts of the compound.

Likewise, for WOODEN SPOON, LARGE may appear to be an emergent component not contained within the relevant prototypes that constitute WOODEN or SPOON. However, I have seen a limited number of large wooden spoons in kitchens, although I have not had enough experiences with them for LARGE to be stored in my prototype knowledge in either of the lexical concepts that make up the compound. Regardless, I have exemplar mental representations of particular wooden things or of spoons that are about particular large wooden spoons I have encountered in my life. As the relevant exemplar is itself constituted by components that represent features such as *large*, the apparent emergent component of the compound WOODEN SPOON does come from the relevant constituent concepts.

There are also studies on standard concrete concepts supporting theory knowledge in concept combination. On Johnson and Keil's (2000) theory knowledge model, they found that participants listed many apparent emergent features for certain compounds. For instance, for *arctic bicycle*, subjects listed the feature *spiked tires* even though they did not list this feature for *arctic* or *bicycle*. Upon finding these results, they then ran other studies asking participants to fill in the blanks of, for example:

> Since the ARCTIC ________________________________
> and since BICYCLES________________________________
> then arctic bicycles have spiked tires.

They found that participants filled in the blanks generally with longer phrases that were not included in the prototype feature-listing task and that contained causal background theory knowledge. For example, one participant said that bicycles require traction to move. Then the experimenters asked the subjects to rate how likely supposed emergent features would belong to a compound category before and after the removal or denial of the relevant theory knowledge. For instance, subjects were asked to rate how likely arctic bicycles would have spiked tires. Then they would be informed that arctic bicycles are jet propelled. Subsequently, they would be re-asked to rate how likely arctic bicycles would have spiked tires. They found that participants substantially lowered the likelihood that the compound category would still contain the supposed emergent feature. This study provides evidence that at times, theory knowledge is at work in concept combination for standard concrete concepts.

The above studies establish that depending on the circumstances, prototypes, exemplars, and theory knowledge are appropriately at work in concept combination for standard concrete concepts. Previous chapters of this book have also established that in order to explain moral categorization, there is empirical evidence that moral concepts generally have prototype, exemplar, or theory structures, among others. Moreover, humans do in fact combine moral concepts all the time. There are compound moral concepts in which two constituent concepts are moral or so called thick moral concepts, such as: SENSIBLE KNAVE, MORAL SAINT, CHIVALROUS GENTLEMAN, VIRTUOUS LADY, DEVIOUS CROOK, HONOR

AMONG THIEVES, KIND BENEFACTOR, and MALICIOUS CRIME. Moreover, there are compounds that contain only one moral concept, such as: BRAVE WOMAN, JUST STATEMENT, IMPUDENT CHILD, and GENEROUS MAN. Since we frequently do combine moral concepts, the knowledge stored in our concepts should be doing the work at many times in these cases for how we understand complex thoughts. As it has been shown that prototypes, exemplars, and theories in varying circumstances do the work for standard concrete concepts in concept combination cases and there is sufficient empirical evidence that moral concepts generally have prototype, exemplar, or theory structures to explain moral categorization, we may draw an inference based on explanatory simplicity that at least such structures also do the specified work for moral concepts at many times in moral concept combination. Given the available evidence that such structures may be at work in concept combination for standard concrete concepts, there is no reason to complicate the explanatory story by supposing that things are different in the moral concepts case. Notice that this inference from simplicity is based on empirical evidence from moral and standard concrete concepts. Since such structures do the combination work for standard concrete concepts and there is evidence for such structures at work in moral categorization, this presents the case that such structures are responsible at many times in the proper way for moral concept combination, where they can be used individually or conjointly depending on the context. Due to this simplicity and that such structures can explain the phenomenon, this pluralistic account of moral concept combination is the best explanation of the phenomenon.

For example, for MORAL SAINT, the typical features I associate with the concept's extension are *kind, honest, perfect,* and *beneficent.* However, the corresponding prototype components are combined from both of the prototype components of my two relevant constituent concepts. For VIRTUOUS LADY, VIRTUOUS contains exemplars such as MY BROTHER HELPING THE POOR YESTERDAY, MY SISTER BEING KIND TO THE STRANGER LAST WINTER, and MOTHER THERESA. LADY is constituted by exemplars of females who are considered to be lady-like, like MY MOTHER and QUEEN ELIZABETH. The constituent exemplars are responsible for why when I token my VIRTUOUS LADY concept, I have the thoughts MOTHER THERESA and MY MOTHER. For JUST STATEMENT, JUST for me is constituted by utilitarian theory knowledge. This knowledge is responsible for the thought MAXIMIZE THE GREATEST HAPPINESS FOR THE GREATEST NUMBER when tokening the complex idea JUST STATEMENT in working memory. Although there are no tests on conative states and combination, the possibility will be left open that future experimentation demonstrates that such states can contribute to combination. For instance, along with other constituents, the non-cognitive pro-attitude contained in my JUST concept may contribute to the overall positive attitude I have for the compound JUST STATEMENT. However, recall from the previous section that it need not be the case that conative constituents take part to account for this desideratum.

9.3 Concept Combination Objections

Jerry Fodor and others (1998) argue that lexical concepts rarely decompose into components that represent non-defining features, such as prototypes (Fodor & Lepore 1996).[1] His first objection claims that the prototype theory cannot account for special phrasal concepts such as: AMERICAN CITIES SITUATED ON THE EAST COAST JUST A LITTLE SOUTH OF TENNESSEE, GRANDMOTHERS MOST OF WHOSE GRANDCHILDREN ARE DENTISTS, and NOT A CAT. Fodor states that the component concepts of the compounds supposedly do have prototype structure, but the compound concepts themselves do not. Prototypes do not combine. Constructing analogous Fodorian examples that in part use moral concepts, we may have: SIN CITIES SITUATED ON THE EAST COAST JUST A LITTLE SOUTH OF TENNESSEE, MORAL GRANDMOTHER MOST OF WHOSE GRANDCHILDREN ARE DENTISTS HELPING THIRD WORLD CHILDREN, and NOT A CRIME.

Whether or not moral and standard concrete prototype concepts can combine with each other is ultimately an empirical question. Although there is no experimental data on the Fodorian moral compounds I have just constructed above as well as on other Fodorian moral compounds we will discuss later, I have provided an inference that moral prototypes, exemplars, and theories can account for combination. Since there are no studies on my constructed Fodorian moral compounds, we may attempt to address Fodor in a more speculative manner in this chapter section, although it is not completely speculative since I already have shown based on categorization studies that moral concepts generally have prototype, exemplar, and theory structures and that the aforementioned knowledge does at many times partake in concept combination depending on the situation. Furthermore, the somewhat speculative manner is warranted in that Fodor just assumes that his special phrasal concepts do not have prototypes without any experimental support.

The first line of response is motivated by Prinz (2002) in his work on standard concrete concepts. If the phrasal concepts are candidates for typicality effects, where some members of the corresponding category are taken to be more typical than others, then this provides suggestive evidence that the phrasal concepts do have prototypes or, in other words, are constituted by a summary or general representation of features. To note, other structures like exemplars can also explain and predict typicality effects. However, either way, whether prototypes or exemplars account for typicality effects, since my overall theory of moral concepts includes both views and I have already established that different kinds of knowledge may be at work in different circumstances, the perceived existence of typicality effects still shows that my overall theory of moral concepts can respond to Fodor's objection.

For SIN CITIES SITUATED ON THE EAST COAST JUST A LITTLE SOUTH OF TENNESSEE, it is plausible that there can be a typicality scale. For example, CHARLESTON, SOUTH CAROLINA may be low on the typicality scale since I perceive it to generally be a sin city on the east coast, but it has some conservative and religious elements. MYRTLE BEACH, SOUTH CAROLINA is high on the scale since it is a well-known beach party destination. What accounts for the typicality scale for SIN CITIES SITUATED ON THE EAST COAST JUST A LITTLE SOUTH OF TENNESSEE may be prototype components such as HAS MANY BARS, HAS GAMBLING, HAS BEACH PARTIES, etc. The perceived existence of typicality effects for this phrasal concept suggests that this compound is constituted by similarity-based knowledge.

For MORAL GRANDMOTHER MOST OF WHOSE GRANDCHILDREN ARE DENTISTS HELPING THIRD WORLD CHILDREN, such a grandmother with less character flaws than another grandmother who also is generally moral is a more typical instance of the class. This typicality scale may be accounted for by prototypes for the compound concept such as GENEROUS, EDUCATOR, KIND, etc. For NOT A CRIME, there are many acts that are not perceived to be crimes at least in our culture, such as: cooking breakfast, helping the poor, walking the dog, and driving to work. However, as crimes are usually perceived as being immoral acts, I may have a typicality scale where the most typical acts that are not crimes are acts that are not at all similar to crimes, such as helping the poor. Meanwhile, telling white lies – kinds of lies that I do not hold to be crimes – is less typical since it shares a little similarity with crimes.

One may wonder what prototypes may constitute the lexical concepts of NOT A CRIME such that these summary representations can be similar to all the countless and diverse acts that are not crimes. It initially appears unlikely that such prototypes exist that can be similar to helping others, telling the truth, walking your dog, mowing the lawn, etc. At the very least, the relevant proposed list of prototypes apparently will be too large and unmanageable given our limited storage capacities in our concepts. In response, we may understand the use of NOT to include a particular operation or cognitive process that alters the function used to measure similarity. Similarity to a negated prototype concept like CRIME is inversely related to similarity to the prototype concept (Prinz 2002). Hence, an act that is well below the similarity threshold of being a crime will be well above the threshold for being not a crime. Therefore, we may think of the relevant list of prototypes for NOT A CRIME to be the list of prototypes for CRIME that are preceded by a negation function that changes the similarity measurement. Another way of thinking about it is that the list of prototypes for NOT A CRIME may be NOT IMMORAL, NOT

CRUEL, NOT HARMFUL, etc. The perceived existence of a typicality scale in the above examples counters Fodor's objection and suggests that my overall theory of moral concepts can handle his contention.

Furthermore, we may add new points to respond to Fodor in that theory knowledge at times can also play an appropriate role in concept combination for the Fodorian compounds. My overall theory of moral concepts allows for the given three different kinds of knowledge to be at work in different circumstances, and such knowledge also may work conjointly with other kinds of knowledge. This also can be a potential response to Fodor in some cases. For instance, for MORAL GRANDMOTHER MOST OF WHOSE GRANDCHILDREN ARE DENTISTS HELPING THIRD WORLD CHILDREN, my GOOD concept in part is constituted by folk consequentialism knowledge. The typicality effects I have for this compound are directly accounted for in cognition by my ethical theory knowledge that one must perform those acts that bring about the best consequences. Relevant grandmothers who bring about better consequences are deemed to be more typical of such moral grandmothers than others.

Another new point is that as mentioned in the second chapter, the prototype and exemplar theories predict that there will be ambiguous cases of membership, whereas the classical view does not. Since prototypes and exemplars are not taken to refer to necessary and sufficient conditions, we should expect that subjects can be unsure at times about whether some items should be classified in one particular category or another. If it is expected that there are ambiguous cases of membership, then this provides further support that the phrasal concepts in question may have prototype or exemplar structure since they predict and explain ambiguous cases of membership. With our particular phrasal concepts, we do see the possibility and likelihood of ambiguous cases of membership, which provides a counter to Fodor. For SIN CITIES SITUATED ON THE EAST COAST JUST A LITTLE SOUTH OF TENNESSEE, I may not be sure whether Wilmington, North Carolina falls within the corresponding category. For, it is a reasonably sized beach city and it has many beach parties which could mean that it is a sin city, but at the same time, from my personal experience, I know there are significant charitable activities occurring in the city. Therefore, I am not sure if it falls in the relevant class or not. Also, recall that in the fourth chapter it was inferred that moral concepts as a class generally do have prototype structure and do produce concomitant typicality effects that provide evidence against the classical view. Thus, the above ambiguity for SIN CITIES SITUATED ON THE EAST COAST JUST A LITTLE SOUTH OF TENNESSEE coupled with the fact that SIN has prototype structure that allows for ambiguous cases of membership, puts forth a case that the compound concept at hand does have prototype structure.

For MORAL GRANDMOTHER MOST OF WHOSE GRANDCHILDREN ARE DENTISTS HELPING THIRD WORLD CHILDREN, I may know a grandmother, most of whose grandchildren are the relevant dentists, but I am not sure if she is a moral person or not. She has some noble qualities but also some questionable ones as well. Therefore, I am not sure whether or not she falls in the corresponding compound category. Also, as further support that this ambiguity may be the case, recall from the fourth chapter that we examined a study that demonstrated that HIGHLY MORAL PERSON does have prototype structure and does produce typicality effects. For NOT A CRIME, many people appear to be uncertain about whether things like abortion are not a crime regardless of what the law in their state may say. Also, recall from the fourth chapter that we examined an experiment that demonstrated that CRIME does have prototype structure and does produce typicality effects such that there may be ambiguous cases of membership for this concept. While ambiguous cases of membership do reinforce the plausibility of a prototype or exemplar analysis as opposed to a classical definitional analysis, insofar as the prototype and exemplar theories predict and explain the existence of ambiguous cases of membership, the strong possible existence of ambiguous cases of membership provides a counter to Fodor's first concept combination objection.

Fodor's (1998) second objection is that there are the previously discussed emergent components to certain compound concepts such as PET FISH. Although Fodor does not discuss this objection in light of moral concepts, the moral compound SENSIBLE KNAVE has the component prototype feature KNOWING WHEN ONE WILL NOT GET CAUGHT. However, this component feature does not appear to be contained within SENSIBLE or within KNAVE when considered individually. My SENSIBLE concept may be constituted by prototype constituents like MAKES GOOD FINANCIAL DECISIONS and MAKES PRACTICAL CAREER MOVES while my KNAVE concept is constituted by prototype representations like DECEITFUL and BAD. KNOWING WHEN ONE WILL NOT GET CAUGHT appears to not be contained in either lexical concept for me. Thus, it appears that there is a problem of concept combination in certain cases for the prototype theory in the domain of moral concepts as well.

The first response that is available for my overall theory of moral concepts is that we may have stored exemplars that may appropriately account for the supposed emergent components. We have already discussed how Hampton and Medin and Shoben have shown that exemplars can account for apparent emergent components in certain instances such as in PET FISH. This may also work for our particular compound moral concept SENSIBLE KNAVE. I have met a few knaves in my life or seen actors play them in movies, some of whom have had good foresight into knowing whether or not they would get caught. However, I have not had enough experiences with such knaves such that the apparent emergent feature *knowing when one will not get caught* is part of the general features I think belong to *knaves*. Nevertheless, such individuals, when understood as exemplar mental representations of particular knaves, can account for the apparent emergent component of the respective compound in that such exemplars are themselves constituted by concepts such as KNOWING WHEN ONE WILL NOT GET CAUGHT. This can handle the emergent features objection in certain cases.

However, Fodor and Lepore (1996) anticipate this exemplar theory move and contend that there are still compounds in which one will not have an exemplar. Even if there are exemplars that can handle the pet fish problem, most people do not have the proper experiences to have relevant exemplars that can in some way handle compounds like PET FISH LIVING IN ARMENIA THAT HAVE RECENTLY SWALLOWED THEIR OWNERS. This particular compound has supposed emergent components such as LARGE and VORACIOUS. Likewise, Fodor and Lepore may claim that the exemplar theory cannot account for apparent emergent components contained in certain compounds that contain moral concepts such as SENSIBLE KNAVE LIVING IN ARMENIA THAT HAS RECENTLY SWALLOWED A NEW YORK STRIP STEAK WHOLE. This compound has the supposed emergent component of LARGE and VORACIOUS that does not appear to be contained within the lexical concepts that make up the compound and where we do not have relevant exemplars of this particular kind of represented individual.

In response to this, we once again can bring in the theory-theory model of combination. For SENSIBLE KNAVE LIVING IN ARMENIA THAT HAS RECENTLY SWALLOWED A NEW YORK STRIP STEAK WHOLE, although the exemplar theory may not work for this instance, KNAVE has a descriptive and a normative component. A descriptive prototypical feature that knaves have is that of being human. We have background explanatory theory knowledge of human beings that if one can swallow things like a steak whole, this individual must be large and have a large mouth. Moreover, this person must also have been voracious. It is the inclusion of background explanatory theory knowledge that can account for concept combination and supposed emergent features in certain cases.[2] As my overall theory of concepts allows for prototypes, exemplars, and theories to work in cognition individually or conjointly on different occasions and in different circumstances, my view has the resources to account for apparent emergent qualities even in circumstances where it appears that certain kinds of knowledge, such as prototypes, relevantly fail.

9.4 Moral Concept Pluralism Established

Recall that moral concepts are the very heart of moral cognition as they are the basic building blocks of moral thought, are responsible for how we understand the moral world, and take part in categorization, induction, deduction, analogical reasoning, planning, etc. However, as of yet, no work has been done on examining all the theories of concepts in light of moral ones. I draw my positive conclusion for my new pluralistic theory of moral concepts based broadly on using an inference to the best explanation that my view best explains the desiderata of a theory of moral concepts. However, at times inductive arguments were used to help build up to the broad abductive argument that finally establishes my theory of moral concepts. In the previous chapters, I systematically have provided positive evidence that my pluralistic view best satisfies and explains the desiderata of a theory of moral concepts; desiderata such as moral categorization, the sense of moral concepts, moral concept acquisition, moral induction, and concept combination. Hence, we have seen that (1) prototypes or representations of virtues, basic rules, reasons for action, and features of moral situations, (2) exemplars or representations of particular acts and persons, (3) theories or representations of ethical theories and causal moral laws, and (4) conative states all together widely constitute our moral concepts. This is the psychological basis of moral judgment. I have established my conclusion in a non-speculative manner and have empirically proven that these structures generally apply to the human mind. I also have shown that the classical theory of moral concepts is not psychologically real and have criticized numerous attempts to contend for a theory of moral concepts, such as from Churchland, Stich, Clark, Harman, Wong, Prinz, Sterelny, Gibbard, and Johnson. I have demonstrated that the above have failed to prove that their proposed moral concept structure(s) is viable. As there are successful prototype studies in the moral concepts literature, my work is the first to empirically establish that more than one theory of concepts applies to moral concepts. I have shown that all four given structures are required to explain moral decision-making, so a concept theory that is lacking in one of these structures is deficient in explanatory power and predictive success regarding the desiderata. It will fail to be the best explanation. The different kinds of conceptual structures on my view can work individually or conjointly with other kinds of knowledge in cognition depending upon the situation, although conative states must always be accompanied by a cognitive state. Also, as with many other empirical claims on the human condition, I allow for aberrations and exceptions to my pluralistic view.

I have in large part drawn concept constitution claims by using experiments that are not explicitly on moral concepts and by combining them with a functionalist identification of what moral concepts are; a move that previously was unforeseen in the literature. Moral psychologists have failed to realize that studies on what mental states causally influence moral judgments can be used with a functionalist metaphysics to draw conclusions on what constitutes moral judgments and on what mental states moral judgments express. Furthermore, I have reworked the theories of concepts for standard concrete concepts to show how they can take into account moral features from the moral domain. Moreover, recall that my theory of moral concepts is also in part buttressed by neuroscience findings showing a consistent correlation between moral decision-making and that of emotional and cognitive brain regions being activated. My pluralistic theory differs from the likes of Hume, Prinz, and A.J. Ayer who contend that our moral concepts are only constituted by emotions as well as from cognitivists like Brink and Shafer-Landau who claim that we have moral concepts that only have a cognitive component.

It also offers a quadruple process theory of moral judgment, where there are four different computational processes involved in moral cognition, such as the linear algorithms of the prototype view and the non-linear algorithms of the exemplar theory. Such computational processes that underwrite decision-making can be viewed as being a more fine-grained version of the more generic dual process theories that espouse the use of cognitive and conative processes in the causal moral judgment field. For, my view contains three cognitive processes and a conative one. However, my theory includes cognitive processes, like those associated with the exemplar theory, that explicitly are not even mentioned by those in the causal moral judgment literature. Furthermore, my quadruple process theory posits computational processes that are individuated at the more fine-grained level that is common and appropriate to mathematical psychology.

It perhaps may be instructive if I contrast my view with a prominent theory of concepts by the psychologist, Susan Carey (1985, 2009). In her earlier works, she is well-known as being an advocate for the theory-theory of concepts, although her focus has largely been on standard concrete concepts. First, since she does not examine specifically moral concepts, she is not justified in drawing a theory view claim for moral concepts, as this would be speculative. However, to her credit, she does not claim that the theory view is viable for moral concepts, and she concurs that experimental evidence on the class of concepts in question is required to warrant a relevant constitution claim:

> These questions must be answered case by case – there is no reason, at the outset, to expect the answers for concepts of causality or human agency to be the same as the answers for mathematical or biological concepts, or for the concepts that articulate our knowledge of chess or baseball.
>
> (2009, p. 3)

As I have argued before, theories of standard concrete concepts do not necessarily apply to moral concepts (§4.1). Proper experiments on moral concepts are at least in part required to sufficiently warrant a moral concept constitution claim.

Given that I am the first to articulate how the theory view will look like in the moral domain, this also indicates that she has not posited the viability of the theory view for moral concepts in her previous work. Furthermore, notice that as with monistic theories of moral concepts as well as dualistic ones that we have discussed and criticized by the likes of Churchland, Stich, Goldman, Sterelny, Wong, Harman, Johnson, Prinz, Hume, etc., even if Carey had somehow shown that moral concepts have theory structure, this monistic view would be severely lacking in explanatory power and predictive success given all the data demonstrating that four different structures appropriately causally influence moral decision-making. Such monistic and dualistic theories will not satisfy and best explain the desiderata of a theory of moral concepts. However, my new tetrad pluralistic view clearly does.

In her later book, *The Origin of Concepts*, Carey (2009) explores mental representations like OBJECT, CAUSE, and MATTER. She concludes that for such concepts, "there are two types of conceptual representations: those embedded in systems of core cognition and those embedded in explicit knowledge systems, such as intuitive theories" (p. 4). "Intuitive theories" are theory knowledge, while core cognition is part of an innate domain specific module that contains information less complex than theory knowledge. For instance, new born chicks when shown a moving ball and a stuffed bird will huddle next to the stuffed bird. Carey claims that chicks have core cognition knowledge such as HEN and STAY CLOSE TO HEN. Once again, Carey in no manner attempts to make a like claim in the moral conceptual domain, but if she wanted to make such a claim, proper data must be collected on specifically moral concepts in order to do so. Also, recall that for moral concepts I have laid down skeptical arguments against humans having an innate moral module (§6.3).

Later in her book, Carey opens the boundaries further and allows for prototype and exemplar structures for her specific non-moral concepts. She writes, "There is no doubt that prototype/exemplar theories account for a great deal of data from categorization experiments, and thus provide insight into the process of categorization" (p. 497), and "[W]e do have summary representations of categories of entities, we do represent specific exemplars ..." (p. 498). This mirrors Machery's theory of standard concrete concepts in that he also maintains that such representations have prototype, exemplar, and theory structures. However, once again, these are not claims about moral concepts, and they have no intention of making such claims for moral concepts given their lack of relevant evidence. If they did attempt to make such claims for moral concepts, they would have much work to do, and it will not be easy. They would have to methodically and laboriously go through empirical support for moral concepts in regard to being able to satisfy the desiderata of moral categorization, sense, concept acquisition, moral induction, and moral concept combination. Most of this evidence will not be explicitly on moral concepts, and they would have to be aware of the causal moral judgment literature and foresee that a functionalist identification can apply to such causal studies to draw moral concept constitution claims. They also would have to know how to appropriately convert the theories of concepts in the standard concrete concepts field to account for moral features for moral concepts, relying in part on knowledge of moral philosophy. Furthermore, even if they had shown that the prototype, exemplar, and theory views were viable for moral concepts, their pluralistic theory still would not satisfy the desideratum of moral categorization given the important role emotions play in this higher act of cognition. Conative structure is also required in an overall theory of moral concepts to satisfy the categorization desideratum. My pluralistic view that includes the conative theory fully can account for the categorization desideratum as well as all the other desiderata for the constitution project. My pluralistic theory of moral concepts is correct because it best explains the relevant phenomena.

With my new empirically confirmed pluralistic theory of moral concepts now on the table, we next turn to what implications my view has in metaethics.

Notes

1 Fodor additionally adds that concepts also do not have definitional structure. Therefore, all concepts are atoms without any structure. Atomism is a view that has fallen out of favor in cognitive science since there is no structure to concepts that can explain the desiderata and decision-making. For example, if there is no structure to our moral concepts, then our moral decisions are not influenced by any mental states. Yet, this is empirically false. Moreover, if concepts are atoms that are primitive unlearned concepts, per Fodor, then this means they are acquired innately, but I have shown that moral nativism is unjustified. For more contentions showing that atomism as a general theory of concepts fails to satisfy the concept desiderata, see Prinz (2002). Regardless, my objection to Fodor's premise that non-defining features cannot account for compositionality shows in another way why this argument for atomism is unsound.

2 Non-default knowledge, such as of *human beings*, at times can account for complex thoughts. Thus, some theories of concepts that only posit default knowledge need not even account for this desideratum at all. Furthermore, for those theories of concepts that posit knowledge that does partake in combination, they need only show that they can account for compound thoughts in some cases and not all the time. Leaving the concept combination desideratum loose, where some concept theories only need to show that they can account for compound thoughts in some but not all cases or perhaps not at all, opens the door and allows for combination to not be invariably compositional, where non-concept-constitutive knowledge also can play a role in combination. It ought to be flagged that this really does mean giving up on compositionality as Fodor et al. have understood it. Not all of our compound thoughts come from the combining of concepts.

References

Carey, Susan. 1985. *Conceptual Change in Childhood.* Cambridge, MA: The MIT Press.

Carey, Susan. 2009. *The Origin of Concepts.* Oxford: Oxford University Press.

Fodor, Jerry. 1975. *The Language of Thought*. Cambridge, MA: Harvard University Press.

Fodor, Jerry. 1998. *Concepts: Where Cognitive Science Went Wrong*. Oxford: Oxford University Press.

Fodor, Jerry and Lepore, Ernest. 1996. "The Red Herring and the Pet Fish: Why Concepts Still Can't Be Prototypes." *Cognition* 58, 253–270.

Hampton, James. 1987. "Inheritance of Attributes in Natural Concept Conjunctions." *Memory & Cognition* 15, 55–71.

Johnson, C. and Keil, F. 2000. "Explanatory Understanding and Conceptual Combination." *Explanation and Cognition*. Ed. by F. Keil and R. Wilson. Cambridge, MA: The MIT Press, 327–359.

Lopez, A., Atran, S., Coley, J., Medin, D., and Smith, E. 1997. "The Tree of Life: Universal and Cultural Features of Folk Biological Taxonomies and Inductions." *Cognitive Psychology* 32, 251–295.

Medin, D. and Shoben, E. 1988. "Context and Structure in Conceptual Combination." *Cognitive Psychology* 20, 158–190.

Murphy, Gregory. 1988. "Comprehending Complex Concepts." *Cognitive Science* 12, 529–562.

Osherson, D.N., Smith, E.E., Wilkie, O., Lopez, A., and Shafir, E. 1990. "Category-based Induction." *Psychological Review* 97, 185–200.

Prinz, Jesse. 2002. *Furnishing the Mind*. Cambridge, MA: The MIT Press.

Rips, Lance. 1975. "Inductive Judgments About Natural Categories." *Journal of Verbal Learning and Verbal Behavior* 14, 665–681.

Smith, Edward and Osherson, Daniel. 1984. "Conceptual Combination with Prototype Concepts." *Cognitive Science* 8, 337–361.

10 Cognitivism/Non-Cognitivism and Motivational Judgment Internalism/Externalism

We have seen how my pluralistic theory best explains the desiderata of a theory of moral concepts. However, there are even further philosophical implications beyond those discussed in previous chapters. Other relevant issues are the cognitivism/non-cognitivism and motivational judgment internalism/externalism debates in metaethics. It is to these issues that we now turn, where I offer new arguments on these matters based on my pluralistic theory of moral concepts.

10.1 Hybrid Cognitivism and Non-Cognitivism

Cognitivists like Plato and Kant generally hold that moral judgments can express beliefs, and such judgments are capable of being true or false in a more substantial way as compared to a deflationary theory of truth. Beliefs generally refer to properties, propositions, and they also can represent facts. For instance, the belief GEORGE WASHINGTON IS THE FIRST PRESIDENT OF THE UNITES STATES represents the fact or proposition that George Washington is the first president of the United States. As the proposition that George Washington is the first president of the United States is true of the world, the corresponding belief is true. Hence, if moral judgments express beliefs, then such judgments also may be capable of being true or false. Cognitivist theories of truth include views like objective and relativistic theories of moral truth. On the other hand, non-cognitivists like Ayer (1936) and Simon Blackburn (1998) generally maintain that moral judgments express emotions, non-representational attitudes, and/or desires.[1] Such non-cognitive conative states do not refer to or are not about genuine moral properties and facts, so moral judgments are only capable of being true or false in a deflationary way.[2] Generally on a deflationary view, to characterize a moral judgment as being true is not to attribute a further property to the judgment such as that it corresponds to objective moral facts of the world, it is what ideal observers would believe, or it is part of a coherent set of beliefs of a culture. Rather, unlike a cognitivist view, to characterize a judgment as being true is not to attribute any such further genuine property to the judgment at all. For example, saying "'Stealing is wrong' is true" is equivalent to just saying "Stealing is wrong." Moral judgments are incapable of being true or false in a substantial or robust way. To note, this characterization of cognitivism versus non-cognitivism is just a loose generalization, and there are more complex versions of non-cognitivism that are harder to distinguish from cognitivist views (Horgan & Timmons 2000, Gibbard 2003). For instance, Horgan and Timmons propound a non-cognitivism view in which moral judgments express non-representational cognitive beliefs only; an empirically false view in light of my pluralistic theory of moral concepts.[3] Furthermore, as we will discuss below, there also are hybrid non-cognitivist accounts in which non-representational moral judgments express both beliefs and conative states.

While here we will not be concerned with the element of the cognitivism/non-cognitivism debate that focuses on theories of moral truth as it will be discussed in the next two chapters, my pluralistic theory of moral concepts leads to the a posteriori claim that moral judgments widely express beliefs and conative states. I use the term 'widely' because there may be certain exceptions, such as certain patients in abnormal psychology like psychopaths that may make moral judgments without expressing conative states. Furthermore, there are certain psychologically abnormal patients, such as those with alexithymia who have severe deficiencies in affect, that we currently must remain agnostic on since future research is required to see whether or not they can make moral judgments without expressing conative states. Also, there are those with a temporary psychological illness or temporary deviation from normal functioning, such as experiencing a period of apathy, a bout of depression, exhaustion, or an emotional disturbance. If such agents do not make moral judgments that express an emotion, they largely still have a sentiment. The emotional disposition will require a return to normal functioning such that it may be activated. Recall that my view on moral concepts is a general claim about the human condition in which there may be aberrations and exceptions. I write that moral judgments "widely" express both kinds of states also to allow for the possibility that there may be some psychologically normal agents who are aberrations as well. For instance, there may be such an agent that does not express an emotion or sentiment but only a belief with the judgment. The empirical evidence from previous chapters does warrant the inference that *all* psychologically normal persons express both states in their moral decisions. However, I perhaps overcautiously allow for the possibility of anomalies in the psychologically normal population.

My theory of moral concepts leads to a specified hybrid view on this debate. This is because moral judgments like RAPE IS WRONG contain moral concepts like WRONG. Insofar as moral judgments contain moral concepts and moral concepts widely are constituted by both cognitive and conative states, moral judgments widely express both kinds of mental states in virtue of being constituted by such states. There is a hybridism. As this hybrid position immediately falls out of my pluralistic theory of moral concepts, my positive arguments for this position already have been posited in all of the previous chapters. However, more specifically, we should understand my hybrid position as being a weak hybrid view. Understood strongly, hybridism can be perceived as claiming that all moral judgments express cognitive and conative states. However, insofar as I allow for limited exceptions, my hybridism is a weak one. Notice that my view does not fall properly within the purely cognitivist (Brink 1989, Shafer-Landau 2003) or non-cognitivist (Ayer 1936, Gibbard 1990, Blackburn 1998) camp concerning what mental states our moral judgments express. For, since I argue that moral judgments widely express both states, a view that pure cognitivists and pure non-cognitivists will utterly shun, then my position more naturally falls within the hybridist camp.

To note, remember that since conative states always are accompanied by a cognitive state, so long as a moral judgment is constituted by a conative state, it also expresses a cognitive state (§8.5).[4] There is a hybridism. However, if an emotion does not constitute a judgment, then recall that the judgment generally is still constituted by a sentiment or disposition to feel an emotion. In this respect, such a judgment still leads to a hybrid view as the given judgment expresses a cognitive state and a sentiment.

Some of the others who have held a hybrid position on this debate are Charles Stevenson (1944), R. M. Hare (1952), and Michael Ridge (2014), although their approaches are more a priori. Among hybridists, there is variance as far as adopting a cognitivist versus a deflationary theory of moral truth, where this variance largely turns on whether the hybrid theorist views the cognitive or non-cognitive component of a judgment as being primary.[5] Also, notice that up to now, the likes of Haidt, Greene, and Nichols who have advocated that cognitive and conative states influence moral decision-making cannot and have not adopted a hybrid position on the cognitivism/non-cognitivism debate. For, in order to do so, one would have to see the connection between the causal moral judgment literature, a functionalist identification from the philosophy of mind, and the concepts field. One would have to reach the further inference that moral concepts in moral judgments are constituted by both states.

10.2 Motivational Judgment Internalism/Externalism

Motivational judgment internalism (MJI) generally is the claim that there is a necessary connection between someone making a sincere moral judgment and this judger having some degree of motivation to act on the judgment. The roots of MJI can be traced back to antiquity when

Plato's Socrates in the *Protagoras* claims that among potential options for action, if someone truly judges an act to be good or better than other acts, then this person must be overridingly motivated to perform said action. As MJI is commonly and generally conceived, it claims that motivation is internal to the judgment itself, where the judgment all by itself motivates. We may therefore interpret the generally understood MJI view as claiming that all moral concepts in all genuine moral judgments are at least in part constituted by a motivational state, such as a conative state like an emotion or desire. If the concepts are so constituted, then motivation stems from and is internal to the judgments themselves. Therefore, in order to see whether MJI is right or not, we should examine whether all moral concepts are at least in part constituted by motivational states. Meanwhile, motivational judgment externalism (MJE), held by the likes of David Brink (1989) and Russ Shafer-Landau (2003), denies this necessary connection between judgment and motivation.

Within MJI, there can be many variants. For instance, on a strong version of MJI, the accompanying motivation is always overriding such that one will always act on the judgment. This view implausibly does not allow for cases of akrasia or weakness of will, where at times our motivation to act on a sincere moral judgment may be overridden by competing motivations. On a weaker version of MJI, the motivation is present but can be overridden. Still, some other variants claim that there is a necessary connection between making a sincere moral judgment and either having a defeasible motivation to act on the judgment or a disposition to act on the judgment that may not be realized (Blackburn 1998, Gibbard 2003). This can be viewed as being a conditional weak MJI claim in that when a judgment is only constituted by a disposition for motivation that is not realized, the connection between judgment and motivation is severed. Christine Korsgaard (1986) and Michael Smith (1994) argue that when one makes a moral judgment, one is necessarily motivated unless one is practically irrational. Generally, one is practically irrational when one's motivation fails to match one's belief about what one has reason to do. This also can be viewed as being a weak conditional variant of MJI in that it severs the necessary connection between judgment and motivation for those who are practically irrational. As we can see, certain weak MJI views can blur the line between MJI and MJE but still attempt to maintain the general flavor of MJI.

The MJI/MJE debate is often argued on the a priori grounds of whether the existence of the amoralist is conceivable. Some philosophers have attempted to argue against MJI by introducing the notion of the amoralist. For example, Brink (1989) argues that the MJI advocate fails to take the amoralist seriously, where we can conceive of an amoralist that makes sincere moral demands but still remains unmoved. Indeed, he notes that there even may be real life examples of such individuals, such as psychopaths. Meanwhile, opposing philosophers contend that such an amoralist is not making a sincere moral judgment but an inverted commas judgment. When the amoralist claims that murder is wrong, he or she is not really judging that murder is wrong and that one ought not to commit murder. Rather, he or she is merely saying something like "people in this society judge that murder is wrong."

However, a significant part of the history of the cognitivism/non-cognitivism debate specifically regarding whether our moral concepts and judgments express beliefs and/or conative states is rooted as an empirical claim (Hume 1738/2000). The same holds for the MJI/MJE debate. For instance, recall from the first chapter that Hume is an empiricist and believed that in order to avoid fruitless debates in ethics, we must rely on observation when making claims in moral psychology about moral concepts. By relying on empirical evidence from introspection of one's own mental events, where empiricists typically allow for introspection or reflection to be a provider of experience along with the senses, Hume can be read as arguing for MJI in the following famous passage:

> Take any action allowed to be vicious: Wilful murder, for instance. Examine it in all lights, and see if you can find that matter of fact, or real existence, which you call vice. In which-ever way you take it, you find only certain passions, motives, volitions, and thoughts. There is no other matter of fact in the case. The vice entirely escapes you, as long as you consider the object. You never can find it, till you turn your reflection into your own breast, and find a sentiment of disapprobation, which arises in you, towards this action.
>
> (1738/2000, Book III, Part I, Sect. I)

However, currently, the MJI/MJE debate is predominantly an a priori one. For instance, it is an a priori issue as to whether one can conceive of an amoralist that makes genuine judgments or not. If one can conceive of such an amoralist, then there is no modal necessary connection between making a sincere moral judgment and motivation since one can conceive otherwise. It does not hold in all possible conceivable worlds. If one cannot conceive otherwise and one also cannot in other relevant cases as well, then there is a necessary connection across all possible worlds since one cannot conceive otherwise. This issue focuses on the concept of a sincere moral judgment. A priori, does the abstracted notion of a concept of a sincere moral judgment necessarily entail a degree of motivation to act on the judgment or not across all possible worlds?

This is a different subject matter from the empirical psychological inquiry of trying to determine whether a motivating mental state actually constitutes a particular moral concept in an actual moral judgment in the real world that is in one's mind. For example, in my mind, I have the judgment RECYCLING IS MORAL, whether it be a sincere moral judgment or an insincere moral judgment. In trying to determine what mental properties constitute the MORAL concept in my judgment, empirical data is required on this specific empirical claim in cognitive science. One needs empirical evidence as far as determining what specifically constitutes my MORAL concept in this case in the real world. Recall that concepts are constituted by those default mental states that play a specified causal role in cognition, so causal evidence is required to determine what specifically constitutes a concept when using a functionalist identification.

Hume has shown us that causal claims only can be known via a posteriori rather than a priori means. Causal claims are not found a priori because we always can conceive otherwise for a causal interaction. For example, I can imagine that the relevant pool balls never will move at all when struck by the cue ball in a game or that the cue ball simply may disappear when struck. Without relevant experience with the world, there is no a priori reason to believe one option will occur rather than the other. It is arbitrary from an a priori vantage point. It is only through experience that we learn the way pool balls ordinarily move, that bread nourishes, that lions kill, or that water drowns. Furthermore, based on Haidt's previously discussed dumbfounding studies where people may introspectively believe that conscious reasoning influences their moral decision-making, such as when making judgments against brother–sister incest, but such reasoning at many times does not influence judgment and is post hoc, we need experimental causal data rather than mere introspective empirical evidence of what we think influences our decision-making to justify the relevant specific causal claims that are used to draw concept constitution ones in a functionalist identification. This need for experimental data for causal claims is further buttressed by the fact that at many times subconscious influences could really be at work that are contrary to our conscious awareness of decision-making processes. Moreover, the fact that our standard concrete and moral concepts do not have classical structure despite the fact that for millennia we have believed that they do provides further reason to require experimental data regarding making relevant moral concept constitution claims rather than relying empirically on introspection of our own mental events. Finally, the experimental data from Hampton's study discussed in the fourth chapter also demonstrates how leery we must be of positing speculative claims and not relying at least in part on experimental evidence directly on moral concepts themselves when drawing specific concept constitution claims for moral concepts (§4.1).

Proper empirical evidence is required in order to appropriately justify a specific concept constitution claim on my MORAL concept in my judgment about recycling in the real world. To draw a specific constitution conclusion on my MORAL concept purely a priori would be to tell a just-so story analogous to just-so stories in evolutionary biology (§6.3). Both cases of just-so stories are similar in the sense that they are unjustified as the relevant scientific fields have demonstrated that they require the requisite empirical confirmation. To quickly and further see how what constitutes moral concepts in the real world is an empirical claim and answerable to empirical investigation, imagine a scenario in which one argues a priori that moral judgments express conative states and then claims that many moral judgments in the real world express conative states. Yet, in this situation, let us say that neuroscience does not show a correlation at all between conative brain regions lighting up and moral judgment. Without correlation, there is no causation. Empirical data would overturn the claim at hand. This is dangerously too easy, and here, the a priori theorist that attempts to make actual claims on the nature of moral mental representations in the real world occupies an exceptionally precarious position. This hazardous position shows that proper experimental evidence is required to really justify a specific moral concept constitution claim in the actual world. The situation is too perilous otherwise. Building on top of this, what becomes more transparent is that one still needs experimental causal evidence because what specifically constitutes such a concept is an empirical claim about a natural phenomenon. Thus, quite simply, from the scientific method, an empirical scientific claim requires the requisite empirical confirmation.

Analyzing a priori what needs to constitute the MORAL concept in the moral judgment for the judgment to count as a sincere one is one thing. However, it is a different question and an empirical matter as far as determining the separate issue of what actually constitutes the MORAL concept in my judgment in my mind in the real world. For instance, one might hold a general a priori MJI view and believe that *if* a judgment is a sincere one in the real world, then it must be constituted by a motivating mental state. However, it strictly is an empirical question to see if my MORAL concept in my environmental ethics judgment actually is constituted by a motivating mental state such that one perhaps might then deem the judgment to be a sincere judgment or an insincere moral judgment.

I take it that most if not all moral philosophers who make purely a priori claims on the MJI/MJE and/or cognitivism/non-cognitivism debates, either implicitly or explicitly, also attribute their views as applying to certain moral judgments in the real world. However, unbeknownst to them, they make an unwarranted leap over a logical gap. They jump from the world of a priori conceivability to a just-so world. They make up a just-so story about the actual world that relevant mental states do or do not constitute certain judgments. Yet, this can be nothing but deception, illusion, and fallacious reasoning. For a philosopher, like a non-cognitivist, to posit that the moral concept in judgments in agents' minds in the real world is actually constituted by a particular mental state, like a motivating conative one, a priori and without the proper experimental support is to tell merely a just-so story; a story whose repute should be cast among the lot of other narrations that come from the mouths of storytellers, fablers, and fabulists.

Also, along with one endorsing a general a priori MJI thesis, to additionally put forth the empirical introspective claim that one's present judgment in one's mind is a sincere one, which could be false given one's subconscious, in order to then try and reach the conclusion that one's MORAL concept in one's judgment in the real world is constituted by a motivating state that influences the judgment is to rely on an empirical introspective premise. This is not a purely a priori contention. However, let us look deeper at such a contention since perhaps causal experimental data may not be required to make the relevant causal claim.

(P1) If a priori MJI is true and one makes genuine moral judgments in the real world, then motivating mental states appropriately causally influence the genuine judgments.
(P2) A priori MJI is true.
(P3) One does make genuine moral judgments in the real world.
(P4) Motivating mental states appropriately causally influence the genuine judgments in the real world.

This argument may allow for reaching a causal claim in moral psychology in the real world without relevant causal experimental data. However, the first premise at first glance appears mysterious. If the antecedent of the conditional is true, how does a causal claim follow in the consequent, especially when it initially appears that there is no mention of causation in the antecedent? In response, let us look even more closely at the MJI phrase in the antecedent of the first premise: "a priori MJI is true." This implicitly also is saying that a sincere moral judgment necessarily is appropriately causally influenced by at least a motivating mental state. In so being influenced, the motivating mental state at least in part constitutes the moral concept in the judgment given the functionalist identification of concepts, and therefore, motivation is internal to the judgment. Understood in this fashion, the consequent in the first premise now seems to follow given the truth of the antecedent of this conditional. The first premise appears to be true.

However, recall that the above standardized argument is precarious as it swiftly can be overturned by experimental data, such as a neuroimaging scan that shows no correlation between motivation and judgment or empirical results demonstrating that motivational states do not influence decision-making. These perhaps may show that one really is not making a genuine judgment even though one consciously thinks one is, or if it independently is a posteriori established beyond mere introspective evidence that one is making a sincere judgment in the real world, disparate empirically confirmed causal data on sincere judgment that runs contrary to a priori MJI can show that a priori MJI is false. I will make a certain version of this latter kind of argument later in this chapter. The situation for the a priori MJI theorist is too perilous to allow for sufficient justification of a concept constitution and causal claim without experimental causal evidence. Once again, what specifically constitutes a concept and influences judgment in the real world is a scientific issue in cognitive science that requires the appropriate degree of causal experimental confirmation for sufficient justification due to a variety of reasons.

To note, I have stated above that proper causal experimental data is required to sufficiently justify a *specific* moral concept constitution claim. However, through observation and absent of such causal data, we still can be justified at times in making more *general* constitution claims that two people likely have mostly different constituents in a given case without specifically stating what those constituent mental states and psychological structures are. For, moral concepts play a causal role in decision-making and behavior. Thus, for example, two observed individuals displaying significantly different moral decision-making and behavior, absent of suspicion of akratic behavior, provides evidence that these two individuals likely have significantly different moral concept constituents. While in such a case, we cannot conclude at the specific level that a particular cognitive or conative state constitutes a concept because this requires appropriate causal experimental evidence, we still can infer that they largely have different moral concept constituents granted that the relevant provisos have been met, such as that the given judgments are observed under conditions that pass the possible mental error test. In this respect, historians, cognitive anthropologists, political scientists, and the like can make general empirical claims that certain people have very different moral concept constituents across time and location. However, based on such observations alone, they cannot be justified in making specific claims that particular mental states, such as the feeling of anger and the prototype HAS CAUSED ME HARM, in fact constitute the relevant moral concept and causally influence(d) the judgment.

Despite the fact that the MJI/MJE literature today is primarily based on a priori argumentation, there are those who in more recent times have addressed the MJI/MJE debate a posteriori (Gibbard 1990, Roskies 2003, Prinz 2007, 2015, Kennett & Fine 2008), and one should view my primary contribution to this issue as being an a posteriori contingent claim about the real world, which is the most important world. My pluralistic theory of moral concepts leads to the conclusion that when making genuine moral judgments, we widely either have a defeasible degree of motivation to act on the judgment or we have a sentiment or disposition to be motivated to act on the judgment. This follows since I have a specified pluralistic view on moral concepts, where moral concepts widely are constituted by both cognitive and conative states. Since I have shown that moral concepts in *all* kinds of moral judgments widely are in part constituted by, for example, emotions or sentiments, then motivation is internal to the very judgment itself for such decisions.

I state that moral judgments "widely" are constituted by motivating mental properties because motivation may not be internal to all moral judgments. For instance, certain psychologically abnormal agents like psychopaths with blunted affect may provide examples of individuals who at times can make moral judgments without being motivated or even having a disposition to be motivated to act on the judgment. Observation indicates that some of such patients consistently are not motivated at all to act in accordance with their judgments, so they even lack the disposition to be motivated.[6] For instance, they judge stereotypical moral transgressions in the West to be morally wrong (Blair et al. 2005, Aharoni et al. 2012), such as hitting others, lying, and stealing, but many psychopaths with blunted affect lack the motivation to act accordingly. Also, as my theory of moral concepts is a general claim about the human condition, I also allow for the possibility of aberrations within the population of the psychologically normal. Moreover, those suffering from certain temporary psychological maladies, like a bout of depression, exhaustion, apathy, etc., may not have a degree of motivation to act accordingly, but if so, they largely do have a disposition to be motivated that may be realized when they return to their normal psychological state. When experiencing such maladies, at least a conative sentiment is being expressed.

Since I allow for exceptions to MJI, where motivation is not internal to all sincere moral judgments but it is for an overwhelming majority of them, my pluralistic theory of moral concepts can be read as leading to an a posteriori weak conditional MJI view that severs motivation and judgment for certain limited cases. My conditional weak MJI view falls in the same category as certain other weak conditional MJI views that blur the boundary between MJI and MJE, such as those discussed above, in that they allow for certain exceptions where motivation is not internal to judgment. As my contingent MJI position immediately falls out of my pluralistic theory of moral concepts, my positive arguments for this view also have been posited in all of the previous chapters. To note, some may think that conditional MJI views are really MJE views since they sever the connection in certain cases between judgment and motivation. If so, I have no problems with someone calling my a posteriori position an MJE view. For, in the end, what matters not is the name of the position one espouses, which is just a name, but rather, the content of the claim itself.

10.3 Objections

To begin the first anticipated objection, many philosophers have addressed the MJI/MJE and even the cognitivism/non-cognitivism debate a priori. For example, a non-cognitivist may claim as a first premise that a generally understood MJI is a priori true, where all sincere moral judgments are constituted by motivating mental states. As a second premise, motivational Humeanism is posited as an a priori claim, where only conative mental properties are motivating mental properties but beliefs supposedly are not, nor can beliefs all by themselves lead to motivation. Moral motivation cannot come from belief alone. Motivational Humeanism entails that the relevant concepts in motivating judgments must be at least in part constitutively linked to some conative state, while anti-Humeanism entails that at times the relevant concepts in motivating judgments or judgments that lead to motivation are not constitutively linked to some conative state. Thus, since sincere moral judgments are constituted by motivating mental states (MJI) and only conative states are motivating mental states (motivational Humeanism), this non-cognitivist then concludes a priori that sincere moral judgments necessarily are constituted by conative states. *If* a moral judgment is a sincere one, then it must express a non-cognitive state.

The relationship between the a priori versus a posteriori investigations of the two issues at hand has not always been made clear, so I will attempt to explore this relationship more deeply. It may seem that those taking the a priori route on the cognitivism/non-cognitivism and/or MJI/MJE debates versus the a posteriori routes are focused on wholly different domains and inquiries. For instance, for the cognitivism/non-cognitivism debate, if it is an a posteriori contingent truth that all moral judgments express conative states and beliefs in the real world, then this can be consistent with the a priori conceptual claim that it is possible that genuine moral judgments do not express both states. For, there could be a possible world that is not the real world in which moral judgments do not express both states. Both of these seemingly conflicting claims stemming from different methodologies need not conflict. Likewise, for the MJI/MJE debate, if the generally understood MJI view is an a posteriori contingent truth in the real world, then this can be consistent with an a priori MJE position. This is because for this MJE view, there can be a possible world that is not the real world in which there are many moral judgments that are not constituted by a motivating mental property.

However, it is possible that both kinds of inquiries can overlap. For instance, if moral judgment on one hand and relevant beliefs and conative states on the other, both are rigid designators and designate the same property across all possible worlds, then the a posteriori discovery that moral judgments are identical to certain kinds of beliefs and conative states for the cognitivism/non-cognitivism debate will lead to an a posteriori necessary truth that moral judgments are constituted by both mental states across all possible worlds. This would be like how it is commonly held to be an a posteriori necessary truth that Hesperus is identical to Phosphorus.

Saul Kripke (1972) claims that HESPERUS is a proper name concept that rigidly designates *the evening star* across all possible worlds. Meanwhile, PHOSPHORUS rigidly designates *the morning star* across all possible worlds. Early on, people did not know that such concepts referred to the same star. People thought that both stars were different. It was later empirically discovered that Hesperus really is the same thing as Phosphorus, and this could have only been known a posteriori. The two mental representations are co-referential. Since the relevant concepts are rigid designators, given the a posteriori discovery, it then follows that such concepts are co-referential across all possible worlds. It is an a posteriori necessary truth that Hesperus is Phosphorus. For moral judgment, the a posteriori necessity conclusion in regards to judgment, belief, and conative states would have an immediate wholesale impact on the a priori inquiry in that it would involve all possible worlds, although I have serious reservations that an a posteriori necessity claim is a viable option when taking the a posteriori route. This is because it may be the case that MORAL JUDGMENT does not rigidly designate the same property across all possible worlds, but rather, the compound concept refers to different properties depending upon culture. As we saw in the seventh chapter when analyzing the moral/conventional distinction (§7.2–7.2.3), moral judgment is not a natural kind, and MORAL JUDGMENT may refer to different categories for different people rather than always referring to the same category across all possible worlds. Moreover, in subsequent chapters, we will discuss theories of reference for moral concepts based in part on experimental philosophy studies I have run and see that there is variability in the extension of such concepts.

Likewise, for the MJI/MJE debate, if it is an a posteriori necessary truth that the generally understood MJI view is true and all moral judgments are at least in part constituted by a motivating mental state across all possible worlds, then this will have a direct impact on the a priori approach to this field. However, the same reservations I have above about the reference of MORAL JUDGMENT apply here as well.

Also, for an a posteriori contingent claim, such a claim pertains only to the real world. This has some overlap with an a priori necessity claim that holds in all possible worlds in that such a claim includes the real world. Thus, for instance, those who address the cognitivism/non-cognitivism debate from an a priori vantage point may object to my weak hybrid position that their conclusion supersedes any conclusion drawn from an a posteriori methodology. An objector may respond that if a supposed moral judgment is consistent with an a posteriori-drawn conclusion on the cognitivism/non-cognitivism debate, but is not consistent with the a priori-drawn conclusion, then this judgment is not a sincere moral judgment. For example, the a posteriori conclusion drawn from my methodology is that cognitive and conative states are widely expressed in moral judgments. A pure non-cognitivist may counter and state, for example, that it is a priori necessarily true in all possible worlds, including the real world, that sincere moral judgments only express motivating conative states alone and are influenced by them. Any judgment that in any way deviates from this is not a sincere moral judgment. Thus, judgments that are empirically discovered to express, for example, both beliefs and emotions are not sincere moral judgments. I may have empirically proven as a contingent truth that moral judgments in the actual world widely express, for instance, beliefs and conative states, but such subjects really are not making sincere moral judgments. They are making insincere moral judgments.

One response to this objection is that it can lead to an unreasonable outcome at times, such as in my case with my pluralistic theory of moral concepts. If the empirical evidence shows that when the pure non-cognitivist, his or her mother, as well as everyone else the non-cognitivist knows makes seemingly sincere moral judgments, such as RAPE IS WRONG and MURDER IS WRONG, that express both mental states, then such an a priori theorist must conclude that they themselves and pretty much everyone else they know have never made a genuine moral judgment ever. In fact, they would have to conclude that human beings widely have never made a real moral judgment since we know based on empirical fact that our judgments widely express two different kinds of mental states rather than only conative states. There is a grand worldwide illusion and delusion that most, if not all, psychologically normal people appear to make genuine moral judgments, but throughout their lifetimes, they do not. However, this appears unreasonable as there are many individuals who appear to have made sincere moral judgments in the real world, such as perhaps your mother when telling you to share with your siblings when you were a child, a minority protester chanting that racism is wrong, a sex slave uttering that slavery is immoral, a pro-life advocate judging that abortion is unethical, or perhaps a priest when advocating for the Ten Commandments to his congregation.

What helps support this point that many people in the real world make sincere judgments is a different a posteriori inquiry for addressing when a person is making a sincere moral judgment or not. For, in the real world, we empirically at times try to assess whether someone is being sincere, insincere, sarcastic, is just joking, or is telling a lie, and at many times, we are empirically justified in our beliefs about sincerity and insincerity, such as for parents in evaluating the statement of their unruly child or for detecting sarcasm within the context of a conversation. Having such abilities also can be life-saving at times when crucial matters are at stake. Moreover, in criminal trials, juries and judges attempt to assess the sincerity of testimony and displays of remorse and sorrow; fathers the sincerity of their daughters' suitors.

For my general empirical approach to both debates, we also can use relevant empirical means for inductively analyzing whether someone is making a genuine moral judgment or not. For an a posteriori contingent claim, there are various factors that, when some of them are combined and satisfied, can help lead to an inductive inference as far as whether a person is likely making a sincere judgment or not. Based on experience, we have learned that these conditions that are not necessary and sufficient conditions can be associated with making sincere/insincere judgments. The conditions can include but are not limited to: (1) Making sure the judger is not in an altered state of mind from his or her norm, such as being under the influence of drugs. (2) Making sure the judger was not extraneously induced with mental states by an experimenter or by something else before even beginning to entertain a moral dilemma. (3) Examining whether the judgment is generally consistent and coherent with the agent's other moral judgments. Testimony from those who know or who have met the subject can be relevant here. (4) Using a polygraph test. (5) Waiting to see if the judgment is quickly retracted. For instance, someone filling out a moral questionnaire may erase and change their answer on a problem, where they leave their new answer as being the final decision. In this case, the first judgment likely is not a sincere judgment. (6) Making sure the judger is not forming a decision in a situation where there is self-gain or self-interest, such as financial reward, for the judger to make insincere judgments. (7) Making sure the judger is not forming a decision in a situation where there is a kind of comedic environment that may promote subjects providing judgments only in jest. (8) Making sure the judger is not a pathological liar or is delusional. If the judger is such a liar or is permanently delusional, then further precautions from a psychologist or psychiatrist must be used to determine what their real judgments are, if any or if possible. (9) Testing to see if the judger can successfully pass the moral/conventional task relative to his or her culture when given particular kinds of acts to categorize as falling in either the moral or conventional domains.

Once again, these are not necessary and sufficient conditions. For example, one may be under the influence of drugs, be extraneously induced with mental states by an experimenter, be in a situation where one is financially bribed to make a particular moral judgment, or be in a comedic environment, but one still may be able to make a sincere judgment in such situations. A polygraph test may be faulty or mistaken. A person may provide a coherent set of judgments but such a set is based on a lie, somewhat similar to how some identity thieves temporarily yet coherently take on the identity of another. One may have changed one's original answer on a questionnaire, but such a change was made due to a subconscious mental error such that the latter judgment is not one's genuine judgment. An agent is not a pathological liar, among other things, but she still may make an insincere judgment. One may not be able to sufficiently score high enough on the moral/conventional task relative to one's culture, but one was still able to get some questions right. On only those successful issues, along with the possible satisfaction of some of the other above conditions, one might still make a sincere moral judgment on them.

If, for example, (1), (2), (5), (6), (7), (8), and (9) are satisfied, which is the case on the studies on psychologically normal people that I relied upon to help support my pluralistic theory of moral concepts, then this permits an inductive inference and a charitable interpretation that their judgments are likely sincere ones. To be sure, there can be defeaters even though many conditions are satisfied. For example, someone may give inconsistent judgments, refuse to take a polygraph exam, and have the incentive to lie in order to keep one's job or attain a new post. However, many of the other conditions are satisfied for this agent, such as being in a normal state of mind and not being in a comedic environment. In such a situation, with all else being equal, we cannot with sufficient confidence attribute the judgment in question as being a sincere one, although future strong evidence might allow us to later change the verdict. Yet, in the absence of such defeaters, which generally is the case for participants in the causal moral judgment literature that I relied upon to establish moral concept pluralism, the satisfaction of many of the criteria does allow for the justified inference that their judgments are sincere ones. Also, recall from prototype experiments that subjects' moral concepts are not constituted by components that suggest that they are making inverted commas judgments that moral values are understood only descriptively as simply being what a society believes (§4.2). While many people believe *prescriptively* that moral values are true and ought to be followed relative to their culture, normal subjects widely are not making strictly descriptive inverted commas judgments when making moral decisions. Rather, they are making straightforward normative moral judgments. All of the above provides sufficient justification that sincere judgments commonly made by psychologically normal agents widely express both cognitive and conative states.

Empirical evidence on psychopaths generally may satisfy these seven criteria as well. Psychopaths are pathological liars, however, studies on them have been run by professional psychologists who at many times have designed their experiments in ways to diminish the possibility of deceitful responses, such as informing psychopathic subjects of the number of moral and conventional issues so that they do not try to impress others by elevating all norms to moral ones. Furthermore, recall that there is evidence that psychopaths can make the moral/conventional distinction relative to their culture (§7.2).[7] To note, there still can be counterexamples even if the above list of conditions is satisfied, where someone still may be making an insincere judgment. Yet, meeting many of such criteria still allows for a justified inductive inference that the judgment is likely a sincere one. The strength of the induction comes in matters of degrees depending upon how many conditions are satisfied. Given the satisfaction of the given seven criteria, this provides strong reason to believe that psychopaths' relevant judgments that are not constituted by motivating conative mental states are sincere ones.

All in all, it is simply false that we widely have never made a real moral judgment in our lives. Rather, we richly make sincere judgments about how we ought to live our lives throughout our lifetimes. In this case, the relevant a priori theorist would be wrong, for example, to think that all sincere moral judgments only express conative states. For an a priori theorist to claim necessarily that genuine moral judgments contrarily can only express some other arrangement than mine and that normal agents in the real world widely never make sincere moral judgments leads to nothing but folly. Such a view is empirically false. My above a posteriori claim on the cognitivism/non-cognitivism debate is not subservient to a priori conclusions on the issue, and we can see how a priori conclusions on this debate at times even can bend the knee before a posteriori ones.

Of course, this a posteriori claim, like any a posterior claim, is still reliant on certain theoretical elements such as a theoretical framework for interpreting the data; elements that may be a priori affairs. Hence, I further qualify my point in that an a posteriori conclusion on the cognitivism/non-cognitivism debate itself can be reliant on certain more metalevel a priori issues. However, I still conclude that an a posteriori conclusion on the debate is not subservient to any a priori conclusion specifically on the cognitivism/non-cognitivism debate due to my above given reasons.

Likewise, for the MJI/MJE debate, an a posteriori contingent claim about the real world has some overlap with an a priori necessity claim in that this latter claim applies to all possible worlds, including the real one. More particularly for our purposes, my a posteriori contingent conclusion for my specified MJI can have some overlap with a robust a priori MJI claim that specifically states that in all possible worlds, including the real world, genuine moral judgments always are constituted by motivating mental states.[8] In the real world, I have argued that there are certain individuals whose genuine judgments are not so constituted. However, the robust a priori MJI advocate may state that their view overrides my conditional and contingent weak MJI position as psychopaths do not make sincere judgments since their judgments are not constituted by a motivating mental state, like a conative one.

However, as previously argued, just as a police officer can be empirically justified in believing that an insensible knave is being insincere or that a witness with no conflict of interest and with a coherent story is being sincere, we are inductively justified in believing that psychopaths make sincere judgments. My contention is an inductive claim of probability or likelihood. However, like other well-supported inductive claims, one is still justified in believing it. This claim is ensconced within my wider empirically confirmed pluralistic theory of moral concepts. Seeing is believing, and my inductive claim based on observations that any person with eyes can perceive overrides a contrary a priori claim on the issue. A posteriori claims can override a priori ones. For instance, quantum mechanics overturns certain a priori claims in classical logic in the micro-world, such as the distributive law and the law of non-contradiction, and Einstein's theory of relativity overturns Euclidean geometry in the macro-world.

Also, there is an unsurprising lack of consensus on the long-running a priori MJI/MJE debate. David Bourget and David Chalmers (2014) have administered a survey asking professional philosophers what their views are on a host of philosophical issues. They found that 35% of the sample population believes in MJI, 30% hold MJE, and 35% maintain some other view. Moreover, there are conflicting and inconclusive results on experimental philosophy studies testing lay intuitions on this debate. Nichols (2002) found that most hold MJE, while Michael Ridge (2014) found that most hold MJI. The inductive evidence that psychopaths can make genuine judgments coupled with the fact that there embarrassingly is far from any general consensus on the a priori MJI/MJE debate in part helps us to infer that some psychopaths do make sincere moral judgments without being motivated or being disposed to being motivated to act accordingly.

Michael Smith (2008) also may object that the cognitivism/non-cognitivism and MJI/MJE debates are inherently a priori conceptual claims, so my a posteriori conclusions do not really speak to the debates at all. In a certain sense, this is right that my contingent claims do not speak to the conceptual debates as they do not even pretend to apply in all possible worlds. However, they do impact the conceptual debates in the sense that they are true of the actual world, and they will countermand contrary a priori necessity claims; claims that purport to include the real world in its purview. Second, this lack of making a claim about all possible worlds should not be so bothersome because my positions are claims about the most important and meaningful world: the real one.

Moreover, to claim that the cognitivism/non-cognitivism and MJI/MJE debates concerning what mental states constitute our moral concepts are inherently an a priori endeavor is a false hagiography magnifying and projecting a narrow and peculiar era of analytic philosophy that understands the primary methodology of these debates to be from the armchair. It is to ignore and to do violence to the history of the debates and the empirical claims by British Sentimentalist empiricists on the issues like Hume, Adam Smith, and Hutcheson.

More broadly, I remind the reader from the first chapter that using empirical evidence to make claims about the mind and/or ethics is no stranger to philosophy. Descartes, the founder of neuroscience, readily dissected brains to map out its anatomy and claim that the pineal gland is the seat of the soul. William James is considered to be one of the fathers of modern psychology, and the building that houses the psychology department at Harvard University bears his name. John Stuart Mill, who was an empiricist, held an empiricist view of psychological concepts, where concepts, such as moral ones, only are acquired through the senses. He also criticized Kant's a priori method for conducting normative ethics because to use a priori reasoning is to merely put forth one's own subjectively biased and prejudiced judgments. Rather, he argued that we need to philosophize about right and wrong empirically using an external standard, such as by considering the greatest happiness for the greatest number. My hybrid view is an empirical claim like the claims of Hume and Adam Smith; a company of which need bear no ignominy or shame.

10.3.1 Objections Against Hybrid Views

Moving on to other objections, there are significant perceived benefits of a hybrid theory that seemingly are more difficult to attain on a pure cognitivist or pure non-cognitivist framework. For example, cognitivist views have a difficult time attempting to account for the motivation that generally appears to accompany the making of sincere moral judgments. When people make sincere judgments, such as I SHOULD CHANGE THIS YEAR AND VOTE FOR THE DEMOCRAT RATHER THAN REPUBLICAN, agents generally seem to have some motivation to act on their genuine judgments or at least have a disposition to so act. If moral judgments are beliefs, then how can such judgments motivate, especially if the default Humean theory of motivation is true? However, espousing a hybrid position in which moral judgments also express conative states, which are motivational mental states, seemingly alleviates this problem. This appears to give the hybridist an advantage in the field of moral motivation compared to the pure cognitivist.

On the other hand, pure non-cognitivists tend to have difficulties accounting for the well-noted Frege-Geach problem, although they put forth intricate attempts to address the issue (Blackburn 1985, 1998, Gibbard 1990). When moral judgments are put in an unexpressed context such as in the antecedent of a conditional statement, the meaning of the judgment in this unexpressed context will differ from when this judgment is put forth in an expressed context. For instance, in the argument below, from a non-cognitivist perspective, the first premise contains a judgment that expresses a conative state. However, in the second premise, 'murder is wrong' does not express a conative state.

(P1) Murder is wrong.
(P2) If murder is wrong, then getting my brother to murder is wrong.
(P3) Getting my brother to murder is wrong.

Since the judgment, 'murder is wrong,' supposedly has different meanings in the first versus the second premise, the above argument is not a valid argument, and it commits the fallacy of equivocation. However, intuitively, this argument is a deductively valid one, and it commits no such fallacy. On the other hand, hybridism can escape the Frege-Geach objection since it allows for a cognitive component to moral judgments that apparently permits a continuity of the same cognitive meaning in moral judgments in both expressed and non-expressed contexts. This degree of supposed shared meaning is sufficient such that the judgment contained in both premises can be said to share the same meaning. The fallacy of equivocation does not come into play. Also, even if a disparate causal theory of reference for moral concepts is true, the Frege-Geach problem still can be handled by the particular hybridist who maintains that moral concepts refer to moral properties. For, the moral concept in the expressed and unexpressed context will refer and will have the same extension given the general causal connection to moral properties. They will share the same meaning and content, so the fallacy of equivocation will not be committed.

However, Mark Schroeder (2009, 2010) raises objections and warnings against certain hybrid accounts. He points out that the non-cognitive attitude expressed in the conclusion of a Frege-Geach modus ponens argument must also be contained somewhere in one of the premises. This is in part required for one to be rationally committed to accepting the conclusion. It is easy to see that the belief components of the two premises logically commit one to accepting the validity of the belief element of the conclusion of the modus ponens contention. However, on a hybridist picture, there is another component to moral judgment that must be taken into account. What also is required for one to rationally be committed for maintaining the conclusion that getting my brother to murder someone else is wrong is having the negative non-cognitive attitude that in part constitutes the conclusory judgment. This is because such an attitude is also a component of the conclusory judgment on a hybrid picture. In order to accept the conclusion, one must have the belief and the attitude. Yet, Schroeder notes that one way to resolve the issue is that if the negative attitude is already being expressed by the agent in a premise, such as in the first premise that murder is wrong, then the agent making the modus ponens inference already has the negative attitude to readily accept the non-cognitive component of the conclusory judgment. The agent then need only draw the descriptive inference in the modus ponens to accept the conclusion.

Concerning this worry, my hybrid picture can account for it in that the feeling or sentiment of disapprobation that is in part expressed in the conclusion is the same as that which is in part expressed in the first premise. 'Murder is wrong' and 'Getting my brother to murder is wrong' both express the same emotion as both are about the same general act of murder. Hence, my hybrid view can account for Schroeder's concern as well as the Frege-Geach problem, whereas pure non-cognitivist theories face serious difficulties.

Second, Schroeder notes that some hybridists understand moral concepts as being like pejoratives, such as racial slurs (Copp 2001, Boisvert 2008). A racial slur term has a descriptive component that describes the relevant race, but it also contains a contemptuous attitude toward members of that race. There is a descriptive and conative component. Also, recall that I have shown that there is a cognitive normative component to moral concepts as well (§8.5). Adherents of the pejorative model for hybridism tend to claim that every judgment containing WRONG will express the very same desire-like attitude in any context. Moreover, you only can accept a judgment that involves the notion that *x* is wrong if you have this exact desire-like attitude. Thus, everyone must share the same desire-like attitude since we all have made or accepted moral judgments before that something is wrong. Schroeder rightfully objects that this is an extraordinary empirical assumption that we all have the exact same attitude for our WRONG concept in every context of making judgments about wrongness. I agree. While WRONG can express the same emotion in the first premise and conclusion within the confines of a Frege-Geach modus ponens as the statements are about the same general act, it is not the case that this concept always expresses the exact same conative attitude in every context for every person. When I make judgments against murder, I at least in part may express anger. When I make judgments that my brother's failure to recycle is wrong, I at least in part may be expressing disappointment. When I make a judgment against my rival, I at least in part may express jealousy. When I tell my brother that lying is wrong, I at least in part may be expressing a sentiment of anger. This is broadly consistent with my aforementioned position that different mental states that constitute a concept can be used or not used depending on the context or situation. My pluralistic account of moral concepts should not be understood as strictly adopting the pejorative model, and my view perfectly allows for different conative states being expressed in different contexts. This is a much more plausible picture of the moral mind, and it escapes Schroeder's criticism.

Schroeder continues his attack against the pejorative model by stating that it does not have an advantage over pure cognitivist theories in the realm of moral motivation. He says that if everyone has exactly the same desire-like attitude for WRONG in any context, then this widespread conative state may allow the pure cognitivist to account for moral motivation as well, where people generally have a degree of motivation to act upon their genuinely held moral judgments. The hybridist will not have an advantage over the cognitivist in this regard. On the pejorative model, everyone has this specific pervasive attitude. This allows for a pure cognitivist picture that moral judgments express only beliefs, and the pervasive attitude is a background conative state that accounts for the motivation that generally exists when people make sincere judgments. For the cognitivist, the widespread desire-like attitude that for them is external to and not part of the judgment leads to a degree of motivation to act. Hence, allowing for a pervasive desire-like attitude when anyone makes a "wrong" judgment will not provide an advantage for the pejorative-based hybrid theorist over that of the pure cognitivist regarding moral motivation. This is because if everyone has such a motivational mental state, the pure cognitivist can use it as a pervasive external background mental state to account for the motivation that seems to at least generally accompany the making of sincere moral judgments. Motivation is external, not internal, to judgment.

My response is that I do not maintain the pejorative hybrid model, so I do not claim that there is a single and specific widespread conative state that is tied to judgments of wrongness. However, as psychologically normal people have the capacity to experience various moral emotions and the empirical data shows that emotions are rampant in such moral decision-making, perhaps the cognitivist may make the same above move except use emotions instead. Moral judgments only express beliefs, and the background moral emotions that lie external rather than internal to moral judgment provide the motivation. However, this is false. Since concepts are functionally defined as playing a specified causal role in decision-making, moral concepts just are those psychological structures that appropriately realize the causal role. Given the appropriate influence of emotions, among other states, in moral cognition, relevant moral judgments are in part constituted by sentiments or emotions and therefore, express them. A pure cognitivist view is empirically false. In fact, given that moral concepts are defined as being those mental states that appropriately influence moral decision-making, only a hybrid account can explain and predict the fact that both cognitive and conative states appropriately influence such decision-making. This is a direct, decisive, and empirically confirmed explanatory and predictive advantage a hybrid theory has over that of pure cognitive and pure non-cognitive accounts. Pure cognitivist and pure non-cognitivist accounts are all empirically false.

Moreover, if a Humean theory of motivation is correct, my hybrid account can explain how the good and strong-willed person is morally motivated. However, the pure cognitivist cannot. Consistent with the likes of Confucius and Aristotle, the good and strong-willed person is automatically motivated to act upon her judgments. Highly virtuous agents have inclinations, emotions, and desires that are aligned with acting in the right way. Motivation flows automatically in virtue of making the judgment itself. My theory can explain the general motivations of highly virtuous persons in that moral judgments are in part constituted by emotions. On my view, motivation is *internal* to the judgment itself. On Schroeder's setup that assumes motivational Humeanism, the cognitivist cannot say this because for them, moral judgments only express beliefs. For cognitivists, the motivating emotions, if present, are *external* to the judgment. The emotions are an extra mental state in addition to the judgment. Thus, on the cognitivist picture, where emotions are external and in addition to judgment, there is "one thought too many" in moral motivation. This is not how highly virtuous persons perceivably act, but rather, they do the right thing seamlessly, naturally, immediately, and effortlessly. Motivation seemingly flows automatically from their convictions. In other words, emotions appear to in part constitute their moral judgments without the need for additional external mental states that aid in motivation. Only within the confines of Schroeder's setup, this is another explanatory virtue tied to the issue of motivation my hybrid theory may have over a pure cognitivist account. To note, this alone is not sufficient to establish moral concept constitution claims and the influence of motivating mental states on judgments from the highly virtuous as, for example, causal experimental data is required. It is too precarious otherwise. However, this point might provide some more limited additional support for my view.

Schroeder raises another worry for pejorative models in that they claim that moral concepts always express desire-like attitudes even when embedded in linguistic expressions such as 'believes that' and 'thinks that.' For instance, when I have the thought ANNETTE THINKS THAT BILL IS WRONG, on the pejorative model, I must be expressing and experiencing the negative desire-like attitude that is contained within WRONG. However, I actually am not judging that Bill is wrong in this case. I am merely describing the thoughts of someone else named Annette. Yet, on the pejorative model, I must be expressing the relevant attitude in any context whatsoever if I am using WRONG. In this case, I must be expressing the relevant attitude against Bill as if I were in fact making the moral judgment myself against Bill even though I am not. On the pejorative account, if I do not have the negative attitude, then I really cannot be using this word even to describe what other people think. However, this is preposterous. I can have the thought ANNETTE THINKS THAT BILL IS WRONG while not simultaneously having the relevant attitude as I am not necessarily making a moral judgment against Bill.

In response, as I do not maintain the pejorative model, I do not claim that moral concepts necessarily are constituted by emotions at all times when embedded in the above relevant linguistic expressions; expressions such as 'thinks that.' Rather, consistent with my hybrid theory, the concept WRONG in ANNETTE THINKS THAT BILL IS WRONG, is in part constituted by a sentiment and not necessarily an emotion. This disposition to feel an emotion can become activated in the proper context such as when WRONG is not embedded in such linguistic expressions that merely describe someone else's thoughts but rather, belongs to a moral judgment that one is actually making, such as MURDER IS WRONG.

10.4 An A Posteriori Claim is Sufficient

By relying on my pluralistic theory of moral concepts and the a posteriori arguments it took to justify it, I have provided novel contentions for a qualified weak hybrid position in the cognitivism/non-cognitivism debate and for a specified weak conditional MJI view on the MJI/MJE debate. These are direct means for addressing these issues, understood as a posteriori investigations, so much so that the final outcome of utilizing this methodology should be understood to be quite decisive. Direct experiments for testing a hypothesis have provided decisive evidence in the past. For instance, the study of the deflection of light from stars passing near the sun during a solar eclipse in 1919 provided such evidence in favor of Einstein's theory of relativity. Although there were other kinks and problems to be worked out and there still are to this day regarding relativity, the empirical test in 1919 was sufficient to set the general agenda for macrophysics, and Newtonian physics for the macro-world was unquestionably overthrown.

Likewise, the functionalist identification of moral concepts along with the many other kinds of arguments I have provided are a direct method that provides such decisive empirical confirmation regarding the relevant aspects of the two debates at hand. Even though there may be kinks and other future discovered problems to work out on the relevant aspects of the cognitivism/non-cognitivism and MJI/MJE debates, such direct empirical confirmation that comes out of my methodology is sufficient to set the general agenda on these issues concerning what psychological states sincere moral judgments express and are constituted by in the real world. For, it is an empirically established truth that our genuine moral judgments generally express cognitive and conative states. Such paradigm shifts should occur, and we should focus our efforts on tinkering with my theories and resolving any kinks, problems, or puzzles that may remain. These subjects, understood as a posteriori inquiries that produce contingent truths, may finally be resolved or be close to being resolved given my new contentions.

What should happen may be somewhat similar to the metaphysical debate as to whether the universe has a beginning or is infinite and has no beginning. This issue, understood as an a priori investigation, was debated by philosophers for millennia without reaching any consensus, to the chagrin of Kant. However, while the conceptual debate unsurprisingly still continues to this day in philosophy, understood as an a posteriori contingent inquiry concerning only the actual world, it was empirically resolved in physics by the Big Bang theory, where the universe began to exist about 13 billion years ago. I take it that this is a fascinating point that should draw extreme interest in philosophers and physicists; that in the real world we live in, the universe began to exist. The a priori conceptual debate is countermanded by empirical investigation in regard to the domain of the real world and is largely a moot point. For, if philosophers' end game is not to ultimately try and draw various conclusions about human existence, the real world, and our place in this real world, then I see no point in being a philosopher in the first place.

Likewise, I perceive that my arguments for my pluralistic theory of moral concepts along with the functional identifications of moral concepts are key philosophical insights that will lay the relevant aspects of the a posteriori cognitivism/non-cognitivism and MJI/MJE debates generally to rest as far as whether or not in the real world we live in, our sincere moral judgments express beliefs, conative states, or both and whether or not our genuine moral judgments and concepts are constituted by motivating mental states, respectively. Some philosophers may want to continue the a priori investigation to examine whether my particular qualified a posteriori hybridist and MJI conclusions hold beyond the real world in all possible worlds or not. However, this is purely academic. I take it that my conclusions from my a posteriori investigations sufficiently will capture the main point of interest for philosophers and psychologists in regards to the psychological basis of moral judgment.

Notes

1 This view will be shown to be empirically false in that moral judgments also express conative states. Moreover, later chapters will demonstrate that moral concepts are representational.

2 Non-cognitivists once held that moral judgments are incapable of being true or false *tout court*. More recently, non-cognitivists tend to maintain that moral judgments are capable of being true or false in a deflationary way in order to try and account for the seeming truth-aptness that purportedly underlies moral discourse.

3 In the empirical realm, such complex versions also can be a posteriori tested for by using my functionalist methodology and examining if the relevant mental states influence decision-making in the appropriate way.

4 Given the wide use of cognitive states in moral cognition, even if a particular judgment did not express a belief, we still can say that it is constituted by a disposition to express a cognitive state. The judgment still expresses two states: A conative state and a disposition to express a belief.
5 Ridge (2014) more recently has claimed that his hybrid non-cognitivist position, called "Ecumenical Expressivism," can espouse a cognitivist or deflationary theory of truth. It is not committed to any particular view on moral truth.
6 This still holds even if one is an anti-Humean on motivation and maintains that beliefs can at times motivate. Their relevant beliefs are not motivational. If one is an anti-Humean on motivation and holds the strong view that moral beliefs always provide a degree of motivation, then studies on psychopaths provide a direct counterexample to this position.
7 Recall that on other moral/conventional task studies that were not as well-designed in which psychopaths failed at the task, they still got some right. If such results were true, psychopaths may still make genuine judgments on those relevant issues.
8 The purview of robust a priori MJI views does not include the theories of Korsgaard and Smith as they are consistent with my a posteriori MJI claim. Psychopaths simply are not practically rational on their account although they are making genuine judgments, so there is no necessary connection for psychopaths.

References

Aharoni, E., Sinnott-Armstrong, W., and Kiehl, K.A. 2012. "Can Psychopathic Offenders Discern Moral Wrongs? A New Look at the Moral/Conventional Distinction." *Journal of Abnormal Psychology* 121, 484.

Ayer, A.J. 1936. *Language, Truth and Logic.* London: Gollancz.

Blackburn, Simon. 1985. "Errors and the Phenomenology of Value." In *Morality and Objectivity.* Ed. by T. Honderich. London: Routledge & Kegan Paul.

Blackburn, Simon. 1998. *Ruling Passions.* Oxford: Oxford University Press.

Blair, R., Mitchell, D., and Blair, K. 2005. *Psychopath: Emotion and the Brain.* New York: Wiley-Blackwell.

Boisvert, Daniel. 2008. Expressive-Assertivism. *Pacific Philosophical Quarterly* 89, 169–203.

Bourget, David and Chalmers, David. 2014. "What do Philosopher's Believe?" *Philosophical Studies* 170, 465–500.

Brink, David. 1989. *Moral Realism and the Foundation of Ethics.* Cambridge: Cambridge University Press.

Copp, David. 2001. "Realist-Expressivism: A Neglected Option for Moral Realism." *Social Philosophy and Policy* 18, 1–43.

Gibbard, Allan. 1990. *Wise Choices, Apt Feelings.* Oxford: Clarendon Press.

Gibbard, Allan. 2003. *Thinking How to Live.* Cambridge, MA: Harvard University Press.

Hare, R.M. 1952. *The Language of Morals.* Oxford: Clarendon.

Horgan, Terry and Timmons, Mark. 2000. "Nondescriptivist Cognitivism: Framework for a New Metaethic." *Philosophical Papers* 29, 121–153.

Hume, David. 1738/2000. *A Treatise of Human Nature.* Ed. By D. Norton and M. Norton. Oxford: Oxford University Press.

Kennett, Jeannett and Fine, Cordelia. 2008. "Internalism and the Evidence from Psychopaths and 'acquired sociopaths.'" In *Moral Psychology Vol.* 3. Ed. by Walter Sinnott-Armstrong. Cambridge, MA: The MIT Press, 173–190.

Korsgaard, Christine. 1986. "Skepticism About Practical Reason." *The Journal of Philosophy* 83, 5–25.

Kripke, Saul. 1972. *Naming and Necessity*. Cambridge, MA: Harvard University Press.

Nichols, Shaun. 2002. "Is it Irrational to be Immoral? How psychopaths threaten moral rationalism." *Monist* 85: 285–304.

Prinz, Jesse. 2007. *The Emotional Construction of Morals*. Oxford: Oxford University Press.

Prinz, Jesse. 2015. "An Empirical Case for Motivational Internalism." *Motivational Internalism*. Ed. by G. Bjornsson, C. Strandberg, R.F. Olinder, J. Eriksson. Oxford: Oxford University Press, 61–84.

Ridge, Michael. 2014. *Impassioned Belief*. Oxford: Oxford University Press.

Roskies, Adina. 2003. "Are Ethical Judgments Intrinsically Motivational? Lesson from 'Acquired Sociopathy.'" *Philosophical Psychology* 16, 51–66.

Schroeder, Mark. 2009. "Hybrid Expressivism: Virtues and vices." *Ethics* 119, 257–309.

Schroeder, Mark. 2010. *Noncognitivism in Ethics*. London: Routledge.

Shafer-Landau, Russ. 2003. *Moral Realism: A Defense*. Oxford: Oxford University Press.

Smith, Michael. 1994. *The Moral Problem*. Oxford: Blackwell Publishers.

Smith, Michael. 2008. "The Truth about Internalism." In *Moral Psychology, Vol.* 3. Ed. by W. Sinnott-Armstrong. Cambridge, MA: The MIT Press, 207–216.

Stevenson, Charles. 1944. *Ethics and Language*. New Haven and London: Yale University Press.

Part II

The Semantic Project and Moral Relativism

11 Moral Semantic Relativism

It is now time to move on to the next project. Up to now, we have discussed the constitution project for moral concepts. We have examined theories of concepts, what mental states constitute moral concepts, and what ramification this has in various domains of moral philosophy. Let us now explore what I called in the first chapter the "semantic project" for moral concepts. For our purposes, this inquiry in particular will focus on what is in principle the distinct issue of what the reference of our moral concepts is.

11.1 Theories of Moral Truth

It first will be helpful to lay out some basic demarcations on theories of moral truth since as we shall see, theories of truth are tied to moral semantics. The naming conventions of the various theories of moral truth can be different for different philosophers. Hence, I stipulate my own meanings of the terms and will attempt to stay consistent in their use throughout. *Objectivist theories* will be understood here as ones that posit that moral judgments on many particular cases are capable of being true or false for all people across location and time.[1] Many of such judgments are objectively true. For example, on any objectivist view, there is only one correct answer to the question of whether abortion or euthanasia is morally wrong or not, and this correct answer does not vary from culture to culture even though different cultures, as a descriptive matter, do take opposing stances on the issue. *Non-objectivist views* claim that objectivism is false and that for all moral issues there is not one correct answer, where moral judgments can correspond to such objective facts. Some examples of such theories are *error theory*, *non-cognitivism* with its deflationary account of moral truth, and *moral relativism*. Error theory maintains that all moral judgments are false. One of the main arguments for this view is that moral concepts purport to refer to objective moral properties that provide reasons for action to all, but such properties are mysterious and do not exist (Mackie 1977, Joyce 2001). Hence, all moral judgments are false. Meanwhile, we already have discussed how on a deflationary account, moral judgments are incapable of being true or false in a genuine or robust way, and such judgments do not refer to genuine moral properties as such properties do not exist (§10.1). Error theorists and non-cognitivists are eliminativists on moral properties.

Moral relativism can be thought of as an umbrella category that contains different tokens. What unifies them all is that they do not maintain that there is an objective moral truth, but rather, the attribution of truth or falsity to a judgment must always be relativized, such as to an agent or group. One kind of relativism is that there is a *group* or *cultural relativism.* This is where moral judgments are true or false only relative to a group, such as to a cultural or subcultural group. Notice that this is not a descriptive view merely stating that people have different judgments in different groups. Rather, it makes a statement about the different truth conditions – or the conditions under which a judgment is true – that apply to different groups based on differences in social practices or institutions. What normatively is true or false is relative to a group. On this picture, there is an incommensurability of moral concepts, where such concepts have different referents or extensions. Moral concepts are like indexicals in that their content or reference shifts depending upon the context of who is making the judgment and what group he or she belongs. Indexicals, like 'I,' in sentences like "I am happy" and "I am not happy" have different contents depending upon who is uttering the sentence. If you utter "I am happy" and I utter "I am not happy," 'I' has different extensions for both utterances, and as such, we both can be correct relative to ourselves. They have different truth conditions to their judgments as they are about different people. There is no contradiction in both utterances even though there initially may appear to be conflict. For group relativism, moral concepts are like indexicals that can have different contents based on group membership. There is no genuine disagreement between groups but only apparent or verbal disagreement, although there are genuine disagreements within groups. If moral concepts across groups refer to different extensions or, in other words, have different contents, then they also are talking past one another. Reference must coincide for two peoples' concepts to be commensurable with each other. For example, if you say, "The bank is at this point on the map" and I say, "No, the bank is at that point on the map," we both can be correct since by 'bank' you are referring to a financial institution, and by 'bank' I am talking about the slope by the side of a river. Our 'bank' terms have different contents and are about different things, so we both can be correct. There is no genuine disagreement. Likewise, when one says, "Genocide is 'bad'" and another says, "Genocide is not 'bad,'" if the 'bad' terms are about different things, like apples and oranges, then they are talking past one another, and they both can be relativistically correct. There is no genuine disagreement. The above is a classic contention for group relativism in moral philosophy that has been used in other domains of philosophy as well.

Another kind of relativism view is *subjectivism*. This theory claims that judgments are true or false relative to an individual subject rather than group. It is an indexical-based view like group relativism. For subjectivism, the content of moral concepts shifts based on the context of the relevant subject. Generally understood, subjectivism maintains that an action is right when the speaker or agent approves of the action, and a moral judgment is true relative to a speaker or agent if it accurately reports the sentiments and desires of the aforesaid speaker or agent, respectively. Subjectivism itself can be further split into *speaker* and *agent subjectivism*, where speaker subjectivism tends to be the default position. Speaker subjectivism, which also can be known as appraiser subjectivism or contextualism, holds that moral truth is relative to the speaker making the judgment. For agent subjectivism, moral truth is relative to the agent about whom the judgment is being made. This bifurcation between speaker versus agent also can apply to group relativism, where moral truth is relative to a speaker's group or agent's group. Insofar as group relativism and subjectivism are indexical-based theories, we will understand them to be in the subcategory *indexical moral relativism*. Indexical relativism is a subcategory of moral relativism that contains group relativism and subjectivism.

The notions of "moral relativism" and "relativism," especially in the 20th century, have been tied to an indexical-based theory. However, there is another newer kind of relativism, where truth is relative to a context of assessment (MacFarlane 2005, 2014). This kind of moral relativism, which will be called *assessment sensitivity relativism*, claims that judgments refer to the same propositions and properties. This is not an indexical-based relativism, where JUSTICE and GOOD have different referents and there is an incommensurability of such concepts. As an example of assessment sensitivity relativism, I may judge PIZZA IS TASTY, but you may judge PIZZA IS NOT TASTY. In this case, both of our TASTY concepts have the same extension. However, the truth of our judgments is relative to a context of assessment, like to a judge or standards parameter. Hence, my judgment is true relative to the context of assessment where my standards of tastiness are operative, and your judgment is true relative to the context of assessment where your standards of tastiness are operative. Assessment sensitivity relativism allows for our concepts to refer to the same property. Thus, there is sufficient communication between individuals when discussing ethics, and agents even from very different cultures are not talking past one another. There is genuine disagreement across cultures, but moral truth is still relative. At many times, adherents of this view call themselves "relativists" and call indexical-based theorists "contextualists," doing violence to prior established usage of terms and opening the door for much confusion. However, we shall understand this new approach as merely one kind of relativism: assessment sensitivity relativism.

11.2 Narrow Versus Wide Content

Although I illustrated in the first chapter how the constitution project in principle differs from the semantic project, it will be instructive for this chapter to revisit it again but in greater detail. In so doing, I will explain the narrow/wide content distinction and provide examples of both kinds of views. Regarding moral semantics, there is a distinction in the philosophy of mind and language that will be crucial. It is the narrow/wide content or semantic internalism/externalism distinction; a semantic internalism/externalism that is distinct from motivational judgment internalism/externalism, reasons internalism/externalism, or any other internalism/externalism distinction. The narrow content view or semantic internalism claims that the meaning and reference of a concept is solely determined by or supervenes narrowly upon internal mental states in one's head. Such mental states may be non-representational or representational, and they can involve functional roles of mental states in cognition too. One such narrow view that has many variants is *descriptivism,* where generally understood, it claims that the referent of a concept is that entity that satisfies the mental descriptions associated with the concept in question. Sense determines reference. For instance, my DOGS concept may be constituted by the concepts BARKS, PLAYS FETCH, WAGS ITS TAIL, HAS FOUR LEGS, etc. On a *cluster descriptivism* view, my DOGS concept in my mind refers to, represents, signifies, or is about those objects in the world that satisfy most or over half of the constituents of the concept but not necessarily all of them. For, if this number of over half is not specified, then it will be possible for two obviously distinct properties to be the referents of a single concept. However, the actual number of descriptions that a property needs to satisfy in order to be a concept's referent will be left unspecified somewhere over the threshold of half the descriptions in that it appears unlikely and perhaps even foolhardy to think that we can nail down the precise number of descriptions that need to be satisfied for determining the reference of all various types of moral concepts. Leaving the number of descriptions unspecified also accounts for the plausible idea that there are degrees of meaning. The issue of whether or not meaning is interpersonally shared is not a black and white issue. Rather, there are degrees of shared and unshared meaning, where at times whether or not two people in a discussion share a sufficient amount of meaning in their respective moral concepts may be a gray and unclear matter.

Moreover, the referent of the concept must satisfy some of the important heavily weighted descriptions associated with the concept as well. On a cluster descriptivism view, an entity need only satisfy most of the descriptions in order to be the extension of the concept along with some heavily weighted ones.

Meanwhile on a *classical descriptivist theory,* an entity needs to satisfy all of the descriptions to be the referent of a concept. For classical descriptivism, one's set of descriptions for a concept is a necessary and sufficient condition for determining the reference of the concept. While the extension, content, or referent of my DOGS concept is *dogs*, the meaning of this concept is something different. For descriptivism, the mentally represented descriptions that constitute my DOGS concept are the meaning of this concept. The sense of a concept is its meaning. Meaning is in the head, so to speak, where meaning determines reference. Meaning and reference supervene only narrowly on internal mental properties. Generally, on an overall descriptivist theory, the meaning of a concept is ontologically distinct from the referent of the concept. BARKS, PLAYS FETCH, etc. is ontologically disparate from *dogs*. Here, we can see that a theory of meaning and a theory of reference can be distinguished from each other and are not necessarily the same thing. Thus, in principle, for example, one may espouse a descriptivist theory of meaning but not a descriptivist theory of reference or vice versa. To note, as we shall see, I base my moral semantic view in significant part on experimental philosophy studies, and I primarily have run such studies on theories of reference rather than of meaning. Hence, regarding my positive project, I primarily will be concerned with establishing a theory of reference in this book.

As an example of a narrow view, Frank Jackson and Philip Pettit (1995) offer a neo-descriptivist "network analysis" account in which the meaning of moral concepts is descriptions, or more precisely "platitudes," that are obvious intuitive moral truths that speakers have an implicit understanding of (Jackson 1998). The long conjunction of all the platitudes is taken to be an implicit necessary and sufficient condition definition of the moral concept that determines the reference of the concept. Jackson and Pettit's view is an analytic naturalism, where they attempt to posit an analytic definition of moral concepts in terms of natural ones. Such an a priori definition is supposedly true by meaning alone. However, recall that classical or definitionist structure to our moral concepts is not psychologically real. Such concepts are not constituted by representations of necessary and sufficient conditions. Since Jackson and Pettit propound a moral semantic theory that presupposes that we can mentally represent necessary and sufficient conditions that are the meaning of our moral concepts, they have put forth an empirically false semantic view.

A narrow analytic naturalism view also was the target of G.E. Moore in his naturalistic fallacy when criticizing reductive naturalistic metaethical positions that claim that moral properties are reducible to naturalistic ones. Moore argued that there is always an open question as to whether a moral concept can be analytically defined in terms of naturalistic ones. For example, if one attempts to define goodness in terms of pleasure, an ordinary speaker may always still question whether goodness is in fact pleasure. For instance, one can still raise the question, "I know this act is pleasurable, but is this act good?" The question is open, and we can still doubt the definition. Yet, if GOODNESS and PLEASURE share the same meaning, where PLEASURE is a represented necessary and sufficient condition for goodness, then there should be no open question. A naturalistic definition does not appear to capture the complete meaning of goodness. Since Moore, who assumes a narrow theory of content and classical descriptivism, maintains that moral concepts are not synonymous with naturalistic concepts due to this open question, he contends a metaphysical thesis that it must then follow that moral properties cannot be identical to natural properties in the way water is identical to H_2O. Moral concepts and the relevant natural ones are not co-referential since meaning determines reference and their meanings differ. This can be contrasted with how the concepts WATER and H_2O co-refer. Co-reference of relevant concepts is required for property identity. Hence, Moore states that to define a moral concept in terms of a natural one is to commit the naturalistic fallacy.

As an aside, we may respond to Moore's open question argument given that moral concepts do not have classical structure. Rather, they have, for instance, prototype or family resemblance structure, where the constituents of a concept refer to statistically frequent features of members of a category. Given that concepts like GOODNESS are not constituted by mental representations of necessary and sufficient conditions but rather by things like prototypes, it should come as no surprise that there are open questions when we psychologically think about whether goodness is defined in terms of natural properties. For, our conceptual minds are structured to think that there are open questions when rigorously entertaining the definition of things like *goodness, game, fruit,* and *vegetable* since our relevant concepts are not constituted by representations of a strict definition or necessary and sufficient conditions; conditions whose existence would lead us to think that such questions are closed when satisfied. Rather, our moral concepts are in part constituted by family resemblance representations that have fuzzy boundaries and that allow for ambiguity. Recall that the prototype view accurately predicts the phenomena of ambiguity. This means that we should expect and predict there to be open questions when attempting to arrive upon a definition of goodness. Hence, moral concepts still may be defined in terms of a cluster of natural concepts, such as based on a prototype and cluster descriptivism view, which is perfectly compatible with there being open questions. In this case, it is possible that moral concepts are properly defined in terms of natural concepts, where the meaning is properly captured despite the presence of open questions. On an overall cluster descriptivist theory, if meaning is sufficiently shared between moral and the relevant natural concepts, where meaning determines reference, then there is co-reference and a naturalistic reduction.

On the other hand, the wide content view or semantic externalism maintains that the meaning and reference of a concept is at least in significant part dependent on properties external to one's mind. To note, since there are already a variety of internalism/externalism distinctions in metaethics, from here forward, I will rely on using the "narrow/wide" terminology when drawing the relevant semantic distinction in order to avoid confusion.

There are a variety of wide content views. Remember that Boyd holds a wide content theory in which the referent of a moral concept is a natural property, such as *human need* and *well-being*, which causally and epistemically regulates the use of our moral concepts and our moral decision-making. Given the causal connection, over time, our moral decision-making or that of a group's should more closely align with the purported objective moral facts. This synthetic naturalism view attempts to arrive upon a definition of goodness through empirical investigation, such as by examining what benefits or harms may arise in societies that give women equal rights to see whether having such rights enhances overall well-being. Recall that Boyd's proposed natural definition of GOODNESS, which includes such constituents as FRIENDSHIP, LOVE, and FREEDOM, does not refer to necessary and sufficient conditions.

However, one problem with Boyd's view is that there are cultures who have maintained their values for hundreds of years, if not for millennia, without changing them to align with what Boyd conceives as being objective moral facts; supposed facts which are unsurprisingly generally aligned with his culture's Western Christian-based values. If there is a reliable or stable causal connection between objective natural moral facts and moral decision-making woven into the fabric of the natural world, then we should expect significant movement in the direction toward "good" over a large expanse of time. However, this is not so in many cases. As just a few examples, although there are many others discussed throughout this book, the Gahuku-Gama of New Guinea claim it is morally permissible to kill non-group members as do the Ilongot of Luzon in the Philippines who will kill innocents to relieve stress or cope with depression. The Yanomamo kidnap women to be their wives. On an island in northwest Melanesia, one ought not to work with others nor share (Bendict 1934). Those anomalous agents who like to work with and help others are considered to be insane and are thought to be living an undesirable life. These norms have held in such cultures since time immemorial, where the supposed reliable causal connection should have altered their judgments by now if such a connection actually exists. 96% of those in Malaysia and 93% of those in Indonesia believe that a woman should always obey her husband despite readily available evidence of how Western women live through various media, pop culture, and the internet (Pew Research Center 2013). Note that moral concepts are very unlike other concepts that Boyd applies his theory of content to like SNAKE or LION that are reliably and accurately tokened across cultures when in the presence of a snake or lion, respectively.

A more palatable causal theory of reference comes from Prinz (2007). A dominant wide content view for natural kind concepts in the philosophy of mind is a causal informational theory, which has some similarities to Boyd's account. Although, there are numerous variations and refinements of causal-informational views, such theories generally may be understood to claim that mental representation R represents C so long as R is reliably caused by C. Prinz espouses this view for moral concepts, where moral properties are secondary qualities that are powers to cause (rather than merit) emotions in us. For Prinz, acts such as murder have the property of moral wrongness since they have the power to reliably cause certain negative emotions in many of us, but perhaps not in others. Since moral concepts only are constituted by sentiments or emotions for Prinz, secondary qualities reliably cause the tokening of sentiments, so therefore, moral concepts refer to secondary or moral qualities. The WRONG concept in MURDER IS WRONG refers to the property of *being wrong* since this property is a secondary quality that reliably causes me to feel disapprobation, where the disapprobation just is the WRONG concept. Therefore, when I judge MURDER IS WRONG, for Prinz, I only express a non-cognitive sentiment of disapprobation but not any beliefs. Yet, given an informational view, I still represent a fact that random killings have the property of *being wrong*.[2] On Prinz's view, a judgment against the morality of random killings is true relative to the relevant subject so long as one has a sentiment of disapprobation toward such acts. On the other hand, if someone else has a sentiment of approbation toward random killings, then a contrary judgment in favor of them also may be true relative to the relevant subject. Notice that this view can handle cases like the Gahuku-Gama, Ilongot, Yanomamo, and relevant Melanesian people. Prinz's proposed reliable causal connection is much more reliable than Boyd's for influencing the great variability in moral judgment-making, and therefore, it is much more plausible. Prinz uses his semantic theory to argue for a moral subjectivist position.[3]

As an aside, one problem with Prinz is that if his causal theory of reference is true, moral properties reliably cause us to have both cognitive and conative states rather than just conative states. This has been empirically verified in previous chapters with my pluralistic theory of moral concepts. Moreover, an ontological criticism of Prinz's secondary quality view will be pursued in the final chapter. To note, below I will provide a sweeping criticism of all extant moral semantic theories. Recall, that the current primary aim is to explain why the constitution project is distinct from the semantic project in light of the narrow/wide content distinction; a distinction that is still being introduced.

The common denominator we see with wide content theories is that the reference of a concept is at least in part dependent upon events and properties external to or outside the head. Second, wide content theorists typically adopt a referential theory of meaning, although they need not have to, where the meaning of a concept is the referent of the concept. Meaning and reference coincide and are not separated. For instance, on an informational view, since *dogs* reliably cause me to bring forth my DOGS concept to working memory, my DOGS concept represents *dogs*. While the category *dogs* is the referent of this concept, the meaning of my DOGS concept is also *dogs*. Meaning just ain't in the head and is not, for instance, the set of mentally represented descriptions stored in one's concept of dogs as with descriptivism.

It now should become clear again why the constitution project is in principle distinct from the semantic project. It can be the case that BEING HELPFUL, BEING GENEROUS, BEING HONEST, etc. constitutes my GOOD ACTION concept in part because they influence me to categorize relevant acts as being *good*. However, it may not be the case that they constitute the meaning of my GOOD ACTION concept nor determine its reference as in line with descriptivism. For, it could be the case based on, for example, Boyd's wide causal regulation account that the extension of this concept is *human need* since *human need* reliably influences moral decision-making, not because *human need* satisfies the represented descriptions that constitute GOOD ACTION. Also, the meaning of the concept is *human need* as well. Hence, what constitutes a moral concept can in principle be separated from the issue of what the meaning and reference of a concept is.

The predominant view espoused in moral semantics is the narrow content account, and in so doing, it has had significant effects regarding theories of moral truth. At many times, the narrow content account has been assumed to be true by philosophers without argument. Moral semantics has played a crucial role in metaethics regarding drawing metaphysical conclusions on truth based on semantic premises. For instance, we already have discussed the descriptivist incommensurability argument for an indexical moral relativism as well as Prinz's use of a wide content theory to contend for subjectivism. Ayer's (1936) non-cognitivism claims that moral judgments are merely the expression of one's non-representational emotions, so such judgments do not refer to moral facts. For example, saying "stealing is wrong" means the same thing as "boo to stealing!" because moral judgments are primarily used to communicate feelings rather than state facts. Moral judgments may have emotive meaning but not cognitive meaning. While in the literature, there are more sophisticated and more refined non-cognitivist accounts since Ayer, in that moral judgments are not about genuine moral properties and facts since such judgments are mere emotional expressions for Ayer, such judgments are strictly speaking incapable of being robustly true or false. Moral meaning and reference is determined narrowly by non-cognitive emotional mental states that constitute moral concepts. Hence, moral semantics can lead to a deflationary theory of moral truth. Meanwhile, cognitivists claim that moral judgments express beliefs. Since meaning is in the head and meaning determines reference, moral judgments may have cognitive meaning, and they may refer to moral facts because beliefs may so refer.[4] Judgments can, for instance, refer to objective moral facts or culturally constructed moral facts. Hence, moral judgments can be capable of being true or false in a non-deflationary way. As we can see, the cognitivism/non-cognitivism debate, as it is generally framed, presumes that a narrow content is correct.

Recall that in one of John Mackie's (1977) primary arguments to establish the unique truth value of error theory, where all moral judgments are false, he argues that ordinary moral judgments purport to refer to objective prescriptive moral properties and facts. Moral reference supervenes narrowly on descriptive mental beliefs people have about morality, such as the belief THERE ARE OBJECTIVE MORAL FACTS THAT PROVIDE REASONS FOR ACTION TO ALL. This belief is supposed to determine the reference of moral concepts. However, Mackie contends that since objective facts that provide reasons for action to all are mysterious, such facts do not exist. Hence, all moral judgments do not refer to objective prescriptive moral facts even though they purport to. Therefore, all moral judgments are false. A narrow moral semantics is assumed without argument in order to attempt to support an error theory account of moral truth.

11.3 Moral Semantic Relativism and Experiments on Moral Twin Earth

I will provide a new incommensurability argument in the next chapter using novel semantic premises to arrive upon a metaphysical conclusion on a theory of moral truth. In so doing, I also will provide a new moral semantic theory and levy objections against all extant moral semantic views. The remainder of this chapter mainly will focus on establishing this new semantic view. We begin first by examining the debate between narrow and wide content theories. The predominant means for adjudicating between narrow and wide theories of content is via a priori intuitions on hypothetical and real cases, where intuitions need to reach a wide consensus. The use of thought experiments and a priori intuitions generally is thought to play a major role regarding the narrow/wide content debate and has been wielded with such authority in contemporary and 20th century philosophy of mind and language. As Michael Devitt notes:

> The received view is that we should test theories of reference, indeed any semantic theory, by consulting our intuitive judgements about language, our metalinguistic "intuitions". It would be hard to exaggerate both the apparently dominant evidential role of such intuitions in the philosophy of language and the agreement among philosophers that these intuitions should have this role. This emphasis on intuitions reflects, of course, a widely held view about the methodology of "armchair philosophy" in general.
>
> (2015, p. 34)[5]

Concerning Twin Earth style hypotheticals such as Moral Twin Earth, Horgan and Timmons write that they are based on intuitions which can be empirically verified:

> Since semantic norms are tapped by human linguistic competence, and since the relevant linguistic competence is presumably reflected in one's intuitive judgments concerning Twin Earth scenarios, this outcome [of intuitions] constitutes strong empirical evidence ….
>
> (1992, pg. 166)

One prominent thought experiment in the literature on mental content is Hillary Putnam's Twin Earth (TE) hypothetical. Putnam asks us to imagine that there is a planet called TE that is exactly like our own planet in every which way except that a chemical substance composed of XYZ, which has all the observable characteristics of water, replaces water everywhere. Thus, for instance, the lakes and oceans on Twin Earth are filled with XYZ rather than H_2O. People on Twin Earth speak Twin English and their term 'water' appears to be indistinguishable from our own term 'water,' where they believe that 'water' is a clear, odorless, and tasteless liquid that fills up rivers and streams. From this thought experiment, Putnam claims that there is a wide content, where meaning just ain't in the head. 'Water' on Earth refers to and means H_2O while the term 'water' for Twin Earthlings on Twin Earth refers to and means XYZ even though it is the case that what is going on inside both of your minds appears to be the same, assuming that you do not know that what you call 'water' on Earth is H_2O and your doppelganger does not know that what he or she calls 'water' on Twin Earth is XYZ. For three-dimensional natural kind terms, content does not supervene solely upon the internal physical-psychological states of the agent. You and your twin are seemingly internally indistinguishable, but your 'water' terms still refer to different things. Rather, content supervenes upon external environmental factors rather than solely what is going on in the head.

Putnam further argues that if you were to learn that what you call 'water' on Earth is H_2O and then visit Twin Earth and realize that what they call 'water' is really XYZ rather than H_2O, you would realize that you and your doppelganger's respective 'water' terms do not refer to the same things. Therefore, when you and your twin have a discussion about 'water,' both of you really are talking past one another since your respective 'water' terms have different contents. Given that the above is the case, in this hypothetical, Putnam states that it would be appropriate for you to invent a new word such as 'twater' for the XYZ that fills up the rivers and streams on Twin Earth. Due to a difference in reference, at times, a particular belief you have about 'water' theoretically could be true while the seemingly opposite contradictory belief about 'water' in the mind of your doppelganger also could be true. Both of your seemingly antithetical beliefs both can be true relative to your respective planets given differences in content.

Terrence Horgan and Mark Timmons (1991, 1992) have made an analog of Putnam's hypothetical situation pitting narrow versus wide content except it is constructed with the intention of examining moral concepts in light of Boyd's causal semantic theory and account of ethical natural properties. They call their thought experiment "Moral Twin Earth" (MTE). As the general layout, they ask us to imagine and assume that there is a world called MTE that is nearly identical to our own world except that our moral term 'good' is causally regulated in a Boyd-like way by natural properties whose essence is captured by consequentialist properties while the orthographically identical term 'good' for those on MTE is causally influenced by natural properties whose essence is captured by deontological ones. Both those on Earth and MTE understand their respective moral terms to be formally related to the evaluation of actions, persons, and institutions. In other words, moral terms have a narrow functional action-guiding role in cognition in both worlds. For both planets, such terms are understood to be used to reason about considerations of 'well-being' and 'justice,' where considerations about what is 'good' to do are at many times overridingly important on how one should act. What goes on inside the moral minds or heads of you and your twin are quite similar, but they differ at precisely the points we would expect them to given the fact that they are being causally regulated by the different consequentialist and deontological properties, respectively.

Horgan and Timmons conclude that our intuitions in this case are that when there are seemingly antithetical judgments between you and your doppelganger on a particular moral issue, both of your moral concepts really share the same meaning and reference, despite the different causal reference-fixing relations, such that both of you are not talking past one another in this debate. There can be a legitimate and genuine substantive disagreement between the both of you in this case. Therefore, this situation can be characterized as one of a difference in some moral beliefs and moral theories rather than one of a difference in reference given that on Earth and MTE your moral concepts respectively are understood to play a formal or functional role internally in the head in cognition in governing evaluative decision-making and behavior. Horgan and Timmons (1992) call their semantic view "moral functionalism," and as we can see, functional role semantics is a narrow theory. They also articulate other functional uses moral concepts play in cognition, such as carrying great importance in determining how to act and being sensitive to considerations of 'well-being,' that generally fall under the functional umbrella of moral concepts being used for evaluative decision-making. It appears that Horgan and Timmons want to claim that when dealing with moral concepts, reference is determined internally by the functional role of moral concepts in cognition. Meaning and reference are not determined by external factors a la Boyd. For if this were the case, then our intuitions should conclude that those on Earth and MTE have disparate referents for their moral concepts given that such concepts are causally influenced by different properties. However, this apparently is not the case. The supposed narrow intuitions that we have on MTE stand in stark contrast to the purported wide intuitions we have on Putnam's TE thought experiment for natural kind concepts. To note, in their initial writings on MTE, they state that the moral concepts share the same meaning and reference, and I adopt and continually will adopt such terminology in my discussion of MTE. However, in later writings, they espouse a kind of non-cognitivism in which moral judgments are non-representational beliefs (2000).

11.3.1 Experiments on MTE

I ran experiments testing semantic intuitions on the MTE thought experiment. The purpose of this and the below studies I conducted is focused only on the reference of moral concepts rather than on the related but different issues concerning moral truth or disagreement. They are limited and specific in scope. There are no previous experimental studies on the semantics of moral concepts regarding the narrow/wide content debate. As such, this and the other below studies are exploratory. I ran tests on 116 folk subjects across the various regions of the United States (Northeast, South, Midwest, West) with an average age of 45 spanning from 18 to 61 years of age and 102 folk participants across the various regions of Singapore (East, Northeast, North, West, Central) with an average age of 34 spanning from 19 to 73 years of age. English is regarded as the main language of Singapore and is the language used in primary through graduate school. Questionnaires were written in English, and responders were recruited online. I also conducted the test on 52 experts with PhDs in philosophy across the ethics and metaphysics/epistemology divide.

The vignette reads:

> Suppose that scientists make a new discovery of a natural property P on Earth that generally is found to causally influence our 'moral' judgment-making. This is somewhat like how the presence of a rabbit that crosses your path tends to influence people to judge that there is a rabbit. Due to the influence of P, the use of terms, like 'good' and 'right,' are largely influenced and shaped by thoughts of bringing about the act that creates the greatest overall happiness. Here, happiness should be understood as only being the feeling of pleasure. Kyle, who lives on Earth, makes judgments influenced by P.
>
> Also, presume that there is a Twin Earth that is exactly like Earth in almost every way. For example, Twin Earth has the same geography and natural surroundings as Earth. There is a twin of you there, and people in your twin country call their language 'English.' Twin Earthlings have terms like 'good' and 'right.' However, scientists discover as a fact that a different natural property Q on Twin Earth is found to influence Twin Earth 'moral decision-making rather than P. Due to the influence of Q, the use of relevant Twin Earth terms are largely influenced and shaped by thoughts of individual 'rights' like the 'right' to move about freely and the 'right' to life, which cannot be violated even if violating them would bring about the greatest happiness. Kyle's twin on Twin Earth, Twin Kyle, makes judgments influenced by Q rather than P.
>
> When asked to discuss 'morality,' Kyle utters things like, "It is used to evaluate actions, persons, and institutions. It usually carries overriding weight in deliberation on how to act." When asked to discuss 'morality,' Twin Kyle utters things like, "It is used to evaluate actions, persons, and institutions. It usually carries overriding weight in deliberation on how to act."
>
> Generally, whenever Earthlings, like Kyle, utter that an act is 'morally permissible' when presented with a case and action, Twin Earthlings, like Twin Kyle, utter that this act is 'morally permissible' when presented with the same thing. This is because at most times, abstaining from murder, stealing, lying, etc. brings about the greatest overall happiness and they protect individual 'rights.' However, there can be exceptions as there are situations in which the overall greatest happiness differs from individual 'rights.' For example, if there is a new deadly contagious virus that some have, Kyle will utter that it's 'morally permissible' to quarantine them because this leads to the greater happiness. However, Twin Kyle will utter that it's 'morally impermissible' to quarantine them since this violates the individual 'right' to move about freely.

Having read the above story and **assuming that it's 100% true**, when Kyle and Twin Kyle utter the words, 'morally permissible,' when talking on their own planets before the discoveries, what are these utterances about?

(1) Kyle's utterance, 'morally permissible,' is about P. Twin Kyle's utterance, 'morally permissible,' is different in that it's about Q.
(2) Kyle's utterance, 'morally permissible,' and Twin Kyle's utterance, 'morally permissible,' are both about the same thing.
(3) Other ____[6]

The MTE thought experiment itself is long and involved, so I attempted to make it as simple and understandable as possible without sacrificing the important details of the setup of the hypothetical. In order to set it up, there needs to be different external natural properties on both planets, but the internal moral minds of the twins need to be similar regarding ethics having the same functional role of being action-guiding. They both have an evaluative or commending component to their moral concepts. Moreover, to account for the distinct cluster descriptivism option, I made note that there is a high degree of similarity between other internal activities of their moral psychologies, such as both of them judging that most acts of killing, stealing, and lying are'wrong.' Based on the Flesch-Kincaid readability measurement, the MTE scenario scores at a 10th grade reading level for reading comprehension. The Flesch-Kincaid readability test is one of the most widely used and reliable measurements for reading comprehension and for judging the reading levels of school books and textbooks. It correlates 0.91 with comprehension as measured by extensive reading comprehension testing. All subjects, including in other experiments I ran that are discussed below, at minimum have a high school diploma.

Upon providing the MTE hypothetical, subjects were then asked whether an Earthling and the Earthling's twin on Twin Earth will be talking about the same thing or not with their 'morally permissible' terms. They also were given the option to choose 'other' and then write in their own different response. If subjects responded that the utterances are about different things, P and Q, then this is an intuition for wide content since the disparate external natural properties that causally regulate judgments are the referents of the terms. If participants believe that the utterances are both about the same thing, then this seemingly is an intuition in favor of narrow content since some kind of internal similarities between the two are responsible for the shared reference.

I found only one response among all responders where a participant chose "other" and explained that moral concepts do not refer to moral properties because there are no such properties, which is consistent with non-cognitivism and error theory.[7] This participant was a philosopher.

Table 11.1 Number of participants (and percentage) in each sample by answer to the MTE scenario

	US $n = 116$	*Singapore* $n = 102$	*Philosophers* $n = 52$
Both are about different things	81 (69.8%)	63 (61.8%)	21 (40.4%)
Both are about the same thing	32 (27.6%)	39 (38.2%)	21 (40.4%)
Other	3 (2.6%)	0 (0%)	10 (19.2%)

This "eliminativist" response group reasonably can be viewed as being a "noise response group" that occurred by chance, where from a statistical standpoint, it can be ignored. Here, a "noise response group" or "noise" in statistics is reasonably understood as being a category with sample proportions less than 5% and statistically significant evidence for the population's proportion to be less than 10%.[8]

Philosophers appear generally split on MTE. However, there is a statistically significant difference between both folk populations versus philosophers in the wide content response, although there is no such difference between the two folk populations.[9] As we can see from Table 11.1, most of the folk, East and West, had wide intuitions for MTE. Against Horgan and Timmons, even among only philosophers, we do not see that a majority of intuitions are narrow ones. Rather, when combining all the populations East, West, and philosophers, it appears that most people have wide intuitions on MTE.

Furthermore, we see that there is substantial intracultural variation for the folk populations. The minority subpopulations in both folk East and West groups are rather sizable, and moral semantic intuitions on MTE lack the kind of widespread consensus that is found in other staunch a priori domains of inquiry, such as in math and logic. The responses in line with a narrow content are too substantial to be written off as being statistical "noise."[10] As there is an absence of sufficient consensus within a culture, a narrow theory of content seemingly applies to both minority folk subgroups in the East and West, although a wide content purportedly applies for most in both East and West groups. Different theories of reference may apply to different people even within the same culture. This also seems to hold for philosophers on MTE too.[11]

11.3.2 Carl/Ian Hypothetical

MTE is a long, complex, and fantastical thought experiment involving a Twin Earth. It is not as ecologically valid or realistic in light of normal experiences had by test subjects. Although, my setup of MTE is manageable on the Flesch-Kincaid readability measurement, I constructed a similar thought experiment to MTE that is shorter, simpler, and more ecologically valid. It will be interesting to see if the MTE results can be replicated on this different setup. In this scenario, the mental states between the parties are similar to that contained in MTE. However, the disparate causal influences are different external cultural influences rather than disparate natural properties on divergent planets that are represented by variables. The thought experiment is called the *Carl/Ian Hypothetical.* It reads:

> Carl is raised in an English-speaking culture that has taught him to always promote the overall greater consequences for society. Ian is raised in a significantly different English-speaking culture across the world that has taught him to always respect individual rights, like the right to move about freely and the right to life. For Ian's culture, these rights cannot be violated even if violating them would bring about the greater consequences.
>
> Most thoughts Carl and Ian have associated with the term, 'morally good,' appear to be similar. This is because at most times, not killing, not stealing, not lying, etc. brings about the overall greater consequences and protects individual rights. Carl and Ian also believe that the term, 'morally good,' is associated with evaluating actions and with providing everyone with the most important consideration in deciding how to act.
>
> However, they still have some different thoughts associated with the term. For example, due to different cultural influences, if there's a new deadly contagious virus that some have, Carl will say that "it's 'morally good' to quarantine them because this leads to the greater consequences for society." However, Ian will say that "it's not 'morally good' to quarantine them because this violates the individual right to move about freely."

Participants then were given reading comprehension/attention check questions that focused on important story-line details such as that Carl and Ian have different external cultural environments and that most of their thoughts appear to be similar. Only semantic intuitions from those who passed all the reading comprehension/attention check questions were counted. The semantic question is:

> Having read the above story and assuming that the story is 100% true, when Carl and Ian utter the term, 'morally good,' when discussing 'moral' issues in their own home locations, what are these utterances actually about regardless of what Carl and Ian might intend to be talking about?

(1) Carl's utterance is about the socially approved values of Carl's own culture. Ian's utterance is different in that it's about the socially approved values of Ian's own culture.
(2) Carl's utterance and Ian's utterance are both about something that is exactly the same thing for both.
(3) Carl's utterance and Ian's utterance are about nothing at all rather than being about something.
(4) Other ______________________________

Online respondents successfully completing the reading comprehension/attention check questions were 62 folk participants across the various regions of the United States and 54 folk participants across the various regions of Singapore. The average age of U.S. participants is 47 ranging from 21 to 4 years of age. The average age of Singapore participants is 34 ranging from 18 to 58 years of age.

As we can see from Table 11.2, the folk results on the Carl/Ian hypothetical from the East and West generally were found to importantly replicate those folk results found on MTE and thus, provide further support for the relevant semantic conclusions drawn from MTE. Most have intuitions for a wide theory of content, where there is no statistically significant difference between Eastern and Western participants.[12] Moreover, significant minority populations for both have narrow content intuitions, where such responses are not mere "noise."[13] Also, notice that in the Carl/Ian hypothetical, I newly brought out the non-cognitivist and error theory option in the answer choice selection, where their utterances are referring to nothing at all. I did this rather than relying on the more generic "Other" response in MTE to potentially see if participants are non-cognitivists or error theorists. Making the eliminativist possibility more explicit might elicit substantially more eliminativist responses. However, there was no such increase. Also, it is reasonable to consider the single eliminativist response in the Singapore sample as being "noise," and it can be ignored.[14]

Table 11.2 Number of participants (and percentage) in each sample by answer to the Carl/Ian hypothetical

	US *n* = *62*	*Singapore* *n* = *53*
Both are about different things	46 (74%)	43 (81%)
Both are about the same thing	15 (24%)	7 (13%)
Both are about nothing	0 (0%)	1 (2%)
Other	1 (2%)	2 (4%)

11.3.3 Medieval England Hypothetical

I ran another semantic thought experiment called *the Medieval England Hypothetical.* The first goal behind this is to create a situation in which the protagonist has descriptions that seemingly are in ignorance or error. This is a common objection against descriptivist theories of reference. It is that we might have erroneous descriptions associated with a term or be ignorant of enough relevant descriptions such that our corresponding concepts do not refer to their purported proper extension on a descriptivist account. However, our concepts apparently do refer to the seemingly proper extension. Descriptivism appears to fail to make correct predictions in these kinds of cases, and such cases seem to provide evidence for wide content. For instance, I may be largely ignorant of physics such that my main description associated with my EINSTEIN concept is the false description THE PHYSICIST WHO CREATED THE ATOMIC BOMB. Descriptivism seems committed to the claim that my EINSTEIN concept refers to Oppenheimer rather than to Einstein in this case, but my concept supposedly really refers to Einstein (Kripke 1972). To note, this study pits narrow versus wide content, but its intent is to focus primarily on a descriptivist narrow theory rather than Horgan and Timmons' functional role account, although both narrow theories have been represented in prior studies and are in this present one.

A second aim of this hypothetical is to test semantic intuitions on reference in a different way than by directly asking participants what a particular concept is about. Rather, the idea is to give participants a sentence in which a moral term is actually being used by the protagonist in a normal every-day statement in a way that is inconsistent with descriptivism. I then ask whether the protagonist's statement is correct or incorrect. If they respond that it is incorrect, then this is evidence in favor of descriptivism. If participants say that it is correct, then this seems to provide evidence for a wide causal view. I also attempted to construct the hypothetical in a shorter, more ecologically valid, and easier way to understand than MTE. The Medieval England hypothetical reads:

> Medieval English cultural values reliably influenced most Medieval English people to think that the term, 'moral goodness,' is associated with things like conquering others, being courageous in battle, plundering your enemies, being tough, disciplined, uncomplaining, noble, and fierce.
>
> Assume David is a socially awkward 10 year-old Medieval English adolescent who has been raised on Medieval English values. Yet, he's a slow learner in this regard, although he's fine in other subjects. All of his thoughts and descriptions associated with the term, 'moral goodness,' are different from other Medieval English people. For example, only because he's a slow learner on this subject, his full

> description associated with 'moral goodness' in his mind is that "one should never harm or steal from others nor ever go to battle. One should surrender to one's enemies and let them kill you without trying to stop them. One should be soft, undisciplined, complaining, not noble, and timid."
>
> However, in a special way, a teacher clarifies to him the Medieval English views on the term, 'moral goodness,' such that his thoughts associated with the term align with other Medieval English people. David then says, "Oh, now I finally get it. Conquering others, being courageous in battle, plundering your enemies, being tough, disciplined, uncomplaining, noble, and fierce has always been what's really 'morally good' for me."

Participants then were given reading comprehension/attention check questions, such as ones to make sure subjects know that the cultural values are a general reliable influence on community members and that before being taught in a special way, all of David's descriptions associated with 'moral goodness' are different from others. Only semantic intuitions from those who answered all of such questions correctly were included. The semantic question is:

> Assuming the above story is 100% true, recall that David later says, "Conquering others, being courageous in battle, plundering your enemies, being tough, disciplined, uncomplaining, noble, and fierce has always been what's really 'morally good' for me." This statement made by David is
>
> (1) Correct
> (2) Incorrect
> (3) Other

Before being taught in a special way, David's descriptions in his young mind associated with 'moral goodness' are all completely different from fellow community members and are all in error relative to Medieval England cultural values. In this case during this time, due to having all different descriptions, cluster and classical descriptivists are committed to saying that David's 'MORAL GOODNESS' concept refers to different moral facts compared to his fellow community members' 'MORAL GOODNESS' concept. Yet, after David is taught in a special way, his concept then has the same extension as others since his descriptions align. Thus, when asked whether David's statement that conquering others, etc. has *always* been what is really 'morally good' for David, descriptivists must answer that this statement is incorrect. They should balk at it. At an earlier point, David's concept was referring to different moral facts, so conquering others, etc. cannot always have been what is morally good for David.

However, those who espouse a causal theory of reference should say that David's statement is correct since the Medieval English cultural influence is a general and reliable influence on those living in Medieval England before and after David is taught in a special way. David is ensconced in this external environment. On a causal view, the descriptions do not matter. David's 'MORAL GOODNESS' concept always will have the same extension given the external cultural environment based on the wide account. Therefore, it makes sense to say that such cultural values, like conquering and plundering others, always really have been what is 'morally good' for David even though at times, all of his descriptions point otherwise and are seemingly in error.

Those online respondents who successfully completed the reading comprehension/attention check questions were 41 folk participants across the various regions of the United States and 51 folk participants across the various regions of Singapore. The average age of U.S. participants is 48 ranging from 27 to 73 years of age. The average age of Singapore participants is 39 ranging from 20 to 62 years of age.

As we can see from Table 11.3, most lay persons from the East and West have intuitions consistent with a causal rather than descriptivist theory of content with no statistically significant differences between populations.[15] Most say that David's statement that conquering others, etc. has always been what is really 'morally good' for David is correct. Notice that these cross-cultural results generally are consistent with, replicate, and buttress folk intuitions on MTE and the Carl/Ian hypothetical that most maintain a wide view. Also, the results are acquired in a different fashion from asking people what a concept is about as in the MTE and the Carl/Ian hypotheticals. Rather, semantic data is gathered when the concept is actually used in a normal sentence. The overall moral semantic results have been replicated in various ways. However, notice that there is still a sizable portion of participants that bite the bullet and maintain a descriptivism in this case. Statistically, such responses are not mere "noise."[16] This replication study also provides further support that different theories of reference seemingly apply to different people.

Table 11.3 Number of participants (and percentage) in each sample by answer to the Medieval England thought experiment

	US *n = 41*	*Singapore* *n = 51*
Correct	25 (61%)	35 (69%)
Incorrect	15 (37%)	13 (25%)
Other	1 (2%)	3 (6%)

Given the coherence of my interpretation of the Medieval England results with the two prior studies, we will set aside the possible non-cognitivist and error theory response to this Medieval England hypothetical since any possible significant eliminativist response beyond mere "noise" will not cohere with the prior moral semantic results. When looking at the big picture, we can infer that participants are not non-cognitivists or error theorists on these thought experiments.

A descriptivist may respond that most have narrow intuitions. For, participants may have understood David to always hold the description, "It is whatever my teachers or community experts think it is." This continuity of this particular description before and after David was instructed in a special way that defers to social leaders on matters of ethics allows David's statement to be correct. He is always talking about the same thing. This is why most say that his statement is correct as most are descriptivists. However, notice that by hypothesis, the story provides David's full set of descriptions before the special instruction. The description about teachers or experts is absent in the set, so this possible interpretation is closed off.

Moreover, one may try to state that David's moral concept always has an evaluative component to it before and after the special instruction was given, where this evaluative component is representational. This similarity allows his moral concept across time to always be referring to the same thing, and it might lead to the majority "correct" response found in the study. There can be a narrow functional role interpretation of the majority results as well as a wide one. However, the problem is that this possible narrow interpretation of the majority findings fails to be coherent with previous results that the majority do not maintain narrow intuitions on the MTE and Carl/Ian thought experiments. Moreover, as we will see in the next chapter, it also fails to cohere with the data I collected on Hare's classic missionary/cannibals hypothetical, where moral concepts across cultures have the same evaluative role in cognition, but the descriptions and external cultural environments differ greatly. In such a case, most say that the cross-cultural agents have representational moral concepts and are talking about different things. Hence, we are justified in believing my interpretation of the data given its coherence across the variety of studies I have run.

11.3.4 Moral Semantic Relativism

I have found the above kind of substantial intracultural variation replicated on all studies thus far on moral semantic intuitions. Moreover, such intracultural variation also is well replicated in the experimental philosophy of language literature for proper name (Machery et al. 2009, Beebe & Undercoffer 2015, Sytsma et al. 2015), non-moral natural kind (Braisby et al. 1996, Genone & Lombrozo 2012, Nichols et al. 2016), and non-moral artifact kind concepts (Genone & Lombrozo 2012). These well-replicated findings of a lack of pervasive consensus in semantic intuitions in these other concept domains along with such replicated results I have discovered for moral concepts, provide a general unified picture concerning the narrow versus wide content debate. Such unification augments the explanatory power of my moral semantic theory. These many studies in other concept domains provide additional justification, replication, and help contribute to sufficient inductive support that there is significant intracultural variation on moral semantic intuitions on a variety of different cases.

Moreover, my findings that most believe that moral judgments refer to relative moral facts and properties is consistent with the previously discussed findings concerning scope objectivity in the moral/conventional task that most people are moral relativists on truth and believe there is no error in seemingly conflicting judgments in cross-cultural moral discourse (§7.2.1–§7.2.2). This allows my various moral semantic experiments to fit in nicely and bring a greater overall coherence and unification power with the general experimental philosophy studies on folk metaethical beliefs about moral truth. In other words, it adds even further support for my conclusions drawn from my moral semantic studies.

Given the replicated findings across concept domains and various kinds of unification, there is a *moral semantic relativism*, where different narrow versus wide semantic intuitions can be found depending upon the person. Hence, it appears that different theories of reference apply relative to the individual. Here, a theory of reference "applies" to a person in the sense that this theory is what determines the reference of their moral concepts, and it *should* determine such reference given the corresponding semantic intuitions, among other justifying reasons to be discussed below. Moral semantic relativism is a new moral semantic theory, where narrow versus wide content applies relative to different agents. It can be viewed as a second order semantic theory that talks about first order theories, such as particular narrow and wide theories.[17] As a priori intuitions are an important factor for what theory of reference should apply, it is a subject matter of empirical investigation, as I have in part undertaken here, and perhaps future empirical investigation to examine all the various possible contexts when and how intuitions generally may differ across persons.

To note, I also allow for the possibility that it later may be found that there is sufficient consensus in intuitions within a particular culture. However, there is still a moral semantic relativism as significant intracultural variation in intuitions in other cultures still exists, as shown. Due to culture, there may be uniformity in intuitions, but in other cultures, this is not so. Ultimately, we cannot say that there this a first order single unified grand theory of moral reference that applies to all people at all times.

I also leave open and allow for the possibility that it later may be discovered that different situations or cases can trigger disparate narrow/wide intuitions even for the same person. There may be moral semantic relativism based on two factors of the individual and the context or case. For example, in situation A, a narrow content applies for agent 1, but in another case B, a wide content applies for this same agent. Meanwhile, for a different agent 2, a wide content applies for A, but a narrow content applies for B. Proper name, non-moral natural kind, and non-moral artifact kind concept experiments have shown that at times there is a situation-based semantic relativism or ambiguity for such mental representations (Genone & Lombrozo 2012, Pinillos 2015, Nichols et al. 2016), where agents can have different semantic intuitions depending on the context, case, or question. Moreover, the experiments are so designed that one can reasonably understand why agents would have such disparate intuitions, and it is not random.[18] I would not be surprised if it later is discovered that this kind of relativism based on the situation also applies to moral concepts.

Moreover, there are certain hybrid theories that fuse narrow and wide accounts. For instance, Gareth Evans (1977) has such a view in which reference is determined by the causal source of at least most of the descriptions one has of a concept. While this hybrid view incorporates descriptions, the ultimate decisive aspect that determines reference is the causal source. In other words, it is the wide rather than narrow aspect that plays the decisive and dominant role in determining reference. In this respect, we can understand it as being a wide hybrid view. David Wong (1986) posits a moral semantic hybrid theory that is predominantly a narrow view in that descriptions decisively and ultimately determine reference. However, there is a wide element to his theory in that once the reference is fixed, the referent supposedly plays a causal role in explaining the speaker's judgments. Here, we can understand Wong's view to be a narrow hybrid theory. Hence, it could be the case that intuitions consistent with a wide account in my studies are really ones for Evan's wide hybrid theory, and intuitions consistent with a narrow content are actually ones for Wong's narrow hybrid theory. I leave these open as possibilities for future testing that certain people really may be adopting such respective hybrid accounts. However, even if these possibilities are both realized, notice that there is still evidence for a moral semantic relativism in that there are significant populations on both the narrow and wide content sides. Given such significant populations, both hybrid theories may apply depending upon the person. There will be more than one correct theory of reference that applies, and moral semantic relativism is still true.

Also, while we have examined a priori semantic intuitions on moral concepts, there are empirical considerations for a theory of reference as well that need to be addressed. First, a theory of reference needs to allow a concept to refer to the entity that is ordinarily and generally being thought about when the concept is tokened. What people generally understand the referent of a concept to be is an empirical question. There is a *relevancy requirement* where a moral concept cannot just refer to anything, but rather, it must be a reference relation to a relevant property. For example, if one's view claimed that our moral concepts refer to cheesecakes that fall off the Manhattan Bridge, then there is a relevancy problem with one's view. Although defeasible, the relevancy requirement in the philosophy of language is thought to carry heavy weight in most cases. It is important that a theory of reference shows how a moral concept refers to things that are consistent with ordinary thoughts about the concept's extension. Notice that data shows that people generally understand the referent of moral concepts to be something like relative properties or cultural values. Thus, it will be an important desideratum for a theory of reference to allow moral concepts to refer to such cultural values. As we will see in the next chapter, my moral semantic relativism account eventually leads to the conclusion that our moral concepts refer to such cultural values, and the relevancy requirement will be satisfied.

Another empirical consideration for adjudicating between theories of reference concerns behavior, such as moral actions and coordination. A theory of reference receives support by its ability to help explain such behavior. In the next chapter, I will show in more detail how my moral semantic relativism, in satisfying the relevancy requirement, helps to explain the diverse and differentially nuanced kinds of moral coordination and cooperation practices across different societies. To provide a brief rundown, for those in which a wide content applies, a causal theory in which disparate cultural values influence the respective moral decision-making explains diverse moral behavior in different cultures. For those in which a narrow content applies, significantly different descriptive thoughts had by people in different groups that leads to corresponding differences in reference to diverse cultural values help explain disparities in behavior in that such descriptive thoughts constitute moral concepts and thus influence decision-making and action.

11.4 Objections to Moral Semantic Relativism

I now will anticipate several objections. There have been many criticisms of experimental philosophy studies testing semantic intuitions on proper name and non-moral natural kind concepts (Deutsch 2009, Martí 2009, Devitt 2011, Sytsma & Livengood 2011). Yet, generally such findings have shown a remarkable and general resilience as follow up studies and further philosophical investigation on concepts at many times have confirmed or buttressed their overall conclusion on the variability of intuitions (Machery et al. 2009, 2010, Machery 2012, Beebe & Undercoffer 2015, Sytsma et al. 2015). For instance, one may counter that semantic thought experiments test people's intuitions regarding which theory of reference is true rather than how people actually use words (Martí 2009). For example, MTE tests intuitions on the narrow/wide content debate rather than on the reference of moral concepts when people actually use such concepts when making moral statements. Perhaps, one should try asking test subjects questions about terms when they actually are used in real world every day sentences rather than just asking respondents what a moral concept is about. However, follow-up experiments have shown that people's theoretical intuitions in semantics on theories of reference for proper name concepts coincide with how they actually use specific terms in sentences (Machery et al. 2009). If someone believes x refers to y, then the person will judge the truth of a sentence containing x depending on what is said about y. Additionally, my above Medieval England hypothetical tested reference based on how moral concepts actually are used in a normal statement. The results replicated the MTE and the Carl/Ian hypothetical results in that intuitions about reference generally are in sync with the truth value of sentences using the terms.

Also, there can be a difference between speaker or pragmatic reference concerning what a speaker intends a concept to refer to and semantic reference regarding what a concept refers to by the conventions of the language (Deutsch 2009). Notice that these need not coincide. For example, I may judge that MY NEIGHBOR, JACK, IS MOWING HIS LAWN NOW. I intend for JACK to refer to the man who is mowing his lawn next to mine. However, I easily confuse names, and "Jack" is actually the name of my neighbor on the opposite side of my house who is not mowing his lawn. "Robert" is the actual name of the person who is mowing his lawn now. In this instance, the semantic reference of JACK is the neighbor who lives on the opposite side of my house who is not mowing his lawn now. Yet, the speaker reference of JACK is the neighbor who is mowing his lawn now. Perhaps when asking what the parties are talking about with their moral concepts, participants may have provided their intuitions on the speaker reference for the relevant parties' concepts rather than semantic reference. Speaker reference can be incorrect at times, and so this can sully the results. It could be the case that participants generally provided only speaker reference intuitions that the relevant parties are talking past one another. Yet, their semantic reference intuitions generally will be that the parties are talking about something that is the same thing for both.

However, experiments on proper names show that people are not providing their intuitions on the speaker reference of the parties involved in semantic thought experiments on proper names but intuitions on semantic reference (Machery et al. 2015). For example, participants were asked what a term is about regardless of what the speaker in the vignette intends to be talking about when uttering the term. The same results were found. On top of this, my above Carl/Ian hypothetical also asked participants about the reference of moral concepts in this same fashion and generally replicated the results of MTE, which provides evidence that people generally were providing intuitions on semantic reference on MTE.

Another objection utilizing the semantic/pragmatic reference distinction is that even though there is a difference in semantic reference, agents still can be talking about the same thing if they intend to refer to a content that is the same for both (Geirsson 2005). For example, my spouse and I together may be looking out the window and watching Robert mow his lawn. My spouse may say that our neighbor mowing his lawn right now is going to get a basketball hoop for his driveway. Being still confused about names, I may then say that Jack actually decided against getting a basketball hoop. Even though the semantic reference of JACK refers to my other neighbor who is not mowing his lawn right now, my pragmatic intention is for JACK to refer to Robert or to the neighbor who is mowing his lawn now. My spouse picks up on my referential intention, and for the purposes of our conversation, we are talking about the same person. There is co-reference and genuine disagreement about the basketball hoop based on pragmatic reference even though there is divergence in semantic reference. Given this possibility, even though there is divergence in semantic reference on MTE style hypotheticals, there still can be a convergence in pragmatic reference, and this is sufficient for attaining a relevant co-reference and being involved in genuine disagreements where people are not talking past one another.

While this is an interesting objection, the problem is that in order to establish univocity in moral concepts across location and time taking this pragmatic route, it requires that people actually intend their moral judgments to refer to the same moral facts. However, given the prior findings that most people are moral relativists on truth (§7.2.1–§7.2.2), it is by no means a far stretch at all to say that since people largely believe that moral facts exist and are relative facts, when they make moral judgments, they intend to be referring to their own group's respective moral facts rather than some supposed set of objective moral facts. Furthermore, my studies have shown that people generally believe that moral concepts refer to relative cultural values. If there is one single instance where one group intends to refer to different moral facts by their moral judgments than another group's, then this pragmatic move to establish that our moral concepts globally and historically co-refer fails. Moreover, we can turn to empirical observations in international affairs as well. For example, the Asian values debate in the 1990s had several Asian leaders basically stating that they intend to be talking about communitarian Asian values when discussing ethics rather than the distinct individualist values of the West.

The above also shows that my moral semantic relativism is a thesis on semantic, not pragmatic, reference. In the next chapter, I will attempt to show that moral semantic relativism helps lead to moral relativism. However, if one were to take into consideration the pragmatics of a language, this still will lead to my ultimate metaethical aim that there is a moral relativism. At times, people intend to talk about different moral facts. Hence, the relevant agents are literally talking about different things and talking past one another such that different truth conditions apply to their moral judgments. What conditions make a moral judgment true in one group is not the same for another group since they are referring to different things. Therefore, what is morally true is only relativistically true.

Moving on, Joshua Knobe (2019) states that after analyzing a variety of experimental philosophy studies across subdomains, like in epistemology, metaphysics, and ethics, he finds that philosophical intuitions generally are robust across demographic differences; differences such as sex and culture. One might think that this means that there's something wrong with my studies as there should be the same consensus intuitions on MTE-style hypotheticals across demographic groups. However, Knobe does admit that there are exception cases, such as between expert philosophers and lay people. Recall that my first MTE study found such a disparity in intuitions between experts and the folk. Knobe also readily admits that there are differences in intuitions at the individual level; differences in individual cognitive styles (Weinberg 2019). For example, while most lay people across cultures may have wide intuitions on MTE, there still can be significant intracultural variation in semantic intuitions at the individual level within cultures. Hence, Knobe's point really is not an objection against my moral semantic relativism. He perfectly allows for my discovered intracultural differences in semantic intuitions, which is key to triggering moral semantic relativism.

Also, one may object to my contention for moral semantic relativism. Perhaps moral judgments largely do not refer, and a deflationary theory of truth applies. However, the problem with this is that recall that intuitions consistent with a deflationary theory largely were not elicited from the MTE and Carl/Ian moral semantic thought experiments. Moreover, the few actual eliminativist responses found were written off as "noise." This provides a substantial objection against a non-representational interpretation of the results.

Another possible counter is that perhaps there is merely a disagreement in non-semantic facts, such as regarding the storyline descriptions in the moral semantic hypotheticals. Once we get clear on and in agreement with the non-semantic facts, our semantic intuitions will align such that there will be a sufficient consensus. However, given the readability measurement, we can infer that most of the participants, including experts, are clear on the non-semantic facts of MTE and comprehend the scenario. Moreover, in the other hypotheticals that replicated MTE, semantic data only was gathered from those who could pass all the comprehension/attention check questions. This creates a burden of proof against those who believe participants in some way failed to properly understand the hypotheticals. Furthermore, these latter hypotheticals were constructed in a shorter, simpler to understand, and more ecologically valid fashion compared to MTE. Furthermore, the data across all three moral semantic thought experiments are largely consistent with each other and consistent with the findings that most people are moral relativists (§7.2.1–§7.2.2). We can infer that relevant participants were clear on the non-semantic facts of the cases.

One also may object that intuitions from expert philosophers and linguists with PhDs is what really matters rather than intuitions from folk subjects. While folk intuitions might be used as a check on expert intuitions, it is the intuitions of experts that should be trusted; experts who have been trained on the semantics of terms, who fully understand the semantic hypotheticals and what is being asked of them, and who perhaps have a more coherent semantic worldview. This is known as the expertise defense. Since moral semantic relativism is in part dependent on studies examining folk intuitions, it is not justified. In response, if we only rely on professional philosophers' intuitions on MTE, notice that a moral semantic relativism still follows.

Second, whether philosophers' intuitions are more reliable than folk intuitions is an empirical question, and there is much experimental evidence demonstrating that relevant experts' semantic intuitions are not more reliable. Empirical data thus far has shown that as long as the folk understand the subject at hand, their intuitions are just as reliable as expert linguists' intuitions (Schütze 1996, Culbertson & Gross 2009). Also, experts in different areas of semantics, such as in philosophy, historical linguistics, anthropological linguistics, and sociolinguistics, etc., have been discovered to have different background theories that lead them to have significant divergences in theory-laden intuitions on the narrow/wide debate for proper name and standard concrete concepts (Machery 2012). For instance, given the training of historical linguists and anthropological linguists, they are more likely to be semantically attuned to the descriptions of words as compared to philosophers and semanticists whose education is primarily focused on the importance of Kripke's wide theory of content. Such significant disparities exist on experts' intuitions on such concepts because they are too theory-laden and subjectively biased given their differences in education and upbringing. Also, regarding the reliability of moral decision-making of right and wrong, which may be relevant when testing for moral semantic intuitions, remember that philosophers have been shown to be more susceptible to the actor-observer bias than folk participants (Tobia et al. 2013). Moreover, philosophers are equally susceptible to order effects as lay participants on a variety of moral dilemmas (Schwitzgebel & Cushman 2012, 2015). Also, one might think that philosophers will reflect more on thought experiments and thus, provide better responses. However, studies show that those who spend more time on reflection generally do not give different answers from those who do not spend extra time deliberating (Weinberg et al. 2012, Machery 2017).

One may counter that running surveys does not gather people's real intellectual and competent intuitions. Competent intuitions only can be gathered through critical interviews and Socratic dialogues (Kauppinen 2007). Surveys only gather quick initial philosophical intuitions that may suffer from performance errors. However, the problem with this is that it is an empirical claim that lacks experimental support. Rather, data shows that first-off philosophical intuitions from experimental research generally do not disappear after greater reflection and scrutiny (Weinberg et al. 2012, Machery 2017). Moreover, my moral semantic findings have been replicated in various ways that ask the test subjects to entertain moral semantics from different angles. Scrutinizing moral semantics from different angles still leads to the same general results in lay persons, which provides additional inductive support that the philosophical intuitions at hand generally are stable.

A different counter from Deutsch (2009) may be that certain cases that are used to determine what theory of reference applies to concepts do not rely upon a priori intuitions.[19] Rather, they rely on an a posteriori methodology. Semantic judgments are empirical judgments that are inferred from the relevant facts contained within a case. For example, after reading a semantic case, it is possible that one rather quickly can perceive what the reference of the concept in question is without relying on a priori intuitions or gathering data on such intuitions. Those who infer a different semantic conclusion are just plain empirically wrong. For instance, my EINSTEIN concept refers to the noted physicist, *Einstein*. This is simply empirically true. We do not rely on a priori intuitions or need to gather data on such intuitions. Adjudicating between theories of reference potentially can be a quick empirical matter. First, I do believe that empirical considerations are relevant to moral semantics, as noted above. However, Deutsch appears to be contending that adjudicating between theories of reference is solely an empirical matter, where we might rather quickly perceive the answer a posteriori.

While Deutsch's criticism specifically is waged against an a priori approach to proper name and non-moral natural kind terms, it is not immediately clear that we can rather quickly empirically perceive that a given moral concept actually has a particular extension and that a particular theory of reference normatively ought to apply when faced with interesting and challenging situations that pit narrow vs. wide content views. It appears that Deutsch wants to say that it can be a rather direct empirical issue as to what the referent of a term is, where one even can make inferences and arguments by analogy using other like cases where we easily can perceive the referent of the term.

However, the MTE thought experiment has been well discussed and rigorously debated for nearly thirty years without such a consensus among philosophers. Furthermore, a central issue in metaethics is moral semantics, which is an underlying theme in much of metaethics, drawing much attention and work from analytic metathicists, such as G. E. Moore, for over a century. Yet, there is still no pervasive consensus on the meaning and reference of moral concepts. Indeed, the "linguistic turn" occurred in the late nineteenth century, creating a proliferation of vibrant and ardent debates; attracting the brightest minds analytic philosophy had to offer over time, such as Bertrand Russell, Ayer, Wittgenstein, Kripke, and Putnam. Yet, it was predated by work on language in the Modern era by the likes of John Stuart Mill with his referential theory of meaning and Locke with his position that if one has a concept without any descriptive ideas associated with the concept then the concept is meaningless. In the Medieval period, there were the likes of Ockham arguing for a causal theory of reference, and in antiquity there were works on theories of meaning from the likes of Antisthenes and the Stoics. Yet, despite all this time, there is still no pervasive consensus on the semantics of moral concepts across professional philosophers, linguists, cognitive scientists, and from my moral semantic test results. Moreover, if moral semantics is fundamentally an empirical issue in which we might quickly perceive the answer, it is not rocket science. It is far from it. Hence, as most empirical matters tend to reach a consensus, we inductively may infer that it is unlikely that using relevant semantic cases to determine what theory of reference ought to apply is solely an empirical matter that Deutsch claims we might rather quickly perceive the answer to rather than being in significant part an a priori project or else it is likely that a pervasive consensus would have been reached by now at least from semantic experts over the millennia. Rather, we may inductively infer that relying on semantic cases is not solely an empirical matter but is in significant part an a priori issue in which there is substantial variation in intuitions. Although I agree that there are empirical considerations to take into account, the substantial relevance of an a priori element that leads to differences in intuitions is predominantly responsible for the lack of consensus in moral semantics. Deutsch writes that understood as solely an empirical issue, it is fine if there is no consensus on judgments of reference. However, we see that this very lack of consensus creates a problem for his thesis that the semantic solution to all cases might be rather quickly perceived a posteriori. On a separate note, this long history of unyielding semantic inquiry also allows us to additionally infer once again that it is unlikely that there will be a pervasive consensus in moral semantic intuitions.

As another objection, even if this variation in intuitions is established, the question remains as to how this leads to moral semantic relativism. Mallon, Machery, Nichols, and Stich, who together first entertained the idea of the possibility of a semantic relativism ensuing from experimental studies on proper name concepts with substantial intracultural variation on intuitions, reject the semantic relativism option because there needs to be some kind of argument establishing that the semantic intuitions provide any evidence about reference such that the disparate intuitions generate a semantic relativism (Mallon et al. 2009). Why rely on a priori semantic intuitions at all? Are they not unreliable since there is significant variation on them? As there supposedly is no such successful positive argument or answer to these questions, we should not trust semantic intuitions at all, and philosophers completely should abandon arguing for a theory of reference. In response, recall that experiments have shown that people's theoretical intuitions in semantics on theories of reference for proper name and moral concepts coincide with how they actually use specific terms in everyday sentences. This provides sufficient empirical data that semantic intuitions do provide evidence about the reference of our concepts.[20] Peoples' words at many times do refer to things in the world, and semantic intuitions appear to be capturing this in a consistent way.

Moreover, there is further reinforcement that our own thoughts about reference carry at least strong yet defeasible support about the reference of our concepts. As Locke notes, it is arbitrary what words, sounds, or scribble marks we use to represent a particular property or category in the world or else there likely would be a universal language. In a significant way, the reference of a term is up to us and society, so our own thoughts on the issue should matter. If by 'bank' you say that you are referring to the slope by the side of a river rather than a financial institution, this provides strong support that when you use the word, 'bank,' in the relevant context, the slope is in fact the referent of your term. In fact, because of this, recall that a prominent desideratum for theories of reference is that they coincide with what people generally and actually believe is the referent of the term. Hence, given all of the above, it is the case that for at least semantic intuitions, there is importance to them given the peculiarities of the subject matter, and they generally are linked to how our words actually refer. To note, this importance, fruitfulness, and need for reliance on a priori intuitions in semantics does not necessarily apply to other subject matters that tend to rely on a priori intuitions but lack the same peculiarities, such as in the a priori MJI/MJE debate or the compatibilism/incompatibilism debate on free will.

Janice Dowell claims that there is no good reason to think competence in our own language on moral terms gives us any competence in Twin English. Therefore, we cannot tell if there is co-reference or not on moral concepts in the MTE hypothetical (2016). Thus, we should not rely on a priori semantic intuitions because we lack any competence in

Twin English to make a cross-world semantic assessment. However, surely we do have a significant amount of competence in Twin English for at least most of their words, which allows us to competently provide semantic intuitions on MTE. This is just like how adults in the United States generally have the competence to make semantic analysis to certain words in British English and have competence for most words in British English.

Adults in the United States and Great Britain speak variants of English in which there are some differences, which is somewhat similar to the MTE thought experiment. However, adults in the United States and Great Britain still have the competence to tell that the 'football' terms in both locales have different referents. In the United States, 'football' refers to a game in which the ball is rarely kicked, and in Great Britain, 'football' refers to a very different game in which the ball is constantly kicked and is of a different shape. Adults have this semantic competence across locales for other relevant terms, such as 'shag' and 'pants.' What helps make such semantic analysis is that, for example, someone from the United States does have competence in British English of terms relevant to the subject matter of the sports at hand that are directly translatable; terms and phrases such as 'game in which the ball is rarely kicked' and 'game in which the ball is constantly kicked and is of a different shape.' We can rely on immediately translatable terms across both types of English to make decisions about the possible translatability of 'football.' People's semantic intuitions on these kinds of cases, such as on 'football,' can be highly reliable and should not be ignored, which is contrary to Dowell's suggestion. Our semantic intuitions should not be discarded.

Hence, by analogy, the like holds for moral terms on MTE. Against Dowell, we do have competence with most terms in Twin English. Pertaining to moral concepts like GOOD ACTION, we can rely on nonmoral concepts that are directly translatable across English speaking cultures and in which both parties have competence, such as SHARES THE SAME FUNCTIONAL OR FORMAL ROLE, IS INFLUENCED AND SHAPED BY DIFFERENT PROPERTIES, or by descriptions like HELPING and TELLING THE TRUTH, in order to make assessments on co-reference in the MTE hypothetical just as we successfully do for terms like 'football' across U.S. and British English. To note, even more detail on this matter will be discussed and will come up in the next chapter.

Dowell continues her attack by stating that those who rely on the method of eliciting semantic intuitions for adjudicating the narrow/wide content debate hold the view that semantic competence with an English 'moral' term requires an ability to make assessments of co-reference across different English-speaking societies. They can make judgments as to whether terms successfully translate or not. Yet, young children have competence with moral terms as they can make moral judgments, such as against stealing, and they can partake in forms of moral communication and cooperation. However, such children cannot participate in assessing whether moral terms share the same reference across relevant societies. Since children cannot make such assessments, this shows that semantic competence does not require translational skills. In essence, adults have competence with moral terms similar to how children do, but they do not have translational skills across different English-speaking communities. Thus, we should not rely on our semantic intuitions on MTE for the narrow/wide content debate.

In response, we should make a distinction between *simple competence* with a moral term and *competence with the translation* of a moral term. Simple competence involves the ability to make moral judgments, track a term's referent, as well as communicate and coordinate regarding ethical matters, among other possible conditions.[21] Both adults and children have this. Competence with translation involves simple competence, but it also includes, for example, an ability to assess whether one's moral terms share the same reference as the moral terms in other generally English-speaking societies.[22] This latter kind of competence is had by adults as I already have argued for above, but presumably not children. Assuming for the sake of argument that young children do not have competence with translation, they may lack this competence because this competence requires more complex concepts that young children generally do not have yet, such as TRANSLATION and CULTURE. Against Dowell, adults do have competence with translation across English speaking societies, such as regarding terms like 'football' across U.S. and British English. While children do have competence with moral terms as Dowell claims, we should more precisely understand this to be simple competence. As such, we should not expect children to have competence with translation as such competence is not entailed by simple competence. Yet, relevant adults do have competence with translation across English-speaking communities. Dowell later goes on to give a positive account of what it is to have competence, but this account is for only simple competence. The main important kind of competence for MTE is competence with translation, and this is something that adults have.

Another objection from Dowell is that children can learn languages and successfully track a term's referent in a variety of different ways. For instance, a blind child will track the referent of WATER in a different way than a child who lives next to the ocean and who relies predominantly on vision. However, relying on semantic intuitions requires that there is only one single method or theory for determining reference that is had by everyone. Yet, this is highly unlikely given the disparate successful methods children use in determining the reference of their concepts. The problem with this is that Dowell fails to see the possibility of a moral semantic relativism that is in part based on a priori intuitions. Her premise that "relying on semantic intuitions requires that there is only one single method or theory for determining reference that is had by everyone" is false. While it is true that philosophers mostly have thought that there is only one correct monolithic theory of reference that applies for everyone, this need not be so as a semantic relativism in which various theories of reference may be true relative to the individual is a possibility and is still consistent with relying in part on semantic intuitions.

One may be concerned that moral semantics will be disorderly since we have both narrow and wide theories of content on the table. It will be less parsimonious. The response is that yes, moral semantics is not as clear cut, neat, parsimonious, and orderly as previously conceived. This is a consequence of our semantic intuitions. Recall that Ockham's razor only comes into effect when competing theories are equal in respects to factors like explanatory power and predictive success. Greater explanatory power and/or predictive success trumps parsimony. Hence, moral semantic relativism, in being able to explain and predict the experimental semantic phenomena among other empirical phenomena, is still true despite the current objection. However, as I will discuss in the next chapter, there may be some more order than one might initially think in that it is possible for certain people to share the same reference despite differences in narrow versus wide content in a situation.

11.5 Implications of Moral Semantic Relativism to Moral Semantics

With moral semantic relativism on the table, it follows that any proposed moral semantic view that propounds a single first order theory that is supposed to apply to all people at all times is false. The purview of my criticism includes all extant moral semantic theories. For example, Jackson and Pettit's descriptivism, Stephen Finlay's (2014) descriptivism, Ralph Wedgwood's narrow conceptual role semantics (2009), Boyd's causal theory, Mackie's narrow semantic presupposition, Moore's assumption of classical descriptivism, Wong's narrow hybrid view, and Prinz's informational account are all wrong because different narrow versus wide theories of reference are true relative to the agent. There is not one grand moral semantic theory, narrow or wide, that is correct at all places at all times for all people. Rather, whether a narrow or wide account correctly applies can vary based on the individual.

Moreover, the aforementioned argument for error theory and the cognitivism/non-cognitivism debate, generally understood, rests on a mistake because recall that they presuppose a narrow semantic theory, but a narrow semantic view alone is not true because there is a moral semantic relativism. The previously discussed contention for error theory and the cognitivism/non-cognitivism debate regarding theories of moral truth generally rests on the assumption that a narrow semantic theory alone is true, but this is to rest on a mistake. A wide theory of content is also true, where both theories apply for disparate agents.

As an example of the important difference between narrow and wide views, we have seen how on Prinz's wide causal account, even though moral concepts are constituted only by conative states, they do refer to genuine moral properties because certain secondary qualities supposedly reliably cause us to have moral thoughts. A deflationary theory of truth semantically grounded solely on internal non-cognitive mental states does not follow on this view even if moral judgments are non-cognitive and only express sentiments or emotions. For, on Prinz's account, moral concepts do refer to genuine moral properties. This stands in stark contrast to a generally understood non-cognitivism, where moral judgments do not refer to genuine moral properties. The purpose of this example only is to illustrate that whether a narrow or wide content view applies can lead to significant differences in moral ontology and truth.

Non-cognitivists, cognitivists, and error theorists generally make a false presumption of the universality of the narrow content view. Furthermore, many hybrid theorists on the cognitivism/non-cognitivism debate, like Stevenson and Hare, also do so as well, where they presume that meaning and reference primarily supervene upon the non-cognitive rather than cognitive component of moral concepts since the non-cognitive element is semantically primary over the cognitive.[23] They erroneously maintain a narrow theory of content for all moral concepts at all times. On top of this, all prior extant moral semantic theories are false. Empirical data helps demonstrate that we must rethink and overturn much of the landscape of metaethics.

Notes

1 Some understand objectivist theories as ones that maintain that moral judgments are capable of being true or false. On this understanding, a relativist theory is an objectivist one since for relativism, moral judgments are capable of being true or false but only relative to a subject or group. Some understand a universalist position as one that maintains that everyone believes a particular act or rule to be either right or wrong. It is a position that describes peoples' relevant beliefs rather than giving a theory of moral truth.

2 To note, Prinz's view on the representational content of moral sentiments and emotions gets much more complicated than what is presented here. Nevertheless, for our purposes, we need not delve further into Prinz's semantic account.

3 Prinz espouses both appraiser and agent relativism.

4 Remember that one may claim that moral judgments express beliefs, but such beliefs are not representational (Horgan & Timmons 2000). The boundaries between cognitivism and non-cognitivism are not exact and can be blurred.

5 Devitt, himself, posits a general a posteriori approach to semantics, but it ultimately still does rely on a priori intuitions.

6 Note that the questions don't differentiate properly between semantic vs. speaker reference. As I will discuss later, a further study I have run does make the differentiation and is specifically on semantic reference only. This further study provides evidence that folk participants on MTE are providing intuitions on semantic reference given that the study replicated the result of MTE.

7 Responses of "other" varied from, for example, one eliminativist answer to the claim that there is a semantic ambiguity with contrasting intuitions equally pulling in different directions.

8 The sample proportion of the "eliminativist" response from the "other" category is 0.0192. There was significant evidence to conclude that the "eliminativist" response was below 0.10 (P = 0.0282, binomial test).

9 The statistical tests indicate that the difference in proportions between PhD and Singapore populations is statistically significant (z = 2.52, P = 0.0117). Similarly, there is a very significant difference between the PhD and U.S. populations (z = 3.61, P = 0.0003). However, the difference in sample proportions between Singapore and U.S. samples is not significant (z = 1.254, P = 0.2098). Regarding the "same" response category, there is statistically strong evidence to conclude that the proportions in PhD and U.S. populations are different (z = 2.03, P = 0.0425). The difference in proportions between Singapore and U.S. populations is not significant (moderate evidence with z = 1.674 and P = 0.0941). Finally, there was almost no difference between the PhD and Singapore population proportions regarding the "same" response (z = 0.325, P = 0.7452).

10 The category "same" had an equal proportion to the "different" category for the PhD sample population (0.4038 for PhD). There was significant evidence to conclude that the corresponding proportion of the "same" category for the PhD population was above 0.20 (P = 0.0006, binomial test). It had smaller proportions in the other populations but wouldn't be ignored (0.3823 for Sing and 0.2758 for USA). There was significant evidence to conclude that the corresponding proportion of the "same" category for the Singapore population was above 0.25 (P = 0.0021, binomial test) and that of the U.S. population was above 0.20 (P = 0.0305, binomial test).

11 One might object that Boyd's theory of reference has an epistemic constraint in that the causal mechanism has a tendency over time that what is predicated of a term will be approximately true. Perhaps either P or Q over time will bring a convergence in moral decision-making and thought on Earth and MTE. This isn't properly accounted for in my vignette, so I may not be taking into account the possible interpretation that responses that Kyle and Twin Kyle are talking about the same thing may be an intuition for wide rather than narrow content. It could be the case that both are talking about the same thing because the same property is causally influencing both agents such that there will be gradual convergence eventually over time. However, in the next study we'll see a variant of MTE where both agents also are influenced by different natural properties in which neither property has overlap to both agents. The results replicate that of MTE providing further evidence that participants didn't view Q or P to overlap on the planets in the MTE vignette.

12 When comparing the sample proportions from these two populations, the differences in the corresponding proportions were not statistically significant, possibly due to the small sample sizes (P = 0.3734 for the "different" category responses and P = 0.1354 for the "same" category).

13 The proportions in the "different" category dominated (0.8113 for Sing and 0.7419 for USA). The category "same" had smaller proportions but wouldn't be ignored (0.1321 for Sing and 0.2419 for USA). There was significant evidence to conclude that the corresponding proportion of the "same" category for the Singapore population was above 0.05 ($P = 0.016$, binomial test) and that of the U.S. population was above 0.15 ($P = 0.0382$, binomial test).

14 For Singapore, the "nothing" or "eliminativist" response had sample proportions less than 5%. There was strong evidence to conclude that the corresponding proportion is less than 0.10 ($P = 0.0258$, binomial test).

15 Even though there was a difference in the sample proportions (0.0765), it was not statistically significant to conclude a difference in the population proportions ($z = 0.77$ and $P = 0.441$). Similarly, the difference in the proportions of "incorrect" categories was not significant ($z = -1.15$ and $P = 0.25$).

16 In both Singapore and U.S. populations, the "correct" category dominated with proportions 0.6863 and 0.6098, respectively. The proportions for the "incorrect" category were not that small: 0.2549 for Singapore and 0.3659 for the United States. Binomial tests regarding the corresponding population proportions showed strong evidence that Singapore "correct" proportion is above 0.55 ($P = 0.0333$), insignificant evidence that U.S. "correct" proportion is above 0.50 ($P = 0.1055$), strong evidence that Singapore "incorrect" proportion is above 0.15 ($P = 0.035$) and U.S. "incorrect" proportion is above 0.20 ($P = 0.001$).

17 What I call "first order *theories*" are also known as metasemantic theories that make a second order claim on what theory we should use to determine how terms refer. This is contrasted with a first order claim that states what the reference of a particular term actually is. However, metasemantic theories like descriptivism and a causal theory are subject to a more meta level of analysis or what I call a "second order *theory*" as to whether such views are objectively true for all people or not. This meta level is analogous to metaethics that can state whether theories like utilitarianism and deontology are objectively true or not.

18 Interpreting MTE and the Carl/Ian hypotheticals as being predominantly for wide content and the Medieval England hypothetical as being mostly for narrow content, as discussed and entertained above, would be random without clear reason as to why participants would make such a shift.

19 For further objections against Deutsche's point, see Machery (2017).

20 Machery (2017) later allows for the possibility of semantic relativism in *Philosophy Within Its Proper Bounds*. In his discussion of parochialism, he allows for the situation that due to differences in semantic intuitions and theories of reference, concepts can refer to different properties, where people are talking past one another. If this is so, philosophers should not focus on semantics and the extension of one's concepts, but rather, Machery claims they should focus on which of the different extensions will allow them to meet their philosophical goals. However, for ethics, if people are talking past one another and there is an indexical moral relativism, then what is most important is one's group's moral concepts and their particular extensions. For, what is morally true is relative to your group. Hence, philosophers primarily should focus on moral semantics in light of their own group's particular referents.

21 These can be represented by prototypes.

22 These can be represented by theory knowledge.

23 We will see Hare's argument for this in the next chapter.

References

Ayer, A. J. 1936. *Language, Truth and Logic.* London: Gollancz.

Beebe, James and Undercoffer, Ryan. 2015. "Moral Valence and Semantic Intuitions." *Erkenntnis* 80, 445–466.

Bendict, Ruth. 1934. "Anthropology and the Abnormal." *The Journal of General Psychology* 10, 59–82.

Braisby, N., Franks, B., and Hampton, J. 1996. "Essentialism, Word Use, and Concepts." *Cognition* 59, 247–274.

Culbertson, Jennifer and Gross, Steven. 2009. "Are Linguists Better Subjects?" *The British Journal for the Philosophy of Science* 60, 721–736.

Deutsch, Max. 2009. "Experimental Philosophy and the Theory of Reference." *Mind & Language* 24, 445–466.

Devitt, Michael. 2011. "Experimental Semantics." *Philosophy and Phenomenological Research* 82, 418–435.

Devitt, Michael. 2015. "Testing Theories of Reference." In *Advances in Experimental Philosophy of Language.* Ed. by J. Haukioja. London: Bloomsbury.

Dowell, Janice. 2016. "The Metaethical Insignificance of Moral Twin Earth." *Oxford Studies in Metaethics* 11, 1–27.

Evans, Gareth. 1977. "The Causal Theory of Names." In *Naming, Necessity, and Natural Kinds.* Ed. by Stephen Schwartz. Ithaca: Cornell University Press.

Finlay, Stephen. 2014. *Confusion of Tongues.* Oxford: Oxford University Press.

Geirsson, Heimir. 2005. "Moral Twin-earth and Semantic Moral Realism." *Erkenntnis* 62, 353–378.

Genone, James and Lombrozo, Tania. 2012. "Concept Possession, Experimental Semantics, and Hybrid Theories of Reference." *Philosophical Psychology* 25, 717–742.

Horgan, Terrence and Timmons, Mark. 1991. "New Wave Moral Realism Meets Moral Twin Earth." *Journal of Philosophical Research* 16, 447–465.

Horgan, Terrence and Timmons, Mark. 1992. "Troubles for New Wave Moral Semantics: The 'open question argument' revived." *Philosophical Papers* 21, 153–175.

Horgan, Terry and Timmons, Mark. 2000. "Nondescriptivist Cognitivism: Framework for a New Metaethic." *Philosophical Papers* 29, 121–153.

Horgan, Terry and Timmons, Mark. 2009. "Analytical Moral Functionalism Meets Moral Twin Earth." In *Essays on the Philosophy of Frank Jackson.* Ed. by I. Ravenscroft. Oxford: Blackwell, 221–236.

Jackson, Frank. 1998. *From Metaphysics to Ethics: A Defense of Conceptual Analysis.* Oxford: Oxford University Press.

Jackson, Frank and Pettit, Philip. 1995. "Moral Functionalism and Moral Motivation." *Philosophical Quarterly* 45, 20–40.

Joyce, Richard. 2001. *The Myth of Morality.* Cambridge: Cambridge University Press.

Kauppinen, A. 2007. "The Rise and Fall of Experimental Philosophy." *Philosophical Explorations* 10, 95–118.

Knobe, Joshua. 2019. "Philosophical Intuitions are Surprisingly Robust Across Demographic Differences." *Epistemology & Philosophy of Science* 56, 29–36.

MacFarlane, John. 2005. "The Assessment Sensitivity of Knowledge Attributions." *Oxford Studies in Epistemology* 1. Ed. by T. Szabo Gendler and J. Hawthorne. Oxford: Oxford University Press, 197–233.

MacFarlane, John. 2014. *Assessment Sensitivity*. Oxford: Oxford University Press.

Machery, Edouard. 2012. "Expertise and Intuitions about Reference." *Theoria. Revista de Teoría, Historia y Fundamentos de la Ciencia* 27, 37–54.

Machery, Edouard. 2017. *Philosophy Within Its Proper Bounds*. Oxford: Oxford University Press.

Machery, E., Deutsch, M., Mallon, R., Nichols, S., Sytsma, J., and Stich, S.P. 2010. "Semantic Intuitions: Reply to Lam." *Cognition* 117, 361–366.

Machery, E., Olivola, C.Y., and De Blanc, M. 2009. "Linguistic and Metalinguistic Intuitions in the Philosophy of Language." *Analysis* 69, 689–694.

Machery, E., Sytsma, J., and Deutsch, M. 2015. "Speaker's Reference and Cross-cultural Semantics." *On Reference*. Ed. by A. Bianchi. Oxford: Oxford University Press, 62–76.

Mackie, John. 1977. *Ethics: Inventing Right and Wrong*. New York: Penguin Books.

Mallon, R., Machery, E., Nichols, S., and Stich, S. 2009. "Against Arguments From Reference." *Philosophy and Phenomenological Research* 79, 332–356.

Martí, Genoveva. 2009. "Against Semantic Multi-culturalism." *Analysis* 69, 42–48.

Nichols, S., Pinillos, A., and Mallon, R. 2016. "Ambiguous Reference." *Mind* 125, 145–175.

Pew Research Center. 2013. "*The World's Muslims: Religion, Politics and Society.*" http://www.pewforum.org/2013/04/30/the-worlds-muslims-religion-politics-society-women-in-society/. Last visited February 28, 2019.

Pinillos, Angel. 2015. "Ambiguity and Referential Machinery." In *Advances in Experimental Philosophy of Language*. Ed. by Haukioja, Jussi. London: Bloomsbury Academic, 139–172.

Prinz, Jesse. 2007. *The Emotional Construction of Morals*. Oxford: Oxford University Press.

Schütze, Carson T. 1996. *The Empirical Base of Linguistics*. Chicago: The University of Chicago Press.

Schwitzgebel, Eric and Cushman, Fiery. 2012. "Expertise in Moral Reasoning? Order Effects on Moral Judgment in Professional Philosophers and Non-philosophers." *Mind & Language* 27, 135–153.

Schwitzgebel, Eric and Cushman, Fiery. 2015. "Philosophers' Biased Judgments Persist Despite Training, Expertise and Reflection." *Cognition* 141, 127–137.

Sytsma, Justin and Livengood, Jonathan. 2011. "A New Perspective Concerning Experiments on Semantic Intuitions." *Australasian Journal of Philosophy* 89, 315–332.

Sytsma, Justin, Livengood, Jonathan, Sato, Ryoji, and Oguchi, Mineki. 2015. "Reference in the Land of the Rising Sun: A Cross-cultural Study on the Reference of Proper Names." *Review of Philosophy and Psychology* 6, 213–230.

Tobia, K., Buckwalter, W., and Stich, S. 2013. "Moral Intuitions: Are Philosophers Experts?" *Philosophical Psychology* 26, 629–638.

Wedgwood, Ralph. 2007. *The Nature of Normativity*. Oxford: Oxford University Press.

Weinberg, Justin. 2019. "Philosophical Intuitions and Demographic Differences." *DailyNous,* December 2, 2019. http://dailynous.com/2019/12/02/philosophical-intuitions-demographic-differences/.

Weinberg, J.M., Alexander, J., Gonnerman, C., and Reuter, S. 2012. "Restrictionism and Reflection: Challenge Deflected, or Simply Redirected?" *The Monist* 95, 200–222.

Wong, David B. 1986. *Moral Relativity.* Berkeley, CA: University of California Press.

12 Moral Relativism

Given the various semantic results on the many MTE-style hypotheticals as well as for other reasons like replicated results in other concept domains, we have seen how there is a moral semantic relativism. We will continue discussing my moral semantic theory and show how it leads to a group moral relativism. Across time, there have been many philosophers that have held some version of relativism (Harman 1975, MacIntyre 1984, Williams 1985, Wong 1986, 2006, Dreier 1990, Copp 1995, Prinz 2007, Schroeder 2007, Street 2008, Velleman 2013, Finlay 2014).[1] However, I will offer novel arguments based on new premises for a particular kind of moral relativism. To note, from here forward in this book, we will understand 'knowledge' in the epistemic sense rather than in the psychological sense of being an information-carrying mental state.

12.1 From Moral Semantics to Moral Relativism

As we have a moral semantic relativism, where narrow and wide theories of content apply depending upon the person, a causal theory of reference for when a wide theory of content is at work and a cluster descriptivism when a narrow content applies appear to be strong candidate views for narrow and wide theories. It need not follow that a moral relativism ensues from moral semantic relativism as narrow and wide theories of content could converge on the extension of moral concepts for all people. In this respect, people will not be talking past one another in moral discourse, and there will be the same truth conditions to people's moral judgments. However, I will demonstrate how moral semantic relativism along with other premises do lead to moral relativism.

12.1.1 Wide Content and Moral Relativism

Let us first discuss wide theories of content for moral concepts. Recall that Boyd's causal theory of reference based on *human need* and *human well-being* will not work since they do not reliably or, in other words, stably causally regulate moral judgments across diverse cultures. However, notice that culture serves as a very reliable causal influence generally for people's moral judgments. At most times they influence judgment. On a causal theory of reference, there must be an external natural property that reliably influences moral judgment. Culture is the reliable influence *par excellence.* We have seen many examples throughout this book of why this is so in light of the cultural variability of ethics. For example, it can handle why Western moral philosophers largely hold broadly Christian moral values even though most are atheists (Bourget & Chalmers 2014), and it can account for the warrior value judgments held by the Yamamomo and Ancient Spartans. Moreover, as previously discussed, given moral concept acquisition, our moral judgments widely are historically contingent upon our moral upbringing, culture, prior cultural shifts, political revolutions, environment, and circumstance. Cultural or subcultural values reliably causally influence judgments, so moral concepts refer to group level moral properties. To note, we will have a deeper look into the nature of moral properties in the next chapter on moral ontology. As it is various cultural values that reliably impact respective moral judgments and thus, are the respective referents of moral concepts on a causal view, a group relativism is a stronger fit for this wide theory of reference than a subjectivism given the extension of moral concepts. Notice here that we have our first argument for a group moral relativism. Experimental data demonstrates that a causal theory of reference applies to many people. Hence, moral properties should be certain causally efficacious natural properties rather than, for example, abstract properties that lack causal powers since they do not exist in spacetime. Moreover, we know that there is a reliable natural causal influence on judgment that holds in most cases; namely, culture. Hence, relevant moral concepts refer to group level properties. This leads to the conclusion that for those in which a causal theory of reference applies, people in different groups have moral concepts that refer to different culturally constructed moral properties and facts. Notice on this framework that not only is subjectivism off the table but an assessment sensitivity relativism is as well since moral concepts are incommensurable with each other. Moral concepts are incommensurable or individuated from each other when the theory (-ies) of reference that applies to them demonstrates that the concepts have disparate extensions.

For those in which a causal theory of reference applies, as there is an incommensurability of moral concepts since such agents' representations can be referring to different things, in relevant cases, people are talking past one another. They are literally talking about different things, like apples and oranges, since their moral concepts are not co-referential. As such, they have different truth conditions to their judgments, and a moral relativistic theory of truth ensues. Moral judgments are true and false only relative to a group. If two groups with incommensurable moral concepts from each other are debating the ethics of genocide and appear to provide conflicting conclusions on it, both can be correct relative to their own respective groups. This is like the previous example of how we can have different referents for the word 'bank.' Given differences in reference, we can both be correct about the location of the 'bank' relative to ourselves even though our judgments appear to conflict.

An objectivist may counter that there is no reliable causal influence for moral judgments on a causal theory of reference. In response, that culture is a reliable causal influence such that it holds at most times is amply backed by fields like history, political science, religion, anthropology, sociology, and psychology. On a causal theory of content, moral concepts refer to relativized group level properties, and the relevancy requirement is satisfied. Given the reliable influence of cultural values and that a causal theory does indeed apply at many times, relevant people in different groups literally will be talking about different things such that there will be different truth conditions to their judgments. Thus, there can be no objective moral properties and facts that apply to all people across location and time as this is inconsistent with an established group moral relativism.

Furthermore, if there is no reliable causal influence, this will not help the objectivist because then the relevant moral concepts will fail to refer since a causal theory of reference applies with no causal influence, and a non-cognitivism will ensue. The objectivist may reply that moral concepts can refer to objective moral properties when a descriptivist theory of reference applies. However, the fact that a causal theory of reference at many times does apply and that the reliable influence of moral decision-making is clearly one's own culture demonstrates that an incommensurability does exist at times, where there are different truth conditions to judgments and different moral facts relative to groups on what are perceived by many to be core moral issues. This is wholly inconsistent with moral objectivism, and thus, objectivism is blocked off.

12.1.2 Narrow Content and Moral Relativism

Let us next discuss promising narrow theories of content. First, relying on the narrow non-cognitive evaluative component of moral concepts to determine reference, where moral concepts do not refer to moral properties, will not work since semantic intuitions are that moral concepts do refer to moral properties. Hence, we need to rely on cognitive components to moral concepts, such as cognitive descriptions, to make sure that moral concepts refer to moral properties. A cluster descriptivism will employ prototype descriptions or representations of things like virtues, rules, and reasons; exemplar descriptions or representations of particular persons or acts; and theory descriptions or representations of ethical theory master principles. Recall that exemplars themselves are constituted by representations of more generalizable attributes (§2.3). Hence, for example, group members can have different exemplar representations of virtuous persons in their VIRTUOUS PERSON concept, such as MY MOTHER and MY FATHER, given their different life experiences. Yet, they still can share many concept constituents interpersonally because representations of the generalizable attributes that constitute exemplars, such as BEING NICE and BEING HONEST, can be held in common interpersonally.

A cluster descriptivism rather than a classical descriptivism view can allow for greater univocity within a group even though group members may have some differences in the cognitive representations that constitute their moral concepts. A classical descriptivist theory will not allow for such univocity and publicity within a group because members must have all of their concept constituents match in order to have commensurable moral concepts. This is highly unlikely. Hence, a cluster descriptivism is a better fit as it is much easier for group members to have co-referential moral concepts such that they are not talking past one another. From here forward, "descriptivism" will refer to cluster descriptivism. Moreover, recall that for descriptivism, those who have large disparities in roughly most of their descriptive ethical representations and/or complete divergences in the heavily weighted descriptions will have incommensurable concepts that fail to co-refer. They will have individuated moral concepts.

An incommensurability thesis for moral relativism also can be based on those in which a descriptivism applies. We already have discussed countless examples of significant cultural variation in moral systems where it appears that people in these different cultures have significantly different descriptions associated with ethical concepts. As more possible instances in which a descriptivism can allow for incommensurability, our current Christian-inspired moral values in the West of kindness, humility, and peacefulness differ from the command and conquer moral values held by many of those in the ancient, medieval, and imperialistic worlds. In prior eras, at many times invading, conquering, enslaving, and submitting other peoples to one's will was one of the highest virtues. Alexander the Great was great precisely for his conquests. Even though the moral paradigm has since shifted in Western society and some may look down on today's war mongers with moral indignation, we still acknowledge Alexander's greatness and apply the standards of days gone by to him. In Ancient Rome under the Republic (509-27 BCE), wars were waged almost every year. The highest moral duty of every male citizen was to serve in the military, and it was only in combat that one could display that most highly prized moral character trait in Rome of *virtus* or the quality of being *vir*, which is to display manliness or virility (Kaster 2010). If one was *virtus*, then one had the physical courage to be a hero in battle and reach the highest pinnacle of excellence that this "noble" culture had to offer. Notice how being *virtus* does not carry primary weight anymore in the West for being virtuous. Rather, being nice and kind carry greater weight in our Christian "slave" moral system. Genghis Khan, who founded the largest empire the world has ever known, stated that "The greatest happiness is to vanquish your enemies, to chase them before you, to see their cities reduced to ashes, to see the faces of those dear to them bathed in tears, to clasp to your bosom their wives and daughters" (Al-Din 1306/1995). Others like Napoleon and Moses, where the latter was nothing less than a genocidal maniac and led an army that gallivanted across the holy land exterminating, raping, pillaging, and plundering nonbelievers like the Canaanites and Amalekites,[2] achieved hero status even to this day for their dominance, ambition, courage, intellect, and "virtue."

Ecological factors also can play a role in the different descriptions we associate with moral concepts. For example, the scientist, Jared Diamond, describes two groups, the Maori and the Moriori (1997). The Maori colonized New Zealand around 1000 AD. Shortly thereafter, a group of Maori colonized the Chatham Islands and became the Moriori. Over the centuries, they lost contact with each other and evolved in different directions. While the Maori were farmers, the Moriori could not be farmers since the Maori tropical crops could not grow in the cold climate of the Chatham Islands. The Moriori reverted to becoming a hunter–gatherer society. Since they could not produce crop surpluses for storage, they did not have the means to support and feed non-hunting specialists such as chiefs, professional armies, and bureaucrats. As a result, they did not have a more complex political structure that would enhance their organizational abilities, nor did they have more military power. Furthermore, the Chatham Islands are small and remote islands that can carry a population of only about 2,000 hunter–gatherers. Without any other nearby islands, the Moriori remained on their island and had to learn how to get along with each other. In order to do this, they constructed a moral system that renounced war, where they even castrated some male infants in order to address the inevitable conflicts that arise from growing populations. The Moriori were a small peaceful anti-war population without strong leadership, organization, and without a strong military.

On the other hand, the Maori lived on the large island of New Zealand, where their population exploded to over 100,000. They were farmers and had crop surpluses that allowed them to feed chiefs and professional soldiers. Moreover, they were surrounded by competing neighboring groups with limited resources, which led to ferocious wars and a moral code that supported warfare. As the Maori and the Moriori lost contact with each other for centuries, in 1835, Australian seal-hunters notified the Maori of the Chatham Islands that contained a peaceful people that did not know how to fight. The Maori then sailed to the Chatham Islands and told the Moriori that the Moriori were now their slaves. The Moriori decided to not fight back, but rather, they offered peace and a sharing of resources. However, the Maori, trained in the cooperative practice of warfare, attacked and killed hundreds of Moriori, cooking and eating their bodies. They enslaved the rest. Although the capacity to think morally may have the function of cooperation, this function can be multiply realized in various ways. Even though the Maori and Moriori came from the same genetic stock, so to speak, how morality's function is multiply realized can be significantly dependent upon environmental factors such as ecological conditions and cultural transmission. Having a peaceful cooperative moral system may have been advantageous in terms of fitness before the 1835 invasion for the Moriori given their conditions, but having a warrior cooperative moral system, especially to defend themselves, may have been advantageous for the Maori given their disparate circumstances on New Zealand.

Examples of significant differences in thoughts as well as weightings across cultures that pervade history, anthropology, political science, sociology, and religion may provide supporting evidence that leads to disparities in reference between groups and an incommensurability for those in which a descriptivism applies. Recall that differences in behavior and decision-making allow us to draw general inferences that there are corresponding differences in what constitutes moral concepts since concepts play a causal role in decision-making and behavior (§10.2). However, such evidence does not allow us to make more specific claims absent of causal experimental data, such as that a particular cognitive and conative state rather than a different set influences judgment-making. Taking this into account, the vast evidence from the social sciences of differences in moral decision-making show that there may be too many differences in the descriptions and/or heavily weighted descriptions across relevant groups such that the moral concepts from the two groups fail to co-refer for those in which a descriptivism applies.

Although relevant examples are suffused throughout this book, further data comes from a cross-cultural study on 223 different countries amassing 39.61 million different recorded moral decisions on what autonomous cars should do when faced with a multiplicity of situations when an accident is unavoidable, such as when having to decide to save one life versus many, a young life versus an old one, or a jay walker versus someone who is crossing the street legally (Awad et al. 2018). They found substantial differences in these scenarios across cultures. For instance, Eastern cultures are significantly more likely to choose to save an elderly person than a young person as compared to Latin American cultures, perhaps due to the emphasis of respecting one's elders in Eastern cultures. Those from wealthy countries and who have strong political institutions that tend to maintain the rule of law are more likely to favor saving the person who legally crosses the street over the jaywalker as compared to members of poor nations with weak political institutions that do not maintain the rule of law. Perhaps relevant cultural disparities are responsible for the differences in judgments in this case. As we can see, members from different cultures at many times hold very different moral judgments. Along with the fact that I have shown that all moral concepts in part are constituted by cognitive states and moral emotions always are accompanied by corresponding cognitive states, this allows us to infer that for the relevant parties, their cognitive descriptions are mostly different as well. For those in which a descriptivism applies, this leads to disparities in reference.

Also, concrete causal data comes from the previously discussed prototype study on GOOD PERSON (Smith et al. 2007), where for example, most of the prototype features, such as INDEPENDENT and TOLERANT, for the Taiwanese are not found in the list of features for the Palauan, a list that includes represented features like RELIGIOUS and NOT TALKATIVE. This cross-cultural study encompassed seven different cultures including the U.S., Chamorro, Philippines, Venezuela, and Turkey. The experimenters write, "If the frequencies reflect the implicit folk theories of what is good,…the theories in effect in different cultures diverge considerably" (357).[3] This wide difference in prototype concept constituents also allows an inductive inference that it is likely that the represented general features that constitute their exemplars, such as INDEPENDENT and TOLERANT, will be different between both cultures since the general prototype features are so different. Moreover, since theory representations underwrite prototype representations, the wide disparities in prototype constituents across cultures mean that the held theory representations between the Taiwanese and Palauan very likely also will be quite different as well. Hence, we may inductively infer that the relevant moral concepts fail to co-refer, and the Taiwanese and Palauan will be talking past one another if they were to engage in moral discourse. Hence, coupled with the rich data from history, psychology, anthropology, political science, sociology, and religion, a relativistic theory of moral truth applies. Thus, we have our second contention for moral relativism. Descriptivism itself does at times lead to an indexical-based moral relativism, and the relevancy requirement is satisfied.

12.1.3 Objections

An objectivist may counter that on a narrow account, if the sets of descriptions from different cultures have mostly different descriptions but at least share formal properties such as sharing the same functional role in cognition of evaluating actions, persons, and institutions, then their concepts are still co-referential. Here, unlike Horgan and Timmons, the objectivist may understand this role and the evaluative component of moral concepts to be representational. Having great differences in descriptions does not matter so long as they share the same functional role. However, recall that since the causal theory applies at many times, there are relative facts on core moral issues such as killing and stealing. This is incompatible with moral objectivism and blocks an objectivist contention that is grounded on descriptivism. Remember that for the MTE and the Carl/Ian hypotheticals, where both interlocutors use their moral concepts for evaluative purposes, most people across cultures claim that both are talking past one another rather than talking about the same thing or talking about nothing. Moreover, later we will discuss Hare's missionary/cannibals hypothetical in which I found that most intuit that a Christian missionary and cannibal with very different descriptions for their moral concepts but with the same evaluative functional role are referring to different moral properties rather than to the same thing or nothing at all.

Also, for a narrow theory of content, basing one's theory of concept individuation on sharing only one mental property between agents' concepts for co-reference, such as having an evaluative component or role, is dangerous because this can lead to the concepts referring to things that they are not supposed to. Remember that to avoid this worry, cluster descriptivism requires that somewhere over half of the descriptions must be shared in common for co-reference because if it is less than half, then it will be possible for two distinct properties to be the referents of a single concept, where one of these properties actually may not be a proper referent. Moreover, some heavily weighted components must be shared as well.

Take for instance the traditional Dyirbal language, which is an aboriginal language in Australia that is dying as their youth are learning English as a primary language due to compulsory Western schooling. Hence, the youth and young adults only speak an extremely oversimplified version of Dyirbal. Traditional Dyirbal has four general categories for classifying everything in the universe (Lakoff 1987). One of these four category names must precede every noun when speaking the language. *Bayi* includes human males and animals, *balan* is the category for water, women, fire, and dangerous things, *balam* for non-flesh foods, such as vegetables and fruits, and *bala* is the grouping for everything else not in the other classes, such as rocks and language. While the underlying rationale for these four categories is quite complex, we need not delve into this issue. For our purposes, what is important is that what Westerners understand as being the *morality* category appears to be part of the *bala* category for the Dyirbal. The components the Dyirbal have for *bala* can include formal properties of ethics like having an evaluative component such that it is functionally used for making evaluations. However, it also includes countless other narrow components that are not related to the Western notion of *morality*, such as descriptions of rocks, language, dirt, air, clouds, grass, etc. *Bala* is clearly a socially constructed category that only really applies to the Dyirbal. Yet, if only matching the functional role is sufficient for determining reference, then on a narrow account, my moral concepts are also referring to the Dyirbal socially constructed category of *bala*. However, my Western concepts obviously do not have this extension. Therefore, having a similarity match in the functional evaluative role in moral cognition is not sufficient for establishing co-reference.[4] Thus, for this and other reasons, the entertained objection at hand fails, and moral relativism is true.

Notice here that for a narrow and wide theory, both can lead to moral concepts referring to moral properties relativized to a group. Recall that on a causal theory of reference, moral concepts refer to culturally constructed norms. When a descriptivism applies, moral concepts also can be referring to the relevant cultural norms. The advantage of this arrangement is that even when members of the same group may be relying on disparate narrow versus wide theories of content, they still can be referring to the same thing and not talking past one another. There is an underlying moral truth relative to their group such that one of them may be mistaken. This allows for a greater univocity, where group members using divergent theories of content are not talking past one another and are literally talking about the same thing.[5] There can be genuine disagreements in such cases. Moreover, we should expect peoples' concepts to refer to the norms of one's culture on a descriptivism account since culture will have played a highly influential role in shaping peoples' descriptions. Most of one's descriptions very likely will mostly describe the reasons and values that pertain to one's culture. Meanwhile, the cultural norms that causally influence judgments on a wide account will be the referent for those in which a wide content applies.

One may object that for those in which a descriptivism applies, there may be cases of exceptions where certain peoples' concepts do not refer to their overall cultural norms as their set of descriptions may be too different. The overall cultural influence, although reliable, can have exceptions where it did not have a significant impact on shaping certain peoples' descriptions. In this case given their widely different descriptions, they may belong to a particular subculture, where their descriptions were significantly influenced by the relevant subculture. Here, a subculture still can be thought of as being a part of the larger culture either because they may share certain non-individuated moral concepts with the larger culture but not other moral concepts or because the subgroup is demographically located within the larger group. To note, although rare, it is possible to have a group or set of only one in which a novel individual has disparate descriptions from others but is not externally influenced by culture or a group.

This general possibility of subgroups is a problem that is faced with any descriptivist theory for moral concepts given the diversity of thoughts people can have about ethics, especially for descriptivist accounts that properly account for the requirement that there must be over half of a similarity match between sets of descriptions, among other things, for co-reference. However, the group moral relativist need only say that this subculture is a subgroup that has at least certain incommensurable moral concepts with those of the majority subgroup. In this situation, there is a lack of univocity or commensurability in the culture at large, but the incommensurability still allows for a group moral relativism at the subgroup level. Those in the majority subgroup either have descriptions generally in league with the majority subcultural values or have moral concepts causally influenced by the majority subcultural values. Meanwhile, those in the minority subculture have a significantly different set of descriptions such that their relevant concepts are referring to their minority subcultural values, or, on the other hand for a wide account, perhaps their moral concepts are being reliably causally influenced by their minority subcultural values.

Another possible objection is that in order to claim that moral concepts across different groups are incommensurable, this presupposes the possibility of comparative studies across groups, especially for those in which a narrow content applies (Moody-Adams 1997). Yet, how is this comparison possible when the relevant moral concepts are incommensurable and cannot be compared, like apples and oranges? The answer is that the presumed cross-cultural comparison is to determine what mental states and concept constituents people have in mind for their moral concepts. One can be involved in this *non-moral* endeavor that may be of interest to a cognitive scientist without being involved in the *moral* endeavor of trying to compare values across groups in order to see whose values are "morally better." These clearly are two different projects. Hence, there is no problem to partake in the non-moral comparison of seeing what mental states constitute moral concepts in different minds across groups. Being involved in this project does not commit one to also partaking in the unfruitful moral project of determining which group has a more "ethical" system when the parties in question have incommensurable moral concepts.

Along similar lines, a possible fourth objection is that it is incoherent to say that a different culture has incommensurable moral terms and then go on to describe such terms at length in one's own language (Putnam 1981, Davidson 1984).[6] If others' moral terms are untranslatable into one's own language or are incommensurable, then they cannot be expressed using one's own language. There is a seeming paradox and self-defeating element in that the moral terms of a supposedly untranslatable language are articulated in the very language into which translation purportedly fails. Given that humans, such as moral relativists and anthropologists, can articulate other groups' supposedly incommensurable moral terms, such terms really are not incommensurable.

However, one response is that there is only local incommensurability. It is not the case that entire languages are incommensurable with each other across groups but only small subsets of terms; namely, for our purposes, only moral terms. Thus, there can be general translation across groups of non-normative descriptions, such as TAKING THE LIFE OF OTHERS and DOING WHAT YOU SAID YOU WOULD DO, which are relevant to moral discourse. Measuring the similarity of descriptions and other narrow states across groups is possible. Untranslatability of moral terms across languages is a relation between sublanguages within total languages. There are only localized translation failures. Hence, the contention that two sublanguages are not translatable can be given in a portion of language that is disparate from the language in which translation fails. The sublanguages can be the subject of discussion carried out in some other part of the language or what can be considered a metalanguage. We can have two incommensurable moral sublanguages MSL and MSL*. They are sublanguages of a broader metalanguage L in the sense that one can use L to speak of the semantic relations between MSL and MSL*. It can be argued in L that a particular term *t** of MSL* cannot be translated into MSL. Using L as a metalanguage, *t** can be shown to be indefinable in MSL without itself being expressed in MSL. Moreover, during the course of argument, there is no need to express the meaning of *t** in MSL. For, *t** can be defined in L, which is used as a metalanguage for MSL without expressing the meaning of *t** in MSL.

For example, for those in which a causal theory of reference applies, we simply need to know that the moral concepts were influenced by different external properties to generate an incommensurability, regardless of what the nature of those natural properties may be. The non-moral notion of 'being influenced by different properties' is translatable across groups and can be discussed in L. Second, for those in which a descriptivism applies, the descriptions associated with *t* and *t** across MSL and MSL*, respectively, largely are translatable across groups and are a part of the metalanguage L. In this respect, we can use L to argue for incommensurability in that there are too many different descriptions and/or too many differences in weights between *t* and *t**.

The fifth objection is that translation is necessary for interpretation (Putnam 1981). If a language is untranslatable, then the ideas in the language cannot be understood. Hence, it is incoherent to describe incommensurable moral terms in different groups as relativists attempt to do. However, one need not translate a foreign expression into one's own home language in order to understand it. For, then it would be impossible to learn and understand one's very first language. Also, an interpreter may start out with only having one language, but in examining a different culture, the interpreter can learn a new language. They can pick up new individuated moral terms relevant to a different culture and language. These new terms may not be translatable into the interpreter's native language, but the interpreter still can understand the new terms. Therefore, the premise that translation is necessary for interpretation and understanding is false.

Michele Moody-Adams (1997) may object that people across groups must have a lot of moral descriptions in common such that it is even possible for them to have an apparent moral disagreement in intercultural dialogue and debate. Intergroup debates in ethics and politics do occur, and the seeming disagreement that is involved requires that the parties at least share most of their descriptions. Hence, their moral concepts are commensurable with each other. However, recall that at many times, a causal theory of reference applies in which people are being influenced by different cultures. In such cases, there is an incommensurability, and people are talking past one another regardless of how similar their descriptions may be. Furthermore, there is experimental data on moral concepts showing that descriptions can differ across cultures such that there is a moral relativism. Moreover, the apparent disagreement in intergroup debate can occur because both parties share formal properties in common such as that their respective moral concepts are used to evaluate actions, persons, and institutions. This is enough to make it perhaps initially appear to some that there is genuine disagreement. However, for those in which a descriptivism applies, I have already demonstrated that this alone is not sufficient to allow for commensurability. Rather, given the incommensurability of moral concepts, the seeming disagreement between groups is only a verbal disagreement rather than a genuine one.

In summary, the above provides a new kind of incommensurability argument for group moral relativism based in part on experimental philosophy studies and moral semantic relativism. Insofar as moral concepts refer to group values, we have a group moral relativism rather than a subjectivism or assessment sensitivity relativism. Moreover, all moral objectivist theories are false, and there are no objective ethical values, such as an objective meaning to life. From here forward, we shall understand 'moral relativism' in its traditional sense, where it is shorthand for group speaker moral relativism.

Furthermore, the conclusions for moral relativism and the study of metaethics are not purely theoretical. Although many political philosophers and politicians have toiled over developing a thesis on universal human rights, such as having equal rights for minorities, an end to sex slavery, the prohibition of torture, and the right to life, such a thesis is false. There are no objective moral facts like the proposed rights in the Universal Declaration of Human Rights that are independent of a relativity clause. Such "rights" are remnants of Western imperialism; in particular, cultural imperialism. Such judgments can be true in a certain sense relative to a group, but not objectively true across all time and location. Any view that is based on an objectivist metaethical theory is false.

Notice that there are other benefits to my moral relativism conclusion. It is consistent with the widespread phenomenon of fundamental moral "disagreement" in ethics (Mackie 1977, Tersman 2006, Wong 2006). In what is typically known as the "argument from disagreement," there is interminable discourse on many moral issues. Such unyielding debates on many moral issues across cultures and subcultures separates ethics from other fields such as science, math, and logic, where in these latter fields, there generally is a much greater degree of consensus on issues, and debates usually get resolved. Rather, in many cases after long moral debate and agreement on the non-moral facts, separate parties are merely left to table slamming that "I am right, and you are wrong." What best explains this empirical phenomenon of interminable and fundamental moral conflict is that there are no objective moral facts.[7] For example, members of different cultural or subcultural groups can agree on all the relevant non-moral facts on an ethical issue but fundamentally cannot agree on the same ethical verdict. People can be aware of and agree upon all the relevant and surrounding biological, political, economic facts, etc., such as on the abortion debate between professional philosophers. However, they fundamentally cannot reach a normative consensus on an issue. What best explains these ready phenomena is that there are no objective moral facts. My moral semantic relativism and moral relativism views are consistent with fundamental "disagreement" in that such parties have individuated moral concepts and are talking about different things, like apples and oranges. There is no genuine disagreement but only verbal disagreement. This explains why there is such fundamental irresolvable "disagreement" in these cases, and moral relativism agrees that there is no objective morality.[8]

12.2 Folk Relativism and More New Arguments for Moral Relativism

More objections may be raised against moral relativism in that it denies objectivism. Some moral objectivists claim that their position on truth values does not lie in conflict with the supposed phenomena that people generally acknowledge that there can be moral error and people also generally are moral objectivists (Brink 1989, Smith 1994, Shafer-Landau 2003, Parfit 2011, Enoch 2017). Concerning truth values, that moral truth is actually objective lies in accord with the apparent fact that people believe there is the possibility for moral error and that there is a presumed underlying objectivity to ordinary moral discourse. Meanwhile, non-objectivist truth values problematically conflict with the appearances concerning these two supposed phenomena. These points are the basis for two intertwined a posteriori contentions commonly used to support moral objectivism and to counter non-objectivists views: The problem of moral error and the problem of folk objectivism (MEFO), respectively.

Several objectivists of various stripes claim that objective truth values are in harmony with the fact that people generally believe that there can be moral error, that sometimes moral arguments are incorrect, and that at times a person's moral stance on an issue can be corrected. People generally believe that there is the possibility for moral error in moral discourse and deliberation. The relevant theorists assume that such acknowledgements of moral error even exist in cross-cultural moral discourse. For example, if two interlocutors from different cultures hold opposing conclusions on a moral matter, the folk generally will understand that at least one of them must be in moral error, and both of them cannot be correct. People seem to believe that at many times there can be genuine moral disagreements, where interlocutors are not merely having disagreements on the relevant non-moral facts of the case, having differences in emotions or attitudes, or they are not just talking past one another with incommensurable moral concepts. People seem to believe that we at many times have genuine moral disagreements regarding the supposed objective moral facts of the matter. There is thought to be a genuine disagreement and an underlying objectivity to ordinary moral discourse, where there is a presumed objectivity to moral discussions such that it is possible to make moral errors. *Folk objectivism* is true, where the folk are for the most part objectivists rather than non-objectivists. For this phenomenon of moral error, at times, moral discourse can sway people to change their positions such that there may be final agreement between two interlocutors when previously there was no such consensus. At times, there appears to be corrections for moral mistakes. Objectivists claim that they have the advantage over non-objectivists since objective truth values are in accord with the two intertwined phenomena since corrections for moral error presume that there is an objective truth of the matter toward which corrections may be made and an objectivist theory of moral truth preserves the appearance of objectivity in moral discourse. As contrasted with non-objectivist views, objectivist truth values do not conflict with the supposed fact that the folk believe that there is objective moral truth. Moral relativism denies moral objectivism, so the problem of MEFO applies.

However, one may wonder that even if the folk believe in MEFO, why should we take their views as indicating anything about the true state of metaethics? How does this alone provide evidence in favor of objectivism and against non-objectivists? The argument that many objectivists make is one that pertains to explanatory power. There are the empirical phenomena of MEFO. What metaethical theory can best explain these phenomena? The view(s) that can provide the best explanation will have an explanatory advantage over the others. What supposedly at least in part best explains MEFO is that there actually are objective moral facts. For example, the reason why people believe there is a moral mistake made by one of the interlocutors in cross-cultural discourse when the two judgments conflict is because one of the judgments is in fact objectively false. Many objectivists claim that their position on truth values help to explain the phenomena while non-objectivist theories on moral truth values do not. This purportedly provides at least an initial explanatory advantage to the objectivist and a burden of proof against the non-objectivist, where non-objectivists have to explain MEFO while simultaneously maintaining their respective metaethical theory. Moreover, even though non-objectivists provide a sufficient and more complex explanation since their truth values cannot explain the phenomena, the objectivist likely will have the upper hand of providing a more direct, simple, and elegant explanation. Objectivists likely will provide the best explanation.

One possible counter to the objectivist is that at best, *most* but not all people may be objectivists, but there are still a number of people who are not. If there is some variation in folk beliefs about the status of morality, then the objectivist has the burden of explaining why those who are non-objectivists have such metaethical beliefs, just as the non-objectivist has the burden of explaining why most are objectivists. There is a seemingly equal explanatory burden on both sides of the objectivism/non-objectivism divide. Objectivists generally have not anticipated this counter. However, the objectivist might respond that each individual's metaethical beliefs are a phenomenon to be explained. Since most but not all are objectivists, objectivist truth values can help to explain most of the relevant phenomena in a more parsimonious way while non-objectivist truth values cannot. Hence, there is at least an initial explanatory advantage for the objectivist in that objectivism initially has greater explanatory power in that its truth values can help provide a simple explanation of most of the phenomena and has only a little bit of phenomena left to explain. Meanwhile the non-objectivist truth values have less explanatory power in that they help to explain only a little bit of the phenomena since only a few supposedly are non-objectivists, but they still have a whole lot of explaining left to do since most apparently are objectivists. Moreover, even if non-objectivists do provide such a complex explanation for most of the phenomena, they still will be at a disadvantage compared to the objectivist since most of the phenomena were explained by the non-objectivist in a complex rather than simple way. Assuming the objectivist can explain the minority phenomena that supposedly a minority of people are not objectivists, the objectivist can tout that on their view, most of the phenomena are explained in a simple way based on objectivist truth values. This provides objectivism with the advantage of explanatory simplicity over non-objectivism even though both types of theories can explain all the phenomena.

The phenomena of MEFO are empirically tractable claims that widely have been assumed to be true by metaethicists without proper empirical support. The immediate issue with the problem of MEFO is that the empirical phenomena that it relies upon are false. Given the host of cross-cultural evidence previously discussed in this book in light of scope objectivity and the moral/conventional task (§7.2.1–§7.2.2), most believe that there is no error between interlocutors from significantly different groups as both of them can be correct. Also, most are relativists rather than objectivists. *Folk relativism* is true.

The tables have turned, and the relevant phenomena actually provide *prima facie* support for moral relativism in that moral relativism can provide a simple and elegant explanation of most of the phenomena. Hence, it may provide the best explanation. People generally believe in moral relativism and in the absence of moral error across cultures because moral relativism is actually true. The truth values of relativism can provide a simple explanation of most of the phenomena, providing it with at least a *prima facie* advantage. However, this does not hold for objectivist, non-cognitivist, and error theory approaches. The alternatives may be able to provide a more complex explanation of most of the phenomena as their truth values cannot explain the phenomena, but they will lack the simplicity that moral relativism can provide. Moreover, if moral relativism and the alternatives both can explain all the phenomena, moral relativism still will have the advantage of parsimony. It will be the best explanation. This is a new prima facie-based contention for moral relativism. Moral relativism has the virtues of being able to straightforwardly explain folk relativism and fundamental "disagreement." Moreover, it is backed by a new incommensurability argument that is supported by new experimental data.

As another new contention for relativism that is similar to the one regarding the ability to explain folk relativism, *mutatis mutandis*, moral relativism provides a simple explanation of why most people believe that moral concepts refer to relative cultural moral properties. My replicated experimental results demonstrating these semantic empirical phenomena can be most simply explained by moral relativism because on this view, moral properties are indeed relative cultural ones. This explains most folk semantic beliefs, whereas the moral properties or lack thereof for alternative metaethical theories alone cannot accomplish this. This provides moral relativism with a *prima facie* advantage over its competitors as the competing views will lack the parsimony had by moral relativism. Hence, moral relativism may provide the most simple and best explanation of the phenomena.

Some, like Jonathan Dancy, alternatively may object to moral relativism by stating that our moral experience of how we are disposed to use moral vocabulary in an objectivist way provides a reason to have a defeasible presumption that morality is objective (Dancy & Hookway 1986). It provides a good reason such that the burden of proof is on the non-objectivist. However, this presumes that MEFO is true, but MEFO is empirically false.

The empirical evidence for folk relativism can be wielded to cut a wider swath in metaethics. In what is known as quasi-realism, several more modern day non-cognitivists of varying stripes have attempted to account for MEFO and the supposed objectivist seeming features in everyday moral discourse by trying to meet the above burden put on by objectivists (Gibbard 1991, 2003, Blackburn 1998, Horgan and Timmons 2000, Ridge 2014). However, this very quasi-realist project itself rests on an empirically false assumption and has been for naught. Most of the folk are not objectivists. If anything, such non-cognitivists should attempt to put forth a quasi-relativism thesis that attempts to account for the generally presumed underlying moral relativism in ordinary moral discourse.

Second, recall that error theorists like Mackie (1977), Joyce (2001), and Streumer (2017) claim that the folk are objectivists, where ordinary people's moral judgments purport to refer to objective moral properties and facts. However, although the above error theorists give variations of the same general contention, they basically claim that such properties do not exist. Since moral judgments attempt to refer to objective moral properties but such properties do not exist and are eliminated, all moral judgments are false. This classic argument that has several variations purports to lead to the characteristic truth value for error theory. However, this kind of argument for error theory does not allow the error theorist to claim that all moral judgments are false since the premise of folk objectivism and that the folk believe moral concepts refer to objective moral properties is not true. Hence, the desired categorical claim that all moral judgments are false, which is one of the hallmarks of error theory, in the above kind of contention for error theory cannot be reached. Therefore, this argument is unsound.

To note, even to this day, analytic metaethicists typically assume MEFO is true without second thought despite experimental evidence to the contrary. A like problem of ignorance of relevant experimental data also holds in many other subdisciplines of philosophy as well. As an epistemological matter, in this and other like respects, philosophy can be very much a backward discipline. For MEFO, in metaethics, there is an echo chamber analogous to ones found in the realm of politics, where objectivists, non-cognitivists, and error theorists tout the truth of MEFO, echoing back to each other the same empirically false claims and creating a constantly re-enforcing system of falsehoods willing its truth. Similar to certain politics, this will to power is of the most suspect variety. For, it not only is oblivious to the experimental research, but it lacks the very interest in even trying to find experimental data to back up its false empirical claims.

12.3 Hare's Missionary and Cannibals Thought Experiment

Hare (1952) may raise a different objection against moral relativism that with a hybrid theory on the cognitivism/non-cognitivism debate, moral concepts do not refer to relativized moral properties and facts. Rather, they do not refer to anything at all. A non-cognitivist rather than a relativist theory of truth prevails. Hare maintains that moral judgments have two semantic components. The first is a descriptive component in relation to standards, while the second is an evaluative component that receives a prescriptivist non-cognitive treatment. He argues that the evaluative component is semantically primary over the descriptive component based on the following thought experiment. Imagine that a missionary lands on an island of cannibals with a translation book so that the missionary can speak their language. He finds their most general adjective of commendation that is like the English concept GOOD and uses it in moral discourse. Hare claims that both parties can communicate with each other in this case because they both have a commending element to their respective concepts in regard to putting forth a positive evaluation. To be sure, the descriptive standards the missionary has associated with this concept that constitute the descriptive components of his evaluative judgments are very different from the cannibals. For example, the missionary has descriptive standards such as that the positive evaluative concept applies to those who do not acquire human scalps and who do not want to conquer other tribes, while, on the other hand, the descriptive standards held by the cannibals are that it applies to those who do acquire a lot of human scalps and who do want to conquer other tribes.

Hare claims that even though the descriptive components of the concepts widely differ between the two parties, both still share the same meaning of the words in that for both parties, the concepts contain a commending evaluative action-guiding component. This is very similar to Horgan and Timmons' claim on MTE that since Earthlings and Twin Earthlings both use moral concepts to evaluate actions, persons, and institutions, their moral concepts share the same meaning. Returning back to Hare, the missionary and cannibals both share the same evaluative non-cognitive meaning to their respective moral concepts, and they are not talking past one another. Since both share the same meaning of the concept in this case even though their descriptions significantly differ, the descriptive component is not primary regarding meaning. Rather, it is the evaluative component that is primary over the descriptive because since both parties have a commending or non-cognitive evaluative component to their respective concepts, their concepts supposedly share the same meaning. The descriptive components are irrelevant for determining whether their moral concepts share the same meaning. Thus, meaning is primarily linked to the evaluative component of a moral concept. Since Hare maintains that the evaluative component only contains non-cognitive prescriptive meaning and that a narrow theory of content applies for all moral concepts, moral judgments do not refer to moral properties.

One problem with this is that Hare incorrectly presumes a narrow theory of moral semantics. Rather, empirical data helps show that moral semantic relativism is true. Hence, his contention is unsound. Second, recall that the evaluative component of moral concepts empirically has been shown to contain cognitive evaluative concepts (§8.5). If both parties' moral representations share the same meaning on a narrow view based on the evaluative component of moral concepts, the cognitive normative component helps alongside the non-cognitive component to account for this shared meaning. Hence, it does not follow from Hare's contention that the non-cognitive component is semantically primary over the cognitive component for moral concepts such that moral concepts do not refer. Third, previously discussed experimental data I have gathered in moral semantics suggests that most people will not share the intuition that the missionary and the cannibals have moral concepts that do not refer to moral properties (§11.3.1–§11.3.3). Rather, people generally understand the moral concepts of agents from different cultures to actually refer to disparate cultural moral properties. Hence, Hare's contention fails to demonstrate that the non-cognitive component is primary. Rather, general intuitions are that such concepts refer to relativized moral facts.

As more direct evidence for my third criticism against Hare, I ran online studies on his classic hypothetical. Those who successfully passed the reading comprehension/attention check questions on the story were 52 lay persons across the various regions in the U.S. and 35 lay persons across the various regions in Singapore. The average age of participants in the U.S. is 47 ranging from 27 to 73 years of age. The average age of participants in Singapore is 40 ranging from 20 to 62 years of age. The vignette reads:

> An English Christian missionary lands on a remote island occupied by cannibals attempting to convert them to Christianity. The cannibals have a long history of meeting and speaking with missionaries. Over time, the cannibals have adopted the English term, 'moral goodness,' into their own language adding their own cultural influence to the term.
>
> The missionary and the cannibals both understand the term, 'moral goodness,' to be associated with evaluating and approving actions.
>
> However, despite this similarity, most of the descriptions the missionary and cannibals have in mind for the term, 'moral goodness,' are very different from one another. For example, the missionary describes the term, 'moral goodness,' as being associated with not taking human scalps, not eating humans, and not raiding other tribes. All of the cannibals describe the term, 'moral goodness,' as being associated with taking lots of human scalps, eating humans, and raiding other tribes.

Participants then were given reading comprehension/attention check questions on crucial parts of the story, such as that the missionary and cannibals both understand the term "moral goodness" to have an evaluative element and that most of the descriptions are different between the two parties. Only semantic intuitions from those who passed all of such questions were included. I then asked separate questions on moral meaning and reference.

(1) Having read the above story and assuming that it's 100% true, the 'moral goodness' term when used by the missionary and the 'moral goodness' term when used by a cannibal share the same meaning.
   a. True
   b. False

(2) Having read the above story and assuming that it's 100% true, when the missionary and a cannibal utter the term, 'moral goodness' when discussing 'moral' issues, what are these utterances actually about regardless of what the missionary and the cannibal might intend to be talking about?
   a. The missionary's utterance is about the socially approved values of his own culture. The cannibal's utterance is different in that it's about the socially approved values of his own culture.
   b. The missionary's utterance and the cannibal's utterance are both about something that is exactly the same thing for both.
   c. The missionary's utterance and the cannibal's utterance are about nothing at all rather than being about something.
   d. Other

Here are the results:

Table 12.1 Number of participants (and percentage) in each sample by answer to Hare's missionary/cannibals hypothetical on meaning

	US *n = 52*	*Singapore* *n = 35*
Same Meaning (True)	8 (15%)	5 (14%)
Different Meanings (False)	44 (85%)	30 (86%)

Table 12.2 Number of participants (and percentage) in each sample by answer to Hare's missionary/cannibals hypothetical on reference

	US *n = 52*	*Singapore* *n = 35*
Both are about different things	43 (83%)	34 (97%)
Both are about the same thing	8 (15%)	1 (3%)
Both are about nothing	1 (2%)	0 (0%)
Other	0 (0%)	0 (0%)

Eastern and Western lay participants overwhelmingly maintain that the terms do not share the same meaning and they do refer to disparate relative moral facts and properties.[9] While this result would be surprising to Hare, Horgan, Timmons, and many other philosophers, the cross-cultural results are generally consistent with my prior replicated experimental philosophy results in moral semantics that most believe that moral concepts refer to relative moral facts. It is also consistent with the aforementioned folk metaethics literature that most are moral relativists on moral truth (§7.2.1–§7.2.2). Moreover, the lone response in the U.S. that moral concepts do not refer is mere statistical "noise" and can be ignored.[10] One notable difference between Hare's hypothetical from MTE, however, is that for Hare, the external cultural environment is different between both parties but the narrow mental states also are mostly different. On MTE, such states are mostly the same. There are substantial differences from both a narrow and wide perspective on the missionary/cannibals thought experiment. Hence, I personally do not find it too surprising that the folk seemingly reach a higher consensus that meaning and reference are not shared in this case. Given all of the combined data against Hare as well as my other two previous contentions, Hare's argument fails.

Michael Ridge (2014) uses Hare's missionary/cannibals hypothetical to argue that *ecumenical cognitivism* is false. Ecumenical cognitivists espouse a hybrid position on the cognitivism/non-cognitivism debate while maintaining that moral judgments do refer to corresponding moral facts. Thus, in this respect, I am an ecumenical cognitivist as I am a hybridist and I maintain that moral judgments refer to relativized moral facts. He contends that ecumenical cognitivism has problems providing the needed links between talk of normative agreement/disagreement and talk of normative truth/falsity. Based on intuitions, he claims that there is genuine disagreement between the missionary and the cannibals, and they are not talking past one another. MEFO is true. However, on a narrow semantic account for ecumenical cognitivists who maintain that moral judgments do refer, their moral concepts refer to different properties given the disparate descriptions in the minds of the missionary versus cannibals for their GOOD concept. On the other hand, if Boyd's wide causal theory of reference applies, then their moral concepts still refer to different properties, since their respective judgments are being reliably causally regulated by different properties given their severe differences in moral decision-making even after large expanses of time have elapsed. Ridge notes that the ecumenical cognitivist may want to account for the real disagreement between the two parties by stating that there is a disagreement in attitude. However, this still will not help the ecumenical cognitivist. For the ecumenical cognitivist, when the missionary says that scalping is not 'good,' this is true relative to the missionary's group. When the cannibal says that scalping is 'good,' then this is true relative to the cannibal's group. They are talking past one another regarding the term, 'good.' However, how can it be the case that there is genuine disagreement when the two parties are talking past one another? For, if they are talking past one another, there is no genuine disagreement in this case, only verbal disagreement. Ridge emphasizes that there is a contradiction here linking truth conditions and genuine disagreement for the ecumenical cognitivist. The response to this objection is that experimental data shows that most people do not have the intuition that there is genuine disagreement in such kinds of cases (§7.2.1–§7.2.2). Rather, most understand that both parties can be correct and folk relativism is true. Both concepts still can refer to different moral properties where people are talking past one another but there is no genuine disagreement; a kind of disagreement that would conflict with moral concept incommensurability. In this manner, the contradiction is eliminated.[11]

Notes

1 Some on this list like James Dreier, Mark Schroeder, Jesse Prinz, and Sharon Street are subjectivists rather than moral relativists.
2 There are many places in the Bible where such values promoting genocide, rape, plundering, etc. are promulgated by God to his chosen (1 Sam 15:3, Josh 10:40, Deut 20:16, Num 31:17–18, Deut 20: 10–18).
3 By 'theories,' the experimenters are not referring to the theory-theory.
4 As a different functional or conceptual role semantics view, Ralph Wedgwood (2007) maintains a narrow conceptual role semantics for moral concepts where such concepts get their meaning from their conceptual role in practical reasoning in cognition. In particular, the conceptual role for OUGHT is that it commits one to making a relevant proposition part of one's ideal plans. This leads one to have motivation and an intention to carry out the proposition. Yet, Wedgwood's conceptual role account fails due to this same objection, *mutatis mutandis*, which applies to Horgan and Timmons.
5 Although I do not substantially examine or discuss the in principle different issue of theories of meaning, even if the meaning of their concepts may differ, reference is semantically more important regarding commensurability or incommensurability. If moral concepts between two people share the same extension, then they literally are talking about the same thing despite possible differences in meaning. Thus, they share the same truth conditions, and there is an underlying truth of the matter between them. Conversely, if they have different referents, then they are literally talking about different things and talking past one another even if they might share the same meaning. In such a case, they share different truth conditions.
6 This and the next objection have been given against Kuhn's incommensurability arguments for relativism in the philosophy of science. While I do not necessarily espouse Kuhn's arguments in the different realm of the philosophy of science that relies on non-moral concepts, I rely on Kuhn's (1983) responses to the likes of Putnam and Davidson as provided in the text.
7 Notice that I leave open the possibility that the argument from "disagreement" can be used to support other non-objectivist views other than moral relativism.

8 Although I do not have the space to go into great depth on this argument and defend it as my primary concern has been on providing my own arguments for moral relativism, the argument from "disagreement" has been defended elsewhere (Wong 2006, Tersman 2006).

9 There are only two categories for the study on moral meaning (sufficient to test one category). No significant difference in the corresponding sample proportions was found (e.g. the proportions of "false" categories): $z = 0.141$ and $P = 0.888$. For comparing the "different" or "same" category proportions on moral reference between the USA and Singapore populations, I notice that the large-sample z-test procedure doesn't apply. Instead, I apply a two-sided approximate Agresti-Caffo confidence interval for the difference in proportions. At 95% level of confidence, the interval for p2-p1 is (0.0045, 0.2578) for the most plausible values. As the lower bound is almost zero, the evidence to conclude that the proportions differ is not very strong (barely made it) but there is sufficient evidence to conclude that $p2 > p1$.

10 The sample proportion of the "eliminativist" response is 0.0192 or less than 5%. There is significant evidence to conclude that the "eliminativist" response was below 0.10 ($P = 0.0282$, binomial test).

11 Schroeder (2009) raises a somewhat similar concern against contextualism or subjectivism (pp. 284–287). It hinges on the point that two people with significantly disparate cognitive components to their moral concepts intuitively still will be genuinely disagreeing with each other. Yet, such disagreement is not possible when they are talking past one another. However, experimental data shows that this intuition of the presence of genuine disagreement is not borne out.

References

Al-Din, Rashid. 1306/1995. *A Compendium of Chronicles.* Ed. by Sheila Blair. Oxford: Oxford University Press.

Awad, E., Dsouza, S., Kim, R., Schulz, J., Henrich, J., Shariff, A., Bonnefon, J.F., and Rahwan, I. 2018. "The Moral Machine Experiment." *Nature* 563, 59–78.

Blackburn, Simon. 1998. *Ruling Passions.* Oxford: Oxford University Press.

Bourget, David and Chalmers, David. 2014. "What do Philosopher's Believe?" *Philosophical Studies* 170, 465–500.

Brink, David. 1989. *Moral Realism and the Foundation of Ethics.* Cambridge: Cambridge University Press.

Copp, David. 1995. *Morality, Normativity, and Society.* New York: Oxford University Press.

Dancy, J. and Hookway, C. 1986. "Two Conceptions of Moral Realism." *Proceedings of the Aristotelian Society, Supplementary Volumes* 60, 167–205.

Davidson, Donald. 1984. *Inquiries Into Truth and Interpretation.* Oxford: Oxford University Press.

Diamond, Jared. 1997. *Guns, Germs, and Steel.* New York: W.W. Norton & Co.

Dreier, James. 1990. "Internalism and Speaker Relativism." *Ethics* 101, 6–26.

Enoch, David. 2017. "Non-Naturalistic Realism in Meta-ethics." *The Routledge Handbook of Metaethics.* Ed. by T. McPherson & D. Plunkett. NY: Routledge, 29–42.

Finlay, Stephen. 2014. *Confusion of Tongues.* Oxford: Oxford University Press.

Gibbard, Allan. 1991. *Wise Choices, Apt Feelings.* Oxford: Clarendon Press.

Gibbard, Allan. 2003. *Thinking How to Live.* Cambridge, MA: Harvard University Press.

Hare, R. M. 1952. *The Language of Morals.* Oxford: Clarendon.

Harman, Gilbert. 1975. "Moral Relativism Defended." *The Philosophical Review* 84, 3–22.

Horgan, Terry and Timmons, Mark. 2000. "Nondescriptivist Cognitivism: Framework for a New Metaethic." *Philosophical Papers* 29, 121–153.

Joyce, Richard. 2001. *The Myth of Morality.* Cambridge: Cambridge University Press.

Kaster, Robert. 2010. "Values and Virtues, Roman." In *The Oxford Encyclopedia of Ancient Greece and Rome.* Ed. by M. Gagarin and E. Fantham. Oxford: Oxford University Press, 148–157.

Kuhn, Thomas. 1983. "Rationality and Theory Choice." *The Journal of Philosophy* 80, 563–570.

Lakoff, George. 1987. *Women, Fire, and Dangerous Things.* Chicago: The Chicago University Press.

Mackie, John. 1977. *Ethics: Inventing Right and Wrong.* New York: Penguin Books.

MacIntyre, Alasdaire. 1984. *After Virtue,* 2nd edition. Notre Dame, IN: Notre Dame Press.

Moody-Adams, Michele. 1997. *Fieldwork in Familiar Places.* Cambridge, MA: Harvard University Press.

Parfit, Derek. 2011. *On What Matters, Vol. 1 & 2.* Oxford: Oxford University Press.

Prinz, Jesse. 2007. *The Emotional Construction of Morals.* Oxford: Oxford University Press.

Putnam, Hilary. 1981. *Reason, Truth and History.* Cambridge: Cambridge University Press.

Ridge, Michael. 2014. *Impassioned Belief.* Oxford: Oxford University Press.

Schroeder, Mark. 2007. *Slaves of the Passions.* Oxford: Oxford University Press.

Schroeder, Mark. 2009. "Hybrid Expressivism: Virtues and vices." *Ethics* 119, 257–309.

Shafer-Landau, Russ. 2003. *Moral Realism: A Defense.* Oxford: Oxford University Press.

Smith, Michael. 1994. *The Moral Problem.* Oxford: Blackwell Publishers.

Smith, Kyle, Smith, Seyda, and Christopher, John. 2007. "What Defines the Good Person?" *Journal of Cross-Cultural Psychology* 38, 333–360.

Street, Sharon. 2008. "Constructivism About Reasons." *Oxford Studies in Metaethics* 3, 207–245.

Streumer, Bart. 2017. *Unbelievable Errors.* Oxford: Oxford University Press.

Tersman, Folke. 2006. *Moral Disagreement.* Cambridge: Cambridge University Press.

Velleman, David. 2013. *Foundations for Moral Relativism.* United Kingdom: Open Book Publishers.

Wedgwood, Ralph. 2007. *The Nature of Normativity.* Oxford: Oxford University Press.

Williams, Bernard. 1985. *Ethics and the Limits of Philosophy.* Cambridge, MA: Harvard University Press.

Wong, David B. 1986. *Moral Relativity.* Berkeley, CA: University of California Press.

Wong, David B. 2006. *Natural Moralities.* Oxford: Oxford University Press.

13 Moral Ontological Relativism

Given that we have a moral relativism on the table, which involves the existence of moral properties, it is now time to discuss in greater detail which ontological theory on the nature of moral properties is the best fit for moral relativism. There are moral properties such as *being good*, *being just*, *being virtuous*, and *being immoral* that are properties or qualities of things like persons, judgments, and actions. For instance, relative to my culture, helping one's neighbor has the property of *being moral*, my mother has the moral property of *being kind*, and helping the poor and needy has the quality of *being just*. We can ask ontological questions concerning the nature of an entity such as, "What is water?" The answer to this question is that water is H_2O. We may ask other ontological or metaphysical questions such as, "What is lightning?" In this case, lightning is identical to electrical discharges. Likewise, in metaethics, there is the ontological question of: "What are moral properties?" Can we touch it or point to it in the same way we can point to H_2O or electrical discharges? This chapter answers this question of what moral properties and facts are.

13.1 From Moral Relativism to Moral Ontological Relativism

Since an indexical-based moral relativistic theory of truth has been established and there are relative moral facts, we can conclude that moral properties are relativistic properties. If being morally true is relative to groups in an indexical-based way, then there is a moral ontological relativism in the sense that moral properties are relativized, and what moral properties and facts exist for or, in other words, pertain to one group or community may be different from group to group. For example, there may be a property *moral* that is relative to the Ancient Romans and another different property *moral* that is relative to the Amish. All moral properties are properties relativized to a particular group. Furthermore, the *moral* property and moral facts relativized to the Ancient Romans does not pertain and is not applicable to the community of the Amish. This moral ontological relativism follows from an indexical-based moral relativistic theory of truth because if moral judgments are true only relative to a group, then the moral judgments are referring to relative moral properties. If an indexical-based relativism is true and Ezekiel's judgment KILLING OUTSIDERS IS NOT MORALLY PERMISSIBLE is true relative to his Amish group and Julius' judgment KILLING OUTSIDERS IS MORALLY PERMISSIBLE is also true relative to his Ancient Roman group, then the concept MORALLY PERMISSIBLE in both judgments are individuated and referring to different *morally permissible* properties in order to account for the fact that in their possible discussion they literally are talking about different things and talking past one another such that Ezekiel's judgment can be true and Julius' seemingly contrary judgment also can be true. These different moral properties and values exist in or pertain to their respective different groups. With an indexical-based relativistic theory of moral truth, we have a moral ontological relativism, where moral properties are always followed by some kind of a relativity clause. If moral truth is relative to groups in an indexical-based way, then moral facts and properties are as well. Furthermore, what moral properties and norms exist for a group is different from group to group given disparities in the social construction of such properties.

I favor a constructivist and naturalist position on moral properties. For constructivism, moral properties are mind-dependent in the sense that for their existence, moral properties depend upon human minds to construct the relevant moral facts. We construct moral facts and properties. Constructivists generally maintain that moral properties are not mind-independent and out there to be discovered in the way we discovered that water is H_2O, but rather, they are created or constructed by minds, usually by way of certain ideal conditions or procedures. Without relevant minds, there would be no moral facts.

Meanwhile naturalist views generally maintain that moral properties and facts are certain natural properties and facts. Moral properties are part of the natural world and studied by the sciences rather than being supernatural properties invoked by a god or abstract and eternal platonic properties that do not exist in space or time. To note, I claim that moral properties are natural in the limited sense that they just are certain properties studied in the sciences. However, I do not maintain that moral properties are natural kinds that exist independent of human construction and that carve nature at the joints. Rather, they are social kinds that are constructed by human beings and groups; kinds that can be studied in the social sciences.

Science has tremendous explanatory power and has proved itself to be the most successful branch of knowledge many times over. Such explanatory power is ever increasing. It can explain how human beings first came into existence, how the universe began, planetary motion, how black holes lose mass, the photoelectric effect, and black body radiation. Quite frankly, as an induction, it would be extremely unlikely given its previous and continuing impressive successes that science would not be able to explain morality. Non-naturalists believe that science cannot explain morality. For example, non-natural realists believe that moral properties are simple properties that cannot be broken down further and explained in natural terms. Even though moral properties supervene upon natural ones, science cannot provide an explanation of what moral properties are. Hence, by common definition, this means for ethics, non-naturalists believe in the supernatural. However, I think there can be a natural explanation of moral goodness just as there can be a perfectly natural explanation of what makes a tool, like a hammer, good, or what makes certain foods good.

13.1.1 Wong's Moral Ontology

Before expounding upon my theory, let us critically assess various competing ontological views from moral relativists. Moral ontology tends not to be as deeply as discussed by moral relativists, but we'll examine what I take to be the two most sophisticated ontological views from moral relativists.[1] The first account we will examine comes from David Wong (1986, 2006). Wong (2006) maintains that moral properties are reducible to and explained in terms of reasons that relate to biological human needs and purposes. On this account, moral reasons just are a particular kind of practical reason that relates to the best biological theory of human nature. Hence, moral facts are reducible, but in another sense they are not. For, moral reasons for action are not themselves reducible to non-moral properties. Moral reasons are reducible to natural evaluative reasons, but these normative reasons are *sui generis* and simple properties that cannot be further reduced. Moral properties are not *sui generis* abstract platonic properties but are *sui generis* natural normative properties that relate to human needs, desires, purposes, and a theory of human nature. Wong holds a non-reductive naturalism view in that moral properties are natural normative properties that cannot be further reduced to descriptive natural properties.

A problem with Wong's view is that moral properties are not causally efficacious. It is important that moral properties within our current metaethical framework be natural properties such that they have causal powers especially given that the causal theory of reference applies at many times. Non-natural properties are not causally efficacious as they do not exist in spacetime. Moral properties must be able to reliably causally influence moral decision-making and thus, be the referent of moral judgments. Also, it is thought that when taking the naturalist route, natural properties in scientific theories need to carry their weight in terms of playing a required role in causal explanations. Yet, if moral properties are natural normative properties that cannot be reduced to non-moral properties, like to psychological or sociological facts, then it does not appear that moral properties can causally explain events.

For example, to take a line of reasoning from Harman (1977), if I see hoodlums pouring gas on a cat and setting the cat on fire, on Wong's non-reductive account, the moral wrongness of the act relative to my culture does not need to be cited to causally explain why I judge the act is wrong. Rather, non-moral facts such as cultural sociological and psychological facts of how I was raised in my culture sufficiently can causally explain my judgment. Of course, moral facts supervene or depend upon non-moral facts for Wong, but the two are not identical. Here, we can understand supervenience as being where two situations cannot be different in their moral properties without also diverging in some way in their natural properties. For example, relative to my group, if Jack tells a lie and Jill tells a lie, they both appear to have done something morally wrong. However, if I state that Jack's act was wrong, but Jill's was not, there must be some difference in their physical acts or in the natural circumstances to account for this difference in the attribution of moral properties. For, if their physical acts are the same and all else is equal in the circumstances, then the attributed moral verdicts to such acts also must be the same. In this example, let us say that Jack told a harmful lie, but Jill only told a harmless white lie that accounts for the disparities in moral attributes. For Wong, there is supervenience of the moral on the non-moral, but the two are disparate properties. Hence, all that is needed to sufficiently explain my decision-making are the usual non-moral cultural descriptive facts in fields like sociology and psychology that typically are thought to play a role in causal explanations, and the disparate natural moral facts are causally inert or epiphenomenal. The disparate natural moral fact is not required for the explanation of why I judge that burning the cat is wrong.

One may claim that both non-moral and moral facts play a causal role, however, this then will be a case of overdetermination, where there are two or more sufficient causes occurring at the same time. Yet, cases of overdetermination, such as when a person is killed by getting shot in the heart at the same time by two bullets, are rare. Unless definitively shown that a genuine case of overdetermination is on our hands, which is lacking in this moral case, we can infer that moral properties are epiphenomenal. This not only is disastrous given the prevalence of the causal theory of reference, but it also puts into serious doubt that moral properties are natural properties since they do not pull their weight in scientific explanatory theories. However, as Harman fully admits, if moral properties are identical to or just are non-moral natural facts, facts which are causally efficacious, then this allows moral properties to have causal powers.

Nicholas Sturgeon (1984) objects that we can understand non-reductive moral facts as playing a counterfactual causal role in explanations. Moral property *m* is a cause of judgment *j* if *j* would not have occurred as it did had *m* not occurred as it did. However, Harman (1986) plausibly objects that there needs to be an account of the underlying mechanism for the counterfactual dependence. The only viable way to account for this underlying mechanism is to posit a reductive naturalistic view in which moral properties just are non-moral natural properties, where the latter properties can account for the underlying mechanism. As Wong's non-reductive natural moral properties are not causally efficacious, this leads to a significant problem for his view.

13.1.2 Harman's Moral Ontology

The second group relativistic theory we will examine is held by Harman (1975). Harman claims that moral facts are reducible to non-moral facts about which actions are supported by an implicit agreement of intentions. In order to determine what is relativistically right and wrong, one must look to the implicit interpersonal agreements made between group members concerning how they ought to live their lives. Such implicit agreements will have been reached through the ideal conditions of making mutual adjustments and bargaining, where members will arrive upon a compromise. Moreover, different groups will arrive upon different compromises and construct different moral perspectives. Hence, for Harman, moral properties are reducible to natural sociological properties of human interaction that are constructed based on the ideal conditions of social bargaining, discourse, compromise, and deliberation.

Harman's ontological theory is a reductive account in which moral properties are reduced to certain social agreements. While this allows for moral properties to be causally efficacious and provides a sufficient explanation of why the moral supervenes upon the non-moral due to an identity relation between the two, the problem here is that in identifying normative properties with descriptive properties, the normativity of ethics problematically disappears. This is called *the normativity objection.* The normativity objection against naturalism has been made by numerous philosophers. It basically claims that identifying moral properties to non-normative natural properties takes the normativity out of ethics. For instance, Derek Parfit (2011) contends that the fact that we have decisive moral reason to do an action is in a completely different category than a natural fact. Hence, we cannot state that moral facts are identical to non-normative natural facts due to the differences in categories. For example, for a classic utilitarian, moral properties are identical to the natural property of happiness. Hence, moral properties just are happiness in the same way water is identical to H_2O. However, the normativity objection comes into play because moral properties are normative ones, but happiness is not. Therefore, if you identify moral properties to happiness, then it looks like moral properties are not normative. Per Leibniz's Law, two things are identical only when they share all their properties in common. Moral properties have the property of being normative, but descriptive properties do not. This looks to be problematic for reductive naturalist views and for Harman.

Also, recall that we previously discussed Prinz's relativism view that moral properties are secondary qualities that have the power to cause certain emotions in us. This is a reductive naturalistic theory reducing moral properties to non-moral natural properties that are qualities of having the power to cause us to feel certain emotions or sentiments. Yet, it also runs into the normativity objection, amongst other possible objections to secondary quality views (Blackburn 1985).[2] It looks like the normativity simply disappears when a naturalistic reduction is made from moral to non-moral properties. Moreover, there is a two-horned dilemma here in that if a relativist then attempts to escape the worry at hand by identifying moral properties as being *sui generis* natural normative properties that keeps the normativity intact, like Wong, then moral properties seemingly are not causally efficacious.

13.2 A Non-Reductive and Reductive Token-Token Identity

Natural normative reasons abound in the sciences, such as in medicine. For instance, that water has an essential life-sustaining property provides a medical reason for one to drink water. In economics, when the U.S. is in a recession, the interest rates ought to be lowered. Such normative properties are not mysterious and are part of the natural world. Certain social scientists readily discuss certain moral properties. For instance, anthropologists and historians examine moral norms and what is right or wrong for a culture or era; political scientists the political values of various international communities. With this insight in mind, I claim that moral properties are token identical to a compound entity that consists of (1) the corresponding *sui generis* natural normative social reasons or values of a group *x*, values that are or can be studied in the social sciences, that are inferred from certain rational constraints[3] and (2) non-moral socio-psychological facts that the given reasons have been approved of by group *x* in light of certain rational constraints. This definition is mentally represented by theory structure that occupies an empirically defeasible placeholder position, and the rational constraints that will be discussed shortly are represented by prototypes. This is a new ontological theory of moral properties that identifies moral properties to a compound just as the reduction of water is to a compound of two hydrogen and one oxygen molecules. Moral properties are reduced to a conjunction of *sui generis* natural normative properties of a group and to non-moral natural properties regarding group approval. Moral properties have a complex but natural reduction base. Here, the natural normative property of the compound cannot be further reduced to non-moral properties. Hence, in this respect, there is a non-reductive component. However, there is a reductive component in that moral properties are in part reduced to non-moral natural facts. In this sense, my ontological relativism is both non-reductive and reductive. Similar to water and H_2O, both parts of the natural reduction base for moral properties are bound together and need to be compounded in order for there to be a moral property. The numerous virtues that justify my identity claim will be discussed shortly.

Also, my ontological relativism theory is a token identity. For instance, the moral property of *being beneficent* relative to group *A* just is the natural social value *being beneficent* that was socially approved of by group *A* in light of certain idealized conditions; a natural value that may be studied by anthropologists, historians, or political scientists. Notice that this is a token-token identity of moral properties, where there is a particular token property of *being beneficent* relative to a group *A* rather than *B* that is identical to a particular token socially constructed value *being beneficent* that was socially approved of by group *A* rather than B. Meanwhile, there is a disparate token property of *being beneficent* relative to group *B* that is identical to a particular token natural social value *being beneficent* that was approved of by group *B*. There are many different moral tokens of *being beneficent* that are identical to disparate token natural compounds. Different token moral properties and facts exist relative to different groups. Moral ontological relativism is preserved.

Also, my token identity is different from type identities that are more common for naturalistic views. We can think of a "type" as being a superordinate category of which a "token" is a member. For example, utilitarians claim that the property of *being right*, understood as a type, is identical to *happiness*, understood as a type. On my view there are many different token properties of *being right* that are identical to disparate token compound natural normative properties constructed and approved of by divergent groups.

There are many virtues to my ontological relativism view. My ontological reduction can explain the supervenience of the moral on the non-moral. Supervenience holds because moral properties are in part identical to the relevant non-moral cultural property of being approved of by the group. Whether acts such as a harmful versus a white lie have the property of *being morally permissible* relative to *x* depends or supervenes upon being approved by the group in light of certain rational constraints. *Being morally permissible* in part just is being approved of by the group in light of certain rational constraints. Identity entails supervenience as every moral property supervenes upon itself. Another way of thinking about it at only the level of the natural properties in the reduction base rather than at the level of the moral properties, the natural normative property is always tied or compounded to the relevant non-moral natural property. Such is the nature of the compound just as two hydrogen and one oxygen molecules are compounded together for water. Hence, whether an act has the natural normative property of *being morally permissible* relative to *x* always will depend upon group approval. They are inextricably linked. A white lie relative to group *x* can have the natural property of *being morally permissible* relative to *x* since it is approved by *x* in light of certain idealized conditions, but a harmful lie relative to group *x* only can have a different natural normative property of *being morally wrong* relative to *x* if there is the non-moral difference that such acts are not approved of by *x*.

Moreover, my reduction to the compound escapes the aforementioned horned dilemma in that moral properties are in part reduced to natural normative reasons that are not themselves further reduced. Moral properties are in significant part simple normative properties, and thus, the normativity objection is addressed. Moral properties are in part normative ones, where this normativity does not wash away.

Furthermore, given that moral properties in part reduce to non-moral socio-psychological properties of group or cultural approval, properties which typically are thought to be causally efficacious, moral properties can play a causal explanatory role in influencing moral decision-making. For, moral properties in part just are such cultural descriptive facts. Culture influences judgment. While the *sui generis* natural normative component is causally inert, the non-moral natural component is causally efficacious, which allows the moral property to be so as well. Furthermore, we already have seen that a view where moral properties are at least in part causally efficacious non-moral natural properties is needed for causal theories of moral mental content. By identifying moral properties as being a compound of a non-reductive natural normative property and a reductive non-moral natural property, I can escape the horned dilemma. Given the various virtues and reasons in favor of this theory, we see that there is a scientific explanation of moral properties as we should expect given science's immense explanatory successes.

Furthermore, notice that my view beneficially is ontologically parsimonious in that moral properties just are token identical to a certain compound of natural properties studied in the sciences. I am not adding something in addition to the natural scientific ontology such as Platonic moral facts that are supernatural properties that have somehow existed for eternity. My ontology is neither bloated nor supernaturally mysterious.

Moreover, my ontological relativism is a synthetic naturalism rather than an analytic one as it relies significantly on empirical evidence to identify moral properties in terms of natural ones rather than being purely a priori. The empirical claim that approved cultural values are what reliably causally influence judgment along with a causal theory of reference is what significantly helps lead to establishing the prominence of an indexical-based moral relativism and thus, an ontological moral relativism and my natural identity.

Derek Parfit criticizes synthetic reductive naturalists in that their identity statement is not informative but is trivial. As I have a synthetic reductive component to my view, his objection applies. He claims that since moral facts are identical to natural facts, the identity will be trivial and uninformative. Hence, he believes that reductive naturalists are in essence merely claiming that, for example, "moral properties are moral properties" or "maximizing happiness is maximizing happiness." However, Parfit points out that such an identity is not trivial. Making an identity claim that, for instance, rightness is maximizing happiness must be argued for, and many people must be informed of this identity claim since it is not obvious to them.

In response, a moral fact in part is just a non-normative natural fact. However, this particular aspect of the identity is informative for some in that a theory-theory mental state that constitutes their moral concepts and that contains representations of the ontological status of moral properties does not represent this identity claim. Of course, empirical evidence shows that most of their descriptions still differ from those of other groups, and so an incommensurability, moral relativism, and then moral ontological relativism still ensues on a narrow account. Yet, while the moral and non-normative facts in part are identical, such claims are still informative for some given certain disparities in the sense of their moral concepts and how they understand the moral world to be. Parfit's criticism problematically conflates metaphysics with epistemology or the ontology of normative facts with concept constituents, which in principle can be distinct matters as just shown. The relevant facts are identical, but it still can be informative given the disparate issue of what constitutes concepts and the human understanding.

Bart Streumer (2017) objects against any reductive approach. Since my ontological view contains a reductive component, his objection applies. He says that moral properties cannot be reductive (or have a reductive component) in that on a narrow content account, descriptions even after full reflection at times will differ substantially across communities, such as from a warrior society to a peaceful one. Hence, people's moral concepts will be individuated from each other and there will be different relative moral facts that reduce to disparate descriptive facts depending upon one's community. Any reductive approach on a narrow account will lead to moral relativism. However, he claims our intuitions are that MEFO is true and both groups cannot be correct, so therefore, moral properties do not so reduce. Moreover, he says that if a wide content account is true, different communities are clearly being reliably causally regulated by different properties. For instance, the property of *maximizing the suffering of outsiders* very reliably regulates certain warrior communities, while the property of *minimizing the suffering of outsiders* reliably regulates certain other groups. Hence, one who believes that moral properties reduce to descriptive ones and who maintains a wide content will have to claim that moral facts are identical to certain causally efficacious descriptive facts. These descriptive facts vary by culture. Hence, relevant moral concepts will not co-refer, so both groups' moral judgments are correct relative to their own groups. However, Streumer says this is false since our intuitions are that MEFO is true. Both descriptivism and a causal theory of reference inevitably will lead to moral relativism, but this can't be right since people believe there's an underlying objectivity to ethics. In response, Streumer is incorrect about the general intuitions on MEFO. Recall that folk relativism is true, where most maintain that both can be correct, and MEFO does not hold. Hence, his argument against a general reductive approach is empirically false.[4] Rather, my moral ontological relativism is true.

13.3 Constructivist Constraints

Constructivists typically state that there are certain rational constraints on constructing moral facts, and my view is no different. We must further specify that the moral properties and facts of a group are not merely those that are approved of by a group. It is more sophisticated in that relativized moral facts are those that are part of a coherent and consistent set that is also ideally formed after careful interpersonal and intrapersonal deliberation and sincere reflection ideally with all the relevant and accurate non-moral facts, although we have seen with Haidt's dumbfounding studies that many may hold false non-moral facts but they do not really base their judgments on them. In this regard, they may hold such moral verdicts as being initial considered judgments or intuitions that carry significant weight and that hold regardless of the relevant non-moral facts. For instance, certain people seemingly may justify their misogynistic judgments based on false non-moral claims regarding the mental inferiority of women, but this may be just post-hoc reasoning. Rather, their misogynistic judgments are weighty initial considered judgments and are not really based on the false non-moral claims at all.

Moral relativism is not an "anything goes" kind of view. Relativism allows for moral error by members within a group. People can make mistaken and false moral judgments relative to a group because they hold inconsistent judgments, judgments that lack coherence, judgments that are grounded on false non-moral facts, etc. Also, these norms for the ideal conditions are not moral practical reasons but are epistemic theoretical reasons for arriving upon judgments. In this fashion, I am not begging the question by saying that moral facts are constructed by an ideal procedure, but the ideal procedure somehow already contains within it ethical norms by implicitly or explicitly assuming such norms exist.

Given my constructive naturalism view on the nature of moral properties, we have an ethical idealism, where moral facts are mental constructions in the head by social animals who have evolved the capacity to think morally and cooperatively and who together in groups have put their minds together and constructed moral facts that generally enhance cooperation, dispute resolution, and the resolution of intrapersonal conflict based on things like cultural and ecological factors and conditions. I do not claim that a general idealism holds but only an ethical idealism for moral properties only. However, analogous to how idealism, generally understood, maintains that objects in the world, such as tables, chairs, and animals, are not mind-independently real and their existence depends upon the mind, moral properties and facts do not exist independent of the mind. There is moral ontological relativity and different moral properties and facts exist for different groups since there is ethical idealism and different groups construct and approve of different moral properties and facts. Moral worlds are only created and can be destroyed. Moral facts are constructed and created by minds based on natural evolutionary, sociological, and psychological processes as well as by ideal procedures. Without minds to construct moral judgments such that the judgments then can be put through ideal conditions, there are no moral facts; there is no morality, no justice or injustice. Hence, moral properties and facts are mind-dependent, and they are token identical to corresponding socially approved norms that are constrained by idealized conditions. In this respect, morality is an artifice and contrivance of the mind.[5]

13.4 Open Question Arguments

A prominent objection against naturalist views is Moore's aforementioned open question argument, where this is an objection against analytic rather than synthetic naturalism. However, I have already shown how this can be handled in a previous chapter with a narrow theory of content given the lack of classical structure and the presence of a prototype structure to moral concepts that predicts open questions (§11.2). Moreover, a wide theory of content also can handle this objection. Internally in our minds, it may seem like there is an open question when entertaining a naturalistic definition and our internal represented descriptions, but internal thoughts play no role in reference on a wide account. For, on a wide view, moral concepts still refer to relevant natural properties given a causal connection to such properties that does not rely on what is in the head. In this respect, moral and the relevant natural concepts are co-referential, so therefore, moral and the relevant natural properties are identical.

Yet, even more fundamentally, my naturalism is a synthetic naturalism. Therefore, it escapes Moore's open question argument. I do not claim that an ontological naturalism is true based merely on the meaning of moral concepts alone, but rather moral properties are compound natural properties based significantly on empirical investigation. Hence, there can be open questions with such naturalistic claims, just as there can be with claims like water is identical to H_2O. For, this identity claim on water is true, but scientists still can question it if they are not exactly sure of themselves, such as when the claim about water's chemical composition being H_2O was first initially made.

However, Horgan and Timmons offer a new revised open question argument against a synthetic ethical naturalism that involves a wide theory of content, but this open question argument is dependent on the truth of narrow content intuitions on MTE. There is the question for a wide account: Given that the use of GOOD is causally regulated by natural property *N*, is entity *e*, which has *N*, good? This question will be closed if there are wide intuitions on MTE and an ethical naturalism predicated on a wide theory of content is true. However, Horgan and Timmons state that since our intuitions are narrow ones, the question is an open question, and it therefore, threatens an ethical naturalism that is based on a wide theory of content. Nevertheless, we have seen how their strong narrow semantic claim on MTE is empirically false. Most have wide intuitions on MTE. Horgan and Timmons' premise that our semantic intuitions overwhelmingly are narrow ones is false, so their objection is unsound.

Also, Horgan and Timmons do not foresee a moral semantic relativism, but they falsely believe there is only one monolithic theory of reference that applies to all moral concepts. Yet, given moral semantic relativism, where what theory of reference applies is dependent on the agent, for those in which a wide content applies, Horgan and Timmons' objection fails. Wide intuitions lead to a closed question. Relative to such agents, a wide content naturalism view applies but not a narrow content naturalism. Only for those in which a narrow content applies, however, their objection against a synthetic naturalism based on a wide theory of content is relevant in the sense that there is the above open question. Therefore, a wide content naturalism does not apply to such people, but a narrow cluster descriptivism naturalism still does. One might then object that Moore's open questions argument comes into play for those in which a narrow content applies, but recall that my naturalistic view can handle Moore's disparate open question argument.[6]

13.5 Normative Ethics and Moral Epistemology

The question now arises as to how to proceed with normative ethics and moral epistemology with moral relativism. Although my treatment of this issue only can be brief and incomplete, I will say a few words. Here, we are not concerned with arriving upon a theory of reference as that already has been accomplished with the establishment of moral semantic relativism in a previous chapter. Rather, we are interested in the issue of moral epistemology and how we can be justified in our moral judgments that an act is right or wrong. Recall that I previously alluded to the notion of coherence. With this in mind, there still will be a crucial place for moral philosophers in normative ethics even though there is no objective moral truth. For, philosophers are still needed to specify what the *coherent* set of moral judgments of a group is. This will require substantial work.

Using a coherentist epistemology or reflective equilibrium in order to justify our moral judgments was utilized by Rawls (1971) in constructing and justifying his theory of justice. This view along with my pluralistic theory of moral concepts claims that justification of moral truth claims is reached holistically by working back and forth between a group's (1) intuitions or initial considered judgments about particular cases, particular precedents, and/or particular agents that are constituted by exemplars and/or conative states, (2) principles and ethical theories represented by prototypes and theory concept constituents that may govern the considered judgments, and (3) the relevant background theories, such as social theory, anthropology, psychology, and political history, that can be represented by theory mental representations as well as by theory representations stored in non-moral concepts. Bringing in knowledge from empirical moral psychology especially can help guard against being improperly influenced from psychological biases and heuristics, like framing effects and in-group biases, when deciding right from wrong.[7] (1)–(3) and the component parts therein are differentially weighted in terms of importance. The name of the game is to attempt to reach a sufficient degree of coherence between all three levels by making adjustments and revisions where necessary between levels. Parts of the set of judgments must be tested against other judgments in the set, where one must attempt to make adjustments and tradeoffs at different levels that allow for the widest mutual supporting of judgments. When inconsistencies and challenges arise within one's set of judgments, revisions must be made at various levels to bring coherence to the set. The revisions can be quite significant. Maximum coherence is reached when we are not inclined to further revise our considered judgments, principles, and theories because they currently have the most credibility for us. Once such coherence is reached, then the set of judgments can be said to be at wide reflective equilibrium and all the judgments in the set are now justified for the agent or group.

Coherence means not only having logical consistency in one's judgments but it also means that one's judgments are mutually supporting, where judgments may provide explanations for other judgments within the set. Coherence requires consistency, but it also contains the notions of *connectedness* and *comprehensiveness* (Sayre-McCord 1985); notions represented by prototypes. Connectedness involves the addition of certain judgments that may link other judgments that are already within one's set. For instance, my thoughts HER INTENTIONS WERE KIND, SO SHE IS GOOD and HIS INTENTIONS WERE SINISTER, SO HE IS NOT GOOD can be connected by adding the judgment INTENTIONS MATTER FOR DETERMINING WHETHER SOMEONE IS GOOD OR NOT. Such additions create a more coherent set of judgments. Moreover, connectedness means that one's judgments stand in such a relation to each other that proper inferences are available or may be made to other judgments. Coherence leads to a web of judgments that are mutually supporting.

Comprehensiveness means that we should *ideally* bring in as many relevant judgments as possible into our set in order to rule out false positions and inferences. This comprehensiveness allows for a greater justification in one's judgments as compared to just relying on intuitions alone. For example, in order to determine what political system ought to be instantiated, besides my normative judgments, I ideally should also include background theories such as social theory, facts on human anthropology, political history, and empirical political psychology, etc. to help create a holistic picture that leads to a stronger justification in judgments (Daniels 1996). Inclusion and coherence of such background theories along with one's intuitions, principles, and ethical theories leads to a wide reflective equilibrium.

A coherentist epistemology might be viewed as being a circular form of justification in which all judgments are inferred from other judgments in the set. The infinite regress problem in moral epistemology is that in order to have knowledge that a moral proposition is true, such as that murder is wrong relative to my group, we need to have good reasons for our judgments, such as possibly that murder is wrong because it violates someone's right to life. However, this reason seemingly then itself will require a justification and so on, *ad infinitum*. For instance, why does someone have a right to life? A foundationalist or intuitionist will respond to the challenge by claiming that there are certain foundational judgments or intuitions that themselves are self-evident and require no further justification. Other moral judgments can be inferred or inevitably inferred from such foundations. This stops the regress. I will criticize this approach in the next section. Meanwhile, a coherentist appears to escape the infinite regress by relying on a never-ending circular justification of judgments. For instance, if judgment J1 is justified by its coherence with judgments J2-J100, then J2 is justified by its coherence with J1 and J3-J100. J1 is in part justified by its relation to J2, J2 is in part justified by its relation to J1, J1 is in part justified by its relation to J2, and so on. Hence, there appears to be a never-ending circular chain of justifications, but there is no infinite regress that requires an infinite amount of justifications. We see that coherentism cuts off the infinite regress problem, where J1 seemingly ultimately is in part justified by itself.

One may object that this is a vicious kind of circularity in which one's judgments are not justified. However, coherentists can respond that for coherentism, the main emphasis should be on entire systems of moral judgments being justified. One primarily should focus on entire systems of moral judgments being justified based on systems being coherent. We can speak of individual judgments being justified only secondarily based on the fact that they help form a coherent system, but the main focus is on entire systems being justified. As we can see, this is not a linear form of circular justification, such as saying that "God exists and wrote the Bible because the Bible says so. The Bible is justified because God exists and wrote the Bible. The supposed facts that God exists and wrote the Bible are justified because the Bible says so, etc." Linear circular justifications that reshape a single line or chain of justifications into a circle are vicious. A linear circular justification says that a judgment J1 is justified by another judgment J2. J2 then may be justified by another judgment and so on, but eventually the judgments circle back. However, coherentism does not claim that J1 is justified by J2. Rather, it claims that J1 is justified in virtue of being part of a maximally coherent set of judgments. Coherentism brings a holistic form of justification rather than a linear one, where an entire system of a wide body of judgments is justified based on this entire whole system being consistent, comprehensive, and having connectedness. A coherentist theory of justification does not appeal to a single circular chain of justifications but rather to an entire interconnected web of judgments that is justified in virtue of it being coherent. In this respect, coherentism is not a linear circularity and is not vicious.

For a coherentist epistemology, there can be different yet equally maximally coherent sets of judgments for different groups. For example, two agents from disparate cultures initially can start out with generally different socially conditioned intuitions, principles, and ethical theories at the beginning of the reflective equilibrium process such that at the end of the process, they both coherently maintain very different systems of moral judgments. In this case, both groups can have justified sets of judgments. This is consistent with moral relativism.

As an example of the use of reflective equilibrium, individuals may have various ethical values that need to be made coherent to actually see what a group's justified moral judgments may be. Corrections for moral error and alterations may need to be made relative to the group. Philosophers need to make such values coherent with each other and have them be based on relevant and true non-moral facts from a careful process of deliberation in order to arrive upon their justified set of judgments. For instance, if a fundamental belief of a culture is that there should be equality and liberty, then later judgments that there can be discrimination based on religion, race, sexual-orientation, and sex are unjustified and need to be cast aside. Not anything goes for a group, and there can be corrections for moral error within a group.

Proper moral judgments are those that are coherent with other relevant judgments and are ones that are formed after careful deliberation. Moreover, moral judgments should not be based on false non-moral facts, and one should take into consideration the accurate and relevant non-moral facts when forming moral judgments. Moral philosophers should be in the business of making moral systems coherent such that they can be justified in believing what is morally correct and incorrect for a group. This is how to proceed with normative ethics.

Moral relativism and coherentism make normative inquiry have at least a significant a posteriori component of empirically uncovering, for example, the relevant moral judgments, intuitions, principles, precedents, and ethical theories approved of by a group and then trying to have them reach wide reflective equilibrium and be based on assessing the relevant true non-moral facts through a careful process of deliberation and discussion. Recall that we have seen how what constitutes our moral concepts and thoughts about ethics is elusive and is best examined by experimental methods, where introspection can lead us astray. Determining the values people hold can be better observed by experimentation and by social scientists, such as psychologists and anthropologists. Against Kant, ideally, we should bring in the aid of such scientists at the beginning of the reflective equilibrium process for forming justified judgments of what is morally and relativistically true and false. As we should expect given my ontological naturalist base, the question of how we ought to live our lives is significantly an empirical matter. Also, recall that when doing normative ethics, one's framework must not presuppose the classical theory of moral concepts but should have a structure that is psychologically real (§4.6–§4.7). For example, although one's conception DISTRIBUTIVE JUSTICE will not be able to respond to every counterexample or objection given the nature of the mental representation, one should adhere to that conception that can best handle most and more of the counters.

In a particular respect, my proposal can be perceived as being analogous to Rawls' political philosophy project. Although interpretations on this matter may be controversial, John Rawls can be read as being a moral relativist articulating the political values that are relative to a Western liberal democratic people and those who espouse a system of justice that is based on fairness rather than, for instance, a hierarchical caste system. In his revision of *A Theory of Justice, Political Liberalism* (1993), he states that he merely is building his political philosophy within a particular tradition and history of Western constitutional democracies. Elsewhere, he says:

> [F]or the time being we put aside the idea of constructing…a systematic account of what we regard as objective moral truths…Since

> the history of moral philosophy shows that the notion of moral truth is problematical.
>
> (Rawls 1974–1975, p. 7)

> Even should everyone attain wide reflective equilibrium, many contrary moral conceptions may still be held…[T]he procedure of reflective equilibrium does not assume that there is one correct moral conception.
>
> (Rawls 1974–1975, p. 9)

We still will need moral philosophers to take the values that are relative to a group and form a coherent moral system of judgments with them, as Rawls seemingly attempts to do relative to a Western liberal tradition. This can help lead to moral progress within a given moral framework. Such a system justifiably applies to the relevant group but not necessarily to others. As it is possible to interpret Rawls as being a relativist, regardless of whether he is or not, this relativistic interpretation of Rawls at least demonstrates the importance of normative philosophers in that philosophers are needed to perform quite substantial and enormously important work in taking the relevant ideals and constructing a coherent normative system of judgments.

One may object that I am presupposing the objectivity of norms by espousing norms of coherence, etc. However, notice once again that the norms regarding coherence, taking into account relevant facts and non-moral theories, having careful deliberation and discussion, and forming judgments based on true non-moral facts are *epistemic* rather than *moral* norms. They are norms about proper judgment formation and not about, for instance, how we ought to treat each other. In this fashion, I am not claiming that there are no objective moral norms but somehow trying to sneak in such values in the epistemic process.

One may also object using Hume's law. The law is understood to be an argument concerning how one can derive an *ought* from an *is*. How can one conclude that an action *ought* to be done when the premises seemingly are descriptive claims simply about what *is* the case? Even though psychologists or anthropologists, for example, descriptively determine that a set of judgments is approved by a group, how do we get the "ought" that perhaps such judgments ought to be followed by the relevant group members? There appears to be an unwarranted jump from descriptive premises to reaching a prescriptive conclusion. Nevertheless, one possible solution amongst others is to point out that we start moral epistemology with assessing a group's normative moral values. What the social scientists or even yourself are doing at the beginning of the reflective equilibrium process is, for instance, information gathering about what intuitions, ethical theories, etc. you or others endorse. Next, remember from the previous section that we have independently established that moral facts are in part identical to what has been approved of by the group in light of my rational constraints. This can be used as a bridge premise showing that certain natural facts acquired by scientists and when put through the idealized conditions just are moral facts; a premise that also contains normative terms and ultimately bridges the natural to the moral. Once the cultural normative information is gathered by observers or scientists, then one attempts to reach reflective equilibrium with the information, making adjustments here and there. Once coherence is attained and given the bridge premise that contains moral terms, one has reached a conclusion on what a group ought to do. Since, the process of reflective equilibrium includes normative premises, such as the bridge premise, I am not attempting to derive an "ought" purely from non-normative premises when using this method.

13.6 Moral Intuitionism

The main competitor of a coherentist moral epistemology is moral intuitionism, which is a foundationalist epistemology for justified belief. While this moral epistemology has long been in disrepute, it has undergone something of a recent revival. There are a variety of moral intuitionist views (Shafer-Landau 2003, Audi 2004, Wedgwood 2007, Enoch 2013); however, they generally hold that we can have a priori moral intuition judgments that are non-inferentially justified.[8] The intuition is not or need not be inferred from other moral truths. The intuition is in need of no argument. In this respect, the intuition is self-evident. Intuitions should be formed after careful deliberation, reflection, and assessment of the relevant true non-moral facts. They should be arrived upon when one has a clear mind, and it may require training and lots of time to produce reliable moral intuitions. Moral intuitions need not be obvious, although more traditional intuitionists tend to claim that they do. Intuitions also may be held to be defeasible or indefeasible, fallible or infallible. Intuitions are the foundation from which other possible moral truths may be inferred or built upon.

However, the scientific picture of the mind shows that our judgments are influenced by other mental states either consciously or subconsciously. Throughout this book, we have witnessed a plethora of different mental states impacting our judgment-making. Moral intuitions are not uncaused causers that mysteriously pop into our minds uncaused by anything and can cause us to have other mental states or lead us to action. Consistent with the sciences of the mind, intuitions are causally influenced by other mental states. Hence, it very well could be the case that some or many of our intuitions are influenced by subconscious mental states that justify the intuition. Moral intuitions at many times may be inferentially justified. Nevertheless, foundationalists like Ross can argue that intuitions *need not* be inferentially justified. We perhaps can inferentially justify an intuition judgment by providing an argument for it, consciously or subconsciously. Perhaps we do this many times without our conscious awareness. However, one need not do so for the intuition to be justified. The intuition when considered all by itself still can be non-inferentially justified and self-evident despite the fact that it also can be inferentially justified.

There are many objections to moral intuitionism in the metaethics literature. Regardless, I instead would like to focus on a particular line of objection against moral intuitionism stemming from the work used to establish my pluralistic theory of moral concepts. We have seen in previous chapters how I have shown that emotions generally play a causal role in impacting our moral decision-making. When influencing cognition, recall that emotions are always accompanied by a moral cognitive state. Moreover, emotions need not always be influencing our decision-making as this depends on the context. However, we have seen that overwhelmingly in most if not all contexts, emotions rampantly influence psychologically normal human moral decision-making no matter if we make a positive or negative decision.

Conative states notoriously can be unruly, recalcitrant, and triggered exogenously by factors and situations external to one's body despite one's internal psychological wishes not to feel the triggered conative state. For example, one may have a fear of speaking in public, such as when delivering a talk at a conference. Even though one has every reason to not be afraid and to be confident in one's presentation, every time one gives such a talk, the feeling of fear always is present, pushing one to the borders of panic. Emotions can have minds of their own and can get the best of us, where people can feel them to different degrees and be more or less susceptible to them. The irascible, irritable, passionate, and wistful, emotions can lift us to jubilation and generosity unpredicted but lurk behind every corner pouncing on moments inopportune; allowing us to show the world, as if on a stage, how base and vulgar we really can be.

Given the rampant influence of emotions beyond our voluntary control in moral deliberation at many times, this places a serious threat on the epistemic reliability of our moral intuitions. A moral intuitionist might claim that intuitions when considered all by themselves are justified even though they are influenced by emotions. Yet, the problem is that intuitions are the result of or are causally facilitated by some mental event, so if they are products of unruly emotions, then they really may not be justified. For example, emotions may lead to decisions we regret or to decisions that are different from what we ordinarily will agree. While moral emotions always are accompanied by a cognitive state, this cognitive state may be merely following the leader and aligning itself with the lead emotion. For example, although I am normally a non-violent person, in jealousy of unrequited love, I intuit that it is permissible to physically assault my non-violent rival. This intuition is formed after careful deliberation taking into account the relevant true non-moral facts, and it is made after one has had much training in forming moral intuitions. This decision is influenced by a long-term festering jealousy and the represented rule ATTACK YOUR COMPETITORS. Emotions can be unruly and get the best of us even from the best of us. As emotions broadly influence moral cognition, it may be that moral intuitions are unreliable.

If the moral intuitionist were to claim that only judgments influenced by emotions that play the *appropriate* causal role should be relied upon, notice that this still involves an inferential justification. For, recall that the cognitive state that accompanies the emotion must be in part inferable from the inferential base or most firmly held ethical theory belief in order for the emotion to be an appropriate influence, *inter alia*. Such an inference from the inferential base and investigation must be used in order to justify the judgment on this particular approach by the intuitionist. Hence, we no longer have a non-inferential theory of justified belief.

We also cannot try to reign in emotions by relying on other emotions or by causally grounding one's epistemic theory on only certain emotions since the epistemic problem of being anchored on unruly exogenous emotions will remain. For instance, only trusting intuitions that are grounded in only particular emotions, such as compassion, are not always epistemically reliable. For example, one may be overly compassionate to one's child, withholding the tough love and discipline that the child needs for her future or being too overbearing on the child, relative to one's group. It must be to cognitive states that we must turn to epistemically harness emotions. Thus, as an epistemic normative matter, the best way to reign in emotion-backed intuitions is to reach coherence of emotions with ethical theories, rules or virtues, empirical moral psychology, etc. This is the best option and way out for moral intuitionists on how to handle emotion-backed intuitions. They can be constrained by cognitive representations in order to determine which emotional reactions in a context actually are merited. From an epistemic vantagepoint, conative states influence the formation of our intuitions, but we cannot let them run wild given their unruly nature. Thus, we need to bring in cognitive states. However, once this step is taken, we see that moral intuitionism is untenable as it melts away into an inferential coherentist moral epistemology rather than a foundationalist one. Justification of moral judgments requires coherence and inference from cognitive states.

The moral intuitionist continually may press that even though moral intuitions are justified based on such coherence-based inferences, they need not be so justified. When considered all by their lonesome, they are still self-evident. However, they are not self-evident because they may be the products of unruly emotions and of an unreliable process; shattering the sense of security and reliability one may have held in one's intuition. Intuitions come from somewhere rather than nowhere. When assessing whether an intuition is self-evident in the absence of a coherentist justification, intuition judgments still are natural psychological states that are products of other mental events. What mental events they are products of are epistemically relevant and important. We cannot really assess moral intuitions as being self-evident absent of their causes because in the real world, they are caused by some mental event, and which mental event they are a product of is crucial as to whether the intuition is justified. Even when attempting to analyze an intuition in a dispassionate way in terms of moral correctness or incorrectness, supposedly absent of any inferential justification, we more likely than not are being influenced by an emotion in this moral assessment.

Next, the moral intuitionist may reply that another condition for forming reliable intuitions is to do so only when one is in a non-emotional state. However, recall that I have empirically confirmed that moral judgments, which include moral intuition judgments, widely and overwhelmingly express and are in part constituted by emotions in most if not all cases for psychologically normal humans even when we're not consciously aware of it. The inductive evidence for this is that strong. We tend to call those who don't express emotions when making ethical judgments psychopaths or mentally ill. Hence, even if we attempt to consider a moral intuition in isolation, the intuition most likely in part just is an emotional state, which can be unruly. When we see inductively that moral intuitions in part are expressions of conative states, further steps must be taken to reach a sufficient level of epistemic justification. Hence, it epistemically ought to be the case that emotions enter a wide reflective equilibrium procedure so that one may have justified judgments relative to a group. Hence, it inevitably is from coherence that moral judgments are justified. Moral intuitionism is false.

This ultimate need of reliance on cognitive states for justifying one's moral judgments when emotions are involved in one's epistemology also has been foreseen in the history of philosophy. Only for the sake of providing historical examples of attempting to reign in sentiments with cognitive states in order to attain epistemic justification, specific attempts that I do not necessarily endorse, Hume emphasizes that we need to escape our own personal perspective and put ourselves in others' shoes; others who have a connection or intercourse with the given moral situation. Examining our emotions from these perspectives perhaps may be a beneficial step toward helping us to arrive upon justified sentiments and a common point of view that others in a particular society may gravitate toward. Adam Smith, another sentimentalist, also contends that we need to leave our own personal perspective and the unruly emotions that may lie therein, but he envelopes emotions within an ideal spectator theory.

We should examine the sentiments that would be held by an ideal and impartial spectator who is knowledgeable of the situation. From this perspective, he claims we can justify our moral judgments by relying on sentiments that actually are merited.

13.7 Conclusion

Although not at all discussing what constitutes moral concepts, Gilbert Ryle (1966/1971) claims that ethics involves the "tempers, habits, dispositions, moods, inclinations, impulses, sentiments, feelings, affections, thoughts, reflections, opinions, principles, prejudices, imaginations and fancies" (p. 182). Concepts are the basic units of thought, and by examining ethics at the most fundamental psychological level of exploring what a moral concept is, we see that something like Ryle's claim generally is true. I have put forth a new pluralistic theory of moral concepts and have empirically proven that our moral concepts widely are constituted by cognitive representations of rules, virtues, reasons, hypothetical situations from which we can draw analogies, and ethical theories. They also can be made up of representations of influential myths and legends of heroism as well as of poignant life moments that help shape our conception of right and wrong but also help make up who we are. Our moral concepts also largely are dispositional sentiments, feelings of love, caring, anger, fear, sympathy, and empathy that provide motivation for action. They have an emotional being that brings a vivacity and qualitative richness, typically thought to be lacking in beliefs, of a "what it is like" experience or sensation in making moral judgments, such as making a judgment against one's enemy, to finally take a stand against one's oppressor, to decide to work together in the bonds of friendship against the odds, and to choose to follow your dreams in order to become who you are. Emotions and the qualia that in part constitutes emotions help make the moral highs higher and the lows lower, ever the more augmenting the seeming gravity of our moral lives.

What mental states constitute concepts is significantly shaped by culture and upbringing, where moral truths are socially constructed by moral minds and are sufficiently explained by science. Ethics deals not with the supernatural and the occult but is wholly part of the natural world. Our normative mental capacity plausibly has an evolutionary history and function of promoting cooperation; an evolutionary function that was multiply realized in different successful ways by different communities. In the beginning, to stave off free-riders and defectors of the moral system from overrunning a population, force was required in order for morality to evolve. Ethics is wrapped in the swaddles of bloodshed, violence, mutilation, and punishment. It was to be obeyed in order to avoid pain and despair. Ethics was built on emotions, like fear, anger, and guilt, and on beliefs, like rules and codes. It was then afforded that sanctity that comes with socialization and custom, as it is then attached to greater pleasure, like most habitual and seemingly natural things. It was followed based on free obedience and even a religious-like devotion. When completely woven into the fabric of a society's common sense, it was obeyed on a kind of obviousness and instinct or what today we call "intuition."

As a building block of ethical thought, Hume showed how an entire moral philosophy can be built on the empirical foundations of a scientific account of human nature that centrally focuses on moral concepts and the human understanding. Moral mental representations not only are responsible for how we make moral categorization judgments and understand the moral world but they are a cynosure and foundation from which ethics may be built. They can be the puppet master pulling the strings of the moral universe: Commanding the nature of moral truth, decreeing the relationship between judgment and motivation, and promulgating what mental states moral judgments express. Like a rigid master, it proclaims how we should even think about normative ethics given the psychological reality of our concept's structure, and it helps ordain how we ought to determine right from wrong. This inquiry has been one on the fundamental psychological basis of moral judgment or, in other words, on moral concepts; examining their nature and semantic properties. However, in the end, it has illuminated upon so much more; exhibiting how something so small and miniscule has the influence and power to command a breadth of prodigiousness and girth.

Notes

1 I don't focus on subjectivist ontological views, such as by Dreier or Street, here since I've shown that subjectivism is false, although I'll briefly mention Prinz's subjectivism view in passing.

2 John McDowell also can be described as holding a secondary quality view. However, unlike Prinz, he utilizes the notion of 'merit.' He states that moral values merit certain affective responses, and this is the nature of value. Here, merit is a non-reductive non-natural property for McDowell. Hence, McDowell's view is unlike Prinz's and fails to be an appropriate partner with the prevalent causal theory of reference. McDowell is also an objectivist, but we have seen how any objectivism theory is false given the incommensurability of moral concepts, amongst other reasons.

3 There is a debate in metaethics as to what kind of property is most fundamental, such as reasons or values. Due to space considerations, I remain neutral on this debate here.

4 Streumer also objects that a non-reductive account is false as there needs to be some kind of a reduction if there are any moral properties at all. As my view in part contains a reductive component, I escape this objection.

5 For discussion of plausible natural and evolutionary constraints on possible moral systems, see Wong (2006) and Velleman (2013).

6 Horgan and Timmons (2009) object to a narrow content naturalism theory that leads to moral relativism. They claim that even though the descriptions differ widely across certain cultures, so long as the formal evaluative use of moral concepts is held in common between interlocutors, two people's moral concepts share the same meaning. However, I have already addressed such an objection above (§12.1.3).

7 Notice that when being aware of our innate in-group biases, the possibility is still open that we may still be justified in believing that we should favor the in-group at least at certain times. Also, for further work on how knowledge of empirical moral psychology can help avoid biases and heuristics, see May (2018).

8 This is sometimes known as rational intuitionism. There is an empiricist variant of intuitionism known as moral sense theory. Here, certain moral judgments are non-inferentially justified a posteriori based on sense perception. My attack against rational intuitionism also applies to moral sense theory, *mutatis mutandis.*

References

Audi, Robert. 2004. *The Good in the Right.* Princeton, NJ: Princeton University Press.

Blackburn, Simon. 1985. "Errors and the Phenomenology of Value." In *Morality and Objectivity.* Ed. by T. Honderich. London: Routledge & Kegan Paul.

Daniels, Norman. 1996. *Justice and Justification.* Cambridge: Cambridge University Press.

Enoch, David. 2013. *Taking Morality Seriously.* Oxford: Oxford University Press.

Harman, Gilbert. 1975. "Moral Relativism Defended." *The Philosophical Review* 84, 3–22.

Harman, Gilbert. 1977. *The Nature of Morality.* Oxford: Oxford University Press.

Harman, Gilbert. 1986. "Moral Explanations of Natural Facts – Can Moral Claims Be Tested Against Reality." *Southern Journal of Philosophy* 24, 57–68.

Horgan, Terry and Timmons, Mark. 2009. "*Analytical Moral Functionalism Meets Moral Twin Earth.*" In *Essays on the Philosophy of Frank Jackson.* Edited by I. Ravenscroft. Oxford: Blackwell, 221–236.

May, Joshua. 2018. *Regard for Reason in the Moral Mind.* Oxford: Oxford University Press.

Parfit, Derek. 2011. *On What Matters, Vol. 1 & 2.* Oxford: Oxford University Press.

Rawls, John. 1971. *A Theory of Justice,* 2nd edition. Cambridge, MA: Belknap Press.

Rawls, John. 1974–1975. "The Independence of Moral Theory." Presidential Address to the APA. *Proceedings and Addresses of the APA* 48, 5–22.

Rawls, John. 1993. *Political Liberalism.* Cambridge, MA: Harvard University Press.

Ryle, Gilbert. 1966/1971. "Jane Austen and the Moralists." *The Oxford Review.* Reprinted in *English Literature and British Philosophy.* Ed. by S. P. Rosenbaum. Chicago, IL: University of Chicago Press.

Sayre-McCord, Geoff. 1985. "Coherence and Models for Moral Theorizing." *Pacific Philosophical Quarterly* 66, 170–190.

Shafer-Landau, Russ. *Moral Realism: A Defense.* Oxford: Oxford University Press, 2003.

Streumer, Bart. 2017. *Unbelievable Errors.* Oxford: Oxford University Press.

Sturgeon, Nicholas. 1984. "Moral Explanations." In *Morality, Reason and Truth.* Ed. by D. Copp and D. Zimmerman. Totowa, NJ: Rowman & Littlefield.

Velleman, David. 2013. *Foundations for Moral Relativism.* United Kingdom: Open Book Publishers.

Wedgwood, Ralph. 2007. *The Nature of Normativity.* Oxford: Oxford University Press.

Wong, David B. 1986. *Moral Relativity.* Berkeley, CA: University of California Press.

Wong, David B. 2006. *Natural Moralities.* Oxford: Oxford University Press.

Index